GW00319448

F.R. Leavis

The only method in criticism is to be very intelligent.

T.S. Eliot

The critic who doesn't make a personal statement, in remeasurements he himself has made, is merely an unreliable critic. He is not a measurer but a repeater of other men's results.

F.R. Leavis

F.R. LEAVIS

A Literary Biography

with Q.D. Leavis' 'Memoir' of F.R. Leavis

G. Singh

Duckworth

First published in 1995 by
Gerald Duckworth & Co. Ltd.
The Old Piano Factory
48 Hoxton Square, London N1 6PB
Tel: 0171 729 5986
Fax: 0171 729 0015

A catalogue record for this book is available
from the British Library

ISBN 0 7156 2664 7

Typeset by Ray Davies
Printed in Great Britain by
Redwood Books Ltd, Trowbridge

Contents

Plates between pages 120 and 121

To
the Memory of
Colin Haycraft

Preface

What is presented in this book is, in the strict sense of the term, a literary biography of F.R. Leavis. It deals, for the most part in chronological order, with the whole range of his writings and, at the same time, offers what one might call a fairly representative anthology of the best in his criticism, commented on analytically. More than criticising the critic, it has been my aim to discuss Leavis' books one by one, as well as the various aspects of his criticism as illustrated and exemplified by his well-known critiques and appraisals; and, only secondarily, to appraise such appraisals. English social and university conditions having changed so much, I have tried to show in this book why Leavis' greatest work is more than ever essential and relevant (and should by the disinterestedly intelligent reader be *seen* to be such) and why a contemporary public more than ever needs some guidance as to why and how he matters. In 1995 – the centenary year of Leavis' birth – it is appropriate to trace how his critical work unfolded in context and why this context is beyond, and a corrective to, the familiar and habitual ways Leavis has generally for the last twenty years been treated by academics and referred to in the press, showing that even if they wish to, literary journalists cannot get round Leavis' indisputable critical achievement.

It is an achievement that brought about something like a revolution in the understanding of and critical attitude to Shakespeare and Milton, Swift and Johnson, the Romantics, the 'great tradition' of the English novel (Dickens, George Eliot, Henry James, Conrad and D.H. Lawrence) and the moderns (Joyce, Yeats, T.S. Eliot, Pound) as well as the masters of English criticism (Johnson, Coleridge, Matthew Arnold, D.H. Lawrence and T.S. Eliot). My quoting from Leavis or recapitulating his critical pronouncements is meant to bring into focus the nature and impact of this revolution and the way it was brought about. As an integral part of his criticism, I have also discussed what Leavis has to say on imagery and technique, reality and sincerity, analysis and judgement, style and language in the course of his own 'practical criticism' – something quite different from what the term means in the case of I.A. Richards or William Empson. As to Leavis' non-literary criticism – criticism dealing with education and the university, the reading public, the mass-media, and the 'frightening' problems of modern technologico-Benthamite civilization, 'our civilization' – where he may be said to don the mantle of a modern Carlyle and a modern Matthew Arnold rolled into one, I have treated it as being, from the very outset, an inextricable part of his criticism in general as evidenced by two of his earliest publications – *Mass Civilization and Minority Culture* and *Culture and Environment*. From his lecture on Sir C.P. Snow onwards, this thread becomes increasingly important, so that the literary and non-literary aspects of Leavis' criticism tend increasingly to merge and, at times, even to overlap – which is one reason why Leavis is to be regarded as 'a whole critic'; i.e. a critic of life and society as well as of literature, culture and civilization.

If, here and there in the book, and especially in the Introduction and in Chapters 11 and 15, I have ventured to make some comments on Leavis' life, personality and character, I have done so largely on the basis of what emerges from his own writings and from the 'personal' nature of his criticism – and for Leavis 'a judgement is either personal or it is nothing; you cannot take over someone else's' – and only partly on the basis of what I knew about him through my acquaintance with him during the last fifteen years of his life.

I am grateful to Leavis' son, Dr Robin Leavis of Nijmegen University, Holland and to Miss Gabrielle Barfoot, formerly my colleague and now a member of the English Department, Trieste University, Italy, for having gone through the typescript of this book and for making some valuable suggestions that have been profitably incorporated.

Lastly, it is both my pleasure and my duty to record my gratitude to Queen's University, Belfast, and, in particular, to its present Vice-Chancellor Sir Gordon Beveridge for enabling me to carry on my work on the Leavises, and to finish this book on F.R. Leavis who came three times to Queen's as a 'Distinguished Scholar' and on whom Queen's conferred an honorary D.Litt.

G.S.

Introduction

F.R. Leavis: the whole critic

A critic must be emotionally alive in every fibre, intellectually capable and skilful in essential logic, and then morally very honest.

D.H. Lawrence

In coming to terms with literature we discover what at bottom we really believe.

F.R. Leavis

'Whether the faculty of literary criticism is the best gift that Heaven has in its treasuries I cannot say; but Heaven seems to think so, for assuredly it is the gift most charily bestowed. Orators and poets, sages and saints and heroes, if rare in comparison with blackberries, are commoner than returns of Halley's comet: literary critics are less common'. It was just a year after *Scrutiny* was founded that A.E. Housman opened his celebrated lecture on 'The Name and Nature of Poetry' at Cambridge in 1933, by recalling what he had said 20 years earlier. But Housman, who lived long enough to see the revolutionary impact that *Scrutiny*, and especially its chief founder and inspirer, had started to have on literary criticism, would hardly have recognised in Leavis the type of critic he had in mind. And yet, even though Leavis was not impressed by Housman's poetry, there is some notable affinity between him and Housman. In fact, both Leavis and Housman had identical views concerning a classical scholar's capacity for criticism. There are exceptions, says Housman, but in general,

if a man wants really penetrating judgements, really illuminating criticism on a classical author, he is ill advised if he goes to a classical scholar to get them ... When it comes to literary criticism, heap up in one scale all the literary criticism that the whole nation of professed scholars ever wrote, and drop into the other the thin green volume of Matthew Arnold's *Lectures on Translating Homer*, which has long been out of print because the British public does not care to read it, and the first scale, as Milton says, will straight fly up and kick the beam.

For Housman, as for Leavis, the chief aim of humanistic and literary education is to 'quicken our appreciation of what is excellent and to refine our discrimination between what is excellent and what is not.' Both insist on high critical competence. 'The average man', says Housman,

> if he meddles with criticism at all, is a conservative critic. His opinions are determined not by his reason, – 'the bulk of mankind', says Swift, 'is as well qualified for flying as for thinking', – but by his passions and the faintest of all human passions is the love of truth.

The severity of critical disapproval and indignation in Housman often acquires the same tone and expresses itself in practically the same terms as in Leavis:

> Frailty of understanding is in itself no proper target for scorn and mockery: 'nihil in eo odio dignum, misericordia digna multa'. But the unintelligent forfeit their claim to compassion when they begin to indulge in self-complacent airs, and to call themselves sane critics .... And when, relying upon their numbers, they pass from self-complacency to insolence, and reprove their betters for using the brains which God has not denied them, they dry up the fount of pity.

Housman's judgements on poetry, too, are as forthright and trenchant as those of Leavis. 'Now the centre of interest in a poet', says Housman,

> is his poetry: not his themes, his doctrines, his opinions, his life or conduct, but the poetical quality of the works he has bequeathed to us.

As to his own professional competence, the questions a critic of literature ought to ask himself, according to Housman, are:

> Am I capable of recognising poetry if I come across it? Do I possess the organ by which poetry is perceived? The majority of civilized mankind notoriously and indisputably do not .... If a man is insensible to poetry, it does not follow that he gets no pleasure from poems. Poems very seldom consist of poetry and nothing else; and pleasure can be derived also from their other ingredients. I am convinced that most readers, when they think that they are admiring poetry, are deceived by inability to analyse their sensations, and that they are really admiring, not the poetry of the passage before them, but something else in it, which they like better than poetry.

Both Housman and Leavis conceived literary criticism as a discipline of thought and a training of intelligence and sensibility, very different from, and in some respects in marked contrast to the discipline of classical and philological scholarship. For it was not merely Leavis, but also Housman, the greatest classical scholar of his age, who affirmed that

> upon the majority of mankind the classics can hardly be said to exert the transforming influence which is claimed for them,

and that,

> The special effect of a classical education on the majority of those who receive it, is not to transform and beautify their inner nature, but rather to confer a certain amount of polish on their surface, by teaching them things that one is expected to know and enabling them to understand the meaning of the English words and use them properly.

Leavis, too, while describing literary criticism as 'a discipline of thought that is at the same time a scrupulous sensitiveness of response to delicate organisations of feeling, sensation and imagery', distinguished it from the training and discipline provided by classical studies. Classical and philosophical training, he points out,

> tends, in its very efficacy as formative discipline, to result in something from which intelligence has to escape – if it ever sees the need for escaping. The confident 'finish', the sense of adequacy, the poised and undeveloping quasi-maturity, that commonly results from such a training is what we see represented at an impressive level in Robert Bridges with his Academy interest in language and technique and the assurance of judgement that enabled him to apologise, in the name of 'a continuous literary decorum', for all the manifestations of Hopkins's genius.

In *Education and the University* (1943), Leavis was to discuss at some length the nature of the link between literary criticism and humane education in general – a link that can be maintained and strengthened, broken or weakened, according to whether humane studies are kept closely in touch with, or are virtually divorced from, the training of sensibility as something 'prior and irremissible'.

> Literary study unassociated with it becomes, infallibly, 'academic' and barren – a matter of profitless memorising, of practice in graceful or scholarly irrelevance, of scanning metrical feet and drawing graphs of plots and actions, or of 'discipline' at the higher navvying.

The very sense of tradition in a literary critic is of a different order from the one cherished and cultivated by a classical scholar. For a critical study of literature aims at producing

> a mind that will approach the problems of modern civilisation with an understanding of their origins, a maturity of outlook, and not a nostalgic addiction to the past, but a sense of human possibilities, difficult of achievement, that traditional cultures bear witness to and that it would be disastrous, in a breach of continuity, to lose sight of for good.

For Leavis awareness of a living tradition and awareness of the present are interdependent and inseparable.

> To initiate into the idea of living tradition except in relation to the present is hardly possible. An addiction to literature that does not go with an interest in the literature of today, and some measure of intelligence about it, goes with the academic idea of tradition – traditionalism, that is, in the bad sense.

Leavis quotes Eliot to the effect that an important critic is the person 'who is absorbed in the present problems of art, and who wishes to bring the forces of the past to bear on the solution of these problems' – something Leavis himself consistently did. For one thing, he distinguished literary criticism from much else that goes by its name – literary theory and history, poetics or the poet's philosophical and religious beliefs, study of sources or influences, biography or social, historical or cultural *milieux* – thereby earning for himself the appellation of 'arch-rejector'. Leavis' classical reply to René Wellek's criticism of *Revaluation* – of which more later – is exemplary and very much a case in point. But already in his preface to *Revaluation*, a neat *résumé* of his critical method, Leavis had spelt out the terms and limits within which a critic

> endeavours to see the poetry of the present as continuation and development; that is, as the decisive, the most significant, contemporary life of tradition. He endeavours, where the poetry of the past is concerned, to realize to the full the implications of the truism that its life is in the present or nowhere; it is alive in so far as it is alive for us. His aim ... is to define, and to order in terms of its own implicit organisation, a kind of ideal and impersonal living memory.

The real significance of the literary tradition as Leavis saw it is not something one can theorise about, but something to be illustrated through individual examples of fully realised art. In evaluating such art Leavis' concern has always been with the concrete, as he points out in his preface to *Revaluation*:

... no treatment of poetry is worth much that does not keep very close to the concrete: there lies the problem of method. The only acceptable solution, it seemed to me, lay in the extension and adaptation of the method appropriate in dealing with individual poets as such. In dealing with individual poets the rule of the critic is, or should (I think) be, to work as much as possible in terms of particular analysis – analysis of poems or passages, and to say nothing that cannot be related immediately to judgements about producible texts. Observing this rule and practising this self-denial the critic limits, of course, his freedom; but there are kinds of freedom he should not aspire to, and the discipline, while not preventing his saying anything that he should in the end find himself needing to say, enables him to say it with a force of relevance and an edged economy not otherwise attainable.

Leavis' own criticism severely adhered to this code – a criticism which is distinct not only from philosophy, literary history and academic scholarship, but also from whatever 'the academic mind' stands for:

The professional student of letters, the 'authority' – authority also, it must be remembered, in matters of curricula, instruction and examination at the high seats of learning – is rarely qualified in relation to his subject with one very relevant kind of authority (I had almost said the indispensable kind, but things are as they are), a kind that is not constituted, and need not be asserted or claimed: he is rarely a good first-hand critic – or even a good second-hand one. This is a truth we are often reminded of by the evident limitations of justly respected scholars: a man may do work that exacts the gratitude of us all as readers of poetry who yet betrays a lack of any developed sensibility, any fineness of perception and judgement.

Crossing swords with T.S. Eliot on the latter's deference to scholars in his criticism of Milton, Leavis again commented on the relation between scholarship and literary criticism:

For the purposes of criticism, scholarship, unless directed by an intelligent interest in poetry – without, that is, critical sensibility and the skill that enables the critic to develop its responses in sensitive and closely relevant thinking – is useless. That skill is not common among scholars. Of the 'champions of Milton in our time' who have rectified the 'errors' with 'vigorous hands' and who have opposed the 'prejudices' with 'commanding voices', is there one whose vigour takes effect as a vigour of relevance, or whose arguments command attention because they so unquestionably represent an intelligent interest in poetry?

If so, I haven't come across him. And no intimation of Mr. Eliot's alters my own finding, which is that there can be little profit in arguing with these champions, since, confident as they are in their status as authorities, their critical education has so patently not begun: where poetry is to be discussed, they show themselves unaware of the elementary conditions of talking to the point.

In his review of James Sutherland's edition of *The Dunciad*, too, Leavis pin-pointed the dissociation between scholarship for its own sake and critical appreciation of the text to which so much erudition and scholarly effort have been devoted:

Yes, one concedes grudgingly, overcoming the inevitable revulsion, as one turns the pages of this new edition [The 'Twickenham'], in which the poem trickles thinly through a desert of apparatus, to disappear time and again from sight .... The material is one thing, the poetry another. In fact, the sufficient recognition [of Pope's poetic merit] won't come except in company with the recognition that notes are not necessary: the poetry doesn't depend upon them in any essential respect.

Another thing that Leavis, in his concern for the true nature of literary criticism, is suspicious of is 'the journalistic addiction of our academic intellectuals', as he calls it, and the mode and style of expression warranted by that addiction. Tillyard's comment that Leavis is 'a better critic when he encourages us to read Carew or Pope than when he puts Spenser or Shelley on the index' is, for Leavis, an example of glib literary journalism and of a mode of expression 'that no self-respecting critic should permit himself; it should be left to the Sunday reviewers'. Similarly Leavis criticises the manner of expression that Sir Charles Snow, in his *Two Cultures*, 'found proper and natural' – a mode 'with its embarrassing vulgarity of style'. And his criticism of Snow's style was also a criticism of what lay behind and what made such a style possible.

Few sentences in Leavis' writings sum up so well his relationship with the contemporary academic and cultural world as the following from '*Scrutiny*: A Retrospect' (August 1962):

Well-known dons, thought of widely as distinguished intellectuals, are assiduous journalists, establish themselves as names and authorities by frequent performances on radio and television, and form what Sir Charles Snow calls a 'culture' with the other practitioners of their kind, whether or not these claim academic standing, and the standards they favour will naturally be those by which they feel themselves safe as distinguished intellectuals.

Leavis also challenged F.W. Bateson on what the latter considered to be the role of literary history and its relation to literary criticism. In Bateson's own account of the controversy between him and Leavis occasioned by the latter's unfavourable review of Bateson's *English Poetry and the English Language*, Leavis' point was that

> unless the literary historian becomes a literary critic he will remain an antiquarian, a literary detective, and even this antiquarianism presupposes a certain critical ability. To date the poem or emend it you must have some elementary understanding of it, and even an elementary literary reaction is necessarily critical. Dr. Leavis was right and I was wrong. And once I had accepted this correction – a medicine of humble pie that took a good many years to work its cure – it was natural to turn to Dr. Leavis' own writings as a model of how to combine synthesis with analysis in the study of literature.

But what lies behind Leavis' literary criticism is something deeper and more complex than what the terms literature or literary signify. It is as a result of this sense of commitment to the values and significance of life itself that there is no dissociation in him between the man and the critic. In other words, if as a critic, he was concerned with 'the re-creative response of the individual minds to the black marks on the page', his own response to those marks was inevitably tied up with his response to life itself. Some critics interpret the significance of literature in terms of its relevance to life and experience; some enable us to appreciate the forms of art and technique through which it is conveyed; and some help us discriminate between what is good and bad in literature, original or conventional. Leavis performed all these functions at one and the same time. Hence he was something much more than the Critic as Moralist, as Eliot less than justly called him. He was, what one might say of very few critics, a whole critic (which implies a whole man).

If there is something very 'personal' about Leavis' criticism, it is not so in any narrowly subjective sense, but in the sense that his judgements always presuppose moral courage, and a sense of conviction, integrity and sincerity. If critics have often no 'personal' judgements to offer it is as much due to their lack of courage as to their lack of perception; and courage in criticism is as rare a virtue as originality. Leavis combined both in an exemplary way. There was something both of Dr. Johnson and of Matthew Arnold in Leavis: 'Deliberately, not dogmatically', he raised literary controversy to the level of serious critical inquiry. Equally at home in dealing with the novel or with poetry, he probed into the creative aspects not only of language but also of thought – and for him creative language was essentially and inevitably the language of thought. His own prose was frequently a target for criticism, especially if his critics were not in a position to rebut the force of his logic; and their admiration of what they considered good English was seldom matched by their own ability to write it. If Leavis conceived creative literature as a discipline of thought, 'a vitalizing force', he also considered literary criticism to be more or less the same, since, for him, the judgements with which the literary critic is concerned are essentially 'judgements about life'. Thus, for instance, while characterising *Burnt Norton* as representing 'a sure apprehension of ... the ultimately real', the 'unreality, the unlivingness of life in time' or 'the vibration of a yearning suffered in inescapable remoteness', he interpreted such concepts not only vis-à-vis Eliot and his poetry, but also vis-à-vis himself and what one might call, though Leavis himself did not use the word, his 'credo'. The very language he used in analysing such concepts was indicative of a certain degree of personal involvement on his part in what was being analysed. Thus, for instance, while commenting on Eliot's lines: 'human kind cannot bear very much reality', Leavis reproved him for his 'suggestion of failure on the part of human kind'. His own comment on these lines is that human kind *cannot but ought*'. Similarly, while commenting on the phrase, 'what might have been', Leavis points out how the 'regret', as intimated here, 'is not merely regret, but guilt too; it is a sense of sin' – a comment on the poem which goes beyond the poem, and becomes a criticism of life both as Eliot saw it and as, in a characteristically different and profoundly 'personal' way, Leavis saw it and lived it. Also, while commenting on *Burnt Norton* , which brings out Eliot's inner conflict and irremediable self-division, Leavis implicitly throws light on himself and on what elicited his moral as well as critical praise: profoundest sincerity, instead of self-division, which generally characterises the work of the greatest writers, and which, in spite of Eliot's undeniable greatness as a poet, Leavis found lacking in him. Thus his criticism of Eliot's personality and his tribute to his creative genius go hand in hand, thereby demonstrating once again that his values and criteria are never solely literary or aesthetic. While responding to Eliot's poem, whether he agreed or disagreed with what it expressed or implied, Leavis found 'a sharpening of thought, conviction and resolution', so that his reading of *Four Quartets* came to mean a certain quest of his own deepest self, illustrating what one means by the profoundly 'personal' nature of Leavis' criticism.

And yet it is a criticism emphatically free from any dogma, creed or ideology. Embodying the very 'reverse of an academic and purely theoretical spirit', it studiously shuns any sort of commitment to any system of *a priori* principles or criteria, and the standards it implicitly upholds or points to cannot be translated into conceptual postulates.

This accounts, among other things, for his lack of interest in linguistics, philology, 'philosophy' or 'ideas' and for his indifference to the charge, often levelled against him, of being provincial or insular. And yet, for all the severity and precision with which he defined the frontiers of literary criticism as well as the limits within which he chose to work, Leavis not only wrote on Tolstoy and Montale, but also had a first-hand knowledge of Dante, Leopardi and the French classics, as well as of classical tragedy. It was his single-minded intensity of commitment to literature that some of his critics had in mind when they complained that he never relaxed. But if he had 'relaxed' – and the more one analyses the meaning of the term in the context of Leavis' life, work and personality, the more meaningless it appears to be – the sense of commitment that, among other things, made *Scrutiny* possible, would not have been there. Such a sense of commitment is writ large on everything Leavis wrote, said or did; and so is his commitment both to tradition and modernity. Consequent upon that commitment were the qualities of integrity and disinterestedness which characterised all his writings. There is no intelligence without character, Leavis used to say, and he himself possessed both in equal measure. 'Earnest, responsible, and loyal by nature', he described Wordsworth to be, and the same may be said of him. It is this sense of loyalty and responsibility towards literature and literary criticism as well as towards what he believed and what he stood for that made Leavis' judgements 'personal'.

His critical judgements no less than his personal convictions, like those of Matthew Arnold, had implicitly moral – not moralistic – criteria and assumptions to back them. He never had any doubt as to the worthwhileness of what was at issue in his criticism before arguing about, analysing and evaluating it. This moral standpoint, often referred to as Leavis' puritanism, meant that academicism and literariness had no more use for Leavis than they had for Pound – a critic both temperamentally and in other respects drastically unlike him. Though himself an academic by profession, what was academic 'in the bad sense of the term', as he often referred to it, had the same pejorative significance for Leavis as sham had for Dr Johnson or philistinism for Matthew Arnold. For Leavis first-hand critical perception and intuition as well as personal insight and judgement were one thing, scholarship for its own sake, at times a convenient euphemism for pedantry, leading up to the dead weight of academic authority, quite another. A work of creative literature, whether it belonged to the twentieth century or to the sixteenth, could never be fully assessed except in terms of its connection with and relevance to the literature of the present. That is why Leavis' sense of tradition, like that of Pound and Eliot, was inseparable from his awareness of the present – the one modifying and in turn being modified by the other.

As to critical theories, schools and methodologies, they had no meaning for Leavis, and he could well have said with Eliot that the only method in criticism is to be very intelligent. While pleading his inability to deal philosophically with Shelley's poetry, Leavis, in his celebrated rejoinder to Wellek, pointed out that if he seemed to be modest, he could afford his modesty, for he had other pretensions – namely those of a literary critic.

In fact, he reminded Wellek that a philosophical training could well turn
out to be a handicap for a literary critic.

And yet, for all his being a critic who was anti-philosopher, Leavis not
only did not believe in purely literary or aesthetic values – he characteristically objected to Aldous Huxley's attributing 'literarism' to him as
opposed to Snow's 'scientism' – but he was also profoundly conscious of the
strong thought element in his own criticism. Thinking, he argued, is a
difficult process and it is one that moulds much of Leavis' criticism. For
him great works of literature, even though they are not 'philosophical' in
character, origin or inspiration, are repositories of the best that has been
thought and said; in other words, of thought at its most subtle, complex
and creative. Thus, for example, Wordsworth had, for Leavis, 'if not a
philosophy, a wisdom to communicate', whereas *Four Quartets* is 'a tour
de force of disciplined thinking'. But a critic's way of dealing with such
thought and wisdom, or with what Matthew Arnold called a 'criticism of
life', is definitely not that of a philosopher, since for him concepts, ideas,
thought, and even what is commonly called philosophy are but so many
jejune abstractions, unless creatively realised and concretely embodied in
art. Leavis' own criticism of Wordsworth's *Ruined Cottage*, for instance –
and, in a more elaborate way, of Eliot's *Four Quartets* – is a case in point.
It is a criticism in which the critic as anti-philosopher, while responding
to thought, whether moral, philosophical or religious, that has been creatively realised and concretised, achieves a corresponding degree of
subtlety, delicacy and profundity in his own thought and criticism.

Outline of an essential biography

One is one, but one is not alone.
F.R. Leavis

There is very little in Leavis' life or work, personality or character from
his school, and especially university, days onwards, that can be meaning-
fully discussed or commented on *without* reference to his literary and
critical career, his vocation and achievement. And what there is has
frankly little or no relevance to one's trying to understand what he was,
what he wrote and what he stood for – the main theme and substance of
the present literary biography – which explains both Leavis' and his wife's
aversion to the idea of a 'Biography'. As to his personal and family life,
Q.D. Leavis' notes for her 'Memoir' go a long way towards throwing light
on this as well as on the character, personality and habits of her husband
whom she married in 1929, from whom she had two sons and a daughter,
and with whom she collaborated till the end of his life with devotion and
admiration, and with love as well as with respect.

One of three children, two brothers and one sister, Leavis was born on
14th July 1895. His father, Harry Leavis, a Victorian rationalist of Hugue-

not descent, kept a piano shop in Cambridge. Leavis went to a local grammar school, the Perse, where the headmaster was Dr. W.H.D. Rouse, a classicist and a Sanskrit scholar who, while translating *The Odyssey* into English, corresponded with Ezra Pound, 'as pupil to master', and got the benefit of the younger American poet's advice in rendering Homer into modern prose, more or less as Benjamin Jowett had benefited from the advice of his pupil A.C. Swinburne in translating Plato's *Dialogues*. In his essay 'The "Great Books" and Liberal Education', Leavis paid tribute to his learned headmaster who contributed to a 'comparatively good education' which Leavis describes as follows:

> I left school with a very good start in French and German. I spent a great deal of my time as a schoolboy writing Latin proses, some of which were commended by my headmaster, Ezra Pound's correspondent, Dr. Rouse. I could in those days (so soon left behind!) explain in Greek, observing quantity, stress, and tonic accent (the precise value of which Dr. Rouse knew), that I was late for school because I had a puncture in my back tyre. With my form I read through semi-dramatically the plays of Shakespeare. I worked enough at history (I remember reading, among other things, Trevelyan's *History of the American Revolution*) to win a University scholarship in that subject. At the university I took the Historical Tripos Part I and the English Tripos, both successfully. Then I was able to spend three years in post-graduate research.

In a way one can say that Dr. Rouse was the first man who, if he did not so much 'influence' Leavis, made a certain impact on him, even though Leavis was not and did not become a classicist. In fact his interest in modern literature was so strong that he took out a subscription to the *English Review* edited by Ford Madox Ford, another correspondent and, later on, friend of Ezra Pound.

Soon after Leavis left school, the War broke out. He joined the Friends Ambulance Unit as a stretcher-bearer – carrying in his rucksack a copy of the World Classics edition of Milton. In later life, while answering a question put to him by a young American researcher at Oxford as to the kind of moral impact the 1914 war and especially the tragic events of the Somme made on the country, Leavis recalled his experiences in a way characteristically moving yet impersonal, charged but controlled.

> I replied that, yes, I suppose the country *had* been profoundly disturbed; speaking as one who had found himself trying to tot up from the casualty-lists in the papers, and odd reports, the sum of schoolfellows dead in a morning, I didn't see how it could be otherwise. I added, still dwelling on a recalled particular sense of the general realization of disaster that shook the country, and not meaning in the

least to imply irony – certainly not prepared for the response I drew – that those innumerable boy-subalterns who figured in the appalling Role of Honour as 'Fallen Officers' had climbed out and gone forward, playing their part in the attacking wave, to be mown down with the swathes that fell to the uneliminated machine-guns. The comment, quietly sure of its matter-of-fact felicity, was: 'The death-wish!' My point is that I didn't know what to say. What actually came out was, 'They didn't *want* to die.' I felt I couldn't stop there, but how to go on? 'They were brave' – that came to me as a faint prompting, but no; it didn't begin to express my positive intention; it didn't even lead towards it. I gave up; there was nothing else to do.

The passage – one of the best in autobiographical vein Leavis ever wrote – captures neatly and evocatively the ethos of the war as he saw it and lived it, and the indelible mark it left on his personality. After the war, Leavis went to Cambridge. He had won a scholarship from the Perse school to Emmanuel College, reading History in Part I of the Tripos, and English in Part II. He took a Second in Part I and a First in Part II. At Cambridge he met two teachers who impressed him very much: Mansfield Forbes, a historian, and the distinguished Anglo-Saxon scholar Hector Munro Chadwick. In later life, Leavis would dedicate one of his books – *English Literature in Our Time and the University* (1969) – 'To H. Munro Chadwick and Mansfield D. Forbes to whom the world owes more than it knows'. And Q.D. Leavis published an article in *Scrutiny* (Vol. XIV, 1947) on 'Professor Chadwick and English Studies'. Another teacher at Cambridge whose lectures and practical criticism classes Leavis, together with William Empson, attended was I.A. Richards, whose ideas appealed to him and who may be regarded as the earliest influence on Leavis. In 1924 Leavis was awarded the Ph.D. degree in English. His subject of research was: *The Relationship of Journalism to Literature: Studied in the Rise and Earlier Development of the Press in England.* It was supervised by Sir Arthur Quiller-Couch, the King Edward VII Professor of English, who tacitly admired Leavis and his work and had a higher opinion of him than of many other colleagues in the Faculty.

In 1927 Leavis was appointed for three years as a Probationary Faculty Lecturer. In 1929 he married Queenie Dorothy Roth who had taken a First Class Honours in the Tripos examination of 1928 and was awarded an Ottilie Hancock research fellowship at Girton. Her Ph.D. thesis, published as the pioneering and epoch-making book *Fiction and the Reading Public*, was supervised by I.A. Richards.

From then on, Leavis' career as well as his reputation and impact as a critic advanced uninterruptedly, though in striking contrast with his university career and advancement, for he achieved a full-time university lectureship on a permanent basis only in his fifties and was made a Reader just two years before he retired. The nature of the contrast is highlighted

when one considers his critical achievement in the light of the quick
succession of such seminal books as *New Bearings, Revaluation, The Great
Tradition, D.H. Lawrence: Novelist* and of the achievement of *Scrutiny*, the
most influential literary and critical periodical of the century. One factor
that accompanied Leavis' critical career throughout is the polemical skirmishes he had with various critics and academics such as C.S. Lewis,
E.M.W. Tillyard, I.A. Richards, René Wellek, F.W. Bateson – skirmishes
which offered him a different context and a different incentive (or rather
provocation) for enforcing his point of view 'deliberately, not dogmatically'.
But the most controversial battle Leavis engaged in, towards the end of
his Cambridge university career, was with Sir C.P. Snow with his concept
of 'two cultures'. This was soon to be followed by another historical event
in Leavis' career as a critic – the reprint of the twenty volumes of *Scrutiny*
by Cambridge University Press. Such a reprint triumphantly vindicated
not only the historical importance, but also the intrinsic worth of what the
once 'outlawed' periodical had achieved and for which Leavis, the chief
editorial protagonist, had always stood.

Other events that were to mark his post-retirement period were the
establishment of the Leavis Trust, at first supported, but later bitterly
opposed by Leavis because of the way it developed; the invitation to give
the Clark Lectures; the numerous honorary degrees; the award of the CH.
Not less significant than these events was, no doubt, the publication of two
of his last books which are among the most important by him: *Dickens the
Novelist* (in collaboration with Q.D. Leavis) and *The Living Principle*.

In America, too, Leavis' reputation had been growing steadily. Some of
his books had been published in American editions and from time to time
Leavis also published his articles in *Sewanee Review* and *Commentary*. In
1963 he was elected to Honorary Membership of the American Academy
of Arts and Sciences. In Europe, particularly in Italy, Sweden and Spain,
his works were translated and his position as a critic discussed by well-
known critics in those countries.

And yet Leavis could not but look back in anger and indignation on his
university career and on the machinations of those in the academic world
who were opposed to him and to what he stood for. That he was appointed
an Assistant lecturer in his early forties and a full university lecturer in
his fifties had financial consequences for his retired years – consequences
that, Leavis himself was to point out, 'constitute, in the nature of things,
a fact that I and my wife (who also – though with even less recognition –
devoted a life's service to Cambridge English) can hardly regard as negligible'. It is with such an awareness as well as against the background of
'obloquy, slander and worldly disadvantage', that his books were written,
and his critical powers developed from strength to strength. No wonder
some of his Cambridge colleagues wished he had moved away from Cambridge. Even Eliot – and Leavis was the first to champion him in the early
thirties and on whom he was to write some of the most searching and

original criticism – Leavis considered to be no friend of his. Eliot had said of Lawrence: 'had Lawrence been a don at Cambridge, his ignorance might have frightful consequences for himself and for the world, "rotten and rotting others".' Leavis, as he himself puts it, 'was widely supposed – at Cambridge, anyway, where it mattered – to share the honour of the intention with Lawrence'. In fact, more than most people's, it was Eliot's attitude to Lawrence, even though later on he was to modify it significantly, that gave a fillip to Leavis' defence of Lawrence, and to his assiduous efforts to establish him as the greatest novelist and the greatest critic of the century.

Nevertheless, Eliot remained for Leavis the greatest and the most original modern poet. In the last two books he was to publish in his lifetime – *The Living Principle* and *Thought, Words and Creativity* – Leavis, in his late seventies, was to achieve some of the most penetrating and 'personal' criticism of Eliot and Lawrence, both of whom dominated his literary and critical horizon more than any other modern writer and brought out the best and the maturest in him both as a critic of poetry and the novel, and as a critic of life.

Leavis died in 1978. A few months before, he was awarded the CH. Two collections of his hitherto unpublished or uncollected essays were published posthumously: *The Critic as Anti-Philosopher* (1982) and *Valuation in Criticism and Other Essays* (1986).

Q.D. Leavis' 'Memoir' of F.R. Leavis

During his lifetime Leavis did his best to discourage people from writing his biography. If he came to know that someone was going to write one, he did all he could to nip such a project in the bud. One such attempt was made in the sixties by an American contributor to *Scrutiny*, in collaboration with another (non-American) contributor. In an undated draft of a letter to one of the people at Chatto who knew the American, Leavis categorically expressed his opposition to such a project:

> I had hoped that that dreadful project of writing a book on me and my work had been dropped for good, after my appalled intervention that stopped off Eliot and Faber's all those years ago .... I am horrified by the news of the advancing 'project', and would stop it if I could. Here are two reasons that can be given to explain my horror – with force and tact: 1) My 'life's work' has not only gone down the drain, but is being so sickeningly exploited and perverted by people I trusted that it would be insufferable to have the world reminded of it in any kind of public celebration .... 2) as an American, and therefore hopelessly and unwittingly an alien in relation to the English scene from which 'my work' and thought have been inseparable, he is bound to give my enemies jeering and misrepresenting opportunities which they will take – and also opportunities for the kind of 'support' and 'sympathy' I hate the idea of.

The letter was written while Leavis was busy preparing the Clark lectures – 'when I am clear of the Clark lectures I shall (instead of relaxing) write to him, but I shall have a terribly delicate problem', he wrote in the letter. He wanted his Chatto contact to persuade the American would-be biographer to drop the project. 'You can add,' Leavis suggested to him,

> that, knowing he can't be stopped, I pray that he will have the delicacy and the sense to keep me clear of all suggestions that I have connived, or been consulted either directly or through my friends; and, if he does bring out a book, make it unequivocally 'by an

American observer for an American public', aiming at application to
the *American* problem. You can say that I besought Chatto's not to
accept *any* book on me.

However, after Leavis' death, Q.D. Leavis, the only person really qualified
to undertake such an attempt, set out to write her 'Memoir' of her husband
which was to be included in the volume of F.R. Leavis' hitherto unpublished essays that she was preparing for Chatto. Due to her own death
shortly afterwards, however, the 'Memoir' couldn't be completed and all
that Q.D. Leavis left behind were numerous notes, jottings and more or
less extended comments. For all their sketchiness and lack of organisation, these notes are extremely valuable, providing, as they do, interesting
insights into Leavis' life and personality. They are all the more valuable
in so far as that when she writes about her husband, Q.D. Leavis' comments have the stamp of a rare and unique authority and authenticity.
She had known Leavis as nobody else could in her role – as wife, collaborator and fellow critic. No wonder, in writing about him after his death,
she could not help blending biography with autobiography, the past with
the present, and objective and factual accounts with personal memories
and comments. There was an inevitable element of resentment and admiration in her account of her husband: resentment against Leavis' rivals,
enemies and detractors; and admiration for one who aroused much jealousy and animosity, masquerading as literary criticism, among people to
whom he was considered in common esteem to be both morally and
intellectually superior. Thus, in her 'Memoir' Q.D. Leavis conveys a dual
sense of involvement in, as well as detachment from, what she recalls. In
drawing on first-hand concrete experiences of a lifetime lived together, she
both relives them and evaluates them in such a way that, in spite of the
passage of time and the cumulative impact of the strains and stresses of a
dedicated life, what is recalled does not seem to have lost its edge and thus
keeps the past poignantly present. It is something no biographer or critic
could ever achieve. For, being part of what she remembers and what she
and her husband lived together, the value of what she has written goes
beyond what is merely autobiographical. She had copied three quotes from
Conrad and one from Sydney Smith which were to serve her as epigraphs
for her 'Memoir'. The first is Conrad's comment on Stephen Crane: 'He was
surrounded by men, who secretly envious, hostile to the real quality of his
genius (and a little afraid of it), were also in antagonism to the essential
fineness of his nature. But enough of them. *Pulvis et umbra sunt.* I mean
even those who may be alive yet'. The other two quotes from Conrad are
from *A Personal Record.* 'There have been times in the history of mankind
when the accents of truth have moved it to nothing but derision'; and 'That
complete, praiseworthy sincerity which, while it delivers one into the
hands of one's enemies, is as likely as not to embroil one with one's friends.'
The quote from Sydney Smith is about his founding and editing the

Edinburgh Review. Q.D. Leavis saw a close parallel between what Smith says about himself and what Leavis might have said about his own role and experience in founding *Scrutiny*: 'To set on foot such a journal in such times, to contribute towards it for many years, to bear patiently the reproach and poverty it caused, and to look back and see that I have nothing to retract, and no intemperance or violence to reproach myself with, is a career of life which I think to be extremely fortunate'.

In writing these notes for the 'Memoir' Mrs Leavis asks herself 'Why a Memoir?' – and answers the question thus: 'In going through the piles of letters to him (he kept only those of special interest and destroyed many times that number of tributes and letters from admirers) I have been struck by the number of requests that he should write his autobiography.' What Mrs Leavis sets out to do is not so much to write something that would take the place of that unwritten autobiography, as to give her own impressions of how Leavis' life had been lived – a life she herself shared to the full. Less than a month after her husband's death she started writing this 'Memoir' largely based on personal memories and associations of a lifelong relationship that had come to an end. Such memories and recollections of a distant and less distant past pressed upon her with all the greater urgency in view of her own precarious health.

Q.D. Leavis starts by tracing the origins of the Leavis family. The Leavises were

a Huguenot branch of the well-known family of the Duc de Lévis, (which in the eighteenth century produced men of letters) and came to Norfolk on the Revocation of the Edict of Nantes. They tried to retain the sound of the French acute *é* and the final stress by spelling their name hereafter as Leavis, Lavis, or Leaviss – these forms occur only in East Anglia and the East Midlands. My husband's father's branch had settled in Wisbech. When I knew it before the War it was still a beautiful little town, with Elizabethan inns, picturesque old buildings by the quayside, what Pevsner describes as one of the first Georgian streets in England separated by the river Nene rolling between the two sides (High Brink and Low Brink), the old boys' grammar school on one bank, the girls' school on the opposite shore, the elegant architecture of Peckover House (now open to the public) in the middle of one side which ended in an old brewery beyond which was agricultural country. When I saw it Wisbech looked in one part like the description of St. Ogg's in *The Mill on the Floss*, in another like the market town where Miss Havisham resided, among other literary reminiscences. The Leavises were proud of their charming native place, but none of the name is now known in Wisbech. From Wisbech Harry Leavis left for employment in Cambridge.

As to the family traits and characteristics of the Leavises, they were all, we are told,

> very animal-oriented – cats, dogs, horses, and in my husband's case birds too. His father was also a horse-lover and was used sometimes to go to Newmarket Races (entirely against his principles, of course) to admire the splendid race-horses. His father, Elihu Leavis (no doubt name acquired in the usual pious country style by his parents opening the Bible at random) used to ride about East Anglia on his beloved mare Kitty, in pursuance of his trade of tuning pianos and attending to musical instruments – he remembered when there was no made road along the backs and one entered Northampton Street from the end by riding through a water-splash where the brook crossed the path. But horses were an important feature of country life even long after railways became common, for even after the invention of the safety bicycle the horse was still necessary where no roads good enough for bicycles existed. Frank remembered his father had a valued hoof of Kitty's after her death in use on his desk in some capacity. Dogs were also a great feature of the Leavis family. Frank's father would keep only an Old English sheep-dog or a Norfolk lurcher, as more intelligent than any other kind of dog and better with children. (Lurchers are not a recognised breed, they were a cross between the sheepdog and the greyhound, to combine intelligence with speed and were able to hunt by hand signals alone from their master. They were therefore very well suited to the needs of gypsies and other shady characters who taught them to poach and steal, which these dogs did with enjoyment and cunning, to the occasional embarrassment of the honest owner, as of which I heard stories from the family annals.) The Leavis dogs had one-syllable names – in turn Frank remembered Bob, Tip, and, when I knew him, Quip. Quip and the family cat Nick were treated like spoilt children and slept and ate in the dining-room, something that to the Leavises' astonishment disgusted me: they however thought me wanting in right feelings regarding pets.

Leavis' father was fond of travels ('which were not so usual then') and went to America, Morocco, Spain (twice) and other countries, leaving his business in the charge of his manager and his wife to look after the three children. He was a hero to his sons, and Leavis was to dedicate *New Bearings* to him as well as to his wife. Leavis' own athletic interests and aptitude were inherited from his father and his grandfather.

> Frank skated, swam (fast), went for ten-mile runs three times a week, rowed and punted on the river, sailed, played rugger with enthusiasm (even once for the University after the War), but disliked

tennis and detested cricket, pruned his trees and kept his hedges and bushes trim, scythed the grass in his orchard expertly and preferred to mow his lawns with the scythe, only taking to pushing a hand-mower at eighty, refusing to buy a motor-operated machine on the grounds that he 'needed the exercise'.

But as to other duties and aspects of domestic life, Leavis, like his father, was 'unrepentantly undomesticated' – a circumstance to which Q.D. Leavis 'had to be resigned'. Leavis' mother, Kate, whose maiden name was Moore, was Suffolk-born and bred in its ancient and beautiful capital Bury St Edmunds. Her mother had been a Miss Pettit of Mildenhall and her father's family had come from Ireland long before with Sir John Moore, the hero of Corunna. 'Certainly', notes Q.D. Leavis,

> she had the very dark hair, fine grey eyes and fresh complexion of a classic Irish type (consequently my husband thought all women with grey eyes beautiful by definition – this depressed me as my eyes were brown). I met her only once, soon after we had become engaged, and her speech had retained a Suffolk diction and grammar (she died suddenly in her sleep, very soon afterwards, of a long-standing heart condition). In accordance with the East Anglian practice she would say 'That rain' instead of 'It's raining' and called the domestic animals by their generic, not personal, names (e.g. she would scold 'Oh, cat!' or call 'Get you out, dog') as her father-in-law would call his pair of cats to be fed (they lived in his garden, trained to keep birds off the fruit and vegetables) by clapping his hands and shouting 'Little cats, little cats', when they came running.

As to Leavis' own personality and character, Q.D. Leavis tells us how he could 'light a fire in any conditions from any material, but was completely undomesticated'; how his athletic interests were manifold and how they stood him in good stead till the very end of a life with its interminable battles and conflicts: 'Punting, and rowing and canoeing the river up and down … like everything else he did it was at top speed; I found it exhausting like his walks and rides, but he had so much energy he could never get enough physical exercise.'

As to cycling, it was not merely a form of physical exercise, but also a means of travel, even during the holidays. In an autobiographical vein Q.D. Leavis reminisces about her cycling expeditions with her husband in their early married life:

> We naturally took holidays on *bike* – our tours of East Anglian coast (1929) and hinterland (unspoilt in the 1929 pre War II days) and this time (summer 1930) we took our cycles on the train to Winchester and then cycled through the New Forest (also comparatively unspoilt

then) and along the coast to T.F. Powys country and on to Exmouth when we turned up through Exeter and cycled back through Oxford to Bletchley and thence turned home. Of course being so hard up we stayed each night at small inns or bed-and-breakfast-for-cyclists cottages or farmhouses. The food always seemed, whether 'tea' or breakfast, to be bread and jam (homemade if you were lucky), boiled egg, watercress or lettuce, and ham (at farm-house, sometimes delicious home-cured and boiled), and a big pot of strong Indian tea. Their coffee we soon learnt was undrinkable (made from a poisonous liquid in a bottle) and many an aspidistra we watered with it to spare our landlady's feelings. I often did the same with my cup of tea, as I found it too strong – the only tea I was used to at my home was Russian tea with lemon, as an after-dinner drink, and we breakfasted off coffee, onto which I weaned my husband off tea at breakfast. But he could drink any tea (except Russian and Chinese), however strong, so long as there was plenty of it and plenty of milk and sugar, having learnt to live on this mainly during the First World War. When he and his brother were schoolboys they used to cycle from Cambridge in the summer, starting soon after dawn, to the Norfolk coast where their father had bought a bungalow at West Runton, to join the family who had gone by train with the luggage – they did this long run in one go. He and I used to train to Norwich and cycle from there to the coast, which was quite as much as I cared to do in one day.

Sailing, walking and gardening were, in fact, 'hobbies' for Leavis as well as forms of exercise, in some of which his wife also participated. As to sailing, she jots down: 'The Norfolk Broads. Our honeymoon. Never again.' And concerning Leavis' walking habit, she recalls certain experiences with pictures of a vanished but jealously treasured past:

Walking – long distances and *fast*. I had been well trained by my brother to accompany him on the walks, long and at a good steady pace, through the Holfordshire and Middlesex lanes and hills, but we used to take rest and eat sandwiches and stand and look over gates, and *talk* – F.R.L. kept up a clipping speed and did not wish to talk but to think, he only wanted my silent companionship, but we were a talking family, and our conversation was full of fun and joie-de-vivre, spontaneously witty and laughing a good deal as well as earnestly intellectual. My brother and sister and I were used to dozens of cousins (my mother one of 6, my father one of 10) of all ages, and some married with children, so we had plenty of weddings and births and an abundance of relatives (all interested in our development and happiness) in our lives, and everyone had a lap and a pair of welcoming arms for the babies and toddlers. Presents on birthdays and festival occasions were showered on us, and we saw no distinction between poor and well-off except on grounds of character and abilities.

In some of these notes, Q.D. Leavis, then, sets out to reconstruct Leavis' life before she married him. He was, she writes,

a country boy. East Anglian on both sides – Norfolk and Suffolk parents, Cambridge born, and oriented to Norfolk – grandfather retired to a cottage and large, highly productive vegetable and fruit garden at Denver Norfolk – childhood of Frank spent there a good deal and featured prominently in his memories of childhood. Wild hops etc. (roasting-jack inside chimney, little cats, hamper of produce, hares).

Leavis' father was a self-educated intellectual and musician and Leavis inherited his taste for music. He was a man of remarkable character and personality and exercised a great influence on his son. In what she says about Leavis' parents and their marriage Q.D. Leavis indirectly adumbrates what were going to be the essential features and interests of her own marriage with F.R. Leavis. Although that of his parents, she tells us,

was an ideally happy marriage according to the son, the pattern (of the husband with interests his wife could not share and a wife by definition confined in domesticity) was a sanctioned Victorian one, there were signs of stress – father a prey to mysterious disabling headaches, which he ignored when they occurred, as they often did, when he had demands of a public nature. He refused often-expressed desires that he should stand for public office which, he was assured, would lead to his becoming Mayor of Cambridge, as his admirers and colleagues wished, but preferred to devote his leisure time to his great interest, the Chesterton Institute, one of those Victorian efforts at providing cultural improvement and recreation for working men, and of which Harry Leavis carried the burden as treasurer and promoter. Though an aggressive Victorian rationalist he was willing to work with the local Canon of the Church in this, sinking his principles for the sake of a cause. He and the Canon collaborated on a basis of mutual respect and friendship.

Q.D. Leavis describes life at the Chesterton Hall Crescent home where the Leavis family lived before the First World War – a description that in some ways throws light on life in general in Cambridge at that time. Cambridge was

only a little market-town that happened also to be attached to a

university with which it had then the happiest relations, quality
shops, such as a number of high-class tailors and bespoke shoe-mak-
ers, which could depend on the support of a university clientele –
working-class families glad to get their boys into university employment, whether in college, the University Press, or other branches,
and very proud to have a son who rose to be a college porter or butler.
As soon as his music business was sufficiently prosperous, (and in
those days of booming piano sales and hiring it soon was) Harry
Leavis was sought after as a good master by those wishing to
apprentice sons to the music business (paternalistic master) and the
firm prided itself, as his younger son, a member of it, told me, on
being able to repair any kind of instrument, including the elaborate
mechanical one. They kept superior instruments – prided themselves
on being able to supply for hire grand pianos suitable for visiting
concert performers, and Harry Leavis owned a valuable collection of
violins, his speciality, for he played the first violin himself in a
chamber music quartet that met at his house for very many years –
his younger son Ralph in due course played the violin in it too. Such
a cultural activity was characteristic of Victorian Cambridge tradesmen and must be recognised as qualifying the usual conception of the
term 'tradesman' – there were a number of very good bookshops in
the town then, several of which provided the start for some distinguished national publishing firms (e.g., Bowes and Bowes for
Macmillan and Bowes, Deighton Bell for George Bell's) and there
were at least half a dozen second-hand bookshops of standing. In a
very small town the resident owners of such shops (and Cambridge
tradesmen in those days generally lived over or behind their business
premises) formed an important cultural element. Old Mr Porter, the
active partner in the largely second-hand book business of Galloway
and Porter's (he was known as the best finder of O.P. books in the
country) was a close personal friend of Harry Leavis', and it was due
to this I suppose that when the Cambridge English Faculty had given
the Cambridge bookshops to understand that *Scrutiny* was taboo and
they would not supply or stock it (Heffer's later sold it from under the
counter on demand), Porter's kept *Scrutiny* on display, and they were
also the only firm that put my husband's books in their window as
they appeared (our Dickens book was the first Heffer's ever displayed
in their window, but by then they had moved from their famous Petty
Curry premises and indeed had changed owners and character). The
prosperous tradesmen sent their sons to the excellent Cambridge
Boys' County School before taking them into their business or, if a
boy was more academically inclined, to the Perse school: both schools
regularly put in boys for university scholarships and were often
successful, providing a long list of Fellows of Cambridge Colleges.

Harry Leavis then looked round, when his children were young (there was only a year between each successive child) for a good-sized piece of land near enough to the business but on the edge of the country, on which he could get built a house to his own design and with room enough to plant the orchard and lay out the fruit and vegetable garden, lawns and hedges which, as a countryman, he felt to be a necessity of life. He was able to buy a plot for four houses from the owner of Chesterton Hall (the home of the De Freville family) adjacent to the Hall's grounds. Chesterton Road was then an academically respectable area – even when I moved in in 1929 (and for long after) it still housed old-style academics like Professor G.E. Moore the philosopher and Dr G.G. Coulton the medieval historian, among others. The wide and handsome Chesterton Road shortly petered out in the tow path via tiny Chesterton Village (noted for its Irish type village ratio of public-houses, depending for trade on the colleges, from which they were a pleasant and easy walk). Mrs Leavis remembered that when she first came to live in Chesterton the village women used to go gleaning in the Chesterton fields, and she bought her yeast for their weekly bread-baking from a brewer's there. Her flour came round in a horse and cart from French's Mill (a local windmill long since disused). Wind and water-mills were a feature of the locality, and I remember Newnham Mill and Grantchester Mill (both water-mills) were burnt down early in our married life; Madingley Mill has been restored only as a picturesque antiquity, but the wisdom of the East Anglians used the water and the strong steady winds of the fen country as free power, nor is there anything to compare with stone-ground flour for bread.

Harry Leavis did not think much of the run of home architecture of the Edwardian age, and had decided views of his own as to what makes a comfortable and aesthetically pleasing house, so he designed 6 Chesterton Hall Crescent himself, with a builder to execute it, and his son remembered being taken constantly by his father to oversee the construction – all materials had to be of the best quality and he threw out any bricks he decided were below standard. The material was a quiet variety of the yellow Cambridge brick, a good background with its white paint and red tiled roofs, for the greenery surrounding it on all sides. The doors and doorsteps, window-frames and banisters and stairs and floor-boards were of Australian jarrah wood, a wood so durable that it needed only to be oiled occasionally, and the workmen complained that it was so hard as to turn their tools; door-furniture was of solid brass, all corners of passages and where ceilings met floors and walls, were rounded – then an unusual feature – and all windows were designed horizontally in contrast to the customary vertical windows, giving, like the long roofs making contrasted masses, and with wide eaves, a modern, that is post-War look to the house, which was in my time greatly admired by people of taste. The effect was of an unpretentious large farmhouse, as no doubt was intended. He had a noble idea of a drawing-room – his was 22′ by 23′ with a high ceiling and with architectural effects of flat pillars and a very long deep bay-window in the west wall to let in the afternoon sun (when we settled there I had a south window put in to make it an all-day sunny room, which meant sacrificing the high mahogany book-case that he had designed to cover most of the south wall and hold the books from which he read to his family). The dining-room and master-bedrooms above, were also of good size and had unusual sets of wide semi-circular windows letting in both east and south sunshine. The open fireplaces in the dining-room and drawing-room provided deep recesses each side for cupboards and bookshelves, and all these rooms had an architectural feeling in their windows, aspect and good proportions.

The house, occupying one plot in front, was close to the Crescent, with a high hedge in between and a great acacia tree in plant. The remaining land was behind a high fence and on each side and behind had been carefully laid out and planted and cultivated before the house was built. My husband remembered how on Sundays and holidays the whole family, still living in Mill Road, would go in summer to picnic in the garden, digging up and cooking vegetables from the garden to supplement the provisions they had bought, over an open fire, drawing water from a well in the garden (bricked up when the house was built, for the children's safety). Early in the century, the house being built and the garden well grown, the satisfied owner moved his family there. An ample cloakroom under the stairs, between the dining-room and the drawing-room walls and heated by the back of the always-burning dining-room fire, with a little window looking on the great pear-tree outside, became a happy private study for Frank to do his homework and keep his schoolbooks, his bedroom being an attic up a steep staircase from the second-floor. The rest of the top floor apart from an ample linen-cupboard was a loft made for the apples and pears from the orchard to be stored, in deep straw, and keep all winter in the cold of the open roof (no one worried in those days without central heating bills about heat escaping through the roof). I go into such detail because the house and garden are no longer there – taken over and scrapped by the city as site for old-type bungalows – and because it was a centre of the Cambridge literary culture for so long.

The garden, well matured when we moved in in 1931, in the second year of our marriage, was a paradise: every kind of fruit-tree, and the best variety of each, bore abundantly in those idyllic days before pests, if any, could not be kept down by little red spiders and other natural enemies. The two great greengage trees were weighed down, even to breaking off over-loaded branches, about every third year, there were gage-plums and all other kinds of plums, red, yellow, purple and almost black, delicious to handle with their bloom and oval shapes so that picking was a pleasure, there were three damson trees, cooking apples – some so hard they could be left on the tree till December and always kept till late summer in the loft so that unlike Mr Knightley of Donwell Abbey we never went without apple-pies, and many a variety of juicy sweet or sharp eating apples, some also no longer to be bought anywhere, and three giant walnut trees of the large-nut continental variety, and several kinds of cooking and eating pears, besides the great William Bon Chretien pear-tree which overhung the large balcony on the south wall providing welcome and picturesque shadow, the balcony which Harry Leavis designed to end the turn of the first-floor corridors: the door to it on the landing, like the door at the end of the ground-floor corridors onto the south wall, between kitchen and dining-room, had always to be kept open unless snow, ice or fog made this insufferable (rain was ignored, they were an exceptionally hardy and strong family even then when people were not softened by over-heated houses and spoiled for walking and cycling by motor-cars).

To me, a London child, it seemed unbelievable, but it was only what in that age a country-town tradesman thought right, proper and desirable for him to live in.

As to F.R. Leavis' reading habits and the kind of books he used to read, Q.D. Leavis observes, thereby more or less implicitly bringing out the differences between his reading and hers, between the books that were already in his possession and books she brought along with her: 'I can only remember what books he had when I first had the run of them. Since then they had repeatedly to be thinned and weeded to make room for acquisitions, because some were superseded, or because First Editions would fetch money in bad times.' Leavis' books included *The Icelandic Sagas* of W.A. Craigie – which he had read when he was twenty-six – French, German and English poets, French history, the Elizabethan and Jacobean dramatists, the major Greek and Latin classics and the nineteenth-century English writers. He used to read to her his favourite English poets – Hardy, Edward Thomas, Eliot, Pound (*Hugh Selwyn Mauberley*), as well as Shakespeare, Pope, Wordsworth and Keats; Heine and Goethe; and 'Stendhal's best novels aloud in French in the evenings and wet days when we spent a month in a cottage in Southwold'. Leavis also bought Proust as he appeared, and

the then modern French poets such as T.S. Eliot nourished his verse on in his first period (*The Waste Land and Other Poems*); he used to read me Tristan Corbière, Rimbaud and Laforgue. He had a regular French library. *La Mercure de France, La Nouvelle Revue Française,*

Les Cahiers du Sud and a row of Sainte-Beuve's criticism and all the French classics in verse and prose and drama, and he bought all the new French writers as they appeared. He had all the major Greek and Latin classics, some in scholarly editions, and shelves full of the Classical Loeb edition with translations alongside the texts.

(The Loeb edition was edited then by W.H.D. Rouse, Leavis' headmaster at the Perse School.)

Along with these works Q.D. Leavis found in Leavis' library his beloved authors – Cobbett, Chaucer and Bunyan – lots of dictionaries of classical and modern languages, books on French idiom and versification, all his school books of Latin, Greek and German to which he had added Italian and some Spanish: 'I remember him, at their request, showing some of his young priests how to read Dante.' He had, moreover, all the Mermaid library (the first unexpurgated editions of the Elizabethan and Jacobean dramatists), all 'the more interesting' in Middle English, a shelf full of seventeenth-century theology and sermons, including Lancelot Andrewes. As to nineteenth-century authors, the complete works of Hardy ('inherited from his father, whose delicate signature "H. Leavis" in them all was unexpected from so forceful a character – his marginal marks and comments in them, particularly in his favourite, *Jude the Obscure*, were more what one would expect'). Other collected works Leavis inherited from his father were those of Mark Twain and Dickens, 'both of which he read to his children, and Cobbett and above all Shakespeare'. Leavis also inherited piles of 'those well-printed double-column Victorian non-fictional diaries in paper-covers published by Watts & Co. at low cost – for Harry was a stalwart supporter of the Rationalist Press. It must be remembered that besides circulating the Huxleys and Darwins and Mills it also printed in this form cheap editions of several of Matthew Arnold's works besides *Culture and Anarchy* (a favourite book of both Leavis generations and well-marked by both), several also of Newman's and Carlyle's, besides propaganda works of intellectual enlightenment.'

The list of such books and writers, essential, though by no means exhaustive or even comprehensive, as F.R. Leavis read in his earlier years had important gaps for Q.D. Leavis. For not only were there no books for children, fairy-tales, folk-lore, or books by female writers, like George Eliot and Mrs Gaskell, but also there was no Henry James – who was to be so important from the point of F.R. Leavis' later criticism. Her getting Leavis interested in these writers was to lay the corner-stone of their partnership, in which collaboration on the same author or subject went hand-in-hand with their working quite independently on different authors. 'What I missed from his library', Q.D. Leavis writes,

were the children's classics that had meant so much in my own childhood, but perhaps these had all been passed on before this to his sister's little girls – he certainly had taken trouble to supply them with gifts of well-illustrated children's books until I took over the congenial job of providing for their birthdays or Xmas presents. But if he had ever had such he never spoke of them nor seemed to remember them, and had no tenderness for the nursery rhymes and tales and songs and the folksongs and singing games which from memory I used to hand on to our children in due course. One would have thought his mother, a Suffolk girl who retained touches of that dialect all her life, would have transmitted them, but perhaps her husband disapproved of them, as he did of her church-going.

Among the books she brought with her on marrying Leavis, there were the novels and tales of Henry James – 'a hiatus in his reading, but whose novels had been discovered by my enterprising brother in his schooldays, like the Barchester novels, and which he passed on to his sisters' – and Trollope's novels. Concerning Leavis' attitude to the latter – Q.D. Leavis found Trollope 'important and valuable' and not merely 'for relaxation or for evidence of the social history of the Mid-Victorian Age' – she comments:

Whereas he examined the entire output of any poet who interested him, on whatever grounds and of whatever period, he did not, as I thought necessary, read or at least look through the entire *oeuvre* of a novelist. He had a well annotated *Mary Barton*, but at the most cursory inspection left it at that as far as Mrs Gaskell was concerned, and having looked at *Daniel Deronda* at some early date and found the Jewish part fictitious, he had written his essay on George Eliot originally without any reference to this, I believed, major novel. I persuaded him to give it another try and introduced him to my own copy (given to me by my parents when I was 14) in which all the good things in the 'Gwendolen Harleth' part I had marked marginally so that he should take the points, and mentioned (tactfully but unaggressively) some praise of the achievement as I understood it. This was successful: he was soon convinced that he had discovered a great novel and I then introduced him to my copy of Henry James's *Partial Portraits* in which James's conversational piece about Deronda appeared, until at my suggestion he reprinted it entire in *The Great Tradition*.

As to Leavis' non-literary reading, Q.D. Leavis cites books of history, philosophy of science, history of philosophy, individual philosophers (like Collingwood and Wittgenstein) and – a subject that particularly interested him – the theory of value on which he possessed psychological, philosophical and aesthetic works in several languages, (books 'long since sacrificed to the exigencies of moving to a smaller house'). Among books of

philosophy, Leavis found two books particularly useful: Pear's book on
Wittgenstein ('the most heavily annotated book I ever saw', notes Q.D.
Leavis); and Marjorie Green's *The Knower and the Known*. He also kept
up his history and 'knew where to lay his hand on any historical work he
needed to support an argument'. But what he never read – and in describing and commenting on it Q.D. Leavis reveals some characteristic aspects
of Leavis' mind and personality and, at the same time, makes some critical
observations on Wittgenstein –

> was what other educated people call light reading and justify as
> valuable for relaxation – detective stories, P.G. Wodehouse, and
> such, and I doubt if he had ever more than looked into Trollope,
> having decided after reading *Barchester Towers*, that was the only
> Trollope he owned, that he had no use for Trollope – I brought seven
> into the household, a fanatic within his family. (Wittgenstein, an avid
> and regular reader of detective story magazines from America, so he
> told us, went twice a week to the cinema to see Hollywood films in
> order to laugh and cry, which apparently he could not without such
> aids.) My husband thought this shocking and pointed to something
> wrong with Wittgenstein and deficient in the pursuit of philosophy.
> Having met Professor 'Space, Time and Deity' Alexander of Manches-
> ter, I did not think Wittgenstein's deficiencies necessarily proved
> that a philosopher cannot be a whole man living all his life on the
> same level and that the finest, and in the past, Spinoza, whom I
> greatly admired, seemed evidence of this too. However, when I once
> voiced my disillusion, from a considered Cambridge experience, that
> philosophers were not personally philosophic, so to speak, to our
> friend Mauris Ginzberg of the L.S.E. (himself a good as well as an
> intellectual man) he replied sadly that one only needed to attend a
> meeting of the Aristotelian Society to be assured of this fact, (that
> philosophers are no better than, or different from, other people). I
> still feel that they ought to be. (Wittgenstein himself was touchy,
> domineering, arbitrary and liable to unreasonable anger, in spite of
> his charm and other engaging qualities.) It always surprised me that
> a man with so much capacity for real life as Wittgenstein – architect,
> engineer and sculptor as he had shown himself to be – should devote
> his whole life to philosophy, instead of doing his thinking as a
> by-product of an activity of the whole man, and one that brought him
> into contact with the life of the community. F.R. Leavis felt no need
> to compensate for an inadequate intellectual life by compensation
> with trash – I remember his taking issue with D.W. Harding who, as
> a psychologist, argued that popular (i.e. commercial) entertainment
> (Walt Disney, the commercial cinema, cheap fiction etc.) were valu-
> able for people exhausted by intellectual occupations – and said 'If
> too tired to engage the mind in fresh effort, why not reread a classic

(something worth reading) with which one is already familiar, play good music one already knows, instead of taking in trash?' In his copy of Collingwood's autobiography he had marked Collingwood's complaint about his living and working in a University, which 'is an institution based on medieval ideas, where life and work are still hedged about by the medieval interpretation of the Greek distinction between the contemplative life and the practical life' – against this he (F.R. Leavis) had written 'not mine', and had marked emphatically Collingwood's statement that his 'attempted reconstruction of moral philosophy would remain incomplete so long as my habits were based on the vulgar division of men into thinkers and men of action'. This is why he found D.H. Lawrence so heartening and congenial.

While tracing Leavis' literary career back to his early years at Cambridge, Q.D. Leavis mentions I.A. Richards – her one-time research supervisor – Basil Willey, Brian W. Downes and William Empson (Q.D. Leavis' exact contemporary) – people who were there at that time. The Empson set (as she calls the Cambridge poets of that period) attended F.R. Leavis' lectures, as did she. It was Leavis' favourable review of Empson in the *Cambridge Review* that stopped connection with that organ. This was, we are told, because the *Cambridge Review* was,

in my husband's words, controlled by 'a committee of innominate dons', including one who had a finger in every academic pie, and who was inevitably a dominant figure. He was not only outraged by these Leavis reviews that flouted academic literary values or supported morally undesirable works like *The Waste Land*, the fiction of T.F. Powys and the squibs of D.H. Lawrence, he saw in articles and reviews published in the *Cambridge Review* by other hands proof of Leavis' corrupting influence – e.g. pieces by the inimical L.C. Knights on Baudelaire (of whom then Tillyard probably knew nothing but then a title like *Les Fleurs du Mal* speaks for itself) and nasty Jacobean dramatists. Tillyard, therefore, drew up a black list (as the *Cambridge Review* editor informed the culprits) of people who were not to be allowed to review or write for the *Cambridge Review* in future. Moreover, the *Cambridge Review* was not to review Leavis' books either. This ban lasted, except for *Education and the University* when the *Cambridge Review* found an obscure clergyman to denounce it as undesirable and anyway only repeating what Newman has said in *The Idea of a University*. This book was considered particularly objectionable by the Cambridge English faculty because (a) it challenged and discussed fundamentalists and (b) who was Leavis to have views about university education?

Apart from the rift with the *Cambridge Review*, there was also a conflict

with the Union Library Committee which Q.D. Leavis documents as
follows:

> Leavis, as known to be interested in and widely read in Contempo-
> rary literature, had been early co-opted on to the Union Library
> Committee that recommended new books for inclusion (and had
> large funds) and had taken great trouble and spent considerable time
> reading and sifting new literature for the purpose. He did not recom-
> mend indiscriminately. At this point he was uncivilly ejected – no
> grounds given. However, an academic friend of ours, on social terms
> with the wife of one of the committee members for another subject,
> confided that it was because 'Dr. Leavis recommended such peculiar
> books' – implying moral condemnation. When asked to specify some
> of these the lady mentioned 'books like *The Waste Land* and *The
> Sacred Wood*, authors like D.H. Lawrence and T.F. Powys and those
> war-poets like Sassoon and Blunden'. An unsavoury reputation was
> thus attached to him through Cambridge gossip on a variety of
> grounds. He had built up a good modern English section for the
> Union Library in poetry, fiction and literary criticism that was much
> appreciated by the intelligentsia among the undergraduates, and
> must have gifted the Union Library with many now valuable first
> editions (unless they were worn out in use). We were thus, even in
> the early days of our married life, allotted the status of pariahs,
> which socially and academically lasted our life-time. I may mention
> that no Professor of English at Cambridge, past or present, has ever
> invited either of us to cross his or her threshold,[1] we were never, in
> over half a century of university life here, invited to any university
> or faculty functions (with one exception, the then Master of Downing
> being Vice-Chancellor and my husband a Fellow of the college, we
> were inevitably present at the lunch held in Downing for the honor-
> ary degree recipients). When it became known that my husband was
> slowly dying and I was tied to the house by nursing duties, I received
> a letter from a Faculty member of the younger generation but per-
> fectly secure as to Faculty and college appointments, whom I had
> only met once, – kindly, and uniquely, offering to help if his services
> in shopping, e.g. were needed, but, he wrote, he must stipulate that
> this should be kept strictly private, because of the scandalous gossip
> that he would incur if it were known. What scandalous gossip could
> be attached to such minimal and impersonal contact, where a man of
> 82 and a woman of 70 were in question, I cannot imagine. I mention
> it as a proof that, far from suffering from persecution mania, the
> Leavises suffered very damaging slander and discrimination.

[1] (I should state here that when my husband ultimately was appointed to an
Assistant Lectureship (in his forties) 'Q' felt it obligatory to invite him to dine at
High Table with him – my existence however was never recognised.)

Early Articles, *New Bearings* and *Scrutiny*

The worth of the critic is known not by his arguments but by the quality of his choice.

The honest critic must be content to find a *very little* contemporary work worth serious attention; but he must also be ready to *recognize* that little, and to demote work of the past when a new work surpasses it.

Ezra Pound

Leavis started his critical career by reviewing books and writing articles and pamphlets. Most of the earliest articles and reviews appeared in the *Cambridge Review* and one in the *Bookman*. The most important of them are 'T.S. Eliot – a reply to the Condescending', 'D.H. Lawrence' and 'William Empson: intelligence and sensibility' (published in the *Cambridge Review* in 1929, 1930 and 1931 respectively), and 'The Influence of Donne on Modern Poetry' (published in the *Bookman* in 1931). There is something at once fresh and challenging, convinced and convincing about these articles. The reputations of Eliot and Lawrence were not at that time the assured values they were to become later on, and so it took courage as well as original perception to champion them.

Leavis wrote the article on Eliot as one who was aware of his debt to Eliot, and one purpose of the article was 'to acknowledge the debt and define its nature'. He sets about describing Eliot as 'a poet of profound originality and of special significance to all who are concerned for the future of English poetry', the 'most modern of the moderns' and at the same time 'more truly traditional than the "traditionalists" ', and one whose poetry 'is more conscious of the past than any other that is being written in English today'. The notion of modernity as co-existing with a particular sense of tradition and the two being, to some extent, interdependent, Leavis may be said to have largely derived from Eliot and from what he says about it in the essay 'Tradition and the Individual Talent'. Eliot's comments on the relevance of tradition to modern poetry and to a modern poet like himself find their apt exemplification in his own poetry where 'the poet bears out the critic', and his acquaintance with the past illumines 'both the past and the present'.

In characterising Eliot's criticism Leavis in a way indicates the lines along which his own criticism, at least in its earlier stages, was to develop, even though from *After Strange Gods* onwards, Leavis was strongly opposed to Eliot's critical evaluations of modern writers, especially D.H. Lawrence. Being unlike those 'who prefer prophecy, exaltations and the ardours of the private soul', Leavis sympathised with Eliot's approach to poetry 'commonly by way of technique', and his dealings with 'content' which were always 'rigorously controlled and disciplined' – something that would characterise Leavis' own approach to poetry in *New Bearings, Revaluation* and elsewhere. That is why those who consider Hamlet 'as a man with a life antecedent to, and outside of, the play, a subject for psychoanalysis, feel that Mr Eliot induces cerebral corrugations to no end' – an attitude to Shakespeare that Leavis and other *Scrutiny* writers on Shakespeare were to share; and that anticipated, in a way, their anti-Bradleyan stance.

There are also other aspects of Eliot's criticism Leavis admires – his generalisations, 'explicit and implied', his conception of order, and of European literature as 'an organic whole', his 'elucidation' of impersonality, of the relation between art and the personality of the artist and his account of the relation between thought and emotion. Leavis' admiration of these qualities and characteristics of Eliot's criticism was to have a radical influence – more than that of any other critic, be he Middleton Murry, I.A. Richards or William Empson – on Leavis' criticism. Not that he accepted all Eliot's critical views *in toto* and without qualifications and reservations. For instance, he did not follow Eliot, 'in either sense of the word', when Eliot passed on from literary criticism, as such, to 'the problem of the relation of poetry to the spiritual and social life of its time and of other times' – a divergence that was subsequently to take many forms and degrees of emphasis, and to lead on to Leavis' rejection of Eliot's concept of timeless and transcendental reality in *Four Quartets*.

In the relatively short note on 'The Influence of Donne on Modern Poetry' Leavis presents Donne not only as 'the undisputed chief' of the Metaphysical Poets, but also as one who replaced Milton as an influence on modern poetry, and at the same time symbolised the antithesis of the ethos of nineteenth-century poetry – poetry characterised by the preoccupation with 'the creation of a dream world'. Moreover, it is Donne's poetry rather than Milton's or even Wordsworth's that helps one grasp what is characteristically 'modern' about modern poetry – its 'unpoetical' character, its 'urgencies' and 'stresses' being associated with 'the unescapable environment of urban civilization and its background of modern thought', rather than with 'dawn, dew, flowers or country place-names, or dreams of old romance'. It is with Donne as its main poetic protagonist that the seventeenth century, much more important to modern poetry than the nineteenth, was restored 'to its proper place in the English tradition'. Leavis quotes Eliot's famous comment on Donne, starting with 'A thought to Donne was an experience; it modified his sensibility,' etc., to suggest the relevance of Donne's poetry – 'intellectual and lyrical, cynical and serious, witty and intense at the same time' – to Eliot's. Hence what future poets were to learn from Eliot will be 'as much as anything, how to learn from Donne'. Leavis quotes a poem by Empson – 'Twixt devil and deep sea, man hacks his caves' – to suggest Empson's modernity and at the same time to enforce the point that 'he would not have written in this way but for Donne'.

The note on Empson, 'William Empson: Intelligence and Sensibility', is a review of *Seven Types of Ambiguity* which Leavis finds 'highly disturbing'. The author is using 'his intelligence on poetry as seriously as if it were mathematics or one of the sciences'. Apart from his analytical brilliance, Leavis finds 'a very fine sensibility' in Empson whom he considers to be 'an uncommonly adequate reader of poetry', which, in Leavis' later phraseology, will be the equivalent of 'an uncommonly adequate critic of poetry'. Hence, *Seven Types of Ambiguity* is considered to be 'that rare thing, a critical work of the first order'.

However, as in the case of Eliot, so also in that of Empson, Leavis' view of him was to be modified later on, and what he originally considered to be a slight limitation – 'he is apt to be a little too ingenious in detecting ambiguities' – would later be regarded as a serious handicap. Leavis also disagrees with Empson when he denies lyrical inspiration to Browning – 'I should have thought', says Leavis, himself no admirer of the poet, 'that Browning's power was lyrical or nothing' – and when he says that 'Wordsworth frankly had no inspiration other than his use, when a boy, of the mountains as a totem or father-substitute'. But on the whole the review is favourable and the strictures mild as compared with Leavis' later criticism in general and of Empson in particular. Leavis also reviewed such books as Osbert Sitwell's *England Reclaimed*, F.R. Higgins' *The Dark Breed*, Augustus Ralli's *Critiques*, George Ryland's *Words and Poetry*, Edmund Blunden's *Retreat*, Shane Leslie's *The Skull of Swift*, and *Cambridge Poetry 1929*.

His first publication, in the form of a pamphlet – *Mass Civilization and Minority Culture* – came out in 1930, the first of the series called 'Minority Pamphlets' published by Gordon Fraser at St. John's College, Cambridge. As an epigraph for his pamphlet Leavis chose a quote from *Culture and Anarchy*: 'And this function is particularly important in our modern world, of which the whole civilization is, to a much greater degree than the civilization of Greece and Rome, mechanical and external, and tends constantly to become more so.' It sums up, in a way, the ethos of much of what Leavis was to say in this pamphlet about modern civilization and culture, or what he would, later, call the plight of our civilization. For his belief, formulated for the first time in this pamphlet, that 'culture has

always been in minority keeping' and that 'it is upon a very small minority
that the discerning appreciation of art and literature depends', he could
have cited Pound and Eliot as his allies. Another ally was I.A. Richards
whom Leavis quotes to the effect that criticism is not 'a luxury trade', that
the critic is as much concerned with 'the health of the mind as any doctor
with the health of the body', and that the arts are 'invariably and quite
apart from the intentions of the artist an appraisal of existence'. Thus,
only the minority is capable of appreciating Dante, Shakespeare, Donne,
Baudelaire, Hardy – 'major instances' of creativity upon whom depend 'the
implicit standards that order the finer living of an age, the sense that this
is worth more than that, this rather than that is the direction in which to
go, that the centre is here rather than there'. This sentence epitomises
Leavis' major concern and procedure as a critic – distinguishing major
creativity through critical discernment and discrimination, and linking
'the subtlest and most perishable parts of tradition' with what is living,
original and permanent in the present.

But the pursuit of standards in criticism did not, even at that stage,
seem to be an easy thing to Leavis, in the face of the ever-multiplying
processes of mass-production, standardisation and levelling down. And
equally, if not more ominous was, and is to an even greater degree today,
the part played by the mass media – Leavis' life-long bogies – guilty of
deliberately exploiting 'the cheap response'; as, for instance, through the
use of applied psychology. Already in his first extended piece of writing,
Leavis thus seemed to be alone in fighting his battle, for even those who
would agree with him that there had been an overthrow of standards, that
authority had disappeared, and that 'the currency has been debased and
inflated', did not often seem to realise what a catastrophe this portended.
His aim in this pamphlet was to bring all this home. And his way of doing
so was by examining the role of such contemporary figures as Arnold Bennett 'the arbiter of taste', J.C. Squire, 'specialist in poetry and "himself a
poet" ', Hugh Walpole, J.B. Priestley, H.G. Wells. None of them seemed to
be concerned with defending the standards of criticism – if anything they
unwittingly contributed to their decline – and fighting against the forces
of a standardised civilization arrayed against them. I.A. Richards, whose
opinion, in his younger days, Leavis found 'worth more than most people's'
may have been a cautious optimist, but not so Leavis. For Richards the
present century seemed to be in a 'cultural trough rather than upon a
crest', and he thought that the situation was likely to get worse before it
got better, believing that 'once the basic level has been reached, a slow
climb back may be possible'. Leavis' own instinct led him to entertain no
such hope. Nevertheless, even he had to cling to such a hope and to the
belief '(unwarranted, possibly), that what we value most matters too much
to the race to be finally abandoned, and that the machine will yet be made
a tool'. If, in the light of what he subsequently wrote, especially from the
date of the 'Snow' lecture onwards, we were to reconsider what he had

written in *Mass Civilization and Minority Culture* we would have less reason to be dissatisfied with his less rosy view of things then than with I.A. Richards'.

These convictions of the young Leavis on the threshold of his long and eventful critical and academic career were to find their cogent expression in his first book of criticism *New Bearings in English Poetry*, which was to have such a decisive impact on the development both of English poetry and of English Criticism. Although Gordon Fraser brought out, in 1930, Leavis' first publication *Mass Civilization and Minority Culture*, practically everything else Leavis wrote in book form was published by Chatto and Windus, starting with *New Bearings in English Poetry* (1932), and ending with the first of his two posthumously published books (*The Critic as Anti-Philosopher*, 1982).

In offering his first book to Chatto, Leavis described it as 'short ... but weighty' and 'the fruit of some years' specialization'. In language, with a 'virility regarded as correlative to a mind-state of maturity and poise', as G. Wilson Knight put it, Leavis proposed a chart in *New Bearings* that has proved to be a source of guidance, inspiration and stimulus to many later critics. After covering in the first chapter the history of the 'preconceptions and assumptions' concerning poetry from the great Romantics down to the moderns, Leavis sets out to assess the literary and cultural factors that made the emergence of modern poetry, and especially that of a poet like Eliot, possible. Starting from the conviction, which he shared with Pound, that 'the potentialities of human experience in any age are realised only by a tiny minority, and the important poet is important because he belongs to this (and has also, of course, the power of communication)', Leavis points out that a poet's capacity for experiencing and his power of communicating are indistinguishable. He is, we are told, 'unusually sensitive, unusually aware, more sincere and more himself than the ordinary man can be'. Hence poetry can communicate 'the actual quality of experience with a subtlety and precision unapproachable by any other means'.

With such convictions and criteria in mind, Leavis rejects the nineteenth-century conventions of 'the poetical' – conventions which enjoyed 'the prestige of the Romantic achievement'. But with a change in the situation 'the incidence of stress for the adult sensitive mind shifted', so that however much Tennyson may have wrestled with the problems of the age, his habits, conventions and techniques were 'not those of a poet who could have exposed himself freely to the rigours of the contemporary climate'. The same is true of Matthew Arnold who, in spite of his deep insight into, and his frank recognition of, the predicament of his age, could not achieve that poetic 'criticism of life' to which he so passionately aspired: 'Alas! the past was out of date, the future not yet born, and Arnold's response to these conditions does not differ fundamentally from that of his fellows', as one can see from his use of the conventionally 'poetical', as distinguished from the authentically 'poetic' use of language.

For Leavis, Robert Browning, too, was lacking in 'the interest of an adult sensitive mind', being concerned merely with simple emotions and sentiments. Leavis finds 'the characteristic corrugation of his surface' superficial and not 'the expression of a complex sensibility'. Although his use of spoken idiom in verse proved useful to later poets (as, for instance, Pound), still for Leavis the fact remained that so inferior a mind and spirit as Browning's could not provide the impulse needed to bring back into poetry 'the adult intelligence'.

Meredith, too, with his 'sham subtlety of thought', fails to impress Leavis who dismisses *Modern Love* as 'the flashy product of unusual but vulgar cleverness working upon cheap emotion'. In Morris, on the other hand, there was a hiatus between the kind of life he lived and the kind of poetry he chose, or was indeed able, to write. 'Who would guess from his poetry', Leavis asks, 'that William Morris was one of the most versatile, energetic and original men of his time, a force that impinged decisively in the world of practice?'

Such assessments of the Victorian and Georgian poets served Leavis as a foil to his treatment of Hopkins, Yeats, Eliot and Pound. The key-criterion he invokes in his 'essential discriminations' is the vital co-relation between a sharper and a subtler sensitiveness to and awareness of the problems of existence, and a correspondingly mature, responsible and supple command over expression. Sensibility, Leavis frequently quoted Eliot as saying, 'alters from generation to generation in everybody, whether we will or no; but expression is only altered by a man of genius'. Thus, it was through his new rhythm and new diction that Yeats succeeded, in his later poetry, in achieving poetic originality based on a creative use of such qualities as 'intellectual passion', 'ardent vitality', 'a kind of ripeness in disillusion', and 'a difficult and delicate sincerity, an extraordinarily subtle poise'.

In the chapter on Eliot, Leavis starts by discussing the poems that pre-date *The Waste Land*, and especially 'The Love Song of J. Alfred Prufrock', the publication of which constituted 'an important event in the history of English Poetry'. In this poem a 'subtlety and flexibility of tone' and a striking imagery express 'freely' a modern sensibility, 'the ways of feeling, the modes of experience, of one fully alive in his own age'. Hence Leavis finds the author of the poem to be 'as close to the contemporary world as any novelist could be'. In commenting on Eliot, Leavis' own powers of perception and subtle analytical probing into and interpretation of the text are exercised here for the first time to the fullest. For instance, while commenting on a bunch of feathers blown in the gale in *Gerontion*, he points out how 'it brings home poignantly the puny helplessness of the individual life', how it contrasts with 'the frowsy squalor of finance, crime and divorce' and how, so far as the old man is concerned, it stands for him not only for 'inevitable death and dissolution', but also for 'the strength that he has lost'.

Coming to *The Waste Land*, Leavis demonstrates analytically how both concentration and 'depth of orchestration' are achieved in the poem in such a way that 'the themes move in and out of one another and the predominance shifts from level to level'. Denying that the poem has a metaphysical unity any more than it has a narrative or a dramatic one, he argues how the kind of unity the poem aims at is that of 'an inclusive consciousness' and how the organisation – or rather 'the rich disorganisation' – it achieves as a work of art can be called musical. The poetical and technical use of the references and quotations in the poem contributes to 'a compression, otherwise unattainable, that is essential to his [Eliot's] aim; a compression approaching simultaneity – the co-presence in the mind of a number of different orientations, fundamental attitudes, orders of experience'. In order to characterise the sort of place the Waste Land is, Leavis observes that in such a land 'one is neither living nor dead'. And if Eliot himself thought it to be 'a dead end' for him, it is, for Leavis, 'a new start for English poetry'. In *The Hollow Men* – expressing as well as giving meaning to what Leavis calls 'the fevered torment' – 'the extreme agony of consciousness' goes hand in hand with 'the extraordinary vitality' of expression. The 'terrible closing section, too with its nightmare poise over the grotesque', is hailed by Leavis as 'a triumph of aplomb'. *Ash-Wednesday*, on the other hand, is even more 'disconcertingly' modern than *The Waste Land*, embodying, as it does, modes of feeling, apprehension and expression that can nowhere be found in the poetry preceding Eliot's. Dealing with 'a special order of experience, dedicated to spiritual exercises', the poem initiates a process of self-scrutiny and self-exploration that was to continue right down to the *Four Quartets* and *Family Reunion* and that proves how Eliot's poetical problem is a spiritual problem, in so far as it is 'a problem in the attainment of a difficult sincerity'. What constituted the difficulty for Eliot was his having 'to achieve a paradoxical precision-in-vagueness, to persuade the elusive intuition to define itself'. Leavis' close commentary on the poem brings out its specifically religious significance, epitomising, as it does, a spiritual history, consisting of ambiguities, equivocations and doubts which contribute to the poet's 'spiritual' and poetical discipline.

Pound is another protagonist of the revolution in modern poetry. His work, together with, and to some extent even more than Eliot's, gave English poetry a decisively 'new bearing'. Leavis refers to Eliot's debt to Pound as a man who 'extended' and 'refined' our sensibility and who enabled some poets, including Eliot himself, to 'improve their verse sense'. However, even though Eliot's witness carries authority with Leavis, he found Pound's influence to have been 'secondary' to Eliot's and considered the latter's Introduction to Pound's *Selected Poems* unrepresentative of Eliot the critic 'at his best', even though he wholly concurred with Eliot's praise of *Hugh Selwyn Mauberley* as 'a great poem'. It would seem, then, that from the very outset, in spite of Eliot's admiration for the 'miglior

fabbro', for his earlier poems like 'Altaforte', and for some of the *Cantos*,
Leavis had no interest in Pound's poetry other than *Mauberley*, on which
he was to write what is, in its subtlety and originality of perception and
insight, representative of his own criticism at its best. After dismissing
Pound's 'various addictions' – Provençal, Italian, Chinese – as those of an
amateur, and an aesthete, albeit in the most serious sense of the word,
Leavis comes to *Mauberley* in which a pressure of experience, 'an impulsion from deep within' dictates its rhythms which, in their apparent
looseness and carelessness, are 'marvels of subtlety'. The various sections
of *Mauberley* constitute for Leavis one poem – 'a representative experience
of life – tragedy, comedy, pathos, and irony' – and the whole poem displays
'a subtlety of tone, a complexity of attitude, such as we associate with
seventeenth century wit'. The 'disillusioned summing-up' of the first poem
of *Mauberley* ending with: 'Unaffected by the "march of events",/He passed
from men's memory in *l'an trentiesme / De son eage*; the case presents/No
adjunct to the Muses' diadem', Leavis considers to be 'great poetry as well
as a "criticism of life" in the best sense of the term'. Commenting on the
fourth and fifth poems of *Mauberley* which deal with the war, Leavis finds
them 'a more remarkable achievement than they may perhaps at first
appear'. As to the famous stanza from the fourth poem – 'These fought in
any case', etc. – Leavis observes: 'That is a dangerous note, and only the
completest integrity and the surest touch could safely venture it. But we
have no uneasiness. The poet has realised the war with the completely
adult (and very uncommon) awareness that makes it impossible to nurse
indignation and horror. They [the two poems] represent a criterion of
seriousness and purity of intention that is implicit in the whole. To say
this is to indicate the great gulf between any of the earliest work, archaiz-
ing or modernizing, and *Mauberley*.' This is praise indeed, coming as it
does from one who, unlike Pound himself, experienced the war at first
hand.

Another poem in the *Mauberley* sequence Leavis admires and comments on with characteristic subtlety and perceptiveness is 'Siena mi fè;
disfecemi Maremma'. The irony of the second and third stanzas of the
poem, says Leavis, 'might be called flippant: if so, it is a flippancy that
subserves a tragic effect. Nothing could illustrate more forcibly Mr.
Pound's sureness of touch, his subtle mastery of tone and accent'. Leavis
considers the poem to be 'one of the most daring things in the sequence' as
well as 'rhythmically ... consummate', as in fact is *Mauberley* as a whole.
In other poems of *Mauberley*, too, Leavis admires the 'technical mastery
functioning at the highest level', the 'ironical economy, impersonal and
detached' and the 'superbly supple and varied art'.

But while *Mauberley* was for Leavis great poetry on which Pound's
standing as a poet 'rests securely', he had little use for *The Cantos* which
he considered to be 'little more than a game – a game serious with the
seriousness of pedantry'. We may recognise, Leavis observes, 'what Mr.

Pound's counters stand for, but they remain counters; and his patterns are not very interesting, even as schematic design, since, in the nature of the game, which hasn't much in the way of rules ... they lack definition and salience'.

Hopkins, on the other hand, is 'one of the most remarkable technical inventors who ever wrote'. Had he received the attention that was his due, the history of English poetry from the nineties onward would have been very different. But a poet like Bridges, with his love of a 'continuous decorum', could not understand Hopkins. Decorum, like 'Good Form', has its uses; but both, Leavis tells us, become 'cramping absurdities when erected into ultimate ends'. Hopkins wanted to get out of his words as much as possible 'unhampered by the rules of grammar, syntax and common usage'. Leavis relates Hopkins' essential genius to Shakespeare's rather than to Milton's, since both exploited the resources and potentialities of the language: 'His words and phrases are actions as well as sounds, ideas and images, and must, as I have said, be read with the body as well as with the eye.' Contrasting Hopkins' achievement with that of the other Victorian poets, Leavis points out how his words seem to have 'substance' and are made of a great variety of 'stuffs', which contrast with the intellectual and spiritual 'anaemia' of Victorian poetry.

That Hopkins has no relation to any nineteenth-century poet comes out most vividly in *The Wreck of the Deutschland*, where his linguistic and technical powers are seen at their best: 'the association of inner, spiritual, emotional stress with physical reverberations, nervous and muscular tensions.' As to Hopkins' imagery, we are told that 'nothing approaching [it] in subtlety and strength can be found in any other poet of the nineteenth century'. 'The Windhover' and 'Spelt from Sibyl's Leaves', too, illustrate how in comparison 'any other poetry of the nineteenth century is seen to be using only a very small part of the resources of the English language', which makes Hopkins 'for our time and the future, the only influential poet of the Victorian age, and he seems to me the greatest'.

Thus, Yeats, Eliot, Pound and Hopkins enabled Leavis to demonstrate what he meant by the 'new bearings' in English poetry and, incidentally, also in English criticism. Both the book and the critical revaluations of the four poets it offered were to impinge decisively on later critics and have stood the test of time; and so far as Eliot is concerned, Leavis could justifiably claim that *New Bearings* made of him a key figure. It also made Leavis' fortune as a critic and showed how a sense of relevance and the adherence to the concrete constituted that sense of responsibility without which a critical judgement can have no validity and no authority. It is in the pages of *New Bearings* that Leavis first argued that the poet's capacity for experiencing and his power of communicating are indistinguishable; not merely because we cannot know of the one without the other, but because 'his power of making words express what he feels is indistinguishable from his awareness of what he feels' and because 'his interest in his experience is not separable from his interest in words'.

The publication of *New Bearings*, at the beginning of 1932, was followed by another significant event: the launch of *Scrutiny*. Leavis and his collaborators brought out the first issue of *Scrutiny* by the end of the year. For 'politic' reasons Leavis 'formally' kept out of the editorial board. Most of the planning was done at his house. His own position enabled him, as he put it, 'to supply the special connections that will constitute the differentia of *Scrutiny*'. Thus *Scrutiny* had, from the outset, a wide connection in schools and universities and one of the main reasons for founding it was precisely to maintain such a connection. No wonder *Scrutiny's* impact was felt – and was meant to be felt – both in the educational and the literary world.

Although *Scrutiny* was not intended to be merely a literary review, it was always difficult for its editors – especially for Leavis – to find non-literary specialists in psychology, anthropology, history, philosophy and economics 'who can justify the space' they took. And yet *Scrutiny* dealt with a wide variety of subjects – from advertising to art and architecture, from economics, education and history to music, philosophy and politics, from psychology, religion and science to sociology and town planning. In 'the incomparably rich' field of English literature, authors from Langland, Chaucer, Shakespeare, Milton, Bunyan and Dryden to the Augustans, the Romantics, the Victorians and the contemporaries were dealt with by more than one 'scrutineer' who, as a 'responsible' critic, displayed in what he wrote, relevant research and scholarship together with first-hand critical acumen and perceptiveness. The same combination, if not always to the same degree, was noted to characterise what was written about foreign writers – for the most part French, but also Italian and German: Corneille, Racine, Apollinaire, Mallarmé, Laforgue, Rimbaud, Camus and Valéry; Dante, Petrarch, Boccaccio, Ariosto, Manzoni, Leopardi, Carducci and Croce; Goethe, Hölderlin, Rilke and Thomas Mann. In the field of music, composers like Wagner, Mahler, Purcell, Stravinsky, Vaughan and Britten were discussed with critical acumen as well as professional competence. Among the contributors, though such names as Auden, Edmund Blunden, I.A. Richards, and René Wellek figure once or twice, the most assiduous and – apart from F.R. Leavis and Q.D. Leavis – the most important are W.D. Harding, L.C. Knights, W.H. Mellers, James Smith and D.A. Traversi. The uncompromising severity of critical standards that *Scrutiny* contributors (inspired and, in many cases, trained by Leavis) applied to what they wrote on or the books they reviewed made the *Scrutiny* appraisals both dreaded and coveted. No periodical was more dedicated to the task of hailing what was original and first-rate in creative literature – especially contemporary creative literature – or that of debunking what was sham, conventional or 'academic' in the pejorative sense. This earned Leavis, in the words of a British Council critic, the reputation of a 'cold intellectual ... whose methodical and uncompromising destruction of reputations periodically enlivens the pages of the hypercritical but bracing magazine *Scrutiny*'. But what was at issue was a radical 'revaluation' of past and contemporary literature. Thus, for instance, Leavis pointed out that 'several of the poems [by William Empson] leave one wondering whether the difficulty of constructing what is recondite in them is worth wrestling with', and that he 'seems no nearer than before to finding a more radical incitement to the writing of poetry (or of criticism) than pleasure in a strenuous intellectual game'. The uncritical acclaim of Auden was attributed to the fact that his poetry presumes 'on the reader's readiness to see subtlety and complexity in the undefined and unorganized', and that it is 'too often content to set down what came more or less as it came'. The most damning charge against Auden was that of immaturity, both of technique and of what was offered by way of a criticism of life. Auden's technique, Leavis pointed out,

> is not one that solves problems; it conceals a failure to grapple with them, or, rather, makes a virtue out of the failure. He has made a technique out of irresponsibility, and his most serious work exhibits a shameless opportunism in the passage from phrase to phrase and from item to item – the use of a kind of bluff.

Even Joyce, whose *Ulysses* Leavis admired, is severely dealt with for his linguistic experiments, his 'revolution of the word'. Some critics had compared the liberties Joyce took with English with those taken by Shakespeare. But for Leavis there is this inescapable distinction between the two:

> Shakespeare's were not the product of a desire to 'develop his medium to the fullest', but of a pressure of something to be conveyed ... it is the burden to be delivered, the precise and urgent command from within, that determines expression – tyrannically ... Those miraculous intricacies of expression could have come only to one whose medium was for him strictly a medium ... the linguistic audacities are derivative.

> Joyce's development has been the other way. There is prose in *Ulysses*, the description, for instance, of Stephen Dedalus walking over the beach, of a Shakespearean concreteness ... But in the *Work in Progress*, it is plain, the interest in words and their possibilities comes first ... even in the best parts, we can never be unaware that the organization is external and mechanical. Each line is a series of jerks, as the focus jumps from point to point; for the kind of attention demanded by each one of the closely packed 'effects' is incompatible with an inclusive, co-ordinating apprehension.

Virginia Woolf, too, is not so much dislodged as 're-placed'. Going straight to the core of her technique, Leavis points out how

> Mrs. Woolf's decision to have 'no plot, no comedy, no tragedy, no love-interest or catastrophe in the accepted style' was perhaps to this extent justified, that she hadn't interests rich and active enough to justify what she was rejecting; but neither, we have to conclude, had she interests adequate to the problem of supplying substitutes.

Perhaps one of Leavis' severest criticisms is levelled against Stephen Spender. While reviewing his autobiography *World within World*, Leavis quotes Spender to the effect that what he writes is 'fragments of autobiography: sometimes they are poems, sometimes stories, and longer passages may take the form of novels'. But the fact that the autobiographical bent 'is not a sign of creative power, but the reverse, we do not need Coleridge's authority for believing', Leavis observes. And as to Spender's remark – 'I have no character or willpower outside my work. In the life of action, I do everything that my friends tell me to do, and have no opinions of my own' – Leavis tells us that 'the absence of creative power or impulse needn't mean lack of literary intelligence. But Mr. Spender would seem never to have achieved even the beginnings of what can in any strictness be called an interest in literature.'

He also criticises G. Wilson Knight for not questioning his own ability to approach Dante and Goethe 'on the same easy terms as Shakespeare', and for not showing 'the least sign of uneasiness at having to rely on Cary's *Divine Comedy* and Professor Latham's Faust'. In the *Critical History of English Poetry*, by Herbert J.C. Grierson and J.C. Smith, Leavis finds lack of discrimination to be the root cause of his dissatisfaction with the book, and for him 'discrimination is life, indiscrimination is death'. When Grierson and Smith claim that 'Mr Masefield has not Chaucer's witty touch nor his universality', Leavis remarks: 'As one who thinks that Chaucer comes next to Shakespeare, I can only say that I find such a sentence fantastic, and damning to the kind of catholicity that made it possible.'

Thus, in his reviews, too, Leavis advanced the cause of criticism, offered models of what 'practical criticism' in its fully integrated form ought to mean, and put into practice what he theorised about, as much as he did in those essays and articles of his published in *Scrutiny* and subsequently in his books. In fact, one can say that the foundations of Leavis' critical achievement were laid in the pages of *Scrutiny*, and his influence on other 'scrutineers' was also largely exercised there.

On different occasions and in diverse contexts Leavis referred, with obvious satisfaction and pride, to the history and achievement of *Scrutiny*. He did so especially in his editorial *Valedictory* which opened the last volume of 1953 and, ten years later, in *'Scrutiny* a Retrospect' as a kind of introduction when the periodical was reprinted by Cambridge University Press.

Although she herself was closely involved in running and contributing to *Scrutiny*, Q.D. Leavis, apart from references here and there, did not write about it. But an indirect testimony of what she thought of *Scrutiny* and of the high regard in which she held its chief protagonist was found, after her death, in her copy of *Dickens the Novelist*, where she had transcribed what Sydney Smith, in the Preface to his collected works, had written about his founding and editing the *Edinburgh Review*, as being implicitly applicable to *Scrutiny* and F.R. Leavis.

> To set on foot such a Journal in such times, to contribute towards it for many years, to bear patiently the reproach and poverty which it caused, and to look back and see that I have nothing to retract, and no intemperance and violence to reproach myself with, is a career of life which I must think to be extremely fortunate.

But, after her husband's death, an opportunity presented itself to her to say something about *Scrutiny* when she was invited to review Francis Mulhern's book *The Moment of 'Scrutiny'* (1979). She declined the invitation, but jotted down some criticisms of the book. Mulhern, she points out,

> makes the mistake of assuming that anyone who (even once) contributed to *Scrutiny* represented *Scrutiny's* position and was endorsed by the editors, or at any rate by Leavis. This is so naive as to make one suspect that Mr. Mulhern has never edited a periodical except *The Left Review*. In the desire to spread our contributors we tried people out and this is always a risk: it will be noticed that some names occur only once or at most twice, (for example, Grigson), before being dropped. And as far as the central office was concerned, we suffered from the fact that the other editors could not be prevented from commissioning contributions on their own initiative (for example, L.C. Knights inviting Spender who declined) nearly always with deplorable results, we felt, but we had to print them. Of course a Leavis industry was bound to start up and couldn't be prevented, but ... the irony of the author's being a pupil of Professor Donoghue, and his thesis under Kermode (a leading Public Enemy as regards *Scrutiny* and Leavis) and furthermore, as the blurb tells us, Editor of *The Left Review*! Poor F.R. Leavis! Poor *Scrutiny*!

Q.D. Leavis also challenges Mulhern's statement that F.R. Leavis was 'one of Richards' freelances', and dismisses it as a 'ridiculous account of the Leavis genealogy'; or that *Fiction and the Reading Public* was 'the logical successor of *Mass Civilization and Minority Culture*' which was, in fact, 'compiled from my data and ideas rehearsed to F.R. Leavis before writing down in full my thesis which left me with a bone ending, for the material and ideas of *Mass Civilization and Minority Culture* and *Culture and Environment* were my final chapter';[1] or that Leavis 'approved the manifesto that Knights had drafted for it'; for it was, in fact, Leavis who wrote it 'after redrafting theirs'.

[1] Moreover, Mulhern doesn't cite – what perhaps he doesn't know – 'Thompson's statement (in print) that *Culture and Environment* was already written when he arrived at our house'.

For Continuity, Culture and Environment and Determinations

Civilization becomes admirable when people begin to prefer a little of
the best to a great deal of the pasty.

Ezra Pound

A year after launching *Scrutiny*, Leavis brought out in *For Continuity* the
best of what he had so far published in that periodical plus *Mass Civilization and Minority Culture* and *D.H. Lawrence* which had appeared independently as 'Minority Pamphlets'. *For Continuity* also included the
'prefatory' essay 'Marxism and Cultural Continuity', 'The Literary Mind',
'What's Wrong with Criticism?', 'Babbitt Buys the World', 'Arnold Bennett:
American Version', 'John Dos Passos', 'D.H. Lawrence and Professor Irv-
ing Babbitt', 'Under Which King, Bezonian?', 'Restatements for Critics',
'This Poetical Renascence' and 'Joyce and "The Revolution of the Word" '.
The selection, impressive both in terms of the variety of subjects treated
and in terms of their historical as well as intrinsic merit, exemplifies the
ethos and approach of Leavis' criticism and brings out what is 'the reverse
of an academic and purely theoretical spirit'.

In 'Marxism and Cultural Continuity', Leavis challenges Edmund Wilson's assumption that Marx was concerned about literature and art, by
pointing out that Marx's concern was, in fact, 'for a simplification involving, as an essential condition, the assumption that literature and art
would look after themselves'; and that, for most Marxists, the attraction
of Marxism is simplicity: 'it absolves from the duty of wrestling with
complexities' – complexities unavoidable in discussing 'the cultural values
– human ends –' which need more attention than they get in 'the doctrine,
strategy and tactics of the Class War'. Generally speaking, Leavis finds in
the Marxists 'that oblivion of, indifference to, the finer values which are
thought to be a characteristic of the "bourgeois" world'; an incapacity or
unwillingness to believe that 'there *can* be intellectual, aesthetic and
moral activity that is not merely an expression of class origin and economic
circumstances' and that 'there *is* a "human culture" to be aimed at that
must be achieved by cultivating a certain autonomy of the human spirit'.
For his own part, Leavis' criticism of Marxism and Marxists becomes an
occasion for an implicit assertion of his own faith in the nature, substance

and values of a culture that is something more than 'a mere function of the economic conditions, of the machinery of civilization', and for his insistence on 'the function of critical scrutiny'.

In 'The Literary Mind', his first contribution to *Scrutiny* in the form of a review article on *The Literary Mind* by Max Eastman – 'one of the first "good" things I did', Leavis would recall in 1974, 'in which I expound my present theme (Practical criticism, and what it covers "associatingly") all those years ago' – Leavis formulates his own critical convictions and criteria as well as outlining the nature of what he, in opposition to Eastman, understands by a 'literary' mind. Characterising Eastman's view of the literary mind as something 'too naive and muddled in its complacent philistinism to be seriously discussed', and something attesting to 'the decay of literary culture', Leavis nevertheless analyses some of his comments and affirmations not only to contradict and demolish them, but also to expose their essentially uncritical nature. Thus, in his first contribution to *Scrutiny*, we see Leavis doing what he would repeatedly be called upon to do both in its pages and outside, namely to 'criticise the critic'.

By linking together names like Allen Tate, Ezra Pound, T.S. Eliot, Ivor Winters, Edith Sitwell, Robert Graves and Laura Riding, whom he supposes to have led a 'classical movement', Eastman simply cannot see the difference 'in intellectual status' between Mr Eliot and Miss Sitwell and prefers her to him, as being 'the most gifted of the modernist poets'. But for all her 'modernist garnishings', Sitwell offers only what her admirers expect to find in poetry – 'sentimental reveries, reminiscences of childhood, and so on'. For the purpose of criticism, she does not exist, 'either as a poet or a critic'. A still more damning proof of Eastman's critical naivety and obtuseness is his view of *Ash Wednesday* – an 'oily puddle of emotional noises' – and his explanation of why 'modernist' poetry is unintelligible. It is unintelligible, according to Eastman, because 'science has withdrawn itself from literature' and has left the poet nothing more serious to do than 'to engineer, as a defensive bluff, a revolt against meaningful language'. Leavis finds such a position 'amusing', but what public, he asks, 'can one count on to find it amusing?' – a public that can see through Eastman's 'innocent self-exposure', his 'complacent illiteracy', his deficiency in taste and sensibility, the 'uncritical looseness' with which he uses such key words as experience, interpretation and meaning. It is in criticising Eastman's faults and deficiencies that Leavis implicitly brings out the virtues and qualities that ought to characterise critical thinking as well as critical prose. He not only finds 'a pervasive debility, a lack of tension, outline and edge', but also a lack of 'that sensitiveness of intelligence without which all apparent vigour of thought is illusory'. In noting the absence of 'a certain fidelity to concrete particulars' in Eastman, he draws our attention to that quality of prose as well as of critical thought that was going to be crucially relevant to his own criticism and analysis of prose as well as of poetry. Analysing what he considers to be good prose,

Leavis shows how 'its virtues are a matter of the negative presence of the concrete and particular; it is not merely absence, but exclusion, an exclusion felt as a pressure. Exclusion implies a firm and subtle grasp; to exclude, the writer must have experienced, perceived and realised'.

Such qualities are the hall-mark of what Leavis calls critical intelligence – intelligence which, while appreciating Empson's *Seven Types of Ambiguity*, can still see that the author's zest 'has sometimes kept him going too long and too ingeniously in the pursuit of ambiguities'; which can stand up to Pound's 'perverse, but fruitfully provocative, pamphlet', *How to Read*; and which can convincingly argue that a Shakespeare play – *pace* Bradley – is not primarily 'a pattern of characters (or persons), with their "psychologies", in action and interaction', but that it is *we* who 'form these by abstraction from Shakespeare's words – that he didn't create persons, but put words together'.

Such a concept of literary criticism and a rigorous discipline in practising it is also exemplified by Leavis in his discussion of Wordsworth. Wordsworth, he tells us, 'invites us to discuss his "philosophy". It is disastrous to accept', because his philosophy

> simply does not exist to be discussed as such. If you find anything to discuss, to a great extent you put it there yourself ... But the only way to fix anything for discussion in the shifting verbosities of his abstract 'thinking' is to start from the concrete and never lose touch with it. What is successful as poetry is obviously 'there'; its abstractable implications, or those encouraged by a general knowledge of Wordsworth, may be coaxed out as far as seems discreet into the Wordsworthian philosophic fog and the poetry made the solid nucleus for such organization in terms of 'thought' as seems worth attempting. But we ought never to forget that Wordsworth matters as a 'thinker' only (if at all) because he is a poet.

But what is true of poetry is, for Leavis, equally true of the novel – especially when the novelist in question is D.H. Lawrence. Lawrence was a 'prophet', says Leavis, but it is only because he was 'an artist of genius that his "prophecy" matters'. In dealing with Lawrence, criticism of his 'doctrine' is inseparably tied up with judgements concerning the literary success or failure of his work.

Leavis' review of Eastman's *The Literary Mind* thus turns out to be a closely reasoned exposition of his own views on the literary mind, the critical intelligence, the critical sensibility, as well as on culture and tradition.

The most substantial piece in *For Continuity* – and in some respects the most interesting – is the essay 'D.H. Lawrence', a 'Minority Pamphlet' (1932). It appeared in the same year as *Mass Civilization and Minority Culture*, and is the first piece of Leavis' writing about Lawrence. What he

writes here stands in sharp contrast with anything else he was to write
later about Lawrence. In fact, in his later essay, 'Lawrence After Thirty
Years', Leavis practically renounced much of what he says in this essay,
as a result of what he himself considered to be due to his 'unintelligence
about Lawrence'. And yet Leavis considered himself to be less unintelli-
gent than T.S. Eliot, E.M. Forster or Middleton Murry – names that
represented critical authority at the time of Lawrence's death. 'What other
names', Leavis asks, 'can one put with these?' For, even in that early
article, Leavis considered himself to be different from Lawrence's 'subtly
malicious deprecators'; compared Lawrence with Blake, being both 'concerned with the vindication of impulse and spontaneity against "reason"
and convention'; considered Lawrence mature in *Sons and Lovers* in the
sense of being 'completely himself', and thought he had independently
arrived at the 'main conclusions of the psycho-analysis'. And yet he found
Sons and Lovers 'difficult to get through', and *The Rainbow* even more
difficult. Lawrence's fanatical concern for the 'essential', he tells us, 'often
results in a strange intensity, but how limited is the range!'. *Women in
Love*, too, in spite of its embodying the 'mature' conclusions, 'hardly
"informs and leads into new places the flow of our sympathetic consciousness". To get through it calls for great determination and a keen diagnostic
interest.' Even the characters in the novel tend to 'disintegrate into swirls
of conflicting impulses and emotions'. What a far cry this is from what
Leavis would subsequently affirm about Lawrence in general, and about
Women in Love in particular!

As to the charge against Lawrence of suffering from sex-obsession, we
are told that 'there can hardly have been a sterner moralist about sex than
Lawrence'. In *Lady Chatterley's Lover*, where Lawrence's artistic success
'validates' his teaching, there is 'no loose prophecy or passional exegesis,
and no mechanical use of the specialized vocabulary'. But this success is
'conditioned by narrowing down: criticism must take the form of the
question: How comprehensive or generally valid is that solution? Can we
believe that even the particular, personal problems facing Connie and the
gamekeeper are permanently solved (for the gamekeeper is after all not
D.H. Lawrence)?'. In any case, *Lady Chatterley's Lover* represents for
Leavis 'greater health and vitality than *A Passage to India*'.

In 'Under Which King, Bezonian', Leavis deals with the challenge to
Scrutiny to show its colours; i.e. indicate where it stood in political terms.
In meeting that challenge Leavis combines his argumentative and expository skill with his critical and analytical powers. 'The more seriously one
is concerned for literary criticism', he tells us, 'the less possible does one
find it to be concerned for that alone.' Even though primarily and most
importantly a literary periodical, *Scrutiny* did not confine itself to literary
criticism. But to identify *Scrutiny* with a social, economic or political creed
or platform would be 'to compromise and impede its special function ... the
free play of intelligence on the underlying issues' – something akin to, but

at once more flexible and more comprehensive than Matthew Arnold's 'application of ideas to life'.

In 'Restatements for Critics', Leavis again takes up the issue of *Scrutiny's* commitment and what it is committed to. In a review of *Scrutiny* in the *New English Weekly*, it was stated that 'The *Criterion* judges; *Scrutiny* scrutinises. Compared to judgement, scrutiny is a non-committal occupation'. In dealing with what amounts to an implicit charge against *Scrutiny* of its being less committed, Leavis retorts with his own question in one of his most cogently argued exposures.

> Forbearing the inquiry whether *Scrutiny* has committed itself less often and less decisively than any other journal in particular judgements, let us ask what, where judgement is in question, the criterion is: what are the standards? The values of intelligence, tradition and orthodox Christianity? But judgement is not a matter of abstractions; it involves particular immediate acts of choice, and these do not advance the business of judgement in any serious sense unless there has been a real and appropriate responsiveness to the thing offered. Without a free and delicate receptivity to fresh experience, whatever the criterion alleged, there is no judging, but merely negation. And this kind of negation, persisted in, with no matter what righteous design, produces in the end nullity: the 'criterion', however once validated by experience, fades into impotent abstraction, the 'values' it represents become empty husks. The safety sought in this way proves to be the safety of death.

In 'This Poetical Renascence', Empson, Auden, Spender and Day Lewis are discussed as representing the 'poetical renascence' which, for the critically alert, seems to be more a fiasco than any promise of the poetical renascence. Empson's work, we are told almost with prophetical intuition, 'is becoming less and less likely to develop. He seems no nearer than before to finding a more radical incitement to the writing of poetry (or of criticism) than pleasure in a strenuous intellectual game.' In the case of Auden – 'the dominating force in the new movement' – 'uncritical acclamation' has been his misfortune, as has been 'an unignorable element of something like undergraduate cleverness' in his work. Concerning Spender, Leavis is even more dismissive. Commenting on the blurb which said of Spender's poems that 'technically they appear to make a definite step forward in English poetry', Leavis bluntly states: 'Whoever was allowed to write it knew nothing about poetry – though that, perhaps, the public being what it is, was after all no serious disqualification.' For Spender's technique is 'very immature and unstable', and certain passages from his poems are quoted to show not only their 'underlying immaturity', but also 'the absence of any realised personal response, of any precise, consistent feeling or vision to communicate'.

Offering, as it does, the best of what Leavis had so far published in *Scrutiny* and in 'Minority Pamphlets', *For Continuity* may easily rank as a book in its own right, and not merely a collection of essays – a book where the literary and the critical aspects of Leavis' writings are as well represented as the polemical, the theoretical and the cultural ones.

In the same year appeared another book, *Culture and Environment: The Training of Critical Awareness*, in collaboration with Denys Thompson. It was originally offered to and accepted by a publisher 'with an educational connection', but was eventually published by Chatto in 1933. In conceding its publication to Chatto, Leavis, in a letter to Ian Parsons, mentioned the book's link with *Scrutiny*, and how, he thought, the one would help the other.

> You will know what I mean in saying that *Culture and Environment* is designed to give serious effect in the educational field to the *Scrutiny* 'drive'. As you are probably aware, *Scrutiny* has a wide connection in schools and universities (to maintain such a connection was one of the main reasons for founding *Scrutiny*). We know that there is a demand for *Culture and Environment*, and you won't think I'm talking idly if I say that we hope, not without some confidence, that the book will be a signal in an educational 'movement'. Numbers of things are correlated, and we're surprised by the response that has been evoked already in academic circles in the country at large.

And with characteristic conviction and self-assurance, he added:

> This will anyway give you an idea of the spirit in which we bestow the book upon the world. And we do really expect that *Culture and Environment, Fiction and the Reading Public* (which you will see we refer to a great deal) and *Scrutiny* will help one another: it isn't a mere solitary forlorn hope.

Though designed for school use, the book had a wider appeal. It was practically written by Leavis alone – 'Thompson did nothing' – as is borne out by the unmistakable tone and substance of the book. With *Mass Civilization and Minority Culture, New Bearings* and the experience of having launched *Scrutiny* behind him, Leavis' key ideas and concerns regarding the training of intelligence and sensibility, as well as of critical awareness, were reflected in this book.

For instance, in the section 'Progress and the Standard of Living' the prevailing note in advertising is described as optimism, since optimism 'favours free spending'. Magazine editors, too, insist on optimism in their instructions to contributors: 'Stories must have a strong feminine element and a happy ending is essential. Sad and sordid stories are not wanted.' That such an optimism is not a good thing is proven by the example of

America where, 'on the approach of difficulties, optimism was made a public duty, and it became an offence against society to recognize that anything was wrong' – a good example of what Leavis would subsequently call 'monstrous unrealism'. Another advertising gimmick that is exposed is 'the attempt to give the Good-mixer-Business ethos a moral and religious sanction in the name of "Service" '. Optimism and 'Service' – 'the religion of "forward-looking" men' – are intimately related to the idea of Progress which advertising inculcates in the 'crudest forms'.

A year later these two books were followed by *Determinations* – a selection of essays from ten *Scrutiny* contributors, namely James Smith ('Metaphysical Poetry'), William Empson ('Marvell's Garden'), D.W. Harding ('I.A. Richards' and 'A Note on Nostalgia'), L.C. Knights ('Notes on Comedy'), John Speirs ('Burns'), W.A. Edwards ('John Webster'), Ronald Bottrall ('XXX Cantos of Ezra Pound'), Denys Thompson ('Our Debt to Lamb'), Michael Oakeshott ('The New Bentham'), J.L. Russell ('The Scientific Best Seller'), and Leavis himself ('The Irony of Swift'), together with his Introduction to the volume. Leavis had intended the selection, which was originally to be called *Cambridge Criticism* or *From and For 'Scrutiny'*, to be really a book, and not a mere collection of essays. The preliminary selection had included M.C. Bradbrook ('Hero and Leander' and 'Notes on the Style of Mrs Woolf '), Henri Fluchère ('Surrealism') and Q.D. Leavis (with a piece she was to decide on). But these three were dropped and Michael Oakeshott and J.L. Russell brought in. The omission of Q.D. Leavis was largely due to her ill health, aggravated by the psychological climate of Cambridge which was so depressing for her.

Leavis was eager for the book to appear before the echoes of John Sparrow's *Sense and Poetry*, recently published, had died down. Sparrow's book had been recommended by the Book Society and was blurbed by Hugh Walpole. Leavis himself regarded the book as better than one could have hoped for, but he could not understand why Walpole should have said in the *Bookman* that 'it makes Mr and Mrs Leavis ridiculous for ever'.

As to the quality and importance of the individual essays in *Determinations*, although Leavis considered each one of them as representing the *Scrutiny* ethos, he thought particularly highly of Harding's 'I.A. Richards'. He thought it was 'extraordinarily well done', with its perfect 'delicacy of touch and restraint', and exemplifying the author's 'rare combination of qualifications'. Empson's Marvell essay, on the other hand, he considered to be 'least of anything in the book', 'brilliant' though it was. Leavis himself was represented here by 'The Irony of Swift' (later included in *The Common Pursuit*) and by his Introduction. As its epigraph the book carried a quote from T.S. Eliot (from 'The Function of Criticism').

Here, one would suppose, was a place for quiet co-operative labour. The critic, one would suppose, if he is to justify his existence, should endeavour to discipline his personal prejudices and cranks – tares to

which we are all subject – and compose his differences with as many
of his fellows as possible in the common pursuit of true judgement.

In his Introduction Leavis describes the underlying unity of approach
that characterises the various essays. It is not so much 'a common programme or credo', as the fact that they have all appeared in *Scrutiny* and
therefore each, in one way or another, enforces 'a clear and full conception
of literary criticism, its function, its scope and responsibilities'. And for
Leavis, criticism, so conceived and practised 'not merely expresses and
defines the "contemporary sensibility"; it helps to form it'. But as no
serious interest in literature can be 'merely literary', so no literary criticism can be without 'a perception of – which must be a preoccupation with
– the problems of social equity and order and cultural health'. That is why
curiosity regarding the 'currents of thought outside literature' and the
intellectual and moral climate of the contemporary epoch is an indispensable factor in literary criticism, as Leavis' own criticism shows.

As to some of the 'theoretical' essays in the volume – for instance, those
on 'Nostalgia', 'Metaphysical Poetry' and 'Comedy' – Leavis notes that 'the
keener one's interest in the profitable discussion of literature, the less
easily does one assume sharp distinctions between theoretical and practical criticism' – a comment the validity of which no critic has exemplified
with such convincing subtlety as Leavis himself. If the authors of the
above-mentioned essays themselves generalise, there are 'particular perceptions' to back their generalizations; for, Leavis argues, 'without a fine
capacity for particular, immediate response to art there can be no good
"theoretical critic", just as the merely "practical" critic is hardly conceiv-
able'. It is the best praise that Leavis, or anyone else, could have bestowed
on the various contributors to *Determinations*.

3

Revaluation and *Education and the University*

> I would rather discuss the function of the university with a mathematician or a physicist than with an academic humanist.
>
> F.R. Leavis

Encouraged by the success of *New Bearings* and *Scrutiny*, Leavis started working on what was going to be a new book – *Revaluation* – which could well be regarded as a background to *New Bearings*. But he had other things on hand as well – *Determinations*, running *Scrutiny* and teaching ('more teaching than anyone else in the English School' and the duties of a Professor without the status and salary). Hence the book could come out only in 1936. Most of the essays in it had already appeared in *Scrutiny*, since Leavis, in common with other collaborators, used *Scrutiny* for 'producing the matter for books', which was an essential part of their original project. He dedicated the book to Downing and described himself as 'Lecturer in English at Downing College'. It was a debt to Downing he was glad to pay, for it was their courage and generosity that had 'staved off the foundering of the ship, till the finishing of this book, anyway'.

However, uncertainty about his position at Downing continued to be a source of worry and anxiety while Leavis was working on *Revaluation*. He was afraid that 'the gentlemen of Cambridge' might bring off 'the final blackballing', and thus deprive him of his position, which would make it practically impossible for him to make a living. He found Quiller-Couch, his Professor, 'friendly, but apparently helpless', which made the whole thing 'all very squalid, and, for me, worse'.

The prospect of having to go round looking for a job could not but interfere with his ability to concentrate. Nevertheless *Revaluation* turned out to be as solid, coherent and closely woven a book as he thought he would ever be able to write. 'It's to be the book', he had written three years earlier to Parsons, while announcing it, 'Richards should have written to justify his title *Practical Criticism*: that is, it's to be all representative analysis, theory being completely subordinate and ancillary'. In spite of his not unjustifiable fears and suspicions, Leavis was appointed Assistant Lecturer in the University and a Fellow of Downing just before the book came out.

In the course of tracing the tradition and development in English poetry, the book dealt with poets from Donne to Keats. Donne was treated as a 'contemporary – obviously a living poet in the most important sense'. For, coupled with his 'magnificent' handling of the stanza-form, there were 'the inexhaustible subtleties' of his use of the speaking voice and the spoken language which account for his historical and, even more, for his intrinsic importance. Milton, on the other hand, offered Leavis the occasion for one of his most drastic criticisms – a criticism which, even though based on grounds now commonly recognised as valid, has been greatly resented, and not only by Milton specialists. These grounds are: a lack of proportion between Milton's magniloquence and the effect it produces; the failure of his diction to weld itself with the stuff of poetry (feelings, perceptions, sensations etc.); and his exhibiting 'a feeling for words rather than a capacity for feeling *through* words', as a result of which there is in him 'so complete and systematic a callousness to the intrinsic nature of English', an absence of pressure behind the words he uses, a 'rhythmic deadness' and 'mechanical externality'.

No wonder, in spite of his moral grandeur and moral force, Leavis finds Milton

> disastrously single-minded and simple-minded .... His volume of moral passion owes its strength too much to innocence – a guileless unawareness of the subtleties of egotism – to be an apt agent for projecting an 'ordered whole of experience'.

In his dealings with Milton the relation between poetry as a criticism of life and the language of poetry as the ultimate crucible of the poet's moral, aesthetic and human sensibility and his inward maturity, depth of feeling and complexity of thought is seen to be at its most vital and significant; and in Leavis' case, as in Arnold's, concern for the creative vitality of language is one with a concern for moral wholeness, complexity and sanity.

On Pope, Leavis offers 'an intelligent orientation' and Pope's 'subtle complexity' is seen to co-exist with his 'correctness', so that he can be at once polite and profound. The particular quality of his sensibility – as embodied in his best work – is something one looks for in vain in other poets – with the exception of Shakespeare. For it is a quality that co-exists with wit, so that 'a completely serious poetic effect should be able to contain suggestions of the ludicrous such as for Gray, Shelley or Matthew Arnold would have meant disaster'. Leavis analyses Pope's technique to show how, in his hands, it is something more than a matter of social elegance, and becomes 'the instrument of a fine organization' through which the 'pressures and potencies' of intense personal feeling are transformed.

In the Wordsworth chapter Leavis assesses the strength, qualities and resources of Wordsworth's poetry. 'If not a philosophy', he argues, Wordsworth 'had a wisdom to communicate', and his best poetry is richer in spiritual undertones and inferences than his so-called philosophical or didactic poetry.

Thus, in his essay on Wordsworth, Leavis is concerned with discriminating not only between Wordsworth's poetry and his philosophy, but also between a critical recognition of Wordsworth's greatness as such and its 'current acceptance, the established habit of many years'. He agrees with Arnold that Wordsworth's philosophy is an 'illusion' and sets out to demonstrate what constitutes its reality and its greatness. Leavis' own strength and originality as a critic lies in the fact that while dealing with Wordsworth's poetry, he did not feel called upon then, as René Wellek had hinted in his criticism of *Revaluation* he should have, to discuss and interpret that wisdom in terms of abstract moral, philosophical, or ethical concepts or assumptions; nor did he evaluate the poetry merely as a vehicle of that wisdom. It is precisely what is unparaphrasable about that wisdom, and the way it works into and through Wordsworth's poetry, that engages Leavis as a critic. Even the 'convincingly expository tone and manner' of Wordsworth's philosophical poetry evokes in him a primarily critical rather than a philosophical response. Such poetry might give one the impression of offering 'paraphrasable arguments', but a real critic cannot paraphrase it and it would be worse than futile to try, because Wordsworth's triumph is precisely 'to command the kind of attention he requires and to permit no other'. What that kind of attention means it takes a literary critic, the 'complete' reader, to perceive and determine, and this is what Leavis does in this essay so superbly.

He works his way into what he calls 'an essential Wordsworthian habit' – namely, that of producing 'the mood, feeling and experience', and at the same time appearing to be 'giving an explanation of it'. Such a habit enabled Wordsworth to register his kinship with the universe, 'inwardly through the rising springs of life and outwardly in an interplay of recognition and response'. Without insisting on the demarcation between poetry and philosophical argument as such, Leavis assumes the demarcation when he comments on the most overtly philosophical and discursive passages of *The Prelude*. For instance, he notices how the verse 'evenly meditative in tone and movement, goes on and on, without dialectical suspense and crisis or rise and fall' – verse in which not only is thought presented in disjunction from poetry, but where even the language in which it is presented fails to exercise its own discipline on the thought expressed. It is by virtue of this discipline that creative literature becomes the language of thought, and Wordsworth is bracketed by Leavis with Eliot. For 'the withdrawn contemplative collectedness of Wordsworth's poetry' and what it represents, finds its correspondence or counterpart in Eliot's poetry as exemplified by such a line as 'Thus devoted, concentrated in purpose'. Wordsworth and Eliot had not merely effected a revolution in poetic diction; they were also engaged in 'thinking' creatively in and through their poetry, and the presentation of 'thought' in Wordsworth's poetry, as in Eliot's, demanded, 'not only what the full attention of the working mind suggests', but also 'a sustained and alert delicacy of attention, a quick and delicate responsiveness of full apprehension'.

Leavis himself displays this kind of attention in his dealings with Wordsworth. To be aware of the varying degrees and manifestations of this attention is itself a proof of one's being instinctively in sympathy with the critical grounds on which Leavis advances Wordsworth's claim to greatness and originality. One factor that made a fundamental difference to Leavis' attitude to Wordsworth is the latter's embodying in his poetry 'a type and a standard of human normality, a way of life'; so that what Leavis would say concerning the theme of time in *Four Quartets* – 'an attitude towards time is an attitude towards life' – can be applied to Wordsworth's 'preoccupation with sanity and normality ... at a level and in a spirit that it seems appropriate to call religious'. Hence one can say that Wordsworth's attitude to sanity and normality stands for his attitude to life. Coupled with, and to a large extent both determined by and determining this preoccupation, was Wordsworth's handling of his own thought and experience in poetry, which entailed a creative use of language. And for Leavis the language of poetry, at its most subtle and perceptive, is the language of thought and has a bearing upon life, upon actual living.

That is why, in his attempt to give a 'satisfying' account of Wordsworth's greatness, Leavis did not lay as much stress, as perhaps Wordsworth himself would have done, on the mystic element in his poetry, or on 'the visionary moments' or 'spots of time', but on 'essential sanity and normality' – the sanity and normality of one who was, unlike Shelley, 'surely and centrally poised', and whose firm hold upon the world of 'common perception' was the more notable because he knew 'fallings from us, vanishings, blank misgivings' ('when the light of sense goes out'). And yet there was nothing complacent about such sureness in Wordsworth. It rested 'consciously over unsounded depths and among mysteries, itself a mystery'. The analysis of what constitutes the sanity and normality in Wordsworth's poetry is part of Leavis' account of Wordsworth's poetic greatness, and of his critical demonstration of how Wordsworth's 'inveterately human and moral preoccupation' leads to the creation of thought no less than of poetry.

Another element in Wordsworth's poetic greatness is his 'maturity' – a pivotal criterion in Leavis' criticism. 'If the strength of Wordsworth's poetry', he tells us, 'is that it brings maturity and youth in relation, the weakness is that the experience from which it draws life is confined mainly to youth, and lies at a distance', – a remark that throws as much light on the underlying ethos of Leavis' own criticism as on the poetically realised link between 'the impersonality of Wordsworth's wisdom and an immediately personal urgency'. One characteristic, and critically pregnant, passage in Leavis' essay on Wordsworth is where he defends him against the charge of 'averting his ken from half of human fate'. If Wordsworth did so, observes Leavis, it was not a matter of weakness or cowardice, nor was his heart 'unoccupied by sorrow of its own'. It was because 'a disciplined limiting of contemplation to the endurable, and, consequently, a withdrawal to a reassuring environment became terrible necessities' for him. To drive home this point and its relevance to Wordsworth's creativity, Leavis deals at some length with the story of Margaret in Book 1 of *The Excursion*, which he considered to be 'the finest thing that Wordsworth wrote and certainly the most disturbingly poignant', and to which he was to return in his 'Bicentenary Lecture'. His critique of this poem brings into play the key concepts and criteria which encompass the whole gamut of his moral and critical sympathies. After having indicated 'the emotional sources of Wordsworth's poetry' and its 'creative pressure and incitement', Leavis goes on to distinguish between Wordsworth's 'equipoise' and the 'settled habit' and 'inertness' to which that equipoise gradually led, as well as to analyse the way Wordsworth's 'inner voice' was transformed into a public voice. 'The intimately and particularly realized experience of an unusually and finely conscious individual', we are told, was replaced by the sentiments and attitudes of the patriotic and Anglican Wordsworth, and what resulted from such a transition (or deterioration) is poetry that is at once 'external, general and conventional', and its medium is 'insensitively Miltonic' – 'not felt from within as something at the nerve-tips, but handled from outside'. The same may be said of most of Wordsworth's sonnets, the worst of them being 'lamentable claptrap', and the best 'distinguished declamation', but hardly 'distinguished poetry'.

In contrast to Wordsworth's poetry, Shelley's suffers from the absence of something which accounts for its 'peculiarly emotional' quality. It is poetry that 'induces – depends for its success on inducing – a kind of attention that doesn't bring the critical intelligence into play: the imagery feels right, the associations work appropriately, if (as it takes conscious resistance not to do) one accepts the immediate feeling and doesn't slow down to think'. But if one does, one soon comes to realise how weak Shelley's grasp upon the actual is, how, in much of his poetry, 'nothing is grasped, no object offered for contemplation, no realized presence to persuade or move us by what it is', and how Shelley's 'quivering intensity of inspiration', his 'elusive' imagery and 'high-pitched' emotions all turn out to be 'a mere tumbled out spate of poeticalities', which can be enjoyed only if thought is suspended.

In order to illustrate the nature of this divorce between feeling and thought and what it entailed, Leavis compares Shelley and Wordsworth. Both were 'romantic', undramatic, and lacking in variety; and in both 'thought', implying 'overtly active energy', was hardly 'an assertive presence'. With Wordsworth's definition of poetry – 'emotion recollected in tranquillity' – in mind, Leavis goes on to explain what is missing in Shelley's poetry: 'emotional discipline, critical exploration of experience, pondered valuation and maturing reflection.' These terms – and they are frequently recurrent in Leavis – do not stand for any preconceived or *a priori* critical formulae applied, as it were, from without, but for first-hand perceptions about and reactions to 'the black marks on the page'. There is no direct or indirect reference to any authority implicitly assumed or explicitly invoked other than that inherent in one's own response to the text.

Shelley's 'Mont Blanc', for instance, illustrates his 'ecstatic dissipation', as, by contrast, Wordsworth's 'The Simplon Pass' illustrates his 'grasp of the outer world' and 'the unobtrusiveness with which that "outer" turns into "inner" '. Wordsworth, Leavis observes, 'seems always to be presenting an object (wherever this may belong) and the emotion seems to derive from what is presented'; Shelley, on the other hand, 'at his best and worst, offers the emotion in itself, unattached, in the void'. Inspiration in his case means nothing more than a 'surrendering to a kind of hypnotic rote of favourite images, associations and words'. For instance, the 'mellifluous mourning' in *Adonais* is seen to be 'a more fervent luxury than in *Lycidas*, and more declamatory', and the poem itself, 'in the voluptuous self-absorption with which the medium enjoys itself ', is seen to be nearer to Tennyson. Thus, for Leavis, as for Eliot, however intoxicating reading Shelley's poetry at fifteen might have been, it is now impossible to read it at any length with pleasure, for the effect it produces is one 'of vanity and emptiness ... as well as monotony'.

From criticism of Shelley's poetic habits, Leavis proceeds to criticism of his personality:

> The antipathy of his sensibility to any play of the critical mind, the uncongeniality of intelligence to inspiration, these clearly go in Shelley, not merely with a capacity for momentary self-deceptions and insincerities, but with a radical lack of self-knowledge.

'The Triumph of Life', however, is a poem still worth going back to when much of Shelley has become generally unreadable. It is marked by 'a profounder note of disenchantment than before, a new kind of desolation, and, in its questioning, a new and profoundly serious concern for reality'. However, even this poem is, in effect, 'a drifting phantasmagoria bewildering and bewildered ... and the failure to place the various phases or levels of visionary drift with reference to any grasped reality is the more significant because of the palpable effort'.

However, Keats, all told, fares better, although even in his case essential discriminations and reservations have to be made. In 'Ode to a Nightingale', for instance, which Leavis examines in close detail, while praising such qualities as sureness of grasp, 'extraordinary intensity of realization', fine and complex organism and 'an extremely subtle and varied interplay of motions, directed now positively, now negatively', he finds that the pang in the poem has little to do with moral and spiritual stress, for 'the pain with which his heart aches is not that of a moral maturity, of a disenchanted wisdom born of a steady contemplation of things as they are; it is itself a luxury'. Leavis distinguishes Keats' aestheticism from that of the Victorians (from Rossetti down to the *fin-de-siècle* poets) in order to bring out Keats' extraordinary force of genius and his characteristic vitality as manifested in 'Ode on Melancholy' and, even more so, in 'Ode to Autumn', which is regarded as being Shakespearian, rather than Tennysonian. For example, a phrase like 'moss'd cottage trees' represents what Leavis calls 'a strength – a native English strength' which is beyond the scope of a poet like Tennyson, who aimed to make English 'as like Italian as possible'.

Another poem closely examined by Leavis is 'Ode on a Grecian Urn'. The urn is considered to be 'the incitement and support to a day-dream' for Keats. Unlike so many scholars and specialists, Leavis is not impressed by the supposed 'subtleties and profundities' of the famous concluding pro-nouncement of the 'Ode' – 'Beauty is truth, truth beauty – that is all/Ye know on earth, and all ye need to know'. It should cause, we are told, 'no metaphysical tremors of excitement or illumination, and needs no great profundity or ingenuity of any kind to elucidate it'. In fact, the word 'truth' in the context corresponds to the attitude towards reality that is concretely embodied in the poem – an attitude Leavis himself analyses in terms of the contrast between life as it is, with its 'discordant and indocile facts', and life as it ought to be or as, with the help of the Grecian urn (a permanent incitement to warm imaginings of an ideal life, a purely beautiful reality) it can be felt for a moment to be.

Leavis makes some illuminating comments on Keats' aestheticism and his 'very subtle and embracing' concept of beauty, distinguishing it from Tennyson's, as expounded in 'The Palace of Art', and from Rossetti's or Pater's. For Keats' attitude to beauty, unlike that of the later poets, does not require one to turn his back on the actual world and get involved with 'fantasies of an alternative'. In order to illustrate this, Leavis analyses the difference between Keats and Rossetti. In reading Rossetti 'we are assist-ing at devotions – aesthetic-religious devotions. There is a sacred hush, and an effect of candles or of light through stained glass, of swinging censers, and of rites before a veiled altar. The poetic otherworld has been turned into a higher reality in the most effectual of ways: "Life is ritual".' Such an attitude to beauty, cutting off, as it does, 'the special valued order of experience from direct vulgar living', and thereby shutting out what is uncongenial cannot but lead to devitalisation.

And yet Tennyson, Rossetti and Pater all looked back to Keats as their leader and inspirer and considered him 'the great Aesthete – the one aesthete of genius', even though, thanks to his unique vitality and creative power, he is 'so much more than a mere aesthete' and his critical intelligence and his character prevent him from taking dreams for reality. Leavis relates Keats' critical intelligence to his sureness of touch and grasp, as he relates the firmness of his art to his grasp of the outer world as superbly exemplified by 'To Autumn', and also by 'The Fall of Hyperion'.

Leavis had some difficulty in getting *Revaluation* reviewed in *Scrutiny* by a 'scrutineer', and he did not want to invite an outsider to do so, with the result that it was merely announced in *Scrutiny*. A way was soon opened, however, when René Wellek, at that time working in the London School of Slavonic Studies, offered to write some criticisms of *Revaluation* which he hoped Leavis would answer. Leavis took the offer as constituting a 'suitable substitute for a review'. Wellek's criticism appeared in the March number of *Scrutiny* and Leavis' reply, 'Philosophy and Literary Criticism', which was to acquire a classical status, in the following number.

With *New Bearings, For Continuity* and *Revaluation* behind him, Leavis was now thinking of writing another book – a book of 'my practical criticism'. But with regard to this particular book Leavis was faced with a problem that was to dog him throughout his career – the problem of obtaining permission to quote from contemporary authors such as Auden and Spender, or from *The Shropshire Lad* and Georgian poetry. The same problem was to arise when he published his longest critique of *Four Quartets* (in *The Living Principle*).

The book Leavis had in mind was to deal with imagery, sincerity, sentimentality, impersonality etc. in terms of particular analysis, but it never materialised. Only essays on 'Reality and Sincerity', 'Imagery and Movement' and 'Thought and Emotional Quality' appeared in *Scrutiny*, and were later included in *The Living Principle* under the general title: 'Judgement and Analysis'.

What *did* materialise, however, was the publication of *Education and the University*, the 'essence of twenty years of work', which aimed at making current Leavis' attitude to post-War Reconstruction. Everything in the book, Leavis wrote to Basil Willey, 'relates immediately to a radical pondering of fundamentals, without any long drawn-out elaboration of theoretical grounds'.

As to the contents of the book, Leavis commented on them in such a way as to throw light on his own standing as a critic both in the academic and the literary world. For instance, he did not consider himself to be 'stocksize left, or stocksize anything' – Humanist or 'religionist', although, to his surprise, he had acquired a considerable following in the Catholic educational world. However he found the devotion of his Catholic pupils reading Arts at Cambridge 'a bit embarrassing', since they regarded his critical approach as integrating perfectly well with Thomist philosophy. Nevertheless he suggested that copies of *Education and the University* be also sent to the *Dublin Review, Blackfriars* and *Anglican Theology*.

Practically the whole of the first half of the book dealt with the problems that had formed Leavis' 'main occupation for twenty years' – the idea of a university, the 'English School' within it and the study of literature as a discipline of intelligence and sensibility. In the second half, consisting of three appendices, he dealt with Eliot's later poetry and included 'How to Teach Reading' – an elaborate corrective of rather than a rejoinder to Ezra Pound's pamphlet *How to Read* – and *Mass Civilization and Minority Culture*. While deploring the 'futilities, misdirections and wastes' in academic literary studies as well as the 'glib superficiality' of those *milieux* in which literary fashions are 'the social currency', Leavis castigated the way the frequenters of such *milieux* 'cultivate quickness on the uptake, knowingness about the latest market quotations and an impressive range of reference, all at the expense of real intelligence and disinterested understanding, or interest in anything but kudos'.

In the first chapter, 'The Idea of a University', Leavis discusses liberal education which 'doesn't start with a doctrinal frame of mind, and is not directed at cultivating one', the way 'advancing specialization' defeats such an education, and how to produce specialists who are 'in touch with a humane centre, and to produce a centre for them to be in touch with'. All this, nevertheless, had a less palpable influence on the University world, than the second chapter, 'Sketch for an "English School" '. In fact, the influence of this sketch was slowly but steadily absorbed by the university departments of English not only in Britain, but also abroad, especially in the British Commonwealth and in India, and came to be seen as an integral part of Leavis' influence as critic. He argued in favour of English being recognised as 'chief of the humanities', of English literature being 'emancipated' from linguistics and philology, and of the essential discipline of an English School being 'the literary-critical one', without which literary education itself is 'null and worse'. But the kind of critical training he had in mind could be carried out only if applied to works in English literature, and not to the Classics. 'If (being English-speaking)', he observed, 'you cannot see how impossible it is to read Aeschylus (in English or Greek) as you read Shakespeare, then you cannot really read Shakespeare, and if you cannot read Shakespeare, then your intelligence has missed an essential training – however rigorous the linguistic, logical and philosophical trainings you may have had.' Training in the Classics, including the ability to read Aeschylus in Greek, as well as Philosophical training, may confer on one a certain superiority, but such a superiority, Leavis argued, tends to have 'heavy drawbacks', resulting in 'the confident "finish", the sense of adequacy, the poised and undeveloping quasi-maturity' from which 'intelligence has to escape – if it ever sees the need for escaping'.

In the chapter on 'Literary Studies', Leavis considers literary history, in so far as it consists of 'facts about' and accepted critical (or quasi-critical) description and commentary, as 'a worthless acquisition'. Instead, he

recommends the training of a literary capacity through 'practical criticism', which should be the training of perception, judgement and
analytical skill. But even this training should be directed towards 'the
sensitive and scrupulous use of intelligence', otherwise the analytical
exercise would become 'a substitute for the use of intelligence upon the
text'. Hence he cited the example of Empson's *Seven Types of Ambiguity*
where we have both 'the profitable and the unprofitable, the valid and the
vicious', and which abounds in instances of ingenuity 'that has taken the
bit between its teeth'. I.A. Richards' *Practical Criticism*, too, is seen as
'another mixed provision of the stimulating and the aberrant', where, in
spite of the author's ambition to make analysis 'a laboratory technique',
the actual analysis is 'little more than show'.

Having adduced two well-known examples of what literary critical
discipline is not, Leavis offers a detailed illustration of what it is, by
analysing Matthew Arnold's sonnet 'To Shakespeare' and by showing how
'there is a general debility that is manifested throughout the sonnet in the
dead conventionality of the phrasing – in the lack of any vital organization
among the words'. What the sonnet suffers from is 'a radical absence of
grasp', since the poet had 'nothing in particular that he was intent on
realizing'.

Leavis continued the same exercises in close criticism in the first of the
three Appendices which constitute roughly the second half of the book. In
'T.S. Eliot's Later Poetry' – up to *The Dry Salvages* (*Little Gidding* was yet
to be published) – he comes up with certain key concepts that were to be
more elaborately developed in his later criticism, and especially in his
full-length critique of *Four Quartets* in *The Living Principle*.

In so far as Eliot's concerns in his later poetry are of a more overtly
religious, theological and metaphysical character, Leavis finds himself
asking if the field of literary criticism is 'so delimitable as to exempt him
from the theological equipment he can lay no claim to'. In view of his
conviction that poetry is to be judged as poetry and that the theological
equipment on the part of other critics has tended, if anything, to 'disqualify
them from appreciating the nature of the poet's genius', his answer is yes.
For critics, so equipped, are 'apt to show too great an alacrity in response;
to defeat his [the poet's] essential method by jumping in too easily and too
happily with familiar terms and concepts'. For his own part, Leavis was
interested in demonstrating how 'the poet's magnificent intelligence is
devoted to keeping as close as possible to the concrete of sensation,
emotion and perception', how, instead of saying 'I believe', 'I know', or
'Here is the truth', Eliot's religious poetry is 'a searching of experience, a
spiritual discipline, a technique for sincerity – for giving "sincerity" a
meaning', and how his preoccupation is 'with establishing from among the
illusions, evanescences and unrealities of life in time an apprehension of
an assured reality – a reality that, though necessarily in time, is not of it'.
Although in his later and more elaborate critique of *Four Quartets* Leavis'

mode of referring to and commenting on this reality was to be more negative, leading to his affirmation that Eliot's concept of transcendental reality was not his own, it did not prevent him from analysing it in this essay with characteristic subtlety and perceptiveness. His comments on how Eliot turns 'the unseizableness – the specific indeterminate status of the experience and the elusiveness of the meaning' – into creative concepts and creative poetry attest to his own ability, as critic and thinker, to deal with Eliot's thought, experience and concepts. For, as Leavis himself points out, 'to have gone seriously into such poetry is to have had a quickening insight into the nature of thought and language' so that one achieves, while dealing with Eliot's poetry, 'real vitality and precision of thought'.

In the second Appendix, 'How to Teach Reading', we find Leavis responding to Pound's pamphlet *How to Read*. 'One may quarrel with it', he tells us, 'but that is its value: it is a thing to quarrel with. Some such challenge was badly needed.' 'How to Teach Reading', which is almost twice as long as *How to Read*, was, as Leavis wrote to Parsons, meant to cause 'profitable annoyance', and he wanted his pamphlet to be taken very seriously. The pamphlet, he explained, is 'literary', but 'moves towards "education". It's an unprecedented combination.' On some basic points concerning the spirit with which Pound wrote *How to Read* Leavis readily agrees with him; as, for instance, when Pound dismisses 'with scornful, but not too scornful unceremoniousness the academic handling of literary education' and with his belief that 'the books that a man needs to know in order to "get his bearings", in order to have a sound judgement of any bit of writing that may come before him, are very few'. This, Leavis observes, 'in a sense, is true, and salutarily said. Yet more than Mr Pound indicates here goes to "sound judgement", to education, to competence in literature'. He also agrees with Pound's definition of great literature as 'simply language charged with meaning to the utmost possible degree' – a definition that suggests for Leavis 'a very good corrective to the academic – and general – habit of discussing literature in terms of Hamlet's and Lamb's personalities, Milton's universe, Johnson's conversation, Wordsworth's philosophy, and Othello's or Shelley's private life'. But it is mainly for what he calls 'the perversities' of Pound's recommendations that Leavis takes him to task. For instance, Pound's excluding Shakespeare and Donne from the two categories of important writers in his own classification: (a) the *inventors*, 'discoverers of a particular process or of more than one mode and process'; and (b) the *masters*, 'inventors who, apart from their own inventions, are able to assimilate and co-ordinate a large number of preceding inventions'. He also criticises Pound for being 'an amateur of abstractions', for his misconception of technique, for his views on translation, for his 'more or less elegantly pedantic dilettantism like that which has its monument in the *Cantos*', and for his 'wide-ranging eclecticism'. As against Pound's recommendations, Leavis offers his own 'positive suggestions' under the headings: The Training of Sensibility, Critical Method,

The Approach to Shakespeare, Equipment for Self-Direction, The Idea of Tradition, The Critical Approach to Criticism, Other Literatures, The Classics, etc. And he ends his pamphlet, or what he calls 'this descent into pedagogy' with a brief 'Tribute and Valediction to Mr Pound', justifying that descent as 'a serious attempt to face the problems he raised. He may deny that he raised them, but that he did raise them is the reason for treating his pamphlet seriously, as that he did not know he had raised them is perhaps the radical criticism of Mr. Pound.'

Perhaps Pound, who had protested to Leavis about his comments on *How to Read* in a private letter, had also Leavis in mind when he said in *ABC of Reading* that 'my lists are a starting-point and a challenge .... There have been general complaints, but no one has offered a rival list, or put forward particular poems as better examples of a postulated virtue or quality .... The only intelligent adverse criticism of my *How to Read* was not an attack on what was in it, but on what I had not been able to put there.'

4

The Great Tradition; J.S. Mill and the Victorian Ethos

The achievement in the novel in the English language is one of the great creative chapters in the human record.

What later novelist rendered the inner movement of impulse, the play of motive that issues in speech and act and underlies formed thought, with more penetrating subtlety than she [George Eliot]?

F.R. Leavis

The publication of *The Great Tradition* in 1948 is a landmark in the novel criticism of this century. It is also, if not the first, the most significant evidence of the collaboration between Leavis and his wife. Although in every essential respect, including style and the mode of analysis and evaluation, the book is unmistakably Leavis', his indebtedness to his wife is manifest in, among other things, his attitude to the minor novels and novelists in which she had a keener interest and of which she had certainly greater knowledge than Leavis. In an unpublished letter to Basil Willey (15 January 1950), while acknowledging his debt to her, Leavis went so far as to suggest that the book had been 'very largely my wife's work'.

The Lawrence quote used as an epigraph for the book – 'Isn't it hard, hard work to come to real grips with one's imagination – throw everything overboard' – and the Johnsonian quote '... not dogmatically but deliberately' used as an epigraph for the first chapter 'The Great Tradition', sum up the aim and the ethos of a book which, through drastic reappraisals of well-known novelists, seeks to establish the position of George Eliot, Henry James and Joseph Conrad (to whom he was, in his later books, to add Dickens and D.H. Lawrence) as the main pillars of 'the great tradition' of the English novel. As to the possibility of misrepresentation – and from an early stage of his literary career he had been used to it – Leavis had this to say: 'The only way to escape misrepresentation is never to commit oneself to any critical judgement that makes an impact – that is, never to *say* anything.'

Thus, undeterred by the fear of misrepresentation, Leavis sets out to formulate bold critical judgements which, for all their provocatively heterodox nature, have come by now to form part of the critical orthodoxy. He starts with Fielding, who 'made Jane Austen possible by opening the central tradition of English fiction', challenges the conventional view regarding the 'perfect construction' of *Tom Jones* as 'absurd', finds Fielding's attitudes and his concern with human nature 'simple', and, while crediting him for leading to Jane Austen, observes that to appreciate her distinction 'is to feel that life isn't long enough to permit of one's giving much time to Fielding or any to Mr. Priestley'. Richardson, on the other hand, offers 'a more inward interest' than Fielding, since his strength lies in the analysis of 'emotional and moral states'. And yet what even he has to offer is 'extremely limited in range and variety'. Moreover, the demand he makes on the reader's time is 'in proportion – and absolutely – so immense as to be found, in general, prohibitive (though I don't know that I wouldn't sooner read through again *Clarissa* than À *la recherche du temps perdu)'.

Hence, for Leavis, the first modern novelist, 'the inaugurator of the great tradition of the English novel', is Jane Austen. The second is George Eliot who, in her maturest work,

> handled with an unprecedented subtlety and refinement the personal relations of sophisticated characters exhibiting the 'civilization' of the 'best society', and used, in so doing, an original psychological notation corresponding to the fineness of their psychological and moral insight.

Henry James' greatness is summed up in terms of his registration of 'sophisticated human consciousness', which *'added* something as only genius can'.

As to Conrad's great novels, if they deal with the sea at all, 'they deal with it only incidentally. But the Merchant Service is for him both a spiritual fact and a spiritual symbol, and the interests that made it so for him control and animate his art everywhere'. As an innovator in 'form' and method, Leavis puts Conrad in the same category as Jane Austen, George Eliot and Henry James. The one obvious influence on Conrad is Dickens who, Leavis suggests, 'may have encouraged the development in Conrad's art of that energy of vision and registration in which they are akin'.

If Dickens, although 'a great genius', is not included in the line of great novelists, it is because his genius was 'that of a great entertainer, and he had for the most part no profounder responsibility as a creative artist than this description suggests' – a judgement Leavis was subsequently to revise. In their joint book on Dickens which came out in 1970, both Leavis and his wife demonstrated convincingly why they rated him as the greatest writer in the English language after Shakespeare.

But on other novelists, Leavis' summary judgements as offered in this chapter were to stay. For instance, Disraeli, though not of the great novelists, is 'so alive and intelligent as to deserve permanent currency', –

his trilogy *Coningsby, Sybil* and *Tancred* representing the interests of 'a supremely intelligent politician who has a sociologist's understanding of civilization and its movements'. Defoe is considered to be a remarkable writer, but 'he made no pretension to practising the novelist's art, and matters little as an influence'. While sharing the common view of Richardson's strength in the analysis of 'emotional and moral states', and of *Clarissa* as 'a really impressive work', Leavis, however, sees no use in 'pretending that *Clarissa* can be made a current classic'. As to Walter Scott, he is 'primarily a kind of inspired folk-lorist, qualified to have done in fiction something analogous to the ballad-opera'. Of his books, *The Heart of Midlothian* 'comes nearest to being a great novel, but hardly *is* that: too many allowances and deductions have to be made'.

Meredith and Hardy, too, are dislodged from their status in popular esteem as great novelists. The only novel that comes nearest to sustaining this reputation, and, 'in its clumsy way ... is impressive' is *Jude the Obscure*. However, Leavis finds it 'a little comic' that Hardy should have been taken in the early nineteen-twenties ... 'as preeminently the representative of the "modern consciousness" or the "modern sense of the human situation" '.

Although no chapter in *The Great Tradition* is devoted to Lawrence, Leavis makes some key comments on him describing him as being 'the great genius of our time', 'a most daring and radical innovator in "form", method and technique' and 'so much more truly creative as a technical inventor, an innovator, a master of language, than Joyce'. As to Joyce's *Ulysses*, while admiring it, although not for something 'positively religious in tendency' in it or in Joyce – a factor which recommended Joyce to Eliot – Leavis finds in *Ulysses* 'no organic principle determining, informing and controlling into a vital whole, the analogical structure, the extraordinary variety of technical devices, the attempts at an exhaustive rendering of consciousness, for which *Ulysses* is remarkable, and which got it accepted by a cosmopolitan world as a new start. It is rather, I think, a dead end, or at least a pointer to disintegration – a view strengthened by Joyce's own development.' This explains why Joyce was not included by Leavis as forming part of 'the great tradition' of the English novel.

After such a tightly packed and richly provocative introduction, with so many academically and conventionally consecrated names in the field of the novel discarded or downgraded, Leavis proceeds to examine the various works of George Eliot, Henry James and Conrad with a view to explaining why they constitute 'the great tradition'. In discussing George Eliot's early phase, he challenges Henry James' assertion that for her the novel 'was not primarily a picture of life, capable of deriving a high value from its form, but a moralized fable, the last word of a philosophy endeavouring to teach by example'. Even though pronounced by a practising novelist, such a comment tends to blur and to mislead, and Leavis rightly asks: 'What is the "form" from which a picture of life derives its value? ...

Is there any great novelist whose preoccupation with "form" is not a matter of his responsibility towards a rich human interest, or complexity of interest, profoundly realized? – a responsibility involving, of its very nature, imaginative sympathy, moral discrimination, and judgement of relative human value?' In order to bring this point home Leavis compares George Eliot with Conrad and Jane Austen. Henry James attributes to George Eliot 'robust powers of intellectual labour and ... stamina in the realm of abstract thought' or 'exemption from cerebral lassitude'. But this does not necessarily differentiate her from Conrad. For she has 'no more of a philosophy than he has' and his picture of life also embodies 'much reflective analysis and sustained thought about fundamentals'. But what *does* differentiate the two is the fact that Conrad is 'more completely an artist', because he 'transmutes more completely into the created work the interests he brings in' than does George Eliot, whose novels contain 'unabsorbed intellectual elements – patches, say, of tough or dryly abstract thinking undigested by her art'.

As to the difference between Jane Austen and George Eliot, while being 'unmistakenly very intelligent', Jane Austen can lay no claim to a 'massive intellect' like George Eliot's, capable of 'maintaining a specialized intellectual life'. Moreover, there is about the intellectual George Eliot 'an emotional quality, one to which there is no equivalent in Jane Austen'. Lastly, there is the difference of theme and interest. George Eliot, for instance, deals with the agonised conscience and with religious need as Jane Austen does not.

Even though Leavis finds Henry James' account of George Eliot 'subtler than any other I know', it is not 'worked out to consistency'. He agrees, on the whole, with Henry James' account of George Eliot's novels, according to which after having written her four classics (*Scenes of Clerical Life*, *Adam Bede*, *The Mill on the Floss*, and *Silas Marner*) George Eliot had exhausted her material and, 'in order to continue a novelist had to bring the other half of herself into play – to hand over, in fact, to the intellectual', so that in the later novels 'the intellectual gets the upper hand'. And yet it is *Middlemarch*, one of the three novels written later on (*Felix Holt* and *Daniel Deronda* being the other two), which is one of the great masterpieces of English fiction. According to Virginia Woolf, to whom Leavis accords the merit of having had 'a good deal to do with the established recognition of *Middlemarch*', it is one of the few English novels 'written for grown-up people'. But for Leavis, who agrees with this view of *Middlemarch*, there is 'a certain devaluing to be done' in respect of the earlier novels – something that he himself, in his subtly discriminatory way, undertakes to do. For instance, what makes *Scenes of Clerical Life* 'remarkable' is not its 'charm' as such – charm deriving from the 'atmospheric richness of the past seen through the associations of childhood' – but its 'clumsiness'. Here George Eliot is unsure of herself as an artist. Her histories 'are straight from life: she doesn't invent – she hasn't arrived at a sense of her art that prompts her to do so'.

Although 'unmistakably qualified to be a popular classic', *Adam Bede*, according to Leavis, 'is too much the sum of its specifiable attractions to be among the great novels ... too resolvable into the separate interests that we can see the author to have started with'. Following the distinction made by Henry James between the 'charm' and the 'art' in *Adam Bede*, Leavis argues that the two things are 'not identical', and he describes the 'charm' as an 'idealizing element ... an abeyance of the profounder responsibility'.

But if 'charm' prevails in *Adam Bede* there should be 'another word' for what we find in *The Mill on the Floss*, namely 'a very fine intelligence as to powers of feeling and remembering', 'an emotional tone', 'an urgency, a resonance, a personal vibration, adverting us of the poignantly immediate presence of the author'. But together with the best in the book, dependent upon these qualities, there are also limitations – limitations 'inseparable from disastrous weaknesses in George Eliot's handling of her themes' which are analysed in terms of the emotional quality representing 'a need or hunger in George Eliot, that shows itself to be insidious company for her intelligence'. Leavis examines certain characters in the novel to illustrate these limitations. For instance, he finds that Maggie's make up is done 'convincingly enough; it is done from the inside'. But it is carried out 'too purely from the inside', and he offers a psychologically penetrating commentary on the way it is done:

> Maggie's emotional and spiritual stresses, her exaltations and renunciations, exhibit, naturally, all the marks of immaturity; they involve confusions and immature valuations; they belong to a stage of development at which the capacity to make some essential distinctions has not yet been arrived at – at which the poised impersonality that is one of the conditions of being able to make them can't be achieved. There is nothing against George Eliot's presenting this immaturity with tender sympathy; but we ask, and ought to ask, of a great novelist something more. 'Sympathy and understanding' is the common formula of praise, but understanding, in any strict sense, is just what she doesn't know. To understand immaturity would be to 'place' it, with however subtle an implication, by relating it to mature experience. But when George Eliot touches on these given intensities of Maggie's inner life the vibration comes directly and simply from the novelist, precluding the presence of a maturer intelligence than Maggie's own. It is in these places that we are most likely to make with conscious critical intent the comment that in George Eliot's presentment of Maggie there is an element of self-idealization. The criticism sharpens itself when we say that with the self-idealization there goes an element of self-pity. George Eliot's

attitude to her own immaturity as represented by Maggie is the reverse of a mature one.

A characteristic example of his close analytical and evaluative reading of the prose text – this passage brings out the shrewd judge as well as the discerning critic in Leavis both of the novel and of the novelist, and of life as well as of literature.

Similarly, as in judging *Silas Marner*, 'that charming minor master-piece', Leavis always interprets what is 'charming' from a literary and creative point of view, by linking it with a moral truth, so that if, by comparison, he finds Dickens' *Hard Times* and 'the heightened reality of that great book', more satisfactory, it is because its satisfaction 'depends on a moral significance that can have no relations with charm'.

It is, then, fundamentally how the characters in a given novel are presented, delineated and analysed and what they represent and how, that engages Leavis in his exploratory and evaluative criticism of a particular novel. For instance, we are told that Tito Melema (in *Romola*) 'remains an illustration, thought of, thought out, and painstakingly speci-fied; never becoming anything like a prior reality that embodies the theme and presents it as life', Romola is 'a palpably emotional presence ... another idealized George Eliot – less real than Maggie Tulliver and more idealized'. And since in Leavis' critical vocabulary, the sense of the real is synonymous with the mature, and both synonymous with the concretely realised and technically accomplished, his judgement of *Romola* is what it is: 'Few will want to read *Romola* a second time, and few can ever have got through it once without some groans. It is indubitably the work of a very gifted mind, but of a mind misusing itself; and it is the one novel answering to the kind of account of George Eliot that became current during the swing of the pendulum against her after her death.'

In *Felix Holt*, on the other hand, 'the "reflective" preponderance of the "moral consciousness", working from the "abstract" without being able to turn it into convincing perception, notably manifests itself'. However, it is only in a certain part of *Felix Holt* – the part dealing with the Transome theme 'realized with an intensity certainly not inferior to that of the most poignant autobiographical pieces in George Eliot' – that the author is 'a great novelist, with a great novelist's psychological insight and fineness of human valuation'. The treatment of Mrs Transome's early lapse consti-tutes an example of George Eliot's mature art – an art where 'there is nothing of the Victorian moralist' and 'the atmosphere of the taboo is unknown; there is none of the excited hush, the skirting round, the thrill of shocked reprobation, or any of the forms of sentimentality typical of the Victorian fiction when such themes are handled'. Thus, while relating George Eliot to the Victorian ethos and milieu, Leavis brings out how she transcends that ethos and that milieu, and how, in her mature art, she

achieves an 'intently matter-of-fact directness' which makes *Felix Holt*
'one of the finest things in fiction'.

However, the only book that can, 'as a whole (though not without
qualification)' be said to represent George Eliot's mature genius is *Middlemarch* which, with its 'sheer informedness about society, its mechanism,
the ways in which people of different classes live and (if they have to) earn
their livelihoods, impresses us with its range, and it is real knowledge;
that is, it is knowledge alive with understanding'. George Eliot's great
intellectual powers are fully engaged in this rather than in any other of
her novels. For 'only a novelist who had known from the inside the
exhaustions and discouragements of long-range intellectual enterprises
could have conveyed the pathos of Dr Casaubon's predicament', even
though he is not supposed to have a remarkable intellect.

The one character in the novel with whom George Eliot identifies
herself is Dorothea, though she is 'far from being the whole of George
Eliot'. Another character who could have been created and convincingly
depicted only by one who knew the intellectual life from the inside is
Lydgate. When novelists tell us 'that a character is a thinker (or an artist)
we have usually only their word for it', but it is not so with Lydgate whose
' "triumphant delight in his studies" is a concrete presence'.

Leavis also analyses, with that subtle psychological insight and moral
perception, so characteristic of his criticism of the novel at its maturest,
other characters in *Middlemarch* such as Rosamond, Bulstrode and Mrs
Bulstrode. George Eliot's treatment of Bulstrode, for instance, is seen as
'a triumph in which the part of a magnificent intelligence in the novelist's
art is manifested in some of the finest analysis any novel can show' – an
analysis of the 'merciless kind' that 'only an intelligence lighted by compassion can attain'.

But the weakness of *Middlemarch* lies in George Eliot's depiction of
Dorothea, and in her imposing her own 'vision and valuation' of Dorothea
on the reader – a kind of depiction that has bearings on George Eliot's own
'immature self, the self persisting so extraordinarily in company with the
genius that is self-knowledge and a rare order of maturity'. In probing
what is false or at least unconvincing in Dorothea's self-indulgence as it
comes out in her relations with Lydgate, Leavis, by implication, probes
into George Eliot's own psychology which enables him to demonstrate 'how
intimately her weakness attends upon her strength' – even in the context
of her maturest art. Hence what George Eliot says apropos of Dorothea –
'permanent rebellion, the disorder of a life without some loving reverent
resolve, was not possible for her' – might have been said of herself.

In analysing the implications of this comment as well as of George
Eliot's identification of herself with Dorothea, Leavis sums up George
Eliot's personality and the way her strength and her weakness are seen to
co-exist even in her greatest novel – a summing up that results in one of
the most pregnant critical passages in *The Great Tradition*:

Strength, and complacent readiness to yield to temptation – they are
not at all the same thing; but we see how insidiously, in George Eliot,
they are related. Intensely alive with intelligence and imaginative
sympathy, quick and vivid in her realization of the 'equivalent centre
of self' in others – even in a Casaubon or a Rosamond, she is
incapable of morose indifference or the normal routine obtuseness,
and it may be said in a wholly laudatory sense, by way of characterizing her at her highest level, that no life would have been possible
for her that was not filled with emotion: her sensibility is directed
outward, and she responds from deep within.

But it is in *Daniel Deronda* that the association of the strength with the
weakness is more unfortunate than in any other of George Eliot's works.
Leavis divides the novel into two parts – the good half and the bad half.
While quoting Henry James on the difference between the strong and the
weak in George Eliot as one between 'what she is by inspiration and what
she is because it is expected of her', Leavis points out that it is, in fact,
rather the bad part of *Daniel Deronda* that bears the marks of 'inspiration'. And if, to quote James again, 'all the Jewish part is at bottom cold',
it is precisely because of 'a determining drive from within, a triumphant
pressure of emotion' that this is so. 'The Victorian intellectual', Leavis tells
us, 'certainly has a large part in her Zionist aspirations, but that doesn't
make these the less fervidly emotional; the part is one of happy subordinate alliance with her immaturity.' And he adds: 'A distinguished mind
and a noble nature are unquestionably present in the bad part of *Daniel
Deronda*, but it *is* bad; and the nobility, generosity, and moral idealism are
at the same time modes of self-indulgence.'

Leavis gives to the good part of *Daniel Deronda* the title of *Gwendolen
Harleth*, and compares it with Henry James' *Portrait of a Lady*, which he
feels could not have been written had Henry James not read *Gwendolen
Harleth*. If he finds George Eliot's novel 'decidedly the greater', it is
because 'she is able, unlimited by masculine partiality of vision, and only
the more perceptive because a woman, to achieve a much *completer*
presentment of her subject than James of his. This strength which manifests itself in sum as completeness affects us locally as a greater
specificity, an advantage which, when considered, turns out to be also an
advantage over James in consistency.' That is why James' world of 'best
society' and country house is 'immeasurably less real than George Eliot's'.
James idealises, and his idealising is 'a matter of not seeing, and not
knowing (or not taking into account), a great deal of the reality'. After
quoting a passage which presents Gwendolen's reactions to Grandcourt's
note asking if he may call – and Leavis' ability to quote with felicitous
appropriateness is as impressive as Matthew Arnold's, especially in 'The
Study of Poetry' – Leavis asks: 'What later novelist has rendered the inner
movement of impulse, the play of motive that issues in speech and act and

underlies formed thought and conscious will, with more penetrating subtlety than she?'

Gwendolen's own character as a tragic figure is 'so much pride and
courage and sensitiveness and intelligence fixed in a destructive deadlock
through false valuation and self-ignorance'. If George Eliot's attitude to
Gwendolen is not 'that of the judge towards the prisoner in the dock',
neither is it 'that of *tout comprendre, c'est tout pardonner*. It is, or should
be (with George Eliot's help), George Eliot's own, which is that of a great
novelist, concerned with human and moral valuation in a way proper to
her art – it is a way that doesn't let us forget that what is being lit up for
us lies within'.

Apart from the question of a comparative valuation of *Gwendolen
Harleth* and *The Portrait of a Lady*, Leavis considers James' novel 'an
original master-piece', representing, together with *The Bostonians*, the
phase when 'his genius functioned with freest and fullest vitality'. In
accounting for its greatness, he stresses 'the inclusive harmony (or something approaching it) that it represents – the vital poise between the
diverse tendencies and impulsions'.

James' later work, however, is marred by 'over-subtlety' and 'a loss of
sureness in his moral touch'. But the three novels of his later phase – *The
Wings of the Dove, The Ambassadors* and *The Golden Bowl* – are singled
out as 'books we ought to know – the books he ought to be known by'
together with *The Awkward Age* and *What Maisie Knew*.

Apart from such successes, there were limitations that became increasingly manifest in James' later 'queer development'. For one thing, he
suffered from 'being too much a professional novelist', so that being a
novelist 'came to be too large a part of his living; that is, he did not live
enough'. For another, being essentially in quest of an ideal society, an ideal
civilisation, James knew that the English society in which he lived could
not offer him 'any sustaining approximation of his ideal. Still less, he
knew, could America. So we find him developing into something like a
paradoxical kind of recluse, a recluse living socially in the midst of society.'

There was, then, also 'the trouble' with James' late style – a style
exacting 'so intensely and inveterately analytic an attention that no
sufficient bodied response builds up: nothing sufficiently approaching the
deferred concrete immediacy that has been earned is attainable. We do not
feel in the late style a rich and lively sensibility freely functioning.' And
yet he achieved some 'admirable successes' in that late period, the most
significant of them being *The Awkward Age* and *What Maisie Knew*.
However, even in these two works, and especially in *The Awkward Age*,
Leavis notes 'a disproportionate interest in technique', as a result of which
technique is seen 'usurping ... upon the interest that, in the greatest art,
technique subserves'. And yet, Leavis asks in conclusion: 'What achievement in the art of fiction – fiction as a completely serious art addressed to
the adult mind – can we point to in English as surpassing his?'

The third of the triad dealt with in this book as constituting 'the great tradition' is Conrad, not only a greater novelist for Leavis than Scott, Thackeray, Meredith and Hardy, but also among 'the very greatest novelists in the language – or any language'. In examining his whole *oeuvre*, Leavis makes 'the necessary discriminations and delimitations' in 'a securely critical frame of mind', since Conrad's classical status does not 'rest evenly' on his whole work. *Heart of Darkness*, for instance, is commonly regarded as one of Conrad's best works. But for Leavis, it is marred by certain defects; as, for instance, the novelist's comment in certain places which appears 'as an interposition, and worse, as an intrusion, at times an exhausting one'; his use of 'the same vocabulary, the same adjectival insistence upon inexpressible and incomprehensible mystery' being applied to 'the evocation of human profundities and spiritual horrors; to magnifying a thrilled sense of the unspeakable potentialities of the human soul', the actual effect of which is 'not to magnify but rather to muffle'; his 'adjectival and worse than supererogatory insistence on "unspeakable rites", "unspeakable secrets", "monstrous passions", "inconceivable mystery", and so on' which tend to cheapen the tone; his 'borrowing the arts of the magazine-writer (who has borrowed his, shall we say, from Kipling and Poe) in order to impose on his readers and on himself, for thrilled response, a "significance" that is merely an emotional insistence on the presence of what he can't produce'; his being 'intent on making a virtue out of not knowing what he means'; his need 'to try and inject "significance" into his narrative' and so on. As a result of these defects and limitations, 'the cosmopolitan Pole, student of the French masters, who became a British master-mariner' seems in some respects 'a simple soul' to Leavis, as is also borne out by Conrad's attitude towards women about which there is 'perceptible, all the way through his literary career, something of the gallant simple sailor'.

Conrad's chief strength, according to Leavis, is realised in such novels as *Typhoon* (especially in the presentment of Captain MacWhirr, the chief master Jukes and the chief engineer Solomon Rout), *The Shadow Line*, a kind of 'prose *Ancient Mariner*' (with its 'supremely sinister and beautiful evocation of enchantment in tropical seas'), and *Nostromo*, 'one of the great novels of the language', where Conrad is 'openly and triumphantly the artist by *métier*, conscious of French initiation and of fellowship in craft with Flaubert', and where he achieves his 'supreme triumph in the evocation of exotic life and colour'.

The main 'political' or 'public' theme of *Nostromo* is 'the relation between moral idealism and "material interests" ' – a theme that is dramatically enacted through 'the life-like convincingness' of the characters in the novel – Charles Gould, Emilia Gould, Martin Decoud, Antonia Avellanus, Dr Monygham, Giorgio Viola. However, the 'distinctive impressiveness' of *Nostromo* is 'not a matter of any profundity of search into human experience, or any explorative subtlety in the analysis of human behaviour. It is a matter rather of the firm and vivid concreteness with which the representative attitudes and motives are realized, and the rich economy of the pattern that plays them off against one another.' If there is something rhetorical about Conrad's art in *Nostromo*, it is so 'in a wholly laudatory sense', and even the 'robust vigour of melodrama' in the novel is 'completely controlled to the pattern of moral significance'.

Nevertheless, for all his insistence on the moral pattern of *Nostromo*, and for 'all the rich variety of the interest and the tightness of the pattern', Leavis finds something 'hollow' about 'the reverberation' of *Nostromo*. With 'the colour and life' there is, for Leavis, 'a suggestion of a certain emptiness'.

In the last part of his chapter on Conrad, Leavis deals briefly with *Victory, The Secret Agent, Under Western Eyes* and *Chance*. *Victory* is a novel dealing with the case history of its protagonist Heyst who, ' "up-rooted" (his own word) and unattached', formed by a philosophically disillusioned father, 'in solitude and silence had been used to think clearly and sometimes even profoundly, seeing life outside the flattering disillusion of ever-lasting hope of conventional self-deception, of an ever-expected hope'. Leavis sees a clear affinity between Conrad and Heyst's father, 'a kind of genius of disillusion, and the "Victory" is a victory over scepticism, a victory of life'. The novel answers most nearly 'to the stock notion' of Conrad's genius, whereas *The Secret Agent*, though 'more indubitably a classic and a masterpiece, ... doesn't answer to the notion at all'. What makes *The Secret Agent* 'truly' classical is 'its maturity of attitude and the consummateness of the art in which this finds expression'. Leavis relates *The Secret Agent* to *Nostromo*: for all the great differences between them in range and temper the two works are 'triumphs of the same art' whose effect depends upon 'an interplay of contrasting moral perspectives'. Leavis offers a close reading of *The Secret Agent*, as one of Conrad's 'two supreme masterpieces, one of the two unquestionable classics of the first order' that Conrad added to the English novel.

(The last chapter in *The Great Tradition* is an analytic note on *Hard Times*, to be discussed below in Chapter 8.)

Both Dickens and George Eliot were, in the field of the novel, the most gifted and qualified interpreters, critics and exponents of the Victorian ethos. And so was John Stuart Mill in the field of social, moral and intellectual thought, to whom Leavis devoted an important essay. The essay was written some three years earlier and published in *Scrutiny* in 1950. It came in handy when Chatto, at Leavis' instance, agreed to make Mill's essays on Bentham and Coleridge current and wanted him to write an Introduction. It was not, Leavis intimated, an essay by a professional expounding one of the themes touched on, but 'an attempt to suggest, for the literary student, approach, exploratory freedoms, connections'. It

could, therefore, be used as an Introduction, all the more so since he had
neither time nor inclination to turn it into 'a solider historical essay'.

The Introduction in fact *does* form a solid essay where, while dealing
with Mill's thought as well as with Bentham's and Coleridge's, Leavis
shows an extraordinary ability to expound historical data as well as
intellectual thought in critical terms. And what he says about Bentham
and Benthamism in this essay was to have a crucial relevance to his
criticism of the nineteenth-century novel in general and of Dickens' *Hard
Times* in particular. In fact, one might go so far as to say that no single
essay of Leavis' which is not, strictly speaking, literary criticism was to
have such a bearing on Leavis' later criticism as this Introduction.

Some of the ideas and concepts discussed here, as, for instance, the
problem of liberal education, the academic 'in the bad sense of the term',
the futility of the university exam system, the essential and indispensable
link between literary and non-literary studies, had already been discussed
in Leavis' earlier writings, but in this essay they find a new context and a
challenging one. What is offered here is not merely Leavis' evaluation of
Mill's importance as a Victorian thinker, on a par not so much with Carlyle
or Ruskin as with Matthew Arnold, but also a critical appraisal of Mill
himself as well as of what he says about Bentham and Coleridge. Using
the Introduction as 'a propagandist opportunity' to make Mill's essays on
Bentham and Coleridge 'current classics' for the literary student, Leavis
starts off by distinguishing a serious study of literature which, by its
nature, 'leads outwards into other studies and disciplines, into fields not
primarily literary' from study that amounts to no more than 'an acquiring
and arranging of cliché-material'. The latter kind of study produces a type
of first-class degree man – 'the complete walking cliché', 'the man (it's
often a woman) who unloads with such confident and accomplished ease
in the examination-room because he has never really grappled with anything and is uninhibited by any inkling of the difference between the
retailing of his amassed externalities and the effort to think something out
into a grasped and unified order that he has made his own'. Leavis'
thinking about the 'English school', the examination system and what for
him constitutes the 'good student' – in sum, his whole idea of education –
is invariably prompted by the critical as opposed to the academic approach. When he poses the question as to what constitutes 'the likeliest
lines for promoting, not the usual ready and confident superficiality of the
"good student", but the conscious and intelligent incompleteness which
carries with it the principle of growth; not the canny amassing of inert
material for the examination-room, but the organization that represents
a measure of real understanding, and seeks of its very nature to extend
and complete itself ', the question implicitly contains its own answer.

What such a student would need by way of guidance in his study of the
Victorian background and the main currents of Victorian thought ought,
according to Leavis, to include the two 'key documents': Mill's essays on

Bentham and Coleridge. For even if they had had no great influence, 'they would still have been the classical examples they are of two great opposing types of mind'. Leavis quotes two passages from Mill to illustrate how Mill had 'a very distinguished mind' and how he was different from both Coleridge and Bentham. Mill's essays on them are 'an educative experience' – something that cannot be said of Coleridge's *Biographia Literaria*. Products of 'a disciplined mind', they are 'models of method and manner', and the intellectual distinction that characterises them is also 'a distinction of character'.

One instance of this dual distinction is Mill's analysis of Bentham's limitations, such as his discarding or describing reductively whatever has not been founded on 'a recognition of ability as the moral standard' as 'vague generality'; his lack of sympathy 'in many of the most natural and strongest feelings of human nature'; and 'his deficiency of Imagination'. Mill's analysis of these limitations was to have a formative influence on Leavis' own mode of dealing with and analysing such characters in *Hard Times* as Gradgrind and Bounderby and the utilitarian ethos they embodied. Such an analysis proves that even though Mill considered himself to be a utilitarian, and had suffered 'all the restrictive rigours of his father's educational experience', he could still react against the eighteenth-century ethos with 'a sensitive intelligence, introspective subtlety, wide perceptions and a lively historical sense'. This comes out with 'admirable trenchancy' in his essay on Coleridge. He may have stood with Locke against the transcendentalists, but he was 'no unqualified Benthamite' and could well argue that the Benthams and the Coleridges 'who seem to be, and believe themselves to be, enemies, are in reality allies'.

In order to bring out the kind of importance Mill had in the intellectual history of the Victorian age, Leavis compares him with George Eliot in the sense that he too developed 'out of pure Benthamism into something pretty much in resonance with George Eliot's unsystematized liberalism'. Leavis also contrasts the quality of Mill's thought and mind – a 'pre-eminently disciplined thinker, a trained logician and analyst' – with Carlyle's 'imaginative head and stress'. 'It is hard at this date', Leavis observes, 'to realize why Carlyle in his own time should have been felt to be so great and profound an influence'.

Further evidence of the centrality of Mill's thought in dealing with the ethos of Victorian intellectual life lies in the fact that it assimilated both utilitarianism and Comptism – 'that most developed expression of the characteristic tendency of the age to replace supernatural religion by the service of humanity' – even though Mill 'never swallowed Positivism whole' and his objections to the system were, in essence, the same as George Eliot's. In fact for all his professed socialism, the individual is 'a prior fact' for Mill, and the idea of society is worked out from that.

As an exponent of a 'properly conceived liberal education' as well as of literary training conceived as a 'proper discipline of intelligence', Leavis criticises I.A. Richards' *Coleridge on Imagination* where 'the subtleties of semasiology clothe an essentially Benthamite spirit – Benthamite in a field in which to be Benthamite is to be indifferent to the essential elements (essential at any rate, from the Coleridgean point of view) in the problems one offers to be tackling'. Basic English is thus seen as exemplifying the practical spirit of Benthamism. Both in his literary criticism – especially of Dickens' *Hard Times*, 'the supreme document in creative literature, where Victorian Utilitarianism and its part in Victorian civilization are in question' – and in his criticism of the ethos of present-day civilization, Benthamism was a term Leavis frequently used to denote what he was opposed to, just as Matthew Arnold used the term 'Philistinism'. And the spirit with which he criticised that ethos was the same with which Mill or Matthew Arnold, Carlyle or Ruskin criticised 'all that was most rationally and righteously inhuman in orthodox utilitarianism' which not only turned a blind eye to, but actually countenanced 'the complacent selfishness and comfortable obtuseness of the prosperous classes in the great age of Progress'. But just as of all the nineteenth-century critics of the pervasive utilitarian ethos of the Victorian age, Matthew Arnold is closest in spirit and intelligence to Mill, so is he also to Leavis, with *his* concern for the plight of the technologico-Benthamite civilisation of today. That is why, in the concluding paragraphs of his introduction, Leavis turns to Arnold, both comparing and contrasting him with Mill. Mill and Arnold 'stand for intelligence', but, unlike Mill, Arnold is 'not a systematic thinker, he represents no strict intellectual discipline, he doesn't go in for sharpness and completeness of analysis or full and clear statement of principle, and he is not preoccupied with consistency'. Nonetheless, Arnold exemplifies 'the flexibility, the sensitiveness, the constant delicacy of touch for the concrete in all its complexity, the intelligence that is inseparably one with an alert and fine sense of value' – qualities which are more relevant to a literary critic as well as to the function of criticism. Such a function, as Arnold defines it in his essay 'The Function of Criticism', entails something much more than literary criticism. It entails, as it was to do also in Leavis' case, 'the general function of critical intelligence in a civilized community' – a function 'that extends the habit, the methods and the qualifications of a good literary critic to the more general field'.

5

The Common Pursuit

> By the critic of poetry I understand the complete reader: the ideal critic
> is the ideal reader.
>
> F.R. Leavis

Even before the new edition of *New Bearings* and *Mill on Bentham and
Coleridge* actually came out, Leavis had already started discussing with
Chatto the publication of a new book, which was to appear in 1953, entitled
The Common Pursuit. People were continually writing to Leavis, asking
why he could not make this or that *Scrutiny* essay of his available. There
were also requests for a reprint of his 10,000-word reply to Eliot on Milton
which had appeared in *The Sewanee Review* and which Leavis wanted to
be published in England, as it was generally considered to be as good a
piece as he had ever done. However, it was *Scrutiny's* policy never to
reprint anything, so the only thing he could do was to bring out a new
selection of his essays including his reply to Eliot as well as his well-known
essay 'The Irony of Swift' from *Determinations*. Leavis himself regarded
the latter as 'a classic' and wanted it to go with the Milton and the Johnson
essays. What he had in mind was a book, but it was to be something quite
different from 'the usual run of collected essays'. It was to have its own
'coherence, build-up and development', and its objective was to define 'a
position and a conception' of literary criticism and 'its place in the scheme
of things'. Q.D. Leavis, 'my severest critic', Leavis noted, had gone through
the collection, had helped him select it, and was 'unaffectedly and unwontedly impressed'. He dedicated the book to her.

One snag, however, about such a collection was the difficulty of obtaining permission to include certain items published elsewhere – for instance,
his essay on Hopkins that had appeared in the *Kenyon Review*. 'How odd
Hopkins's business is and how exasperating!' he wrote to Parsons. 'I think
the Society of Jesus ought to bear me some gratitude for enhancing the
value of their property. Did anyone do more than I to establish Hopkins?'
Eventually permission was given and the essay included in *The Common
Pursuit* – a title Leavis had 'hit on – and rested on after much consideration'. It was a phrase from Eliot's essay 'The Function of Criticism' where
the poet is discussing the desirability for a critic to 'discipline his personal
prejudices and cranks ... in the common pursuit of true judgement'.

The Common Pursuit was widely reviewed. Many reviews were of a kind where Leavis noticed – and not without cause – what he thought to be hostility. One reviewer in particular – Noel (now Lord) Annan, writing in the *Manchester Guardian* – was a characteristic example. Annan, Leavis remarked, 'oughtn't to be reviewing literature at all; he hasn't even a show of qualification. But he is one of the younger of Keynes's "choice spirits" and he has a flair ... his review is a portent'.

But although Leavis could not help taking notice of such reviews, he was not unduly perturbed, regarding them as just 'the usual kind of thing about the angry and humourless heavyweight who can't write'. Another reviewer (in *The Tablet*) compared Leavis to Dr Johnson – a comparison that, of course, flattered Leavis: ' "Lord I am not worthy" – but still!' As to the criticism of his style and the implicit charge that he could not write English, Leavis observed: 'Some time it will be pointed out (and later generally accepted – in America first) that I *have* a style, and a style that justifies itself. Even elegance and wit – if you don't mean by these Kings and Connolly.' However, in spite of adverse criticism, Leavis was convinced that *The Common Pursuit* 'won't be a flop. It's something that things have got to such a stage that what the Mortimers and the Raymonds and the System do (and don't do) *has* the effect of a demonstration. When you contemplate it, it bears me out staggeringly. What bad luck that the nice friendly Robson (3rd Programme – he was provoked by Raymond's brazen talk) should be so dull.'

Once the reviewing was over, and the reviewers had had their say, *The Common Pursuit* steadily emerged as a worthy successor to *New Bearings, Revaluation* and *The Great Tradition* and is now generally regarded as among Leavis' best books. There are two dozen essays in it, including some of the more celebrated ones: 'Mr. Eliot and Milton'; 'The Irony of Swift'; 'Tragedy and the "Medium" '; 'Measure for Measure'; and 'Literary Criticism and Philosophy'. The book carries three epigraphs – two from Henry James and one from Robert Graves. In the first, James is affirming his belief 'only in absolutely independent, individual and lonely virtue, and the serenely unsociable (or if need be at a pinch sulky and sullen) practice of the same'; and in the second he is making 'a sort of plea for Criticism, for Discrimination, for Appreciation on other than infantile lines'. The Graves epigraph reports a conversation between him and the spokesman of the college board at the end of his first term at Oxford: 'I understand, Mr. Graves, that the essays that you write for your English tutor are, shall I say, a trifle temperamental. It appears, indeed, that you prefer some authors to others.' Each of these epigraphs is aptly chosen, reflecting Leavis' own attitude to literary criticism and his practice as a critic.

In 'Mr Eliot and Milton', Leavis tackles Eliot's paper on Milton delivered as a British Academy 'Lecture on a Master Mind', and widely acclaimed as a classic of recantation of what he had written earlier on

Milton. Of the two kinds of 'relevant critical competence' that Eliot recognises – that of the practitioner of verse, and that of the scholar – Leavis claims to have neither – his only competence being that of a 'teacher' whose business is to promote the intelligent study and discussion of literature. It is in this capacity, that he not only finds Eliot 'unable to bring to Milton any but a perfunctory interest', but he also finds the deference Eliot exhibits to scholars 'wholly deplorable'. As to competence on the part of the 'practitioner of verse', one can, says Leavis, grant it 'only if one delimits one's practitioner very narrowly'. Consequently, it is not so much what Eliot, as a practitioner of verse, said about Milton that brought about Milton's 'dislodgement', as Eliot's work as critic and poet. For when Eliot began to write, Milton had long been 'prepotent as an influence in taste and practice' and, as a result of Eliot's work, 'he ceased to be'.

In commenting on Eliot's analysis of Milton's use of language, Leavis finds it 'not only surprisingly superficial, but also vitiated by familiar confusion and fallacies', and he challenges Eliot's own use or rather 'time-honoured abuse' of 'music' and 'musical', by observing that while it is true, as Eliot observes, that in Milton's use of the language 'the emphasis is on the sound, not the vision, upon the word, not the idea', one must recognise that 'this "sound" is an entirely different thing from the musician's'. Finding Eliot's antithetical use of sound and vision 'pregnant with fallacy', Leavis proceeds with his own explanation of what the 'emphasis ... on the sound' means or ought to mean. In reading Milton, he tells us, we are 'less exactly conscious in respect of meaning' than in reading Eliot's own poetry, or, for that matter, Wordsworth's *The Ruined Cottage* or Yeats' *Sailing to Byzantium*. In fact, the kind of state induced by reading Milton has, for Leavis, 'analogies with intoxication', a state in which 'our response brings nothing to any arresting focus, but gives us a feeling of exalted significance, of energetic effortlessness, and of a buoyant ease of command. In return for satisfaction of this order – the rhythmic and "musical" – we lower our criteria of force and consistency in meaning'.

Leavis himself then goes on to analyse Milton's weaknesses and inadequacies: his lack of self-knowledge in *Paradise Lost*; and the discrepancy between theory and practice, 'between the effect of a given crucial matter as Milton presents it, and the view he instructs us to take of it'. He follows up this analysis with a survey of the varying kinds and degrees of Milton's influence on the Romantic and the Victorian poets, indicating the wholly questionable and unsalutary nature of that influence on modern poets. 'I find it hard to believe', he concludes, 'that salutary lessons in "verse structure" or in the avoidance of "servitude to colloquial speech" are likely to be learnt from a master in whom "there is always the maximal, never the minimal alteration of ordinary language" – who departs so consistently and so far from speech that the sensitiveness and subtlety of rhythm that depend for an appeal on our sense of the natural run are forbidden him.' Here we find Leavis engaged, not only as a 'teacher', but also as a critic for whom 'an effective concern for the future of English poetry must express itself in a concern for the present function of criticism'.

The two essays on Hopkins – 'Gerard Manley Hopkins' and 'The Letters of Gerard Manley Hopkins' – bring out why Leavis considered Hopkins to be easily the most original Victorian poet. He compared Hopkins with other Victorian poets to bring out his superiority – over poets like Rossetti for example, with his 'shamelessly cheap evocation of a romantic and bogus Platonism', exemplifying 'in a gross form the consequences of that separation of feeling ("soul" – the source of "genuine poetry") from thinking which the Victorian tradition, in its "poetical" use of language, carries with it'. The same applies to Hopkins *vis-à-vis* Tennyson and Arnold – poets 'who often think they are thinking and who offer thought about life, religion and morals'; especially Arnold who offers 'poetically as thought' what is 'dismissed as negligible by the standards of his prose'. The difference between 'the Victorian-romantic addicts of beauty and transience' – Tennyson, Arnold, Rossetti and Swinburne, who 'cherish the pang as a kind of religiose-poetic sanction of defeatism in the face of an alien actual world' – and Hopkins is enormous – Hopkins who 'embraces transience as a necessary condition of any grasp of the real'. This, as well as his power to transcend 'the poetic climate of his age' and his ' "metaphysical" audacity', which is the expression of a 'refined and disciplined spirit' makes him a far more interesting poet than Tennyson, Arnold or Browning and, as his letters demonstrate, 'a spirit so pure, courageous and humane'.

In 'The Irony of Swift' – an essay that became a classic in Leavis' own lifetime – we find Leavis dealing with his subject not merely in his role as literary critic, but also as a moralist and a psychologist. Moreover, it is not *Gulliver's Travels* – even though it is recognised to be Swift's 'most impressive achievement in the way of complete creation – the thing achieved and detached' – that gives him 'the best opportunities for examining his irony', but other works such as *Argument against Abolishing Christianity*, *Modest Proposal*, *Tale of a Tub*, *Battle of the Books* and *Digression Concerning the Original, the Use, and Improvement of Madness in a Commonwealth*. These works reveal the 'disturbing' characteristic of Swift's genius – his 'peculiar emotional intensity', tied up with his 'habitually critical attitude ... towards the world' and 'the negative emotions he specializes in'. The negative element is indeed so endemic that even when his ironic intensity is engaged in defending what he is 'intensely concerned to defend', the effect is essentially negative. 'The positive itself appears only negatively – a kind of skeletal presence, rigid enough, but without life or body; a necessary pre-condition, as it were, of directed negation. The intensity is purely destructive.'

Leavis contrasts Swift's irony with Gibbon's. Gibbon's irony may be aimed against, instead of for, Christianity, but contrasted with Swift's 'it is an assertion of faith', because 'the positive standards by reference to which his irony works represent something impressively realised in eighteenth century civilization'. That is why Gibbon's irony 'habituates and reassures, ministering to a kind of judicial certitude of complacency', whereas Swift's is essentially 'a matter of surprise and negation; its function is to defeat habit, to intimidate and to demoralize'.

The analysis of Swift's irony, undertaken simultaneously on moral, psychological and stylistic planes, leads Leavis to an examination of how it works. The element of surprise in it is 'a perpetually varied accompaniment of the grave, dispassionate, matter-of-fact tone in which Swift delivers his intensities', and the technique which generates 'a remarkably disturbing energy' is analysed by Leavis with superb diagnostic subtlety and acumen.

> But when in reading the *Modest Proposal* we are most engaged, it is an effect directly upon ourselves that we are most disturbingly aware of. The dispassionate, matter-of-fact tone induces a feeling and a motion of assent, while the burden, at the same time, compels the feelings appropriate to rejection, and in the contrast – the tension – a remarkable disturbing energy is generated. A sense of an extraordinary energy is the general effect of Swift's irony. The intensive means just indicated are reinforced extensively in the continuous and unpredictable movement of the attack, which turns this way and that, comes now from one quarter and now from another, inexhaustibly surprising – making again an odd contrast with the sustained and level gravity of the tone. If Swift does for a moment appear to settle down to a formula it is only in order to betray; to induce a trust in the solid ground before opening the pitfall.

This passage, with its analytical grip on the way the irony of Swift, with his 'ant-like energy, the business-like air, obsessed intentness and unpredictable movement', works is characteristic of the whole essay; so too is his way of defining, determining and summing up the genius of Swift whose writings are 'probably the most remarkable expression of negative feelings and attitude that literature can offer – the spectacle of creative powers (the paradoxical description seems right) exhibited consistently in negation and rejection'. Apropos of Swift himself Leavis tells us: 'A great writer – yes; that account still imposes itself as fitting, though his greatness is no matter of moral grandeur or human centrality; our sense of it is merely a sense of great force ... he is distinguished by the intensity of his feelings, not by insight into them, and he certainly does not impress us as a mind in possession of its experience. We shall not find Swift remarkable for intelligence if we think of Blake.'

'The Dunciad' is Leavis' review of the Twickenham edition of *The Dunciad* by Professor James Sutherland, in which 'the poem trickles thinly through a desert of apparatus, to disappear time and again from sight'. Commenting on Sutherland's statement that 'the art which Pope lavished upon this poem has too often been obscured by an unnecessary concern for his victims', Leavis remarks: 'Yes; and more generally, by an unnecessary concern *with* his victims – a concern of a kind that notes, especially obtrusive ones, inevitably encourage.' Again, when Sutherland observes that the criticism of the nineteenth and the twentieth centuries 'has been far too much concerned with moral issues raised by Pope's satire, and too little interested in its purely aesthetic values', Leavis objects to the use of the term 'aesthetic', saying that it is a term 'the literary critic would do well to deny himself. Opposed to "moral", as it is in this sentence, it certainly doesn't generate light.' He then goes on to explain what he considers to be the crux of the matter for a literary critic in dealing with the *Dunciad*:

> Moral values enter inevitably into the appreciation of the *Dunciad*, if it is judged to be a considerable work; the problem is to bring them in with due relevance, and the bringing of them in is the appreciation of Pope's art. How have malice, resentment, spite, contempt, and the other negative attitudes and feelings that we can't doubt to have played a large part in the genesis of his poetry, turned that poetry into something that affects us as being so very different?

In his own dealings with Pope's poetry, the critic, i.e. 'the complete reader' in Leavis, is fully engaged – the critic who, while commenting on the *Dunciad* as a poem, also interprets the poem's social and cultural milieu. Thus, for example, while discussing Pope's use of the word 'order', Leavis tells us that for Pope it is 'no mere word, but a rich concept imaginatively realised: ideal Augustan civilization. It is thanks to his greatness as a poet that he can relate the polite Augustan social culture always present in Augustan idiom and movement with something more profound than a code of manners: a code adequate to being thought of as the basis and structure of a great civilization.'

Also in 'Johnson and Augustanism' (a review of *Samuel Johnson* by Joseph Wood Krutch), Leavis' powers as critic and as historian enable him to link the feelings and sentiments of such a 'robustly individual' writer as Johnson with the ethos of his age. He quotes Johnson on Shakespeare to the effect that 'it is incident to him to be now and then entangled with an unwieldy sentiment, which he cannot well express, and will not reject; he struggles with it a while, and if it continues stubborn, comprises it in words such as occur, and leaves it to be disentangled and evolved by those who have more leisure to bestow on it'. But, Leavis argues, Johnson himself, 'the supreme Augustan writer', never got 'entangled with an unwieldy sentiment' which he could not express, for the mode of creation suggested by 'comprising' anything in 'words such as occur' was something foreign to the Augustan tradition. That Johnson could find himself 'so at home in such a tradition and that it should have so fostered his extraordinary powers, tells us something about the civilization that produced it'.

Leavis also comments on Johnson's inability 'to appreciate the more profoundly creative uses of language', since the only method of language Johnson could understand was that of prose-statement, as distinct from 'the poetic-creative use of language – the use by which the stuff of experience is presented to speak and act for itself'. That is why, while he has difficulty in dealing with the Shakespearean use of the language, he has none in dealing with that of the eighteenth century. In fact, he discriminates, Leavis points out, 'with something approaching infallibility between what is strong and what is weak in the eighteenth century'.

Lastly, while commenting on Johnson's tragic sense of life which was, at the same time, both 'moral centrality and a profound commonsense', and which is so manifestly embodied in *Rasselas*, Leavis explains why this novel had such an influence on the ethos of Jane Austen's work and why it has 'more right to a place in the history of the English novel than Defoe and Sterne together'.

There are four essays in *The Common Pursuit* dealing with various aspects of Shakespeare: 'Tragedy and the "Medium" ' (a note on George Santayana's 'Tragic Philosophy'); 'Diabolic Intellect and the Noble Hero: or The Sentimentalist's Othello'; *'Measure for Measure'*; and 'The Criticism of Shakespeare's Late Plays (a Caveat)'.

Santayana's playing off Macbeth's speech beginning 'Tomorrow and tomorrow and tomorrow' against the passage attributed by Dante to Piccarda de Donati, with the famous line 'E'n la sua volontade è nostra pace', suggests and is intended to suggest that Macbeth's speech was a substitute for such philosophy as Shakespeare has to offer. But for Leavis 'it is not on this extinction after a tale of sound and fury, signifying nothing, that the play ends, and his [Macbeth's] valedictory nihilism is the vindication of the moral and spiritual order he has outraged, and which is re-established in the close'. And when Santayana differentiates between Shakespeare's medium and Dante's – 'in Shakespeare the medium is rich and thick and more important than the idea; whereas in Dante the medium is as unvarying and simple as possible, and meant to be transparent' – Leavis is forced to conclude that the critic 'who falls so complete a victim to the word "medium" as Mr. Santayana here shows himself, doesn't, it is plain, understand the poetic – and the essentially dramatic – use of language that Shakespeare's verse supremely exemplifies. He cannot, then, understand the nature of the organization that goes with that use of language: he cannot appreciate the ways in which the themes and significances of the plan are dramatically presented'. In other words, Santayana is guilty of 'a naiveté about the nature of conceptual thought that is common among philosophers, to their disadvantage as such'. Leavis' regarding himself as an anti-philosopher was probably encouraged by Santayana's inability to appreciate Shakespeare, as much as by

René Wellek's inability to understand the difference between philosophy and literary criticism. It is, no doubt, as a result of such naïvety that a philosopher of Santayana's calibre could treat poetry as a 'medium' for 'previously definite' ideas – something both arbitrary and indicative of 'a radical incomprehension'. Shakespeare's medium, Leavis tells us, 'creates what it conveys; "previously definite" ideas put into a "clear and transparent" medium wouldn't have been definite enough for Shakespeare's purpose'. And when Santayana says that Shakespeare's greatness lay 'in the gift of the gab: in that exuberance and joy in language which everybody had in that age, but he supremely' and that 'the Renaissance needed no mastering religion, no mastering living philosophy' and 'Life was gayer without them', Leavis rebuts him with characteristic frankness and conviction: 'It would clearly be misleading to say that the critic who can express himself thus can properly appreciate Shakespeare's poetry. He clearly cannot appreciate the organization that has its local life in the verse. He has no inkling of the way in which the mastering living theme commands and controls the words.'

In 'Diabolic Intellect and the Noble Hero', Leavis, while discussing *Othello* – 'of all Shakespeare's great tragedies, the simplest' – crosses swords with A.C. Bradley, for whom the effect of the play is 'one of a noble, "classical" clarity – of firm, clear outlines, unblurred and undistracted by cloudy passions, metaphysical aura, or richly symbolical ambiguities'. But for Leavis, *Othello* suffers, as no other of the great tragedies does, from 'an essential and denaturing falsification' in current appreciation, and no one is more responsible for this state of affairs than Bradley, nor is any part of his *Shakespearean Tragedy* 'more extravagant in misdirected scrupulosity' than his essay on *Othello*. And yet Bradley's *Othello* 'is substantially that of common acceptance'.

According to Bradley, the action and catastrophe of *Othello* depend largely on intrigue, and Iago's plot 'is Iago's character in action'. For Leavis the main character is Othello and the tragedy is his character in action, whereas Iago is 'subordinate and merely ancillary'. Bradley thus creates 'the noble hero' with 'an ideal conception of himself '. Othello may or may not suffer from jealousy, but for Leavis there are other faults than jealousy that are 'at least as damaging to a man in the character of husband and married lover'. Not to be able to see those faults, which Leavis analyses with moral conviction backed by psychological insight, amounts to wearing, as Bradley seems to do, such blinkers as to make him assert, with 'resolute fidelity', his conception of Othello's perfect nobility, that 'his trust, where he trusts, is absolute'. Iago's 'prompt success' and Othello's 'immediate surrender' demonstrate, according to Leavis, 'not so much Iago's diabolic intellect as Othello's readiness to respond' – a readiness which Leavis interprets as a defect in Othello himself – Othello the husband of Desdemona. The essential traitor, we are told, 'is within the gates', and Leavis considers him as being 'in his magnanimous way ...

egoistic', with his habit of 'self-approving self-dramatization' which is and which remains till the very end 'an essential element in Othello's make-up'.

Probing into Othello's character and how Iago can work upon it to his own ends, Leavis analyses the significance of the storm. While both the lovers, in their voyage to Cyprus, 'triumphantly outride' the outer storm, it is 'the stresses of the spiritual climate' in the new life beginning at Cyprus that constitute the challenge. These stresses are 'concentrated by Iago (with his deflating, unbeglamouring, brutally realistic mode of speech) into something immediately apprehensible in drama and comparable with the storm'. As a result of this Othello's 'inner timbers begin to part at once, the stuff of which he is made begins at once to deteriorate and show itself unfit'. The way he so easily falls a prey to Iago's persuasions and insinuations, and resolves to take revenge against Desdemona, makes it plain 'that the mind that undoes him is not Iago's but his own'. In analysing the frame and constitution of such a mind, Leavis analyses the nature and origin of love that brought Othello and Desdemona together – 'a marriage of romantic love'. Othello did not really know Desdemona; his love is very largely based on 'ignorance of self as well as ignorance of her: however noble he may feel about it, it isn't altogether what he, and Bradley with him, thinks it is. It may be love, but it can be only in an oddly qualified sense love of her: it must be much more a matter of self-centred and self-regarding satisfactions – pride, sensual possessiveness, appetite, love of loving – than he suspects.'

Such a penetrating diagnosis of Othello's character is conducted by Leavis through a close reading of the text which exposes Othello's 'self-idealization' as blindness, his nobility as 'the disguise of an obtuse and brutal egotism', and self-pride as 'stupidity, ferocious stupidity, an insane and self-deceiving passion'. But then Leavis' response to the text is that of 'the unidealizing reader' – one who considers the poetic skill of Shakespeare as being one with the dramatic. Hence, instead of letting himself be critically beguiled or morally impressed by Othello's concern for justice – 'Yet she must die, else she'll betray more men' – or by his 'self-bracing to noble sacrifice', he sees through them as self-deception. For even after he has killed Desdemona and discovers his mistake, there is no 'tragic self-discovery' in Othello. He is ruined, but he is 'the same Othello in whose essential make-up the tragedy lay: the tragedy doesn't involve the idea of the hero's learning through suffering'. Indeed, Leavis concludes, the fact 'that Othello tends to sentimentalize should be the reverse of a reason for our sentimentalizing too'.

If Bradley's reading of *Othello* serves as a foil to Leavis' reading of it, L.C. Knights' essay on *Measure for Measure* serves the same purpose, stimulating Leavis' illuminating critique as a corrective. The fact that Leavis was replying to a *Scrutiny* collaborator who was also co-editor and co-founder of that periodical made no difference to the critically stringent quality of what he had to say. In fact, this essay may be cited as an example of what Leavis understood by critical collaboration in 'the common pursuit' of a disinterested and objective valuation – something quite different from the coterie spirit so repugnant to Leavis. At the outset Leavis registers his sense of surprise that Knights, the author of *How Many Children Had Lady Macbeth?*, should, like Hazlitt and Coleridge, Swinburne, the *Arden* editor, Sir Edmund Chambers, Desmond MacCarthy, the editors of the *New Cambridge Shakespeare*, and 'innumerable others', feel any 'discomfort' about what is for Leavis 'one of the very greatest of the plays, and most consummate and convincing of Shakespeare's achievements'. For Leavis such a feeling of discomfort cannot but amount to 'that incapacity for dealing with poetic drama, that innocence about the nature of convention and the conventional possibilities of Shakespearean dramatic method and form, which we associate with the name of Bradley'. After quoting half a dozen lines of Claudio's first address to Lucio, starting with 'From too much liberty, my Lucio, liberty', Leavis asks: 'What problem is presented by these lines? The only problem I can see is why anyone should make heavy weather of them.' The aim of Leavis' rebuttal is to invalidate 'the accepted classing' of *Measure for Measure* with the 'unpleasant', 'cynical' and 'pessimistic' 'problem' plays, and he succeeds impressively in his aim.

Evaluating critically as well as morally some of the characters and their attitudes to life and death, Leavis brings to the fore his own powers as a 'whole' critic and a 'complete' reader. Thus, for instance, apropos of Bernardine's indifference to death – Bernardine who, 'for all the appreciative commentaries of the best authorities', is not for Leavis 'a mere piece of self-indulgence on Shakespeare's part' – Leavis tells us that 'those illusions and unrealities which he dismisses, and which for most of us make living undeniably positive and real, have no hold on Bernardine; for him life is indeed an after-dinner's sleep, and he, in the wisdom of drink and insensibility, has no fear at all of death. And towards him we are left in no doubt about the attitude we are to take: "Unfit to live or die", says the Duke, voicing the general contempt'. As a matter of fact, the whole play is 'an implicit criticism of that speech'. Concerning 'the assortment of attitudes to death that the play dramatizes', Leavis characterises Angelo's attitude as that of one who 'stands condemned, not merely in the eyes of others, but in his own eyes, by the criteria upon which his self-approval has been based; when, it may fairly be said, his image of himself shattered, he has already lost his life'. Again, as regards Shakespeare's belief – conveyed through a complexity of attitudes – that law, order and formal justice are necessary, Leavis rejects Knights' view of the 'underlying dilemma' of the play, and offers his own interpretation:

> Complexity of attitude isn't necessarily conflict or contradiction; and, it may be added (perhaps the reminder will be found not unpardonable), some degree of complexity of attitude is involved in all social living. It is Shakespeare's great triumph in *Measure for Measure* to

have achieved so inclusive and delicate a complexity, and to have shown us complexity distinguished from contradiction, conflict and uncertainty, with so sure and subtle a touch. The quality of the whole, in fact, answers to the promise of the poetic texture, to which Knights, in his preoccupation with a false trail, seems to me to have done so little justice.

Another disagreement between Leavis and Knights concerns the resolution of the plot of *Measure for Measure*. For Knights the last two acts, 'showing obvious signs of haste, are little more than a drawing out and resolution of the plot'. Leavis' view is 'clean contrary', inasmuch as he finds the resolution of the plot 'a consummately right and satisfying fulfilment of the essential design; marvellously adroit, with an adroitness that expresses, and derives from, the poet's sure human insight and his fineness of ethical and poetic sensibility'. Leavis analyses the way in which this is done, so that a romantic comedy is transformed into 'a completely and profoundly serious "criticism of life", with a marvellous subtlety, precision and concreteness of detail'. The 'resolution' of the plot, we are told,

> ballet-like in its patterned formality and masterly in stage-craft, sets out with lucid pregnancy the full significance of the demonstration: 'man, proud man', is stripped publicly of all protective ignorance of 'his glassy essence'; the ironies of 'measure for measure' are clinched; in a supreme test upon Isabella, 'Judge not, that ye be not judged' gets an ironical enforcement; and the relative values are conclusively established – the various attitudes settle into their final placing with regard to one another and to the positives that have been concretely defined.

In 'The Criticism of Shakespeare's Late Plays', Leavis offers his own view of *Cymbeline*, *The Winter's Tale* and *The Tempest* by questioning those of two *Scrutiny* critics Fr. A.A. Stephenson and F.C. Tinkler. With their essays in mind, he sounds a cautionary note, saying that 'Shakespeare's methods are so subtle, flexible and varied that we must be on our guard against approaching any play with inappropriate preconceptions as to what we have in front of us. By assuming that the organization is of a given kind we may incapacitate ourselves for seeing what it actually is, and so miss, or misread, the significance.' His own way of reading the essays of these two critics serves to bring home 'that we may err by insisting on finding a "significance" that we assume to be necessarily there'. Hence he finds that although *Cymbeline* 'is not a great work of art of the order of *The Winter's Tale*', its romantic fairy-tale characteristics turn out to be 'the conditions of a profundity and generality of theme', and the pastoral scene in the play is 'something much more than a charming superfluity'.

In his successive books, whether he was dealing with Dr. Johnson, Dickens, Lawrence, Eliot or Joyce, Leavis frequently invoked Shakespeare's poetic art, his dramatic technique, his moral, stylistic and linguistic maturity and, above all, his profound insight into human nature and into the complexities of human motives and behaviour. But he himself never wrote a full-length independent essay on any particular play of Shakespeare's, so that his claim as a critic of Shakespeare rests on these four essays alone.

In 'Literature and Society', 'Sociology and Literature' and 'Criticism and Philosophy', Leavis comes as close to offering the theoretical exposition of his thought and ideas as he ever did – a theoretical, not so much opposed to, as distinguished from a 'practical exposition'. In 'Literature and Society', the substance of an address given to the Students Union of the London School of Economics, Leavis juxtaposes the 'unprofitable' Marxist approach to literature against Eliot's idea of tradition, according to which a literature is 'something more than an accumulation of works'. It has, in Eliot's words, 'an organic form, or constitutes an organic order, in relation to which the individual writer has his significance and his being'. An age that boasts of such a tradition – a tradition in which 'the writer feels himself very much at one with society' – is the Augustan age which was very confident of its 'flourishing cultural health'. And yet such an age which made a writer feel himself 'very much at home with society' was bound to have – and here we note how the critic as historian and the historian as critic combine in Leavis – 'a discouraging effect on the deeper sources of originality, the creative springs in the individually experiencing mind'. In such an age there is bound to be 'a movement of protests' on the part of the creative minds who could not but feel that 'conventional expression – that which, nevertheless, seems natural and inevitable to the age – imposes a conventional experience ... [which is] at odds with their own'. Blake is a case in point. In discussing his originality as an artist, Leavis develops certain concepts fundamental to his own criticism. For example, he talks of Blake's attaining to 'that impersonal realm to which the work of art belongs and in which minds can meet'; the 'inevitable' way in which serious literary interest develops towards the sociological, the doing away, as Blake so effectively did, of the separation between the sophisticated culture and the popular; the reason why 'thinking about political and social matters ought to be done by minds of some literary education' (something similar to what Leavis himself undertook to do in his later writings, especially in *Nor Shall My Sword*); the principle that 'literature will yield to the sociologist, or anyone else, what it has to give only if it is approached as literature'. That is why a sociologist cannot learn from D.H. Lawrence since he is not 'an original critic, adverted and sensitized by experience and the habit of critical analysis'.

In 'Sociology and Literature' more or less the same arguments are applied to the 'sociological medium of literature'. Dr. Shücking's essay, *The Sociology of Literary Taste*, published in Germany in 1931, provided Leavis with an opportunity to argue that 'no attempt to relate literary studies with sociological will yield much profit – unless informed and controlled by a real and intelligent interest – a first-hand critical interest in literature'. Dr. Shücking's attempt to inquire into the social background of Chaucer is very much a case in point, and not merely because he is not inward with, not being born into, the language of Chaucer. Literature, Leavis tells us, 'isn't so much material lying there to be turned over from the outside, and drawn on for reference and exemplification, by the critically inert'; nor is 'real' interest in literature merely a matter of 'practical criticism'; it embraces 'an interest in man, society and civilization'. That is why 'its boundaries cannot be drawn'. Even G.M. Trevelyan's use of literature is nothing 'more than external', as when he uses Chaucer in his *England in the Age of Wycliffe*: 'he knows that literature exists – it nowhere amounts to evidence of much more than that.'

In the last and, in many ways, the most important of the three 'theoretical' essays which, together with the one on *Measure for Measure*, are the most original and characteristic in *The Common Pursuit*, Leavis tackles the concept of literary criticism as something to be sharply and unequivocally distinguished from philosophy. The occasion was René Wellek's review of Leavis' *Revaluation*, published in *Scrutiny* (March, 1937). By virtue of the subtle analytical commentary on and systematic demolition of Wellek's arguments and the impressive array of the counter-arguments advanced by means of the use of delicate irony and incontrovertible logic, this essay, in its devastating effect, might well be regarded as the forerunner of Leavis' attack on C.P. Snow. Moreover, while he deals with Wellek's arguments, Leavis incidentally enunciates the tenets and fundamentals of what one might call his own critical credo more explicitly than in any other essay.

Wellek criticised Leavis on several counts: that in his dealings with English poetry he did not make his assumptions 'more explicitly and defend them systematically'; that he was unaware of the fact that 'large ethical, philosophical and, of course, ultimately, also aesthetic *choices* are involved'; that, 'contrary to Leavis' own conclusion', there was 'the coherence, unity, and subtlety of Wordsworth's thought'; that he (Wellek) did not see why 'the argument of Canto II of the *Prelude* could not be paraphrased'; and, lastly, that *Revaluation* raised anew 'the question of the poet's "belief" and how far sympathy with his belief and comprehension of it is necessary for an appreciation of the poetry'. A question, Wellek added, provocatively, 'which has been debated a good deal, as you know, and which I would not like to solve too hastily on the basis of your book'.

With the calm self-assurance that is a hallmark of his critical tactics, Leavis proceeds to deal with Wellek's charges one by one. He starts by

reminding Wellek that while he is a philosopher, he (Leavis) himself is not
and that he could not 'elaborate a theory that he [Wellek] would find
satisfactory'. And he adds: 'I am not, however, relying upon modesty for
my defence. If I profess myself so freely to be no philosopher it is because
I feel that I can afford my modesty; it is because I have pretensions –
pretensions to being a literary critic' who considers literary criticism and
philosophy to be 'quite distinct and different kinds of discipline'. Even if a
literary critic might be the better for a philosophic training, Leavis argues,
'the advantage, I believe, would manifest itself in a surer realization that
literary criticism is not philosophy'. Leavis then offers the simplest, the
most significant and the most memorable definition of a critic of poetry.
'By a critic of poetry', he tells Wellek, 'I understand the complete reader:
the ideal critic is the ideal reader.' That is why the reading demanded by
poetry is of a different kind from that demanded by philosophy: 'Philosophy, we say, is "abstract" ... and poetry "concrete". Words in poetry
invite us, not to "think about" and judge but to "feel into" or "become" – to
realize a complex experience that is given in the words.' (What Leavis says
here was probably at the back of D.W. Harding's mind when he called his
book *Experience into Words*.) What the words in poetry demand is not
merely 'a fuller-bodied response, but a completer responsiveness – a kind
of responsiveness that is incompatible with the judicial, one-eye-on-the-
standard approach suggested by Dr. Wellek's phrase: "Your *norm* with
which you measure every poet" '. Leavis goes into the nature of the critical
process and how it works and what 'a complete responsiveness' entails. 'As
he [the critic] matures in experience of the new thing he asks explicitly
and implicitly: "Where does this come? How does it stand in relation to ...?
How relatively important does it seem?" And the organization into which
it settles as a constituent in becoming "placed" is an organization of
similarly "placed" things, things that have found their bearings with
regard to one another, and not a theoretical system or a system determined by abstract considerations.'

A philosophic training, Leavis concedes, 'might possibly – ideally would
– make a critic surer and more penetrating in the perception of significance and relation and in the judgement of value'. But the improvement
one would ask for is of the critic as critic, whereas a philosophic training
might well lead to 'blunting of edge, blurring of focus and muddled
misdirection of attention: consequences of queering one discipline with the
habits of another'. Looking for an example of such consequences, Leavis
did not have to go very far. Wellek's own comments on *Revaluation* provide
an ideal example. If, Leavis tells Wellek, he had explicitly enunciated
principles and 'abstractly formulable norms', he would be drawn away
from, instead of remaining as close to the concrete as possible, arriving
thereby at such concrete judgements and specific analyses as any critic
worth the name should aim at. That is why he could achieve 'a relative
precision that makes the summarizing seem intolerably clumsy and in-

adequate'. 'There is, I hope, a chance', Leavis reflects, 'that I may, in this way, have advanced the theory, even if I haven't done the theorizing. I know that the cogency and precision I have aimed at are limited; but I believe that any approach involves limitations, and that it is by recognizing them and working within them one may hope to get something done.'

Another demonstration of 'the irrelevance of the philosophic approach' is offered by Wellek when he talks about the romantic view of the world underlying and pervading the poetry of Blake, Wordsworth and Shelley, and about Leavis' indifference to this view as a result of his lack of interest in philosophy. This accounts for his being unfair to the poets of the Romantic period. As to the romantic view of the world, Leavis retorts, 'yes, I have heard of it; but what interest can it have for the literary critic? For the critic, for the reader whose primary interest is in poetry, those three poets are so radically different, immediately and finally, from one another that the offer to assimilate them in a common philosophy can only suggest the irrelevance of the philosophic approach.'

Similarly, Wellek's attitude to Blake's symbolic philosophy and its importance in interpreting Blake's poetry is sharply opposed to Leavis'. For Leavis, Blake's philosophy is one thing, his poetry another, so that, in his poetry, even when his symbols 'function poetically', they have 'a life that is independent of his "symbolical philosophy" '. But Wellek displays a philosopher's confidence – 'the confidence of one who in the double strength of a philosophic training and a knowledge of Blake's system ignores the working of poetry'. By virtue of his undeflected interest in the working of poetry as such, Leavis, on the other hand, can respond to Blake's thought or philosophy as an organically rooted part of poetry, and not as something that can be extracted or paraphrased.

The last example of where Wellek thinks he is interested in poetry, whereas his main interest is in philosophy, is the way in which he defends Shelley. Instead of paying attention to Leavis' analysis of Shelley's poetry, and especially of the imagery of 'Ode to the West Wind', Wellek offers his own interpretations of certain aspects of the poem which Leavis finds quite unacceptable. But, Leavis observes, 'even if they were otherwise, they would make no substantial difference to my carefully elaborated analysis of the way in which Shelley's poetry works'. And why, he asks, 'should Dr. Wellek suppose that he is defending Shelley in arguing that the tangled boughs of Heaven and Ocean may allude to "the old mystical conception of the two trees of Heaven and Earth intertwining"? Not that I attack the "Ode to the West Wind"; I merely illustrate from it the characteristic working of Shelley's poetry.' And when apropos of Leavis' charge that Shelley's poetry is 'repetitive, vaporous, monotonously self-regarding and often emotionally cheap, and so, in no very long run, boring', Wellek replies by saying that Shelley was an idealist, one cannot help wondering, observes Leavis, 'whether some unfavourable presumption has not been set up about idealism'.

More than defining the nature and function of a critic of poetry, this essay defines, in a fuller and more explicit way than anything else so far written by Leavis, his own criteria and convictions as a critic, and the distinction he draws between literary criticism and philosophy may, to some extent, be indicative of the difference between himself and other critics, since so few critics, whether they are interested in philosophy, sociology, politics or religion, manage to maintain their autonomy and their integrity as critics as Leavis invariably did. No wonder this essay has acquired the status of a classical formulation of what one means by a critic of poetry and how such a critic works in order to keep as close to the concrete as possible. It may also be regarded as a landmark in the sense that Leavis' notion of the critic as anti-philosopher – the title of one of his two posthumously published books – may already have been formed in his mind in the course of writing this essay.

The remaining essays in the book, too, originate from or are, for the most part, Leavis' response to what others had written – a response eventually taking the form of a personal critical evaluation of the subject concerned. Thus, in 'Henry James and the Function of Criticism', it is Quentin Anderson's essay on James published in the *Kenyon Review* (Autumn, 1946) and what Leavis calls his 'radical misconceptions', that are the subject of his critique. While commenting on James' identification with his father's system – something 'pretty meaningless, except as satisfying the particular and emotional needs of the leisure-class American idealist who elaborated it' – Leavis makes an important point: 'intentions are nothing in art except as realized and the tests of realization remain what they are.' His disagreements with Anderson boil down to the fact that in his interpretation of James, Anderson is not 'actively enough a literary critic'. That is why, for instance, for all the light he might throw on James' possible intentions, *The Ambassadors* still seems to Leavis 'a feeble piece of word-spinning'. As to the novels of James' later phase – *The Wings of the Dove* and *The Golden Bowl* – Leavis largely agrees with Anderson's diagnosis and finds them, 'in spite of all our attempts to say what can be said in favour of them', as evidencing 'the hypertrophy of technique, the overdoing ... correlated with a malnutrition'. The malnutrition was due to James' living 'too much as a novelist, and not richly enough as a man'. In analysing the nature, causes and consequences of James' literary upbringing and malnutrition, the literary critic, the social critic and the social historian in Leavis join hands. As a result of his upbringing, James, we are told, was never allowed to take root in any community, so that 'for all his intense critical interest in civilization, he never developed any sense of society as a system of functions and responsibilities. And he spent his life, when not at house-parties of a merely social kind (he was unaware, it would seem, of the Victorian country-house at its functional best), dining out and writing.' This, at least in his last phase, accounts for the separation of his art from life and his 'inherited symbolism' taking over. But it doesn't represent for Leavis 'the structure of interests behind his operative sensibility; it does not belong with his creativeness'.

In the three relatively short essays 'The Wild, Untutored Phoenix', 'Mr. Eliot, Wyndham Lewis and Lawrence', and 'Keynes, Lawrence and Cambridge', Leavis is taking to task T.S. Eliot, Wyndham Lewis and Keynes, as critics of Lawrence. In the first essay, while comparing Lawrence with Eliot, Leavis remarks: 'It seems to me probable that D.H. Lawrence at twenty-one was no less trained intellectually than Mr. Eliot at the same age; had, that is, read no less widely (even if lacking Greek), was no less in command of his capacities and resources and of the means of developing further, and had as adequate a sense of tradition and the nature of wisdom. And it seems to me probable that, even if less sophisticated than Mr. Eliot, he was not less mature in experience of life.' Leavis is writing not so much in a spirit of *parti pris* as out of his own experience and awareness of what constituted the traditional education in England in Lawrence's and in his own time both at school and later, how it contributed to 'a sense of tradition and the nature of wisdom' and how it was conducive to maturity of experience in life. In corroboration of what he has to say in order to counter Eliot's charge of ignorance and the lack of social training in Lawrence, Leavis could well have cited what Hardy, in his poem 'On Declining the Invitation to Visit the United States' says concerning the significance of being brought up and educated in an old culture and tradition where every inch of land is lettered like a tomb, as against a country 'whose riper times are yet to be'.

In the second essay Leavis defends Lawrence against what Eliot calls Wyndham Lewis' 'brilliant exposure' of him in *Paleface* – an exposure which Eliot considers 'by far the most conclusive criticism that has been made'. Leavis' defence turns into a critical evaluation of Lewis himself, who

> in a paradoxically high-pitched and excited way, [stands] for common sense; he offers us, at the common-sense level, perceptions of an uncommon intensity, and he is capable of making 'brilliant' connections. But 'what we ordinarily call thinking' is just what he is incapable of ... though he may stand for Intelligence, he is as unqualified to discriminate between the profound insight and the superficial romantic illusion, as anyone who could have been hit on. His remarkable satiric gift is frustrated by unrestrained egotism, and Mr. Eliot might have placed him along with Mr. Pound among those whose Hells are for the other people: no one could with less injustice be said to be destitute of humility.

'Keynes, Lawrence and Cambridge', too, is more about Keynes – 'a great representative Cambridge man of his time' – and the Cambridge that produced him than about Lawrence who figures in the essay as representing, by contrast, a different set of values, different aspects of civilisation and different criteria of seriousness. Hence Lawrence's repugnance for David Garnett's friends and the Cambridge-Bloomsbury *milieu* – a repugnance that was the result of something more than what Garnett calls 'jealousy'; Keynes himself, in his *Memoir*, refers to what, in his first glimpse of Cambridge, repulsed Lawrence: 'It was obviously a civilization, and not less obviously uncomfortable and unattainable for him – very repulsive and very attractive.' Leavis calls it 'undergraduate' civilisation, which 'should be left behind as soon as possible, and which the most intelligent men should escape'. His strictures against that civilisation which, in a large part, determined the Cambridge-Bloomsbury ethos, have a personal relevance, since he himself – as the founder and the mainspring of *Scrutiny* – suffered because of it. What characterised that ethos Leavis himself diagnoses: 'Articulateness and unreality cultivated together; callowness disguised from itself in articulateness; conceit casing itself safely in a confirmed sense of high sophistication; the uncertainty as to whether one is serious or not taking itself for ironic poise.' And he goes on to ask: 'Who has not at some time observed the process?'

It was both a process and a phenomenon that could not but have repulsed Lawrence, as it was later to repulse Leavis who, in the days of *Scrutiny*, widely regarded in Cambridge as an 'outlaw's enterprise', considered himself and his collaborators as being 'Cambridge in spite of Cambridge'. But, writes Keynes, while recalling the Cambridge and Bloomsbury ethos of his time, 'it did not prevent us from laughing most of the time and we enjoyed supreme self-confidence, superiority and contempt towards all the rest of the unconverted world'. But what Keynes, his compeers and his world illustrated for Leavis was the way 'the power of an ancient university, in some of its climatic pockets, was used to arrest development' and how they found in their intellectual performances 'sanction and reinforcement for an undergraduate immaturity: the more confident they grew in their sophistication, the less chance had they of discovering what seriousness was like'. It is 'the levity of so many petty egos ... each primed with conscious cleverness and hardened in self-approval' that Lawrence encountered and condemned at Cambridge in 1914. With his gift for an aptly chosen quote, Leavis gives us Lawrence reporting on what he found at Cambridge: 'they talk endlessly, but endlessly – and never, never a good thing said. They are cased each in a hard little shell of his own and out of this they talk words. There is never for one second any outgoing feeling and no reverence, not a crumb or grain of reverence: I cannot stand it.'

Together with Keynes, there was another Cambridge and Bloomsbury luminary – E.M. Forster – to whom Leavis devotes a whole chapter in this book. In the sixties Leavis told me that if he were to re-write this essay, he would be more severe with Forster. But even so the essay (written in 1938) starts by noting 'the oddly limited and uncertain quality of his

[Forster's] distinction', though it is a 'real and very fine distinction'. Forster's early novels are considered to be extremely unequal, illustrating the contrast between maturity and immaturity, the fine and the crude, even though what is positively artistic about them suggests 'comparisons with Jane Austen'. Nevertheless, in so far as he is 'pre-eminently a novelist of civilized personal relations', a novelist who feels at the same time 'a radical dissatisfaction with civilization – with the finest civilization of personal intercourse that he knows' – he reminds Leavis of Lawrence rather than of Jane Austen. Examining Forster's novels individually with a view to ascertaining his real distinction and status as a novelist, Leavis finds *A Room with a View*, in spite of certain weaknesses, 'a charming and very original book – extremely original and personal'. However, in comparison with Meredith's *The Egoist*, to which it obviously owes its inspiration, it has the status only of minor comedy, for it is 'essentially trivial'. As to *The Longest Journey* and *Howards End*, they are less successful than *Where Angels Fear to Tread* and *A Room with a View*, which bring out 'the sure easy poise ... of the artist's – the "born novelist's" – control'. Leavis also analyses the weaknesses in *A Passage to India*: 'a curious lack of grasp'; 'the depressed ethos of the book'; the equivocal character of 'the very poise of Mr. Forster's art', which is conditioned 'by its not knowing what kind of poise it is'; his 'extraordinarily lacking in force, or robustness, of intelligence'; his 'general lack of vitality'. And yet *A Passage to India* is 'a classic: not only a most significant document of our age, but a truly memorable work of literature ... a classic of the liberal spirit'.

There are some other essays in this book that have not been examined – not because they are less important or less characteristic of Leavis, but because they do not really add much to what has already been adduced for discussion, analysis and illustration of how, in some fundamental ways, *The Common Pursuit* is a unique book, dealing in two dozen chapters with nearly a dozen different writers and with as many literary and critical themes, issues and concepts. Published a year before the demise of *Scrutiny*, it brings together some of Leavis' best published work, where his critical, analytical and argumentative powers are seen at their maturest and most engaged. With three of his best books and their successive reprints behind him, and others still to come, and with his name and authority as a critic firmly established in England and America as well as in the Commonwealth, *The Common Pursuit* may well mark the heyday of Leavis' critical and university career.

6

D.H. Lawrence: Novelist

> The novel is a great discovery: far greater than Galileo's telescope or somebody else's wireless. The novel is the highest form of human expression so far attained.
>
> D.H. Lawrence

The Common Pursuit was followed, three years later, by another important book: *D.H. Lawrence: Novelist* – fruit of the author's long interest in the novelist, going back to his school days, and especially to his first essay on Lawrence that appeared in the *Cambridge Review* in 1930 (now collected in *Valuation in Criticism*). One could say that as influence and inspiration Lawrence meant to Leavis what Dante meant to Eliot and Joyce to Pound. But whereas Pound's interest in and early enthusiasm for Joyce declined later on, Leavis' in Lawrence increased with the years. In fact he brought out his second book on Lawrence just a year before his death. Whatever the subject-matter or context of Leavis criticism, the one name that was almost invariably invoked was Lawrence. Moreover, apart from Eliot, Lawrence was the only writer Leavis called a genius. He also regarded him as 'by far the best critic of his day'. The notes Leavis kept jotting down till the very end of his life as part of a future book had Lawrence, together with Wordsworth and Eliot, as the main foci of his interest.

In *D.H. Lawrence: Novelist* all that Leavis had so far written, whether by way of defending Lawrence against his detractors, or by way of trying to achieve recognition for him not only as an important creative novelist – the greatest after Dickens – but also as a critic of modern civilisation, was both synthetised and elaborated. Lawrence is placed firmly within the 'great tradition' of the English novel; in fact, the book 'carries on from *The Great Tradition*', even though 'work on it has had a different feel from work on the earlier book ... because of the nearness – in more than one sense – of Lawrence'. But there might well have been another reason for the difference. Whereas in *The Great Tradition* Q.D. Leavis' collaboration played an important part, this book is entirely Leavis' own. Another feature of the book – distinguishing it from *The Great Tradition* – is the kind of emphasis Leavis lays on Lawrence's relevance to modern times – something one does not find – or not to the same degree – in the case of any other novelist in *The Great Tradition.* 'The way things have developed since his death', Leavis makes a point of emphasising, 'has had no tendency to make his diagnostic insight the less important to us, or the positive enlivening and enlightenment – the education – he brings the less necessary.'

It is, therefore, not merely Lawrence the creative artist and the literary critic, but also, to use the Arnoldian phrase apropos of Goethe, Lawrence 'the physician' of our age, that matters to Leavis in his total evaluation of him. Leavis' conviction, arrived at early in his career, and always reinforced by the passage of time, was that Lawrence 'would pay endless frequentation as Joyce would not' and, consequently, 'if you took Joyce for a major creative writer, then, like Mr. Eliot, you had no use for Lawrence, and if you judged Lawrence a great writer, then you could hardly take a sustained interest in Joyce'.

Hence, apart from the critical instinct to interpret and evaluate Lawrence, especially in the face of such unjust and antagonistic treatment of him by influential people like Eliot – Leavis calls them 'the grosser and the absurder falsities' – Leavis feels the need to vindicate Lawrence and win 'clear recognition for the nature of his genius' – something that he, here as well as in his later writings, does almost with a missionary zeal, invariably backed up by telling argument and superb analytical skill.

In the first chapter, 'Lawrence and Art: The Lesser Novels', Leavis comments on the novels as the work of 'incomparably the greatest creative writer in English in our time' who was at the same time 'as remarkable a technical innovator as there has ever been' – especially in his greatest works *The Rainbow* and *Women in Love.* But Leavis' criticism is equally searching and enlightening when he analyses also the weaknesses and limitations of the earlier novels.

Sons and Lovers, for instance, though a work of striking original genius, has not much in it for Leavis to suggest that the author was going to be a novelist; *The White Peacock* is 'painfully callow' and Lawrence has 'no certain grasp of his emotional purpose, and is too much preoccupied with writing a novel'. *The Trespasser*, too, for all its autobiographical and personal character, does not contain 'any clear promise of a great novelist'.

When it comes to discussing Lawrence's two masterworks, Leavis recognises the difficulty of understanding them at first reading, since the methods and procedures used by Lawrence are so original that we fail to recognise what his art is all about. But for Leavis such a difficulty 'is a measure of their profound originality' as well as a challenge to interpret it. And in so far as the technical originality in Lawrence is the consequence of the originality of what he has to say, the worst difficulty for Leavis is what he calls the 'resistance in us' to what Lawrence's art conveys – resistance represented by 'habit; habit that will not let us see what is there for what it is, or believe that the door is open'. Commenting on Lawrence's view of Flaubert and of his conception of art – 'the craving for form' as being not so much the outcome of an artistic conscience as of 'a certain attitude to life' in which 'distaste and boredom have so decisive a part' – Leavis considers both the method and the ethos of Lawrence's art as being 'characteristically un-Flaubertian (and un-Joycean)', and, he might well have added, in some respect un-Eliotian too.

Other novels summarily commented on in this chapter are *Aaron's Rod*, *Kangaroo*, *The Plumed Serpent*, *Lady Chatterley's Lover* and *The Lost Girl* as well as the Tales: 'The Captain's Doll', 'St. Mawr' and 'The Ladybird' particularly. To some of these works – 'The Captain's Doll', 'St Mawr' and the other Tales – Leavis devotes a chapter each in the book where critical assessments, succinctly formulated in the first chapter, receive a more detailed, more elaborate and more analytical treatment. *The Plumed Serpent* is regarded as 'a bad book and a regrettable performance'; *The Lost Girl* is 'unlike any other novel that Lawrence ever wrote ... the work of an unsentimental, more subtle and incomparably more penetrating Dickens'; *Aaron's Rod*, though 'a most lively novel and a work of genius', is not a work of art of the order of *Women in Love*', and clearly illustrates the way 'in which intelligence in Lawrence, marvellous as it was, could fail to transcend the special conditions of experience'. Leavis discusses this novel, both in terms of art and technique and in terms of the light it throws on Lawrence's own life, character and personality. That Frieda, as his wife, had 'no home, and, having abandoned her children, no maternal function', that she was neither maternal in type nor intellectual, and that she had 'no place in any community, no social function, and nothing much to do' are for Leavis 'the disadvantages Lawrence had to contend with as a seeker after normative conclusions about the relations between men and women'. Hence, even though the union between Lawrence and Frieda 'justified itself', it was 'hardly one that provided representative experience for pronouncing normatively about marriage' – something in respect of which the author of *Anna Karenina* enjoys a much greater advantage.

The special circumstances of Lawrence's life, therefore, could not but affect his perception of problems 'in ways he is not sufficiently aware of '. 'The Captain's Doll', 'one of the finest of the tales', demonstrates 'the insidious effect' with 'more ominous significance', when the hero Alexander Hepburn refuses to marry Hannele on the basis of love; 'love conceived as a matter of the man's devoting himself to adoring the beloved and making it the business of his life to make *her* life happy'. Leavis discusses with great subtlety and delicacy the possibilities as well as the difficulties of our identifying Hepburn with Lawrence and Hannele with Frieda, and he quotes Hepburn as saying to Hannele: 'I do want to do something along with men ... I *am* alone and cut off. As a man among men, I have no place. I have my life with you, I know; *et praeterea nihil*', to which Hennele retorts: '*Et praeterea nihil*! And what more do you want? Besides, you liar, haven't you got your writing? Isn't that all you want, isn't that doing all there is to be done? Men! Much *men* there is about them! Bah, when it comes to that, I have to be the only man as well as the only woman.' Leavis' commentary on Hennele's repartee is a good illustration of how the critic, in the fullness and complexity of his response to what is there before him, is both a critic of literature and a critic of life, and presents his critical thought and perception in terms of a morally sensitive and imaginatively subtle assessment of the situation. The voice is unmistakably Frieda's, says Leavis,

> and Lawrence doesn't make any show of finding an answer that wholly convinces himself. Yet it is *of* Lawrence's genius to be conscious of a responsibility – to be conscious of a power that is responsibility – such as makes him feel that writing is *not* doing all there is to be done; his writing is the writing of a man (a 'greater man' and a 'more heroic soul') who feels that. His problem is to determine what, in the concrete, the manifestations of the 'power' and the responsibility should be. And the three novels *Aaron's Rod, Kangaroo*, and *The Plumed Serpent*, are preoccupied with the effort of determination.

In *Kangaroo*, through a day-dream, Lawrence 'tests the idea of becoming a leader in political action'; and records the failure; in *The Plumed Serpent* we have an attempt on his part to prove – 'an imaginative enactment' – that the revival of the necessary religion, the ancient Mexican religion, is possible; in *Aaron's Rod*, there is a 'special' effort on Lawrence's part to 'transcend the peculiarities of his actual situation'.

Coming to *Lady Chatterley's Lover*, 'a courageous, profoundly sincere, and very deliberate piece of work', Leavis finds much that is admirable about it – 'that strong vital instinct of health' – which is the very spirit of Lawrence's genius and the way he 'relates his special theme with great power to the malady of industrial civilization'.

The second chapter, 'Lawrence and Class', deals specifically with the tale *The Daughters of the Vicar* to illustrate Lawrence *vis-à-vis* class and to show in what way he is 'the supreme master' of the shorter forms of prose fiction. It is a tale which has class-distinctions as a 'major element' in its theme, the discussion of which gives Leavis the opportunity of refuting the charges laid against Lawrence by Eliot in *After Strange Gods*: 'alarming strain of cruelty', and the absence of any 'moral or social sense' in the relations between his men and women. The villain of the drama, says Leavis, is class, represented by 'the proud class-superiority of the impoverished vicar's family'. Pride due to class-superiority is the enemy of life, 'starving and thwarting and denying, and breeding in consequence hate and ugliness'. Leavis diagnoses the destructive force of class-superiority – 'destructive of all fineness and nobility' – and yet he finds something heroic about the drama of the Vicar and his family, 'something almost tragic'. The attitude implicit in the presentation of the drama is 'not one that goes with contemptuous exposure or satiric condemnation', but something 'more subtle and poised', so that it is 'incompatible with complacency or cruelty in any form'. A close analytical examination of the words and feelings, the motives and effect of the conduct and actions, of the different characters enables Leavis to show how Lawrence's treatment of class works and how it reveals 'the strongly tender humanity of the tale'.

The next two chapters include Leavis' masterly critiques of *The Rainbow* and *Women in Love* – critiques comparable, in their exhaustively exploratory and expository approach to the works in question, to his later critique of *Four Quartets* (*The Living Principle*). Less analytical, less successful than *Women in Love*, which Lawrence called a sequel, *The Rainbow* is not a 'perfect work of art'; does not have the inclusiveness of scope of *Women in Love*; and in some respects belongs to the same tradition of art as George Eliot.

And yet *The Rainbow* is as much characteristic of Lawrence's genius as *Women in Love* or any other novel, conveying with force and vividness, Lawrence's 'intuition of the oneness of life' and, at the same time, his sense of 'the separateness and irreducible otherness of lives'. In fact, the very intensity of the intuition of the oneness of life takes the form of 'an intensity of preoccupation with the individual', and underlies what Leavis calls 'the supreme importance of "fulfilment" of the individual, because here (if not here, nowhere) is life'. For his own 'fulfilment' the individual has to be involved in personal relations, especially those between a man and a woman, which 'make and validate a marriage'. But for Lawrence, marriage as such has to be 'a mutual acceptance of their separateness and otherness'. With telling clarity and conciseness Leavis sums up Lawrence's view of as well as his attitude to love, marriage and sex. Love, we are told, 'is no more an absolute than sex is his religion'. What strikes us as religious in Lawrence is the intensity with which his men and women, 'hearkening to their deepest needs and promptings as they seek "fulfilment" in marriage know that they "do not belong to themselves", but are responsible to something that, in transcending the individual, transcends love and sex too'.

Leavis examines numerous passages from *The Rainbow* with a view to bringing out, among other things, Lawrence's rendering of the relations between men and women, 'the burden' of his art, which is that life is 'fulfilled' in the individual or nowhere and that without a true marital relation, which is creative in more than the sense of producing children, there can be no 'fulfilment' – the particular concrete terms of 'fulfilment' varying from individual to individual. Hence

to have achieved 'fulfilment' is to find meaning in life in the sense of having found immunity against the torment of the question, 'What for?', and found it, not by falling into inert day-to-dayness, the anaesthesia of habit or automatism, but by achieving what Lawrence elsewhere (and both the context of discourse in *Psychoanalysis and the Unconscious* and the art of *The Rainbow* and *Women in Love* make it much more than a phrase) calls 'spontaneous-creative fullness of being'.

Thus, with Lawrence as his subject, Leavis' criticism itself rises to the Laurentian level of moral perception, psychological insight, and critical acumen, which is the only way he can do justice to the highly charged passages on which he undertakes to comment. Hence one can say that there is something genuinely creative about Leavis' criticism as such.

As to Lawrence's attitude to sex, it comes out, among other things, in the way he deals with the sex desire that torments Tom Brangwen, forcing his imagination always to revert to lustful scenes. Leavis deals with the subject by comparing Lawrence and George Eliot – two novelists who, in more than one way, shared the same ethical and religious tradition. And yet George Eliot 'could not have dealt with the stresses of his [Tom Brangwen's] sexual life as Lawrence does ... She would not have brought them insistently into focus in this way, and she could not have achieved either this natural intimacy and directness, or this inwardness, of treatment.' However, in spite of this difference, Lawrence is, 'as a recorder of essential English history ... a great successor of George Eliot' and his genius is no less related to his upbringing 'in the environment of a living tradition' than is George Eliot's, even though George Eliot's way of relating to such a tradition and Lawrence's are different. Leavis analyses this difference in cultural and historical terms rather than in critical terms. The civilisation and the tradition that associate Lawrence with George Eliot were not 'a residual evangelizing earnestness, or a naive provinciality of ethical temper, or a bent for insisting, in terms of a narrow untheological bigotry, that strait is the gate, and few there are that shall be saved'. Cultural and social history and the way it impinges upon the literary sensibility of a given literary period almost always combines with and gives force to Leavis' critical arguments, appraisals and discriminations. For instance, if the word for George Eliot is 'ethical' rather than 'religious', the same cannot be said of Lawrence, and Leavis argues why, by demonstrating the essentially religious character of the intensity with which Lawrence makes his characters hearken 'to their deepest needs and promptings as they seek "fulfilment" in marriage', while at the same time knowing that they 'do not belong to themselves'. Another thing that differentiates Lawrence from George Eliot is in their way of dealing with the theme of love and marriage. 'It might be said', observes Leavis, as he sets out to analyse the 'complex structure' of Brangwen's need for love, that it is *'mutatis mutandis*, in a general way Maggie Tulliver's. But under that "general" lies the immense difference between the two authors .... Lawrence sees what the needs are, and understands their nature, so much better than George Eliot .... Her strength doesn't lie here.' Understanding those needs implies understanding their effects as well which Lawrence describes with analytical subtlety as well as poetic intensity. For the sake of illustration Leavis quotes a passage from *The Rainbow* where 'the tenderness, reverence, and wonder that are defined ... have an utterly unsentimental strength'. Lawrence's art defines 'the complex and delicate relations that form a marriage' which involves 'the recognition of something beyond love – the recognition that love is "not an end in itself" '.

As while analysing a poem, so also while analysing *The Rainbow* and *Women in Love* – and they are for him dramatic poems – Leavis analyses the significance and the symbolism of certain words like 'fulfilment', 'creative', 'beyond' used by Brangwen as well as by Lawrence himself, and also of the quality of the prose in certain parts of the novel, as, for instance, where Anna's and Will's visit to Lincoln Cathedral is described. 'It is', Leavis observes, 'a poem rising easily and naturally out of the almost incredibly flexible prose in which *The Rainbow* is written.' The discussion between Anna and Will about religion concerns 'a conflict in the inner life of the married pair', and Leavis brings out how 'the defeat or failure on both sides has its significance in a failure of complete "fulfilment" in marriage; a failure to create "a new knowledge of Eternity in the flux of time".'

Leavis also analyses the autobiographical element in *The Rainbow*. Referring to Chapter VIII ('The Child') which renders the young father Will's 'awe, terror, and delight' in a very Laurentian way, Leavis tells us that it is 'something more than the imaginative divination of a young father's response ... it comes with the peculiar directness from the centre of Lawrence himself'. While assessing the relevance of what happened to Lawrence in his boyhood, Leavis discards the general assumption that Lawrence had been 'warped for life or in some way disabled by the strain set up in babyhood'. 'What, for a genius, *is* misfortune?' he asks, and his own view is that one would be 'hard put to it to assemble any weight of critical evidence from the writings' in support of that assumption. On the contrary, there is 'no more impressive mark of his genius than what he did with his "misfortune"; he turned it into insight. It was a triumph of supreme intelligence – the intelligence that is inseparable from imagination and self-knowledge.'

In this respect, the character in the novel Leavis finds nearest to Lawrence is Ursula. But far from finding the substitution of the other sex for the author's to be 'the mark of an impersonality unachieved or insecure, a disguise prompted by a sense of danger', he considers it to be 'the mark of a creative genius, the impulse and the power to transcend the merely personal predicament by the intelligence that is imagination – or the imagination that is intelligence'. He attributes 'an astringent delicacy ... and a clear-eyed subtlety' to Lawrence – something Leavis himself achieves as he deals with the Ursula-Skrebensky and Ursula-Inger relationships, and brings out such significant details as the unobtrusive symbolism of Ursula's and Skrebensky's walk, Skrebensky's inadequacy as a lover and his 'public spirit', and his 'good-citizen acceptance of the social function as the ultimate meaning of life', which provokes Ursula's judgement: 'You seem like nothing to me.' In describing as well as disentangling the various threads of the relationships between various characters, Lawrence shows his 'extraordinary power of the impersonalizing intelligence' which characterises 'the wonderfully original work of a great genius' that *The Rainbow*, in spite of its imperfections, is – imperfections such as 'the absence of an inevitable close', 'the signs of too great a tentativeness in the development and organization of the later part' and, above all, 'the sterile deadlock' between Ursula and Skrebensky which is 'too long-drawn-out'. However, in the light of what has been achieved in the novel, including the 'marvellous invention of form' and the record of 'the spiritual heritage' of an actual society, which makes Lawrence, as social historian, 'unsurpassed' among novelists, these faults, according to Leavis, amount to very little.

Turning to a still greater and more complex as well as more accomplished work – *Women in Love* – Leavis heaps on it and on the author various kinds of praise, throughout critically sustained: 'a formidable originality of method and style'; 'the astonishing variety and force of the enacted life'; Lawrence's power of 'introducing direct discussion of his themes into dialogue that remains convincingly dramatic in every respect'; his study of 'the individual psyche' leading to the diagnosis of civilization; his art being 'fed by an inexhaustible creative flow', and so on. The more Leavis admires a particular aspect of *Women in Love*, the more penetrating and subtle is his own response to it, and the more convincing is his appreciation of the intelligence of one whose 'imaginative achievements are, at the same time, achievements of intelligence'. One manifestation of such intelligence is the way Lawrence probes into the psyche of his individual characters. For instance, 'the plausible ethics of productivity' embodied by Gerald is interpreted by Leavis as representing 'a refusal of responsibility – of self-responsibility, or responsibility towards life'. Similarly, Thomas Crich's idealism is seen as something more than 'a sentimental self-indulgence and an evasion of responsibility'; Gerald's love for Gudrun is judged to be nothing but a 'desperate need and utter dependence' which makes him 'a deadly oppression to her', turning her love for him more and more into malice. Gerald, on his part, also hates her, knowing that 'there is no dominance to be achieved that will ensure his safety'.

Through his close critical and psychological analysis of the moral significance of what is involved, Leavis turns the criticism of the novel into something larger – into a criticism of life itself, as well as of society and civilisation. One of Leavis' most memorable comments is on the failure of the Gerald-Gudrun relationship and what it ultimately amounts to: 'The realization that will and idea and dominant masculinity in Gerald can supply no answer to the question that gnaws from within ("What for?")

leaves Gudrun unable to evade the failure, in herself, of "spontaneous creative life". The failure manifests itself to her in an experience that, suffered from time to time by different actors, recurs in *Women in Love*: an obsessed and tormenting awareness of time as measured by the clock, an endless succession of minutes and hours and days'.

The long drama of the Birkin-Ursula relationship, too, which does not lend itself to dramatic presentation in the normal sense of the term, is dealt with by Lawrence with 'the astonishing originality' of his genius. One manifestation of that originality is the fact that in Lawrence's art significance is 'never a matter of a mere intended "meaning" symbolized; it works from profounder levels and more complex ways' – something that cannot be appreciated by 'the habit-conditioned novel reader' who brings to *Women in Love* 'expectations that certainly do not open him to the possibility of that kind (the familiar kind) of significance', so that he is left with 'a general impression of meaningless chaos'.

Equally subtle is Leavis' commentary on the Birkin-Hermione conflict and on her 'subconscious and intense' hatred of him. 'It is not a mere matter', says Leavis, 'of our being *told* that "her hatred of him was subconscious and intense"; the destructive animus has been defined and conveyed by a variety of inexplicit evocative means. It is there in the hunger of possession with which she besieges him.' While explaining the nature and origin of this 'hunger', Leavis delves into her psyche and will with a degree of imaginativeness, subtlety and insight almost comparable to Lawrence's:

> She *must* know; her will is not her instrument, a power by which she commands: she is under its compulsion, the slave of a malign automatism that is inimical to life in herself as in Birkin. To 'know' is to possess, and to possess is to destroy; it is a self-defeating process. This, far down in herself, Birkin's reply forces her to realize; his 'knowing' is so obviously a different kind of thing, and different in a way that proclaims, implicitly, the impossibility of satisfying her own hunger to 'know': hence the strange quality of her reaction.

Leavis also analyses Lawrence's 'relating the overt expressions of personal life to the impersonal depths' and presenting in the disorder of the individual psyche 'the large movement of civilization'. It is precisely because it gives so much 'that *Women in Love* has been judged to give less than the reader has the right to demand' – a judgement which is a compliment for Leavis.

The last three chapters of the book are devoted to 'The Captain's Doll', 'St Mawr' and the Tales. In the first, Leavis finds some of the characteristic qualities of Lawrence's art impressively exemplified – flexibility, 'marvellous ear for speech', remarkable dramatic range, 'the fresh and easy (it seems) creative, or poetic, power and sensitiveness of the prose, with the unpondered inevitability of its rightness, and the way in which the dialogue, itself so right, works with it'. He also elucidates the significance of the various scenes in the tale, while commenting on them with a real insight into the complexities of the individual psyche as well as of human nature, the human condition and human possibilities. For instance, while discussing the significance of the telescopes and Alexander's interest in the moon, Leavis makes some generalisations which are crucial to the matter in hand. One cannot, he tells us,

> live to make another person happy; and to propose to do so, to take that for a *raison d'être*, is a denial of life that can only breed ill. Again, what we have had presented to us by the whole scene is the face of *otherness*: we cannot possess one another, and the possibility of valid intimate relations – the essential lasting relations between a man and a woman, for instance – depends on an acceptance of this truth.

But Leavis no more propounds or generalises than does 'The Captain's Doll' itself. He merely interprets what his own reading of the tale means or suggests to him. And in doing so, he is implicitly showing how 'again and again Lawrence's art deals with the woman, nerve-worn and strained or lethally sardonic, in whom life has gone wrong because she is committed to the man's part, or to contempt for it, or to living in a mode that gives no place to it'.

However, for all his enthusiasm for the tale, Leavis knows that certain things in 'The Captain's Doll' call for criticism. For instance, the fact that certain possibilities have not been recognised; and that the tale 'raises questions in a way of which the author cannot be supposed to be unaware'. Nevertheless, the tale ends with a suggestive efficacy; with the Captain and Hannele accepting each other – an end Leavis himself comments on with great delicacy and insight.

For all its creative and technical originality Leavis finds 'St Mawr' more remarkable than *The Waste Land*, being, 'as that poem is not, completely achieved, a full and self-sufficient creation'. He quotes various passages from 'St Mawr' to show Lawrence's power of 'easy and inevitable transitions', so that 'what looks like carelessness – the relaxed, idiomatic, and even slangy familiarity', as in the opening pages of the tale – 'is actually precision and vivid firsthandness'. This kind of 'flexibility' and 'creative freedom' which Lawrence shows while writing 'out of the full living language' has, for Leavis, 'no parallel in modern times'. Lawrence's dialogues, too, have a creative convincingness, realism and immediacy about them. Leavis quotes the discussion between Mrs. Witt and her daughter as an example of Lawrence's method of establishing his values and significances. The mother and the daughter discuss what may be called his [Lawrence's] central theme, and while doing so in a wholly dramatic way, bring to the point of explicitness the essential work of the implicit definition that has been done by image, action and symbolic presentation.

Behind such a method is Lawrence's 'deep insight into human nature; [his] clairvoyant understanding of so wide a range of types and milieux; [his] generalizing power which never leaves the concrete'. The dialogue itself, though belonging to the conversational everyday world, is always 'kept in touch with the depths, can blend in one utterance the hard-boiled sardonic with the poignant ... it starts from, and, when it likes, lapses back into, slangy colloquialism, yet, invoking the essential resources of poetic expression, can hazard the most intense emotional and imaginative heightening' – something that, according to Leavis, could not be done outside Shakespearean dramatic poetry.

The Tales, too, attest to Lawrence's creative power. Leavis briefly characterises each one of them, thereby bringing out that quality in Lawrence by virtue of which he is 'radically unlike (the unlikeness being his greatness) not only Maupassant but Eliot, Wyndham Lewis, Pound and Joyce' – whether he is dealing with his central theme (the relationship between men and women, or sex), the 'disquality' of the individual, or 'the complimentary truth ... that without his relations with other lives, the individual is nothing'. Another thing that sets Lawrence apart from other writers is his use of irony, which, for all its astringency, 'never has a touch of animus; never a touch of that egoistic superiority which makes the ostensibly comparable work of other writers seem cheap – so often cheap and nasty' – a difference that is 'one of depth'.

The one writer Leavis specifically compares Lawrence with is Eliot. In the Appendix 'Mr. Eliot and Lawrence', he defends him against Eliot's attack by attacking Eliot himself. Passionately committed as he was to seeing Lawrence recognised as 'the great creative genius of our age, and one of the greatest figures in English literature', Leavis uses such terms as enemy and ally – those who are against Lawrence and those who are for him. Considered by Leavis to have been, all those years, 'the reverse of an ally', 'the essential opposition in person', when others, including most importantly Leavis himself, had been contending that the time for Lawrence's recognition was overdue, Eliot comes in for what may be regarded as the *first* explicit attack on him by Leavis – an attack on his ethos, his prejudices and his limitations, both as a man and as a writer.

In his preface to 'Fr' Tiverton's *D.H. Lawrence and Human Existence*, Eliot could not have exposed in a more searching and forthright way Lawrence's limitations and, incidentally, also challenged Leavis' view of Lawrence, than by depicting him as 'an impatient and impulsive man', 'a man of fitful and profound insights, rather than of ratiocinative powers', and, so far as his religious attitude goes, 'an ignorant man in the sense that he was unaware of how much he did not know'. Eliot also criticised Lawrence for a lack, 'not so much of information, as of the critical faculties which education should give, and an incapacity for what is ordinarily called thinking'. Moreover, Lawrence represents an extreme case of the 'crippling effect upon men of letters of not having been brought up in the environment of a living and central tradition'.

Leavis rebuts each one of Eliot's charges. To begin with he asserts Lawrence's and his own Englishness as against Eliot's non-Englishness. It is, he says,

> when I come to these things in Mr. Eliot that I find myself saying: '*I am a fellow-countryman of D.H. Lawrence.*' Mr. Eliot is not – the fact that in any case is sufficiently obvious insists here for recognition. For no educated Englishman of Mr. Eliot's generation and Mr. Eliot's intelligence, I am convinced, could so confidently have expressed his ignorance.

As to Lawrence's religion, Leavis counter-attacks Eliot's charge by exposing his own ignorance of the nature of the particular religious tradition to which Lawrence belonged, and of how Lawrence turned the earnestness and moral seriousness of this tradition to 'the powering of a strenuous intellectual inquiringness'.

As to Eliot's charge of Lawrence's 'incapacity for what is ordinarily called thinking', Leavis meets it frontally, by asserting authoritatively that Lawrence's thinking is 'so much superior to what is ordinarily called thinking that it tends not to be recognized for thinking at all'. As regards 'ratiocinative powers', if it 'means anything worth having', then Lawrence's again seem to be 'superlative' to Eliot's. For, in terms of 'logical stamina, the power to pursue an organising process of thought through a wide and difficult tract, with a sustained consistency that is at the same time a delicate fidelity to the complexities of the full concrete experience, Lawrence seems to me to be superior to Mr. Eliot (yes, to the author of *Four Quartets*)'.

But when it comes to Lawrence's defects of knowledge about religion and theology, Leavis meets the charge with a 'direct retort':

> I am not, then, impressed by any superiority of religious and theological knowledge in a writer capable of exposing what is to me the shocking essential ignorance that characterizes *The Cock-tail Party* – ignorance of the possibilities of life; ignorance of the effect the play must have on a kind of reader or spectator of whose existence the author appears to be unaware: the reader who has, himself, found serious work to do in the world and is able to be unaffectedly serious about it, who knows what family life is and

F.R. Leavis

has helped to bring up children and who, though capable of being interested in Mr. Eliot's poetry, cannot afford cocktail civilization and would reject it, with contempt and boredom, if he *could* afford it.

Retirement and Post-retirement

The unanswerableness is the 'cruelty' and is what has 'wounded' Snow.
It would have been less 'cruel' if it had been accompanied, as it was not,
by the animus that impels the intention to hurt.

F.R. Leavis

Two Cultures?

A year before his retirement, controversy engulfed Leavis on an unprece-
dented scale – a controversy that had nationwide repercussions and that
crossed the Atlantic and, subsequently, reached Europe. The occasion was
Leavis' Richmond Lecture delivered in the Hall of Downing College,
Cambridge, on 28 February 1962 and published on 9 March 1962 in the
Spectator, and the bitter polemical reaction it aroused in the correspondence column of the *Spectator* and in other periodicals, both English and
American. 'The lecture', Leavis pointed out, explaining its publication in
the *Spectator*, 'was private and representatives of the press who inquired
were informed that no reporting was to be permitted. The appearance in
newspapers of garbled reports has made it desirable that the lecture
should appear in full.'

The Times printed a report of it the following day; the *Observer* (4
March) had their correspondent reporting from Cambridge under the
caption 'Why Dr. Leavis Attacked Snow's "Two Cultures?" ' as well as
David Piper writing in the magazine section under 'Leavis versus Snow –
Round One: Demolition at Downing'; Peter Simple, in the *Daily Telegraph*
(12 March), commented on Leavis' lecture under the heading 'Well Said';
the *Guardian* (20 March) published an article by John Madox on 'The
Significance of C.P. Snow', whereas *Encounter* had a piece by George
Steiner on Leavis (May 1962).

There was, besides, in the correspondence column of the *Spectator*, the
'debate' on Snow, Leavis and the 'two cultures' which continued till 6 April,
1962, and in which various better or less well known people took part:
William Gerhardi, Edith Sitwell, Lord Boothby, G.S. Fraser, Peter Jay,
J.D. Bernal, Ian Parsons, Remington Rose, G.S.A. Guinness, Robert Conquest, J.H. Plumb, Robert Harvey, Charles E. Raven, Robert Kabak and
Neville Denny.

When Chatto published the lecture in book form in 1962, Leavis added a Prefatory Note in which he referred to the mass of correspondence – 'the angry, abusive and strikingly confident utterances of Snow's supporters' – as being hardly worth the name of a 'debate'. 'The abundant adverse comment', he went on,

> directed against my lecture hasn't advanced the argument by leaving me something to answer. *The Spectator* was indulgent when it called the mass of correspondence it printed a 'debate'. I say 'adverse comment' because to say 'criticism' would be inappropriate: the case I presented wasn't dealt with – there was no attempt to deal with it. The angry, abusive and strikingly confident utterances of Snow's supporters merely illustrated the nature of the world or 'culture' that had made Snow a mind, a sage, and a major novelist. 'Without thinking they respond alike'. The confidence is remarkable and significant because the demonstrators see themselves, unmistakably, as an intellectual *élite* and pre-eminently capable of grounded conviction, and yet, when they sense criticism by which their distinction and standing are implicitly denied, can only, with the flank-rubber's response, enact an involuntary corroboration of the criticism.

Some of the letters published in the correspondence column of the *Spectator* (16 March – 6 April 1962) would hardly qualify as 'adverse comment', much less as contributions to a debate. They were simply malicious abuse. Take, for instance, William Gerhardi's two-and-a-half page comment in which he attacked Leavis on three counts: insincerity; incapacity; and envy. He attributed to Leavis 'a mania of persecution', referred to his 'defunct *foolishest* (as Carlyle would say) *Scrutiny* and what it "stood – *and stands* – for" ', rebaptised *Scrutiny* as the *Literary Police Gazette*, and described Leavis as 'the Himmler of literature', 'our closely scrutinising Himmler'. For Gerhardi it was not simply Leavis' lecture on the two cultures but his whole work as a critic that was suspect. For instance, he found Leavis' book on Lawrence

> such an abomination of style (and he argues against Snow that style reveals the man) and that the fact that Leavis could have stomached the swill himself, and even passed it for print, argues an absence of sensibility and taste with which to measure up the shortcomings of others.

For Gerhardi even Leavis' impact as a teacher was bogus and pernicious, in that he was 'a teacher of a band of analphabetics who, young and foolish, applaud his cold contempt for writers he does not understand'. And he concluded by noting that 'in setting out to assassinate another writer's reputation' Leavis had assassinated his own.

Dame Edith Sitwell, for her part, found nothing more illuminating to say than that Leavis only attacked Charles because 'he is famous and writes good English'. A Mr. Stephen Toulmin, a Cambridge man, as he let it be known, found in Leavis' lecture nothing more than 'The spectacle of the sage of Downing pelting C.P. Snow with coke', 'a quite extreme member of the "literary" *Kulturkreis*', and reassured himself and his readers that

> Cambridge is and will remain, not the university of Leavis and Snow, but the university of Isaac Newton and Charles Darwin, of James Clerk Maxwell and Charles Sherrington. And one must at any rate say *this* much for Snow: he recognises that fact, and does not resent it.

For Ronald Millar, too, Leavis' lecture was 'the boomerang of the year'. However, G.S. Fraser found in it 'one of the greatest rhetorical performances I have ever read', and while he considered Sir Charles to be a 'good man' in the sense that Sir Walter Scott was, Leavis struck him as a man of integrity whose 'critical regime could perhaps be called a Robespierrian one, of Virtue and Terror'. Sir Oliver Scott, on the other hand, ridiculed Leavis' prose style by quoting a long sentence from the lecture – the length of which is both sustained and justified by the closely packed thought content and logical rigour – and asked

> if any really cultured gentleman (from Cambridge, preferably) could tell me

> (a) what the quotation from Leavis means?
> (b) if this is an example of good English?

Many correspondents took Leavis' demolition of Snow's thesis for cruelty and attacked Leavis in order to defend Snow, while completely ignoring the merits of Leavis' case, or, for that matter, of Snow's. Detraction by wilful misrepresentation was the common tactic, of which Professor J.D. Bernal's comment is a classical example. 'In my early days at Cambridge', he wrote, ' I.A. Richards upset the English School there by inducing students to read and to understand the texts on which they were supposed to pass judgement. His pupil, Dr. Leavis, found that a better and a far easier way was to pass judgement first.'

Professor (now Sir) J.H. Plumb, too, could find no better way of defending Snow than by charging Leavis of an ignorance of history which he found 'so abysmal that it would require a new *Dunciad* to do justice either to his folly or to his arrogance'. Lovat Dickson, a director of Macmillan – Snow's publishers – also defended Snow against Leavis' 'intemperate outburst' by asserting that not only is Leavis not a novelist, but that his 'strong personal predilections prevent him from being taken seriously as a critic', and that he is 'just about as angry with the public for liking them [Snow's novels] as he is with Snow for writing them'.

There were, of course, some pro-Leavis letters as well – letters protesting against what Ian Parsons, Director of Chatto & Windus, called apropos of the *Spectator* correspondence, emptying 'the rubbish basket ... over Dr. Leavis' head'. Commenting on Gerhardi's description of *Scrutiny* as 'defunct foolishest *Scrutiny*' Parsons pointed out that the Cambridge University Press were 'currently engaged in reprinting *Scrutiny*, in toto'. Similarly, rebutting the claim by Mr. M.S. Deol (whose letter was published in the *Spectator* of the previous week) that Leavis' reputation as a critic was 'a myth created by undergraduates', Mr. Parsons observed:

> If so, there must be an unbelievable consistency in undergraduate opinion, for ... Dr. Leavis' lectures were drawing full houses in the middle Twenties. In point of fact, Dr. Leavis' reputation as a critic was firmly established with the publication of *New Bearings in English Poetry* in 1932, which can hardly be described as 'of late'.

Another correspondent – T.T. Roe – considered attacks on Leavis in the 16 March issue of the *Spectator* as constituting 'a first-rate social document for the condition of our time', a condition described by Ortega Y Gasset, whom Roe quoted as follows:

> in the intellectual life, which of its essence requires and presupposes qualification, one can note the progressive triumph of the pseudo-intellectual, unqualified, unqualifiable and, by their very mental texture, disqualified.

And Mr Roe concluded by suggesting that it was Dr. Leavis who was the truly qualified man.

Another correspondent – J.F.I. Long – admitted 'the basic truth of Leavis' criticism of Snow's work as a novelist and populariser of ideas'. He took 'the cries of indignation' in the letters column of the *Spectator* as an indication that Leavis had 'hit his target'. He wondered why the attack had been so long delayed. And for those who found the attack on Snow cruel – in Plumb's words a 'senseless diatribe' – there was a letter from an undergraduate – Robert Harvey – justifying the attack. It arose, he says, because

> Snow, as representative of a force that commands attention and invites suspicion, has been measured against a positive ideal. It is not an ideal that has been vaguely apprehended and exists only in phantom insubstantiality, but an ideal clearly conceived, which Dr.

Leavis defines concretely in the climax of his lecture, and which he has himself realized. What can one do with critics who arrogantly confess their incomprehension and who wilfully persist in condemning the lecture as obscure and sterile, but wave the lecture in their faces till they read it?

Remington Rose, an American engaged in research at Cambridge, challenged the notion that 'the myth of Leavis, the great critic ... is the creation of undergraduates', and observed:

> The documents are these: *New Bearings, Revaluation, The Common Pursuit, The Great Tradition, D.H. Lawrence* and thirty [sic] years of *Scrutiny*. Having read them, perhaps someone will attempt a clear, rational, and consistently relevant critique of the thought and sensibility which style and judgements illustrate. To date the only intelligent and responsible criticism of which I am aware has come from members of 'the Leavis tribe of logical positivists', those 'analphabetics' who lack Mr Gerhardi's 'unbribable integrity', 'humorous compassion' and particularly his superb, ironical 'detachment'. And no one has yet offered any with regard to the Richmond Lecture.

Another American – Geoffrey Wagner – writing from New York, mentioned Snow's popularity in the United States (which, he says, 'craves a literature of assent') and found Leavis' 'characteristically independent comments ... most timely'. In the face of 'the hosannas obediently continued on this side of the Atlantic', Wagner added, 'both from the Barzun-Trilling syndrome and the Book-of-the-Month Club, the worst of both worlds, as it were, Dr. Leavis' lecture was needed, indeed'.

The most telling comment, justifying Leavis' strictures on Snow's conception of 'the two cultures' and his criticism of his novels came from Charles E. Raven of Christ's College, Cambridge, who wrote:

> the objection which many of us felt to Sir Charles's lecture was ... that the lecture shows no appreciation of the true nature of its subject. Dr. Leavis broadened the issue by demonstrating that the same defect characterized his novels. Anyone who knows Cambridge and the College which is the admitted scene of his principal books will know that instead of encouraging culture these books have debased it.
>
> ... Having participated in three colleges at five magisterial elections I can testify that the canvassing and caballing are grotesquely overdrawn; that no candidate would behave like Mr. Jago (in *The Masters*); and that Sir Charles Snow's one effort at wire-pulling immediately resulted in the crushing defeat of his proposal.

Fellows of Colleges are indeed pledged to education, religion, learning and research. Most of them are loyal to their obligation. Without some such obligation there can be no true culture: Sir Charles offers us only careerism. That is the case against him.

Leavis also received many private letters from people on both sides of the Atlantic, vindicating his thesis (viz. that there *is* only one culture) and praising his courage for having said so. Some came from people he had taught twenty or thirty years before, but mostly from people he didn't know. Here is a sample of their comments:

Thank you for a stimulating and devastating exposé of Snow's pretentions. With the truth of it I am deeply in accord.

How delighted I was to read in today's *Spectator* your wonderful lecture on Snow. Nothing has delighted me so much for a long time. It was splendidly done and so overwhelmingly necessary.

Magnificent! I've just read your Snow lecture in *The Spectator*. It fills me with new life. A really concentrated and vividly illuminating criticism of our whole civilization.

I write to thank you, not just for the Richmond Lecture, or for any piece of work in particular; but for the assurance one is permitted in reading your work (I have only had the opportunity of attending one of your lectures) of deep moral responsibility ... There must be many people like myself, whom you cannot know, and of whom you may only guess, people who do not style themselves your 'disciples', but for whom your critical integrity is a constant inspiration and a positive help, not to say comfort.

There was also a letter from a Professor of Mechanical Engineering and Physics at Princeton University:

It was indeed good news to read your opinions about C.P. Snow. You have a sympathetic audience among many scientists on this side of the Atlantic.

The 30 March issue of the *Spectator* summed up, in its editorial entitled 'The Two Cultures', the pros and cons, merits and flaws of Snow's thesis and Leavis' antithesis, and came out in favour of the more complex and more humane view of culture as advocated by Leavis rather than the one advocated by Snow. It is difficult to quarrel with Snow's thesis, the editorial said, 'inasmuch as it is simply a demand for more scientific education and a rather more general curriculum in the schools; nor did Dr.

Leavis do so'; but what is controversial about the Rede Lecture is Snow's view of the nature of culture. 'Without thinking about it, they respond alike', says Snow of scientists, 'That is what culture means'. 'But is this so?' the editorial asks, and it goes on:

> The history of civilization is surely one of increasing consciousness and increasing variety of cultural reaction. Certain values can be held in common, but within these there is an almost infinite range of response. It is hard not to agree with Dr Leavis when he criticises Sir Charles's view of culture. Such an instinctive unity might possibly be called 'a culture' if it occurred in a primitive tribe (and even a primitive culture is done an injustice by this description), but among more civilized peoples it is crippling – and potentially tyrannical.

As to Snow's affirmation that the scientists have 'the future in their bones', that literary intellectuals are 'natural Luddites', that some of them hold contemptible social attitudes and that they are all smothered in 'the traditional culture', the editorial replied by paraphrasing Leavis. A Dickens, a Ruskin or a Lawrence, it says,

> has been in fact responsible for some of the profoundest utterances on the transformation of the modern world and its social consequences. But for Ruskin 'well-being' or 'welfare' could not conceivably be matters of merely 'standard of living', with the advantages of technology and scientific hygiene.

For the writer of the editorial, if there is one word lacking in the Rede Lecture – a word that alone can give significance to any attempt to bring science and literature together – it is 'philosophy'. 'In its secular significance', we are told, 'this word takes the form of that effort to impart moral direction, which is to be found in the best nineteenth-century English writers' – writers whose appreciation of the human condition and of the human problem has been, in Leavis' words, 'incomparably and poignantly more complex' than that entailed by Snow's conception of history.

Hence, it is the Richmond Lecture, rather than the Rede Lecture, for all its good intentions, that, to quote Peter Simple of the *Daily Telegraph*, 'raised a loud cry on behalf of humanity and civilization against the blind worship of technology. It should be reprinted in leaflet form, translated in every known language, and dropped in millions on every university in the world ... There cannot be much doubt that for the moment at least the world is going the way he [Snow] wants rather than the way Leavis wants. I would rather lose with Leavis than win with Snow.'

Leavis himself was quite sure of the value of his lecture which he considered to be 'a certain classic'. The letters in the correspondence column of the *Spectator* made him and his publisher all the more eager to bring it out as a pamphlet or a small book. But there was the possible risk of Snow taking legal action against such a publication, even though he had allowed the *Spectator* to publish Leavis' Richmond Lecture. Whatever the legal position, Leavis told Parsons (4 July 1962), an action would be disastrous for Snow, even if he won. 'Snow should certainly be told there will be American publication. He can see how discreditable *that* (publication here banned) would be to him.' Eventually, Parsons obtained Snow's assurance that, even if he did not approve of it, he would not take legal action if Parsons republished Leavis' lecture exactly as it was printed in the *Spectator* without Leavis or anybody else altering the text or adding any additional material to it. Chatto brought out the lecture in 1962, printing along with it another essay on Snow's Rede Lecture by Michael Yudkin.

A year later Leavis returned to the subject in his Prefatory Note for the American edition of *Two Cultures?* (Pantheon Books, New York) in which he answered some of his American critics – especially Lionel Trilling and Richard Wollheim. In the *New York Review* commentary (June 1962), Trilling had criticised Leavis' lecture, accusing him of gratuitous cruelty to Snow, without making any attempts, as Leavis put it, 'to deal as a disinterested critic with what I had actually said. That is, no rejoinder was called for; he had my answer there already before him in my lecture.' As to the charge that he 'attacked' Snow – 'attack', says Leavis, 'goes with the suggestion that I have indulged in an unpleasant display of personal animus' – he pointed out that 'the unanswerableness is the "cruelty" and is what has "wounded" Snow. It would have been less "cruel" if it had been accompanied, as it was not, by the animus that impels the intention to hurt.'

Wollheim, on the other hand, accused Leavis of being guilty of insidious and significant evasion in not saying clearly whether he was for a material standard of living or against it. For Leavis the problem could not be reduced to those terms, and for Wollheim to insist that it could, meant that he ignored 'the whole theme, argument and substance of my lecture'.

Given that such misconception of the aims and intentions of the Richmond Lecture was current in the United States, it was no wonder that when, in 1966, the Leavises were invited to lecture at Cornell and Harvard, one of the three lectures F.R. Leavis chose to give was on 'Luddites? or There is Only One Culture'. He started this lecture by observing: 'I am used to being misrepresented, but not resigned to it' – the 'gross and inconsequent' misrepresentation resulting, he pointed out, from 'a large element of willed refusal to see and understand' on the part of 'the publicity-practitioners, the formers of public opinion'.

For Leavis, Lord Snow – or for that matter Lord Robbins – takes a simple view of the development and human significance of industrialisation, whereas whoever, like Leavis himself, takes a more complex view is dubbed 'Luddite'; more or less in the same way as a *Sunday Times* reviewer, while discussing a work on Victorian cities 'not long ago ... reeled off a list of names of distinguished writers as those of notorious Luddites in their attitude towards the new kind of urban development'. Though no useful purpose is served by dubbing Carlyle and Ruskin 'Luddites', he could, says Leavis, 'pass that with a shrug. And if Morris is dubbed "Luddite", it doesn't move me to fierce indignation. But Arnold and Dickens!' – Dickens the 'incomparable social historian'. For it is the great novelists above all who give us our social history; 'compared with what is done in *their* work – the creative work – the histories of the professional social historian seem empty and unenlightening.' It is in characterising Dickens as a social historian that Leavis makes some pregnant comments not only as a literary critic but also as an historian:

> He [Dickens] saw how the diverse interplaying currents of life flowed strongly and gathered force here, dwindled there from importance to relative unimportance, settled there into something oppressively stagnant, reasserted themselves elsewhere as strong new promise. The forty years of his writing life were years of portentous change, and, in the way only a great creative writer, sensitive to the full actuality of contemporary life, could, he registers changing England in the succession of his books with wonderful vividness.

Hence what Dickens' work, or that of any great creative writer, embodies, is an important and indispensable part of the 'cultural tradition', as distinguished from Snow's 'traditional culture' which suggests 'something belonging to the past, a reservoir of alleged wisdom, an established habit, an unadventurousness in the face of life and change'. For Leavis, culture meant something that lives 'in the living creative response to change in the present', which, however, does not mean that one should be blind to the insights embodied by cultural tradition. He quoted from a *Guardian* leader to the effect that 'science is a means to an end', and added sardonically: 'yes – a rising standard of living.' If culture meant something radically different to him from what it meant to Snow, it was because his view of human nature and human need was much more complex than Snow's. Mankind, he said, 'has a need to feel life significant' – which is a consideration of an altogether different order from the notion of a high standard of living, 'a dangerously inadequate notion or criterion of human prosperity'. A hunger for significance, Leavis observes,

> isn't altogether satisfied by devotion to Tottenham Hotspur or by hopes of the World Cup for a team called England or Uruguay, or by space travel (mediated by professional publicists), or by patriotic ardour nourished on international athletics, or by the thrill of broken records – even though records, by dint of scientific training, go on

being broken and the measurement of times becomes progressively finer.

Having such criteria in mind for measuring human significance, human needs and human aspirations in an age of revolutionary and constantly advancing technology, Leavis could not but reject the 'simplifying and reductive criteria of human need and human good' – criteria which 'generate ... disastrously false and inadequate conceptions of the *ends* to which science should be a means'. Nor could he refrain from exposing – in the Richmond Lecture and in his later writings – the cultural effects of mass production and the levelling down and standardisation it entailed:

> Ponder, I find myself saying in England, to academic audiences, the 'magazine sections' of the Sunday Papers (they know which two I mean), and tell yourselves that this, for many dons – and I am thinking of the non-scientists, the custodians of culture – represents the top level: what Arnold meant by 'the best that is thought and known in our time'. It will almost certainly represent the top level for those who, at this time of rapid and confident and large scale reforms, make authoritative and decisive recommendations in the field of higher education. To point out these things is not to be a Luddite.

The repercussions of 'the two cultures' controversy continued to be registered in Leavis' later writings. The public lecture on ' "Literarism" versus "Scientism": the Misconception and the Menace', that he gave at Bristol University in 1970 as the Churchill Visiting Professor, was another attempt to formulate, albeit in a different context and in the face of different challenges, what his own notion of culture was. A challenge was made by Aldous Huxley who had come out with the formula 'Literarism *versus* Scientism' in order to balance Snow's 'scientism' against a 'literarism' attributed to Leavis – both being, as Leavis ironically put it, 'deviations from the centre of truth. What, positively, *was* at the centre of truth Huxley didn't, I thought, make at all plain, except that *he* was there.' It was easier for him – 'cultivated, widely read and voraciously inquiring' as he was – to define and explain the meaning of 'scientism'; but not so with what he meant by Leavis' 'literarism'. 'I neither believe', said Leavis,

> in any special 'literary' values nor am hostile to science ... I don't by the 'one culture' mean what 'literary culture' in either Snow's or Huxley's intention implies .... What I pointed out was that there's only one culture and that Snow merely – and symptomatically – abuses the word (a very important one) when he talks about a scientific culture, generated out of the technical knowledge and the specialized intellectual habits that scientists have.

F.R. Leavis as a young man.
Photograph reproduced by courtesy of Mrs Mary Pitter.

Left to right: F.R. Leavis, Ruth Leavis and Ralph Leavis.
Photograph reproduced by courtesy of Mrs Mary Pitter.

The Vice Chancellor of York University, Lord James *(left)* presents Leavis with his honorary degree.
Photograph reproduced by courtesy of the Yorkshire Post.

Leavis in the grounds of Downing College, Cambridge, in 1948.

Leavis giving a public lecture at Nijmegen University, Holland, in the 1960s.

Leavis in the late 1940s.

The Leavises' house in Bulstrode Gardens, Cambridge.

F.R. and Q.D. Leavis at
home, June 1975.
Photographs © Times
Newspapers Ltd

Leavis in the garden of his home in Cambridge.
Above: Photograph © Times Newspapers Ltd

Leavis in the Botanic Gardens, Belfast, at the time he was awarded an honorary degree by Queen's University.

One of the menaces of 'scientism', as Leavis saw it, was what he called 'the computerologist's prescription – our ruling team's official prescription – for ensuring our survival as a nation'. For Leavis, it amounted to

> saving by cheerfully destroying all that makes survival worth fighting for. It means expediting the process by which the country, not only of Shakespeare, Dickens, Lawrence and Blake, but also of Blake's *bêtes noires*, Newton, Locke and Johnson (I think of all these when I speak of the 'one culture'), becomes just a province of an American world. My saying this is hostility, not to Americans, but to essential Americanization – under which they themselves wilt.

How prophetic these words would turn out to be in the subsequent history of England – *his* England – and of Europe, Leavis was not to know, although with his Blakean vision and intuition, he might well have surmised.

The *Scrutiny* reprint

Another event that marked Leavis' retirement was the publication of the reprints of the twenty volumes of *Scrutiny* by Cambridge University Press. It was a historic event. The Preface Leavis wrote to it, entitled '*Scrutiny*: A Retrospect', describes in close analytical and specific detail, the nature and circumstances of the origin, the significance and the influence of the most important twentieth-century critical periodical in English. The main editorial protagonist, he expatiates on how *Scrutiny* triumphantly vindicated the function of literary criticism, as he and his collaborators had conceived it. Hence the Preface may be regarded as an incomparably valuable piece of critical autobiography, incorporating a vivid and moving account of what Leavis and his wife stood for and what they had given so much of their time and energy to. His life-long concern for maintaining the standards of literary criticism, for upholding the concept of an educated public, for the importance of university education, and especially for the central place of the 'English' school in the university form the backbone of this Preface as of Leavis' life itself.

At the outset of the Preface, Leavis points out that although essentially a Cambridge achievement, *Scrutiny* 'started, established itself and survived in spite of Cambridge', thereby exemplifying the idea of criticism as well as the idea of a university. The kind of opposition that *Scrutiny* had to contend with was represented by what Leavis calls 'academic' in the pejorative sense of the term. *Scrutiny* was, therefore, treated both by the academic and the literary Establishment as 'an outlaw's enterprise', even though a great many of the more important contributors had taken English Tripos – a typically Cambridge phenomenon.

For Leavis was convinced that only at Cambridge could *Scrutiny* have 'maintained the continuous force that made it hated and effective'; only at Cambridge could it have 'survived in spite of Cambridge' and developed the idea of practical criticism as something more than 'just a matter of analytic technique and brilliant exercises'. Taking note of certain precedents and influences – for example, Q.D. Leavis' *Fiction and the Reading Public*, the *Calendar of Modern Letters* (1925-7) and his own *Mass Civilization and Minority Culture* – Leavis outlines the spirit of *Scrutiny* which was to inspire and to be exemplified in the work of the *Scrutiny* collaborators. One of Leavis' own early contributions to *Scrutiny* was an article entitled 'What's Wrong with Criticism?', which he had been commissioned to write by Eliot for the 'Criterion Miscellany'. When Eliot decided not to publish it because 'he knew that such a pamphlet would arouse unforgiving hostility in the dominant literary world, and knew too that it was not at all his vocation to incur such hostility for himself', Leavis' eye, as he puts it, 'lost its respectful innocence' so far as Eliot was concerned. But Eliot was not alone in adopting such a diplomatic position. An advanced Cambridge intellectual – Leavis gave me to understand that it was I.A. Richards – also told him: 'I am not a moral hero.'

More congenial and charged with a greater degree of critical integrity than Eliot's *Criterion*, was the *Calendar of Modern Letters* which, in its brief life of two and a half years, succeeded in establishing 'a strong and lively contemporary criticism', while embodying what were for Leavis some of the fundamental desiderata of a critical periodical as well as of critical reviewing: 'the weight, responsibility and edge given by disinterested intelligence that perceives and judges out of a background of wide cultivation and of acquaintance with relevant disciplines', coupled with 'a quick perceptive responsiveness to the new creative life of the time'. *Scrutiny* owed not only its title, but also part of its ethos and policy to the *Calendar's* 'Scrutinies' (critiques of the modern 'classics' such as J.M. Barrie, Arnold Bennett, G.K. Chesterton, Walter de la Mare, Rudyard Kipling, John Masefield, George Moore, Bernard Shaw, H.G. Wells, John Galsworthy and D.H. Lawrence). There was, however, no question of imitation. The founding editors and collaborators of *Scrutiny* were 'empirical and opportunist in spirit' as well as quite independent and 'conscious of being in a particular place at a particular time'. They were also anti-Marxist because they believed that 'an intelligent, that is, a real interest in literature implied a conception of it very different from any that a Marxist could expound and explain' – a conception which upholds 'a human reality, an autonomy of the human spirit, for which economic determinism and reductive interpretation in terms of the Class War left no room'.

With such a concept of literature in mind, for Leavis and his collaborators, Cambridge had to be the place for such a critical venture as *Scrutiny* set out to be. And when Leavis talks of the periodical's surviving the hostility of the institutional academic powers, he pointedly means the

academic powers at Cambridge, and so the achievement of what he calls
'our quixotic anti-academic design' has a direct bearing on Cambridge.
That is why Leavis could well assert that those who founded *Scrutiny* and
wrote in it represented the 'essential' Cambridge in spite of Cambridge. In
appraising the achievement of *Scrutiny*, he emphasises its anti-academic
nature which enabled it to challenge, on strictly critical grounds and in a
'new critical idiom', a number of conventional judgements and academic
positions, thereby effecting virtually a radical revaluation of English
literature from Chaucer to Eliot. The *Scrutiny* revaluations, in fact,
though 'derided and resented at first', became 'accepted currency' and
gradually came to be seen as 'authoritative'. Those who wrote for *Scrutiny*
were concerned about 'conservation and continuity', as well as concerned
to promote 'that which the academic mind, in the "humanities" hates: the
creative interplay of real judgements – genuine personal judgements, that
is of engaged minds fully alive in the present'. This enabled *Scrutiny* to
make its own reputation and make it 'very rapidly'. The contributors were
not paid, but wrote for honour. For 'there was advantage as well as
satisfaction in being printed in a place that conferred distinction'. There
were well over a hundred and fifty contributors of 'diverse creeds and
outlooks', some of whom (W.D. Harding, L.C. Knights, James Smith, Boris
Ford, Wilfred Mellers, Bruce Pattison, D.J. Enright) later became profes-
sors in different disciplines. *Scrutiny* did not confine itself to English
literature. It examined works and authors from foreign literatures as well
– French above all, but also German and Italian. Leavis refers to *Scrutiny's* work on the Grand Siècle, its reappraisals of Corneille and Racine,
its reports on Sartre and Camus, and singles out such distinguished
contributions as James Smith's essay on Mallarmé, D.A. Traversi's essay
on *I promessi sposi* and D.J. Enright's 'sustained' examination of Goethe.
There were also contributors from other fields. For instance, J.L. Russell
(author of the essay 'The Scientific Best Seller') who dealt with Jeans and
Eddington, and Wilfred Mellers and Bruce Pattison who wrote on music.

However, *Scrutiny's* 'basic' achievement was in literary criticism.
Leavis enumerates some particularly distinguished and influential contributions. John Speirs' work on Chaucer, his essay on 'Sir Gawayne and the
Grene Knight', and his work on 'The Scots Literary Tradition'; L.C.
Knights' and D.A. Traversi's Shakespeare Criticism; Q.D. Leavis' criticism
of Jane Austen; and R.C. Churchill's essays on 'Dickens, Drama and
Tradition' and 'The Great Reviews'. *Scrutiny* also printed an 'immense'
body of 'pioneering' criticism of the novel, 'restored' George Eliot to her
position among the great novelists, classified Conrad as a great novelist
and *Nostromo* as his greatest novel, started the Henry James cult and
published some of the most 'poignant' criticism on him, besides establishing D.H. Lawrence as a great novelist and critic.

Positive revaluations in the case of such writers entailed, by implication, negative valuations in the case of others. For, as Leavis points out,

'there can be no real – no truly creative – performance' that does not entail
much offending 'negative' criticism. Thus, for instance, *Scrutiny* challenged the reputation of Auden, Spender and C. Day Lewis, as the
contemporary 'Glories' of English poetry, pointing out that 'talent and
promise might plausibly be found in only one of the famed cluster –
Auden', even though Auden 'did not develop' – or what development he
showed was not into 'maturity'. As to *Scrutiny's* influence, Leavis
quotes as evidence 'the immense book-making indebtedness to it' – an
indebtedness that was never acknowledged – and the fact that *Scrutiny*
generated the spirit of 'a consistent and undeniable *parti pris*' against
it on the part of such reputable organs of the literary establishment as
the *Times Literary Supplement*, with its air of 'institutional disinterestedness'.

While recalling the circumstances in which *Scrutiny* had to cease
publication – paper restriction which outlasted the war, the impossibility of mustering a sufficient team of qualified contributors, and the fact
that the war had made enlisting and training of recruits impossible and
that when the war ended 'men came back very conscious of the lost
years' and had little or no time for 'gratuitous' concentration on work
for *Scrutiny* – Leavis tells us how 'the struggle to keep going was
desperate' and how such a struggle bore more heavily than before on
him.

As to the possibility of such an enterprise as *Scrutiny* repeating itself,
Leavis considered the task to be practically impossible, and he explains
why: 'The reviewing, in fact (and the system controlling it is much
strengthened by command of the air and the television screen), is more
clique- and mode- and time-serving than ever, and less inhibited, in its
pursuit of its non-critical ends, by knowledge and education, or any sense
of a critical public that might listen or read'. Another problem is the widely
accepted culture of the 'agreeably distracting and time-passing' Sunday
papers which tends to prevail more and more even at the senior levels in
universities. No wonder, well-known dons 'thought of widely as distinguished intellectuals, are assiduous journalists, establish themselves as
names and authorities by frequent performance on radio and television,
and form what Sir Charles Snow calls a "culture" with the other practitioners of their kind, whether or not these claim academic standing. The
standards they favour will naturally be those by which they feel themselves safe as distinguished intellectuals'. Terms such as 'journalists',
'critics', 'dons', 'intellectuals', are used by Leavis with a sense of his own
proven authority both as a critic and as an intellectual who is aware of the
difference between literary criticism as such, and journalism. In defining
the concept and function of literary criticism as exemplified by *Scrutiny*,
Leavis could not but question the standards of the weeklies and the
culture of the Sunday papers as well as 'the value sense and the critical
assumptions of the greater number of dons'. But it needed an 'educated' –

that is, a critically alert and mature – public to be able to perceive the difference between the real culture which forms and embodies 'a community of consciousness and responsibility', and the popular, journalistic, mass-media culture. Such a public may be small but, for Leavis, 'even a very small public may ... be disproportionately influential: *Scrutiny* proved that'.

Editorial protagonist turned chronicler, Leavis, in '*Scrutiny*: a Retrospect', offers a unique piece of cultural and literary autobiography which is, at the same time, also the portrait of an epoch as well as the summing up of an ethos. One might, in a certain sense, say that there is hardly any essay, article or chapter of a book in the writing of which Leavis felt so justifiably proud of his own achievement as in writing this Preface.

His retirement from Cambridge was marked by another momentous event in his life. He was invited as Visiting Professor of English at the new University of York by the late Professor Philip Brockbank, then Professor and Head of its English Department, who had been a student of Leavis' and by Lord James, the Vice-Chancellor of York University and himself an educationalist and admirer of Leavis and his work. While it was a prestigious acquisition for York University to have Leavis lecturing there and many students flocked to read English at York because of it, it was equally important and stimulating for Leavis to continue to be involved in university teaching which gave him a valuable impetus for his own critical activity. After his first year as Visiting Professor, he continued practically throughout the remainder of his life to visit York to teach, to hold postgraduate seminars, and to give occasional public lectures. Some of his lectures went into his book *Nor Shall My Sword* which he dedicated to the students of his new University, who had given him 'a new Blake with clean margins to write in'. The York visits – together with lecturing assignments at other universities – kept Leavis physically as well as intellectually busy and active. For all his frequently reiterated complaints about relentless pressures and an unending drain on his energy, he actually seemed to enjoy these commitments which kept him even busier than he was before he retired.

In fact, after his retirement, Leavis brought out almost as many books as before his retirement: '*Anna Karenina*' and Other Essays (1967); *English Literature in Our Time and the University* (1969); *Lectures in America* (1969) and *Dickens the Novelist* (1970) – the last two in collaboration with Q.D. Leavis – *Nor Shall My Sword* (1972); *Letters in Criticism*, edited by John Tasker (1974); *The Living Principle: 'English' as a Discipline of Thought* (1975) and *Thought, Words and Creativity: Art and Thought in Lawrence* (1976). He also left a fair amount of unpublished material which he was working on in his last two years, most of which was to appear in the two posthumously published collections of his writings – *The Critic as Anti-Philosopher* (1981) and *Valuation in Criticism and Other Essays* (1986). His last writings attest to his undiminished powers as a critic, a thinker and a writer. Though in many of them he returns to authors and subjects he had already dealt with – Blake, Wordsworth, Dickens, Hopkins, Yeats, Lawrence and Eliot; the university and the 'two' cultures – he has always something new to say or something to say from a new angle. This is why his way of dealing with these authors is just as fresh and provocative, as subtle and cogent as ever, and his style has that analytical grasp and critical acumen which one associates with his *Scrutiny* days. In his public lectures, too, Leavis used, with considerable effectiveness, the classroom or seminar technique, so that even a public lecture turned out to be something engagingly direct and spontaneous, where the critic and the educationist, the thinker and the polemicist meet.

'Anna Karenina' and Other Essays

'Anna Karenina' and Other Essays, which Leavis dedicated to the University of York, was published by Chatto in England and by Random House in America. With a shrewd analytical insight into the working of his own mind and into the ethos the book embodied, Leavis had this to say concerning the book:

> I don't think ill of the book. In fact, it impresses me very favourably indeed. It is not, for the temporal range, any the less a book. It's unmistakably mine, yet offers fresh diversity – all tending to concentration and development in definition of my 'stance'. For there is (and in my *oeuvre* as a whole) a decidedly positive 'stance' of a kind that challenges the Moral Sciencers. Not that 'stance' is to imply fixedness; but consistency along with endlessly supple resourcefulness in the concern for precision is in my positive refusal (which is a philosophy) to be a *philosopher*.

However, he predicted, with good reason, that the book would get 'no orchestrated acclamation from the literary boys'. One of the more hostile reviews was by Donald Davie – it was, Leavis said, 'calculated to clinch the general supposition that once a force, and so to be "honoured", I'm now on the shelf among the "authors" relegated; superseded as *Scrutiny* has been superseded by the *Cambridge Quarterly*'.

'Anna Karenina' and Other Essays consists of sixteen essays, reviews, or lectures that had already appeared in various periodicals, both English and American, dealing with such themes as *Anna Karenina*, *The Pilgrim's Progress*, *What Maisie Knew*, *The Shadow-Line*, 'The Americanness of American Literature', 'T.S. Eliot as Critic', 'Johnson as Critic' and 'Pound in His Letters'.

In different contexts, and prompted by situations calling for different degrees of emphasis, Leavis' sense of the importance of literature and its relation to life is what constitutes the implicit unity underlying the various essays in this volume. Thus, while evaluating *Anna Karenina* –

and through it Tolstoy's genius – Leavis argues how it exemplifies the
relations between art and life – the prime requisite of the highest kind of
creativity. But whether he is analysing *Anna Karenina* in terms of art, or
in terms of the didactic impulses behind it – even though the essential
spirit of Tolstoy's art is such that the didactic impulses never get out of
hand – Leavis is invariably concerned with presenting the findings of his
critical analysis in terms of a significance which transcends the distinction
between art and didacticism. And the same applies to his exploration of
what he considers to be the moral sense and significance of the novel,
which he analyses in terms of the individual's moral responsibility and his
social context. Hence both the ethos and the *leitmotif* of the novel acquire
a dual significance – modern and historical – as a result of which
Anna Karenina is seen to be a great novel of modern times and Tolstoy's
essential problems, moral and spiritual, are seen to be ours.

Another important essay in the book is the one on *The Pilgrim's
Progress* which starts with the affirmation: 'It is possible to read *The
Pilgrim's Progress* without any thought of its theological intention' – an
affirmation that neatly separates the literary and artistic merit of the
work from its theological content. Not that Leavis is not profoundly
conscious of its religious import; but his way of being conscious is at once
morally as well as critically more subtle and more complex than that of the
theologically orientated exegetes of *The Pilgrim's Progress*.

In the other works examined – *Adam Bede*, *What Maisie Knew*,
The Europeans and *The Shadow-Line* – Leavis' approach is dictated by his
belief that criticism of the novel and criticism of life are fundamentally the
same, both revolving round the question 'What do men live for?' It is, for
example, the positing of and answering this question that, more than
anything else, makes *The Shadow-Line* the important novel it is, being
central to Conrad's genius as well as being, as Leavis puts it, 'Conrad's
Silas Marner'.

Lectures in America

In 1966 the Leavises went to America on a lecture tour. They were invited
by Cornell and Harvard Universities. Leavis gave three lectures ('Luddites? or There is Only One Culture', 'Eliot's Classical Standing' and
'Yeats: The Problem and The Challenge'), and Mrs. Leavis one ('A Fresh
Approach to *Wuthering Heights*'). Except for the Yeats lecture, all lectures
were delivered for the first time in America. Both Cornell and Harvard
University Presses wanted to publish these lectures, but Leavis wanted
them to appear in England with Chatto as, in fact, they did.

Leavis' first lecture is an extended counter-comment on the attacks
made on him after his lecture on C.P Snow. What is offered here is another
brilliant example of his polemical prowess and brilliance. While counter-
ing the arguments of his British and American critics, Leavis achieves a

masterly prose through which he conveys the positive nature of his concerns and preoccupations about contemporary civilisation.

In 'Eliot's Classical Standing', while discussing the grounds for Eliot's standing and why he is more influential than Yeats or Hardy, Leavis points out that although *The Waste Land* was very impressive in the 1920s, one tended to regard it as a higher kind of achievement at that time than it actually is. But even before the publication of this poem, Eliot had done something by way of altering expression, as in the two early poems of his: 'Portrait of a Lady' and 'The Love Song of J. Alfred Prufrock'. Another later poem Leavis singles out for praise – in fact, a favourite poem of his – is 'La figlia che piange', which represents something very important for Eliot, 'some vital node of experience – something felt as perhaps a possibility of transcending disgust, rejection and protest'. In *Ash-Wednesday*, on the other hand, Eliot's quest – his desperate need, as in *The Hollow Men*, to be able to believe in, to be sure of, something real, something that could claim his allegiance and give it meaning – becomes consciously religious, even though Eliot refrains from making religious affirmations. 'Marina', another favourite poem of Leavis', impresses him for 'its unliturgical and un-Dantean human tenderness'. Referring to what he considered to be Eliot's overdependence or 'illegitimate dependence' on Dante, Leavis criticises him for overvaluing what Dante has to offer and suggests that he might have got from Shakespeare 'a great deal more than is represented by that resonance from *Pericles*'. An essential part of Leavis' evaluation of Eliot's religious poetry is the distinction he draws between what is merely theologically interesting in it, and what can be upheld from the creative and the critical point of view. He considers it to be a high tribute to Eliot, to be able to say that it needs a literary critic, not a theologian, to do justice to him and his poetry – especially *Four Quartets*, the final and most impressive vindication of Eliot's genius.

Leavis' lecture on 'Yeats: The Problem and the Challenge' had originally been given at Queen's University, Belfast, to mark the centenary of the poet's birth. Setting out to re-assess Yeats' poetic achievement as a major twentieth century poet since he first wrote on him in *New Bearings in English Poetry* (1932), Leavis starts by asking 'how much of the fully achieved thing *is* there in Yeats' *oeuvre* – what proportion of the wholly created poem that stands there unequivocally in its own right, self-sufficient?' And his answer is that the proportion is not large, and that there are only a few poems – less than a dozen – in which one recognises that the poetic art locally is that of the great poet who 'altered expression'. Such poems include 'Sailing to Byzantium', 'Byzantium', 'The Winding Stair' and 'Among School Children' – the last being Leavis' favourite poem. As to the element of irony in 'Sailing to Byzantium', and especially in the line, 'Of what is past, or passing, or to come', Leavis calls it the irony of 'a tormenting complexity of experience – a complexity that entails an irreducible and tormenting contradiction of impulsions or imperatives or

verdicts'. In this poem Yeats achieves 'a tense and tentative poise', but it
is 'no index of an achieved stability'. Similarly, while analysing the sardonic bitterness of 'Byzantium' (with its 'I hail the superhuman;/I call it
death-in-life and life-in-death') Leavis asks: 'Which is it? There is surely a
difference. To "Hail the superhuman" as "death-in-life" *and* "life-in-death"
with that air of ecstatic assurance is to transcend the balancing of doubt
and belief in irony; to drop thought in an act, the act being an expression
of intense sardonic bitterness.' However, for Leavis, both 'Byzantium' and
'Sailing to Byzantium' are major poetry, even though they stand apart,
inasmuch as the latter does not come out of 'any wholeness of being or
mastery of experience'. What the poem offers in its totality is a 'poetic or
quasi-musical satisfyingness, though it is no proof of the poet's having
achieved a permanent stability in life'. In evaluating the significance of
this particular aspect of Yeats' poetry Leavis links it with the poet's
personality and background – a link that is crucially important in assessing Yeats' poetic career and his status as a major figure in English
literature.

As to the schematisms, diagrammatics and symbolic elaborations, to
which Yeats devoted so much of his energy, Leavis does not consider it
necessary, as so many Yeats specialists do, to study them in order to
appreciate his poetry. In fact, for a critical appreciation of a poem by Yeats,
according to Leavis, no special knowledge or instruction from outside is
required. In any case, what Yeats has to offer is no comprehensive wisdom,
but a sense of complete disinterestedness and complete sincerity. He had,
Leavis tells us, 'a real integrity and a rare sense of responsibility as a focus
of life' and his ability to perceive and understand was 'undeflected by
egotism or by any impulse to project an image of himself'.

English Literature in Our Time and the University

When the Leavises returned from America, there was another prestigious
honour waiting for F.R. Leavis. He was invited to be a Clark lecturer at
Cambridge in the Lent Term. He gave six lectures with Lord Butler, the
then Master of Trinity, in the Chair. They were 'Literature and the
University: The Wrong Question'; 'The Present and the Past: Eliot's
Demonstration'; 'Eliot's "Axe to Grind", and the Nature of Great Criticism';
'Why *Four Quartets* Matters in a Technologico-Benthamite Age'; 'The
Necessary Opposite, Lawrence; Illustration – The Opposed Critics on
Hamlet'; and ' "Monstrous Unrealism" and the Alternative'. When they
appeared with Chatto, under the title *English Literature in Our Time and
the University*, Leavis had added three appendices: 'The Function of the
University'; 'Rilke on Vacuity'; and 'Research in English'. The book, dedicated to 'The Memory of H. Munro Chadwick and Mansfield D. Forbes to
whom the world owes more than it knows', came out in 1969, with an
introductory essay in which Leavis analysed the concepts and criteria

embodied by these lectures. The very choice of the title reflects his sense of the gravity of what is at issue – the gravity being 'the blankness – the inability, or refusal, to perceive – that characterizes our civilization'. Both what he says in the introductory essay and the substance of his lectures link this book with *Education and the University* on the one hand, and with *Nor Shall My Sword* on the other. Directing his thought in all the three books is Leavis' triple interest – university education, creative literature and the civilisation in which we live. His concept of English literature as a living reality, 'a real and potent force in our time', does not entail any attempt to ignore or underrate the sciences, or other disciplines or specialist studies. In fact an 'English school' is all the better for deserving the respect of those who are 'acquainted with intellectual standards in their own fields'.

From considerations of the nature of the 'English School' and the University, Leavis goes on to examine the ethos of present-day enlightenment, 'the deadly enemy', which has imported into British life 'the portentous total mechanism' of American civilisation. If Matthew Arnold dreaded the danger of England becoming a greater Holland, Leavis dreads that of its 'turning with rapid acceleration into a little America'. His roles as a literary critic and as a critic of civilisation merge in this book, so that it is as much about Eliot and Lawrence, or as much about English literature and the University, as about 'the frightening problems' of our civilisation.

The particular themes and concerns outlined in the introductory essay are elaborated in the course of the book where Lawrence and Eliot are singled out as major creative artists, whose work uniquely illustrates for Leavis both the significance of English literature, past and present, and a radical criticism of modern civilisation. Invoking the Arnoldian concern for preserving the continuity of cultural consciousness through 'a more conscious and deliberate use of intelligence' than is exercised today, Leavis points out how, in the England Arnold was addressing, there was a large and immensely influential educated class. In view of the rapid growth of egalitarianism – another child of modern enlightenment – in practically all walks of life such a class is even more necessary today, even though the community of the educated could never be a majority. In 'The Present and the Past: Eliot's Demonstration' Leavis expatiates on 'English' as a liaison centre in the universities, and the 'English school' as a centre of higher education, with modern literature playing a key role. For, as he observes, 'it is only from the present, out of the present, in the present' that literature of the past can be approached.

In 'Eliot's "Axe to Grind" ', while scrutinising Eliot's critical attitude to Donne, Milton, Dryden and Johnson, Leavis' own criticism achieves some of those qualities he attributes to Eliot – criticism with a 'highly compressed charge of perceptions, intuitions and suggestions'. Thus, for instance, while characterising Milton's genius, he tells us that it is not merely '*un*- but *anti*-Shakespearian',

> The ethos of his stylistic invention denies his verse anything like a Shakespearian relation to the living language. With the absence of the speech-subtlety of movement, tone and inflection that can be commanded only by the poet who appeals to the reader's most delicate sense of what is natural in English speech goes a marked restriction of the part played by evoked sensuous effects and evoked specific varieties of energy – an absence, in sum, of arresting concreteness.

In 'Why *Four Quartets* Matters in a Technologico-Benthamite Age' Leavis starts by demoting the view of Eliot as being primarily the poet of *The Waste Land*, and traces his development as a mature and accomplished poet through *The Hollow Men* (a prelude to *Ash-Wednesday*) and *Ash-Wednesday* to *Four Quartets* where Eliot's poetic mastery, together with his 'power of searching and sustained thought', is fully realised. It is not so much a 'matter of reflecting poetically' (to use Eliot's own phrase), as using for its 'definition and conduct' essentially poetic means and procedures, which accounts for Eliot's religious poetry being so different both from Dante's or Herbert's. And the difference lies primarily in the way it represents 'an insistent challenge to the thinking – the pondering, distinguishing, relating – mind', so that even as a critic what Eliot, like Lawrence, essentially offers are 'modes of thought'.

But while Eliot's poetry fully vindicates his claim to being a poetic genius and a creative thinker, and attests to 'the heroic integrity of his poetic career', his plays – those 'embarrassing plays', Leavis calls them, – do not, in as much as they are written with an eye to success in the theatre and to 'the applause of the best people and kudos that a man of his kind of distinction should surely not be very much concerned for'. The ethos of these plays is determined by, as well as tied up with, the consciousness of the social world, the world where 'social pressures, social suggestion and social "civilization" work (especially on the insecure) in the most insidious ways'. These plays, therefore, constitute for Leavis an unmistakable proof of Eliot's sense of insecurity.

In the following chapter, while dealing with Eliot and Lawrence as critics of *Hamlet* Leavis goes further into the causes as well as nature of Eliot's sense of insecurity, how it affected his writings – especially his plays and criticism – and why he felt an instinctive antipathy towards Lawrence – the antipathy of 'the weak, the uncreative – the anti-*creative*' Eliot who, in his 'brave anti-Lawrence days', with the backing of Bloomsbury behind him, which gave him 'a confidence he wouldn't otherwise have had', took his weakness for his strength. And yet his 'inner disorder and insecurity, and the lack of self-knowledge that went with

them', if it did not altogether disqualify him, 'had grave consequences for
him as a spiritual explorer'. Nowhere does this come out more revealingly
than in his plays, the 'unconscious falsity' of which makes them 'repellent'
to Leavis. This is all the more evident in Eliot's dealing with *Hamlet*,
especially when it is compared with the way Lawrence deals with it. As a
result of 'his own inner disorder', Eliot attributes its nature 'to Hamlet
(and Shakespeare)'. Lawrence's analysis of Hamlet, on the other hand, is
carried out by 'uncompromised intelligence', the agent of 'the whole being',
as a result of which he comes to an altogether different interpretation of
Hamlet. For, even though the play repels him, it is still 'the great work the
world has taken it to be'; the plight of Hamlet is related to what Leavis
calls 'a great change in the European psyche'. He is seen as the outcome
of 'the great religious, philosophic tide, which had been swelling all
through the Middle Ages'. Lawrence's criticism of *Hamlet* (in *Twilight in
Italy*) is by no means 'a full and final account of Shakespeare's play';
nevertheless, Leavis points out, no one 'capable of profiting by the university study of literature will find that it hasn't had a lasting effect on his
reading and thinking' – something one can hardly say of Eliot's essay on
Hamlet, apart from the issue of the general concept of the objective
correlative it incidently raises. In the last chapter – 'Summing Up: "Monstrous Unrealism" and the Alternative' – Leavis re-elaborates the
difference between Lawrence and Eliot, according to which the former
shows in his criticism of *Hamlet* (in *Twilight in Italy*) 'a completer and
profounder intelligence about life than Eliot'.

From Shakespeare Leavis proceeds to the novel, according to Lawrence,
'the highest form of human expression so far attained' – a view Leavis fully
shares – and considers the English novel one of 'the great creative chapters in the human record'. The study of novelists from Dickens to
Lawrence is, therefore, a study that 'entails a study of the changing
civilization (ours) of which their work is the criticism, the interpretation
and the history: nothing rivals it as such'.

Leavis' emphasis on the incomparable richness of English literature in
general and of the English novel in particular has exposed him to the
charge of provincialism. But he considered it his business – or for that
matter any critic's business – to emphasise the difference between 'the
right kind of partialness, patchiness and incompletion and what is favoured by those who dismiss as "provincial" the spirit I have tried to
define. Better, then, be provincial than cosmopolitan, for to be cosmopolitan in these matters is to be at home nowhere, and he who is at home
nowhere can make little of *any* literature – the more he knows, the larger
is his ignorance.'

One consequence of such ignorance is the tendency, in those who decide
what constitutes *The Novel* examination paper for undergraduates, to be
indifferent to 'the considerations that should determine what reading is
worth doing'. As a result Joyce, Proust, Mann, Kafka and the Americans

and the Russians are all added to the list of what an undergraduate should read, thereby betraying 'the monstrous unrealism that prevails, at the senior level, in the field of the University study of literature'. Such all-embracing, or such 'cosmopolitan cures for our provinciality', are, according to Leavis, the 'portent' of the American influence on university 'English' – a growing influence which is certainly a bad one and which 'for America's sake as well as our own, we should resist'. It is both a symptom and the consequence of that influence, for instance, that England 'has taken over, or developed for itself, the American conception of democracy'. Another symptom is the general assumption that America has 'more of a "sense of purpose" than this country has, or is in a more satisfying spiritual – or human – state', an assumption which is 'a characteristic illusion, or symptom, of the civilization we live in'.

English Literature in Our Time and the University thus continues, in a practical form, the broadening of Leavis' interest as a critic of literature, so that it embodies his interest in culture, civilisation and society, as well as in the values of life and in what one lives for.

Dickens and After (1970-1974)

Dickens [is] the Shakespeare of the novel.
F.R. and Q.D. Leavis

Dickens the Novelist

To mark the centenary year of Dickens' death the Leavises brought out their joint book on him. An American publisher had offered Leavis $200 for a contribution to a Centenary volume on Dickens (along with J.B. Priestley and others), but he declined – 'no heroism required', he commented. In the Peregrine Books reprint of *The Great Tradition* in 1962, he had supplied a footnote indicating his changed view of Dickens. In fact, he had been changing his view on him over the last twenty years and by now considered himself to be Dickens' vindicator, contending that 'he created the modern novel.'

The Leavises' book, *Dickens the Novelist*, came out in 1970, with three essays by F.R. Leavis ('The First Major Novel: *Dombey and Son*', 'Hard Times: The World of Bentham', taken from *The Great Tradition*, and 'Dickens and Blake: *Little Dorrit*'), and four by Q.D. Leavis ('Dickens and Tolstoy', '*Bleak House*', 'How We Must Read *Great Expectations*' and 'The Dickens Illustrations: Their Function'), together with six appendices by her ('Dickens and Smollett', 'Done "from a woman's point of view"', '*Oliver Twist, Jane Eyre* and *David Copperfield*', 'Dickens' Exposure Scenes', 'The Symbolic Function of the Doctor in Victorian Novels', and 'Mayhew and Dickens'). The Leavises characteristically dedicated the book to each other as proof,

> along with *Scrutiny* (of which for twenty-one years we sustained the main burden and the responsibility), of forty years and more of daily collaboration in living, university teaching, discussion of literature and the social and cultural context from which literature is born, and above all, devotion to the fostering of that true respect for creative writing, creative minds and, English literature being in question, the English tradition, without which literary criticism can have no validity and no life.

In their Preface they explained what they had *not* undertaken to do in this book – i.e: offer a general survey of Dickens which they regard as being 'merely academic, and unprofitable critically'; why they considered the trend of American criticism of Dickens, from Edmund Wilson onwards, 'in general wrong-headed, ill-informed ... and essentially ignorant and mis-directing'; why Forster's *Life of Dickens* was more important as a source than 'modern, more "correct" biographies, whether British or, still less acceptable, American'; and how, in the case of inept scholars who consider themselves to be literary critics, 'essential ignorance' could 'consort with a great deal of scholarly industry in assembling irrelevant data, and misrepresentation with interpreting the so-called "factual matter" ', as a result of which, the subject often becomes a 'victim'.

What they themselves undertook to offer was a critical evaluation of the six great novels 'in terms of intrinsic interest but in chronological order and in reference to each other'. Their collaboration in this book meant that each wrote his or her respective essays 'guided by the spontaneities of the personal judgement and the personal habit of approach', and each found 'the differences of idiosyncrasy ... an advantage in the execution of the collaboratively conceived project'.

In what some considered to be by far the best book to appear in the Dickens centenary year, the nature of the collaboration between F.R. and Q.D. Leavis brings out, in its complexity as well as complementarity, their different approaches and different degrees of appreciation of the various works of the writer they considered to be the greatest novelist in English, as well as their distinct individuality as critics and their essential affinity through diversity and vice versa. In fact so distinctly individual in its approach and procedure is the criticism of each that the other, while dealing with the same novel (or novels), could not have written it. But for the purpose of this book, only F.R. Leavis' contributions to the book will be examined.

In 'The First Major Novel: *Dombey and Son*' – originally an introduction to the novel and published in the *Sewanee Review* (1962) – Leavis identifies a decisive moment in Dickens' career which represents his first attempt at the elaborately plotted Victorian novel and displays those qualities which one associates with his inexhaustible creativity – 'the vigour of the perception and rendering of life, the varied comedy, the vitality of expression'. His genius is already seen at work here, with its 'unusual intensity' co-existing with 'a control from an unusual depth'. Leavis' own admiration for Dickens' prose brings out the creative aspect of his own prose, with its subtlety and suppleness, its control and firm grip on the specific and the concrete. For instance, he tells us how the theme as Dickens is possessed by it in the novel, is something quite different from what it becomes: 'For he *is* possessed by it: he is possessed by an intense and penetrating perception of the real – his theme *is* that. The art that serves it does not run to the luxuries of pathos and sensation or to redundancies. And it is astonishingly sensitive and plausible.' Leavis' interest in Dickens' language is neither linguistic nor philological, but essentially creative, so that the language is taken as a proof, not only of Dickens' skill and power as a writer, but also of his moral maturity and vision so indispensable to a great artist. What makes Dickens' use of language Shakespearian is its remarkable richness in terms of 'the vitality – the surprisingness combined with felicity, dramatic and poetic – of the speech in which he so largely renders these characters [Susan Nipper, Mr Toots, Mrs MacStringer, Cousin Feenix]'. Such qualities constitute the weft and warp of 'the inexhaustibly wonderful poetic life' of Dickens' prose.

But behind that prose there is Dickens' art – 'a bold, rapid and highly simplifying art' – through which he evokes Dombey, with 'his brand of pride and self-importance, and the cold inhumanity of his egotism – in so brief a space'. And the boldness of his art is one with 'the intensity of the realization, sensuous and imaginative'. With his eye on the definition of the novel as 'dramatic poem', Leavis illustrates the poetic quality and potentiality of the description of the two watches – Dombey's and Doctor Parker Pep's – 'running a race' and the sharp precision with which 'that peculiarly and impertinently insistent noise is evoked ... giving us in immediacy the stillness of the death-chamber, and giving it as the fact and presence of death'. Both the Dickensian detail and Leavis' commentary on it suggest as if it were a passage or an image from a poem that were in question. The very choice of details Leavis quotes in order to comment on them and comment on the way Dickens' poetic as well as narrative genius works suggests something creative about Leavis himself. Thus while assessing what the 'intensity of sensuous and imaginative realization' in Dickens' art gives us, Leavis finds its counterpart to be the moral, psychological and sociological aspects of the Victorian ethos as represented by Dombey's character and situation. Dombey's pride is thus seen to be 'in essence a stultifying self-contradiction; his egotism, in its inhumanity, as inimical to life and inevitably self-defeating'. The moral and social implications of Dombey's confidence in himself – confidence largely based on his wealth and on his belief in what money can do – are so analysed by Leavis as to bring out 'the truly great Dickens, the clairvoyant artist wholly commanded by a profound theme – a Dickens profoundly serious, that is, as well as genially creative'. *Dombey and Son*, like *Hard Times*, deals with 'the hard and hateful ethos' of the Victorian age to which the rampant utilitarian orthodoxy contributed a great deal, inculcating and sanctioning such things as 'money-pride and money-faith egotism, the closed heart and the sense of class as "exclusion" '.

However, while appreciating 'an art so strong, a moral insight and a grasp of realities so sure' as displayed in *Dombey and Son*, Leavis is fully aware of the fact that the novel as a whole is not conceived 'in any unified or unifying imagination', that it is not 'the work of genius which compels our homage in the strong parts', and that 'the creative afflatus goes in other, characteristic and large parts of the book with a moral *élan* that favours neither moral perception nor a grasp of the real'.

In conclusion Leavis alludes to his own description of Dickens in *The Great Tradition* as being that of a 'great entertainer', and comments:

> One cannot, then, rest happily on the formula that Dickens's genius was that of a great popular entertainer: the account is not unequivocal enough .... Dickens was in the fullest sense a great national artist. His genius responded with inexhaustible vitality to the new, the unprecedented conditions of a rapidly developing civilization .... His art was wonderfully original, and no writer was ever more remote from being troubled or guided by scruples that could in any sense be called academic .... And if we are to say that he saw himself as a popular entertainer, it must not be with any suggestion that he did not think of himself, and with justice, as having, *qua* artist, a penetrating insight into contemporary civilization, its ethos, its realities and its drives, that it concerned him to impart. And if we are to talk of fiction as a 'major art', then, faced with explaining what we mean and how the 'art' established its right to be considered in that way, we have to recognize that Dickens had a very important – a major – part in the history.

Coming to *Hard Times* (in the critical note on the novel in *The Great Tradition*, now included as a chapter in this book under the title '*Hard Times*: The World of Bentham'), where Dickens' creative power and inventiveness are convincingly exhibited, what Leavis says practically belies what he had said about Dickens' being the 'genius of a great entertainer'. Not only does the novel present the world of Bentham 'more vividly and more poignantly than any of his other novels', but it is also, of all Dickens' works, 'the one that has all the strength of his genius, with a strength no other work can show – that of a completely serious work of art'. It is a work where one finds the 'Dickensian vitality, in its varied characteristic modes', where 'the creative exuberance is controlled by a profound inspiration', and where Dickens is 'for once possessed by a comprehensive vision, one in which the inhumanities are seen as fostered and sanctioned by a philosophy, the aggressive formulation of an inhumane spirit' as represented by Thomas Gradgrind. In challenging this spirit as well as in exposing its nefarious and soul-destroying consequences, Dickens' art has 'a stamina, a flexibility combined with consistency, and a depth that he seems to have had little credit for'. Other qualities characterising that art are its 'poetically-creative operation', the force with which 'moral and spiritual differences are rendered ... in terms of sensation, so that the symbolic intention emerges out of a metaphor and the vivid evocation of the concrete', 'the astonishing and irresistible richness of life that characterizes the book everywhere' and that meets us 'everywhere, unstrained and natural, in the prose'. Dickens' linguistic flexibility, too, is the flexibility of 'a richly poetic art of the word', even though he does not write 'poetic prose'. No wonder that by virtue of 'texture, imaginative mode, symbolic method, and the resulting concentration, *Hard Times* affects us as belonging with formally poetic works'.

The inspiration behind the novel is summed up in the 'grim clinch' of the title, *Hard Times*, where the qualities of human kindness, 'vital human impulse' and human spontaneity stand out in sharp contrast with such negative manifestations of human nature and behaviour as those represented by Gradgrind and Bounderby, and by 'the spirit-quenching hideousness' of industrialism. With his 'extraordinary energy of perception and registration' Dickens observes 'the humanness of humanity as exhibited in the urban (and suburban) scene. When he sees, as he sees so readily, the common manifestations of human kindness, and the essential virtues, asserting themselves in the midst of ugliness, squalor and banality, his warmly sympathetic response has no disgust to overcome.' Also, the way in which Dickens alludes to the confutation of Utilitarianism by life in the person of Gradgrind is both subtle and illuminating, as is his way of portraying the psychology of Louisa's development. All this contributes to and, in fact, *is* part of the rich complexity of Dickens' art – Dickens whose genius is described by Leavis as being that of a poetic dramatist like Shakespeare, capable of 'concentration and flexibility in the interpretation of life'.

However, it is on Dickens' use of the language, on his command of 'word, phrase, rhythm and image' that Leavis' final stress falls; and 'in ease and range' he finds 'no greater master of English except Shakespeare' – another popular entertainer' as Leavis himself calls him. Elaborating his view that Dickens is a great poet, Leavis points out how his 'endless resource in felicitously varied expression is an extraordinary responsiveness to life', how his senses are 'charged with emotional energy, and his intelligence plays and flashes in the quickest and sharpest perception'. If Dickens' mastery of 'style' is 'of the only kind that matters', it is not because 'he hasn't a conscious interest in what can be done with words; many of his felicities could plainly not have come if there had not been, in the background, a habit of such interest'. However, Dickens is no more a stylist than Shakespeare, and it is not his descriptive evocations that bring out his mastery of expression, but his 'strictly dramatic felicities', so that, in Dickens' case, one talks 'not of style but of dramatic creation and imaginative genius'.

While examining *Little Dorrit*, 'one of the very greatest of novels', Leavis wonders how Dickens, a producer of popular fiction, could have developed into a creative writer of the first order, 'the superlatively original creator'. He analyses the factors that made such a development possible: Dickens' intense interest in contemplating and pondering life around him; his undertaking, here as in other novels, the study of 'the criteria implicit in the evaluative study of life'; and his ability to communicate 'generally valid truths about what can't be defined'.

Concerning Dickens' background, Leavis dismisses Santayana's observation that 'a waif himself, he was totally disinherited', as 'stultifyingly false' and insists that 'Dickens no more than Shakespeare started from nothing and created out of a cultural void'. In fact, he belonged 'to a culture in which the arts of speech were intensely alive' – which was, according to Leavis, 'a good start'. Moreover, Dickens read immensely, 'with the intelligence of genius, and his inwardness with Shakespeare, the subtlety of the influence manifest, and to be divined, in his own creative originality, can't be explained except by a reader's close and pondering acquaintance'. On the basis of such an acquaintance, Leavis brings to bear his own critical perception, intuition and curiosity as well as his historical sense of what the culture and conditions of Victorian England signified for Dickens' development.

But what Dickens personally hated about his age itself became part of his 'inquest into contemporary civilization' undertaken in *Little Dorrit* which might equally be called 'a study of the criteria implicit in an evaluative study of life'. Such a study commits Dickens to 'an enterprise of thought; thought that is in our time of the greatest moment to get recognized, consciously and clearly, *as* thought – an affair (that is) of the thinking intelligence directed to a grasp of the real'. In recognising and analysing such thought – thought 'that asks questions, seeks answers and defines' – Leavis displays his own capacity for thought, both critical and creative, exploratory and analytical. This helps him establish that Dickens' genius as a novelist means 'a capacity for profound and subtle thought' and that *Little Dorrit* is 'a supreme illustration of the general truth about great creative writers, that their creative genius is a potency of *thought*'.

Coming to the analytical probing of Little Dorrit's personality and how 'her genius is to be always beyond question genuine – real ... indefectibly real, and the test of reality for the others', what she is and what Dickens meant her to stand for are happily merged. What emerges is the most perceptive, sympathetic and psychologically convincing account of Little Dorrit who is, for her father and brother and sister, 'the never-failing providence, the vital core of sincerity, the conscience, the courage of moral percipience, the saving realism, that preserves for them the necessary bare minimum of the real beneath the fantastic play of snobberies, pretences and self-deceptions that constitutes genteel life in the Marshalsea .... Incorruptibly innocent and sincere, what does she know – really know? To know would be to recognize and judge: she judges and doesn't judge. She understands enough to be infallible in response.'

Leavis' intuitive insight into the psyche of Dickens' characters, into Dickens' art and into the very nature of 'reality' and 'unreality' takes his criticism beyond the level of what is normally called 'literary criticism'. It becomes something memorably much more than that: becomes an illuminating self-searching through which the exploration and the creation of reality is achieved. Little Dorrit, Leavis tells us, 'like anyone else, needs collaboration in creating the reality she can grasp – more comprehensively, the reality she can implicitly believe herself to be, and that which she can feel with assurance she lives in'; but so, one might say, does the critic whose response to, and recreation of, what a major artist like Dickens or George Eliot, D.H. Lawrence or T.S. Eliot offers is itself an exercise in collaboration between himself and the author. Concerning Little Dorrit's father, we are told that he, too, 'as he exemplifies – with effects of both comedy and pathos – every day, can't get on without collaboration; without it he couldn't have maintained the unreality he inhabited as a gentleman in the Marshalsea (the prison that also protected – as he recognized in declining the turnkey's offer to let him step outside into the street for a glimpse of the world). It was a system of countenanced empty pretensions. But so is that in which he proudly takes his place when he is liberated into Society; the "real" unreality is equally unreal, and, in his own way, equally a prison.'

It is, thus, by virtue of what he reads into the text of the novel and what he recreates on the basis of his own experience and observation of life that a critic like Leavis can appreciate how 'clear-sighted' Dickens is about the social realities of the Victorian age, and how no one has surpassed him in the treatment of Victorian snobbery – indeed, Leavis asks, 'has anyone approached?' But Dickens' insight into the workings of Victorian society and Victorian snobberies could not have had the value and relevance it has, had it not been rooted in his profound apprehension of the workings of the human psyche as well as of what Leavis calls 'the inherited totality of the values, the promptings, the intuitions of basic human need'. For all his evocation of death, time and eternity and the non-human universe, Dickens, Leavis points out, 'has no more bent than Blake towards conceiving life or mankind reductively. His exposure of unrealities is a vindication of human creativity, and an insistence that such a vindication, real and achieved, can (as Daniel Doyce is there to testify) have no hubris in it.'

As to the Blake-Dickens relationship, Leavis notes how, in spite of their affinity, there is a radical difference between them. For one thing, there is no Swedenborg and no Boheme in the case of Dickens, who owed more to Shakespeare than to the 'perennial philosophy'. More important still, the difference is not that Blake is more spiritual than Dickens, but the fact that, lacking 'that essential kind of collaboration which Dickens's relations with his public gave *him*', Blake spent a vast deal of his life and effort wrestling with 'ultimate questions that inevitably defeated him' and 'aspiring to a possession of "answers" that is unattainable'. And yet, so far as their concern for the spirit is concerned, Dickens and Blake, 'whatever the differences in emphasis and accent, [are] religious in the same sense'. In any case, Leavis notes, 'it is not a creative writer's business to be a theologian or a philosopher'. As to Dickens being 'the greatest of the romantic novelists', it is Blake that Leavis is primarily thinking of, as he is thinking of the Romantic movement and of the romantic period as 'the century of the American and the French Revolutions, of the opening Industrial Revolution, and of the inevitable reaction against "Locke and Newton" ' which produced 'changes, challenges and creative incitements enough to make the emergence of a new sense of human responsibility comprehensible, and to explain a notable development of language'. In responding to this development, writers in the English tradition had 'the immeasurable advantage to draw – as both Blake and Dickens did – on Shakespeare'.

Nor Shall My Sword

Soon after the publication of the Dickens book, Leavis started planning a new book – not a collection of essays so much as 'a closely-worked book (appealing for its wider context to *Education and the University* and the Clark Lectures)'. It was to include 'Two Cultures? The Significance of Lord Snow', 'Luddites? Or There is Only One Culture', ' "Élites", Unrest and Continuity', ' "Literarism" versus "Scientism": The Misconception and the Menace', 'Pluralism, Compassion and Social Hope' and 'Élites, Oligarchies and an Educated Public', delivered at various universities (York, Bristol, Wales, Oxford, Cambridge, Durham, Hull) with 'packed audiences and sustained and very emphatic applause'.

He expected such a book to solve the problem, as he saw it, of 'making a higher pamphleteering impact with a pregnant theme that entailed complex and original thought', so that, as he suggested in his 'characteristic modest way', the whole be 'much more a classical achievement ... than the pamphleteering classics of Matthew Arnold – to whom ... I felt too much likened'. He had even thought out the title for the book: *Nor Shall My Sword: Discourses on Pluralism, Compassion and Social Hope*.

Leavis cared very much about such a book which dealt with what he called 'the great modern theme – *my* major theme', and wanted it to come out while 'the actualité is pressing'. He had already started writing the Introduction, of which he tells us that 'there are ideas, and *ahnung* and nisus in my head and lower down. Some things I know *must* be said there. Ideally, the Introduction would greatly add.'

The Introduction increasingly acquired 'something like lecture-length', and came to be 'on a level with other chapters', as Leavis became more and more convinced of the importance of the book. He considered it to be 'not less effective' than anything he had done before – something that would contribute to what he called 'the Great Debate'. He entitled it 'Introductory: "Life *is* a necessary word" '.

After the typescript of *Nor Shall My Sword* had been with Chatto for some months, Leavis started reminding them about its publication. And when a tentative date was given – January 1972 – he found it 'a great assuagement', explaining why he was in such a hurry: 'My *actualité* isn't, I hope, ephemerality, but it does mean that we oughtn't to be in the lag for the launch.' Moreover, he had already started working on another book 'jostled by several others', for 'the impulsions jostle one another'.

But there was a certain hitch before the book came out. Only at the galley-proof stage did Q.D. Leavis come to know both about the title – *Nor Shall My Sword* – and about the inclusion of the last of the six lectures, 'Élites, Oligarchies and an Educated Public', to both of which she was categorically opposed. She not only disapproved of the title, but found the lecture 'gratuitously, embarrassingly and impossibly personal'. In deference to her criticism, and in order not to aggravate her already precarious state of health, Leavis asked his publisher to withdraw both, if possible, and suggested an alternative title *Pluralism, Compassion and Social Hope*. But within a month, largely as a result of 'regrets and protests' on the part of those who had come to know about the original title, Leavis had second thoughts and reverted to it. He also decided to include the last lecture.

When asked for a photograph for a dust-jacket, he suggested the one – 'the best ... for the purpose' – that the *Times Literary Supplement* had used (23 April 1970) when it published his lecture ' "Literarism" versus "Scientism" '. 'It doesn't lend itself ', he commented, 'to the familiar cartoon-contrast with Snow. Snow, of course, doesn't need caricaturing, but the frontal view of me has been improved into the paradigm of "aggressively" cynical intellectuality'. But later he withdrew this suggestion: 'It doesn't suit my present role to be thought of as an ironical aggressor with that nasty superior face ... one can't be *too* corrective. Chatto and Windus typography is the thing: it does all that really needs doing.'

Nor Shall My Sword came out in 1972. The lecture 'Two Cultures?' (included in this book) had marked the beginning of his publicly argued concern with the social and cultural problems and dilemmas of contemporary civilisation, and his diagnostic commentary on them found a cogent expression in *Nor Shall My Sword*. Apart from ' "English", Unrest and Continuity' and ' "Literarism" versus "Scientism": The Misconception and the Menace', much of the discussion in the book centres around the non-literary aspects and problems of today. In fact, Leavis' concern with the problems and dilemmas of our civilisation is a logical corollary as well as an extension of his concern for the values of literature and for the standards of criticism as a discipline of sensibility and intelligence. Striking an effective balance between the critical and the polemical, between tradition and modernity, what Leavis says is at once challenging and illuminating. With his sense of realism and concreteness, and his impressive command of the creative and analytical subtleties of language – in fact, one can say of Leavis' polemical as well as critical prose what A.E.

Housman said of the nineteenth-century English Latinist, Hugo Munro, namely, that 'he wrote English so well that most scholars did not know how well he wrote it' – Leavis tackles the problems of modern civilisation. Both the title and the dedication of the book suggest the key role Blake played in Leavis' thinking about these problems, and especially about the ethos of the times, with 'the hubris of technological-positivist enlightenment' in stark contrast with as well as militating against what is humane and conducive to creativity. Thus against Blake's 'intransigent certainties', what the modern world has to offer is 'a high standard of living in a vacuum of disinheritance'. The sense of such blankness as well as of spiritual Philistinism is summed up under the name 'Pluralism', which denotes 'a sitting-easy to questions of responsibility, intellectual standard, and even superficial consistency, the aplomb, or suppleness, being conditioned by a coterie-confident sense of one's own unquestioned sufficiency – or superiority'. It contrasts with Leavis' own belief that what civilisation needs by way of the creative change 'can't be initiated by majorities, but only by those capable of disinterestedness, essential human responsibility, and grounded conviction'. The only way to combat the spiritual Philistinism of our times, therefore, is to emphasise 'that creative human reality of significances, values and non-measurable ends which our technologico-Benthamite civilization ignores and progressively impoverishes, thus threatening human existence'.

Among the problems and conditions of modern technologico-Benthamite civilisation Leavis includes the menace of leisure, such pathetic 'vacuum-fillers' as bingo establishments, the journalistic addiction of academics and intellectuals and the consequent mistaking of the 'magazine sections' of the Sunday papers for what Matthew Arnold meant by 'the best that is thought and known in our times', 'the professional subhumanities of computeral addiction' and a naively euphoric faith in computerised teaching and computerised assessment of standards and performance, the statesmen's view and treatment of a university as an industrial plant, with the smiling Vice-Chancellors making the students feel that their claims to prescribe their curricula and examine themselves are discussible, and the growing proportion of students qualified to claim university places, but not qualified to profit by them.

Leavis not only sees the role of British universities as changing, but Britain itself as fast becoming merely a province of the American world. And it is above all in the universities that one notes the encroachment of American conditions: 'the rootlessness, the vacuity, the inhuman scale, the failure of the organic cultural life, the anti-human reductivism that favours the American neo-imperialism of the computer'. In the face of such menaces, even Oxford and Cambridge, far from remaining centres of excellence or creative centres of civilisation, are doomed to become more and more 'mushrooms of mediocrity'. The notion that such a view of the American world and American conditions might give the impression that he was anti-American is explicitly dispelled by Leavis himself. For, far from being anti-American, he believed that the 'hope of salvation for America depends upon our success in the creative battle here, where we can still open it, and wage it, and resolve to win (or not to lose)'. The battle, that is to say, against 'the barbarity of reformist enlightenment ... the civilized barbarity, complacent, self-indulgent and ignorant, that can see nothing to be quarrelled with in believing, or wanting to believe, that a computer can write a poem'.

Letters in Criticism

Two years later, in 1974, a selection of Leavis' letters – *Letters in Criticism* – appeared, edited and introduced by John Tasker. Leavis, like Pound, was a prolific letter-writer, having a vast circle of correspondents from all over the world – chiefly the British Commonwealth, America and India. The telling efficacy of his prose style – index of a strong personality and a committed mind – is evidenced in these letters no less than in his criticism. Controversial, for the most part, in tone and spirit, they invariably succeed in enforcing Leavis' point of view, as well as in substantiating and enforcing his critical pronouncements. Hence the organic link between them and his books of criticism. In the last letter (18 January, 1973) included in this book, Leavis corrects the misconception on the part of a *Listener* correspondent regarding the supposed affinity between himself and Wittgenstein: 'I am surprised at the suggestion that there is an affinity between me and Wittgenstein, or any concurrence of "influence" ... I lack intellectual sympathy with Wittgenstein. Real intellectual and cultural life entails the creative play, some of which may find expression as strong as disagreements.' Through such pithy comments, Leavis expresses his personal views on such literary, cultural and social matters as the BBC, left-wing intellectuals, working-class culture, the degeneration of the reading public, the transition from quality to quantity in education, the function of the university at the present time, the 'Great Debate' about joining Europe, etc. For all its 'personal' character, Leavis' epistolary art is never subjective in the narrow sense of the word. For instance, while commenting on Richard Church's review of *New Bearings in English Poetry*, Leavis observes: 'My critical approach, which (to my gratification) leads Mr Church to note that I am "preoccupied with technique", I have always imagined to derive from Mr Eliot as much as from anyone' (9 April 1932); or when (March 1955) he replies to L.D. Lerner's charge that in his discussion of modern poetry he should have added a section on what had been written since 1932. The Epilogue, says Leavis, in fact explains 'why the post-Eliot history of English poetry should be so discouraging – so discouraging that it couldn't be dealt with by taking up again the critical approach of *New Bearings*'. As to Lerner's antithetical use of 'practical' and 'theoretical' criticism, Leavis remarks that he has never liked the term 'practical criticism', that it is no more than 'an academic convenience', that in places where Coleridge's distinctive genius as a critic 'most clearly and notably' manifests itself (ch. XV of *Biographia Literaria*, and of that chapter the second head above all), 'it is impossible to disengage the dealings with principle from the "practical criticism"', and that the master of theoretical criticism who matters is 'the completion of a practical critic'. In another letter ('A New "Establishment" in Criticism') Leavis recalls the history of 'the hostility, overt and covert, intense and wholly unscrupulous, of the academic and literary worlds, or of what I think it reasonable to call the Establishment' to *Scrutiny*, to himself and to what he stood for, and he asks: 'What has my criticism in common with Mr. Wilson Knight's, Mr. Traversi's, Mr. Eliot's or Professor Empson's? .... And if Mr. Holloway ... should suggest that to be known as a pupil of mine or an admirer of *Scrutiny* is a passport to success in an academic career, I should be obliged to say – as of course I shall not – that he was guilty of dishonesty.'

In another letter (to the *Listener*, 3 November 1960), which is a superb illustration of his skill as a polemicist, Leavis defends himself against an attack on him by a leading article (20 October). 'Attack', he tells the editor, 'is perhaps too complimentary a word, since it suggests a boldness of explicit and unequivocal criticism. Your actual method is one of insinuation – with minimal self-commitment.' 'English as a *discipline*', the *Listener* article had suggested, 'cannot be wholly divorced from the historical past.' 'But what excuse have you', asks Leavis, 'for imputing to me the suggestion that it can? ... What distinguishes your own position, it seems to me, is a readiness to rely upon empty phrases and inert preconceptions – which look like something else to you because of your consciousness of enjoying massive support. How does one get access to the "historical past"? – that, surely, is the great problem. But to you it is *no* problem: you see (it appears) no relation between it and that delicate cultivation of perception, sensibility and intelligence which you refer to as "practical criticism".'

Another example of Leavis' fight against insinuation is provided by Professor Frank Kermode's remarks that 'young people are less prone to Donne-intoxication than they were twenty years ago', and that 'Milton and the Victorians are no longer savagely excluded from their permitted reading'. Coming, as it does, from the editor of a book of essays on Milton – *The Living Milton* – to which the editor himself had also contributed, Leavis asks, 'who can fail to have assumed that he had me in mind' in writing that sentence, and adds:

> I do not ask that he [Kermode] should have *read* my criticism – read it for what it says. Without that he could have known, if he had wanted to, what would (I hope) have shamed him out of the impulse to indulge in that slanderous implication. All pupils of mine know that I have always been very far from discouraging the reading of Milton, and that when, twenty years ago, I defended Milton against

an eminent Miltonist, my title was not merely ironical. I have always held that Milton is a very great power, and that without an intelligent study of him one cannot understand English literary history. If one is not intelligent about him, I think it improbable that one will be intelligent about Donne (and certainly that one cannot be intelligent about Eliot). But, if we are to talk about what is, and what is not, permissible, the fact I have to state is that students likely to be thought of as pupils of mine ('disciples', 'Leavisites') have long been afraid to answer on Milton in the examination room. It is the Mummified Milton that such an academic world is bent on preserving.

As in his criticism, so also in his letters Leavis constantly merges history with criticism, factual data with critical perception. The letter to the *Oxford Review* (1 January 1966) generally, and what it says about Johnson as a critic of Shakespeare in particular, is a case in point, illustrating how Leavis' own understanding of Shakespeare's art and of Johnson's criticism of it interact. 'I greatly admire Johnson', observes Leavis,

> but it is certainly absurd to make him the ideal critic of Shakespeare, or to speak of him as one who possessed Shakespeare fully. Though he may sometimes seem to transcend them in non-evaluative characterization of Shakespeare's use of the English language, critically he doesn't escape the limitations of his age: creative expression – the Shakespearean poetic creativity that so utterly and unmistakably defies paraphrase – defeats (or is defeated by) the critical apparatus of preconceptions, assumptions and habits that Johnson brings up. A major consequence is that he can, quite unequivocally (*pace* the Cambridge essayist, who resorts to dishonest and falsifying selectiveness in 'proving' the contrary) exalt Shakespeare's comedy above his tragedy. No critic who does that can be said to possess Shakespeare fully.

Such a state of affairs makes one feel the 'need to have an intelligent and disinterested critical organ' to be all the more urgent – something, Leavis had hoped, the *Oxford Review* was going to provide. But, he adds sadly,

> The more deeply one feels the need, the more wary is one of being made to appear benign, or neutral, in the face of what aims, essentially – not the less so for deferential shows, at the undoing of all one has worked for. And it seems proper to add that I, having been habitually pretty free with my trust, have had in my 'retired' years some seismic shocks of disillusion.

In a letter to *The Times* (22 January 1968), Leavis dealt with another such shock concerning a subject close to his heart – university education. Replying to Lord Annan's letter about the university crisis and his suggestion that 'if the universities are not to be attacked as citadels of privilege, they must give what help they can', such as offering a month-long residential course in the summer for children 'who would have stayed on at school but for the postponement', Leavis argues that the 'privilege' the universities are called upon to surrender is in fact the right (or duty) to maintain the standards proper to a university. But, he adds,

> neither democratic zeal nor egalitarian jealousies should be permitted to dismiss or discredit the fact that only a limited proportion of any young adult group is capable of profiting by, or enjoying, university education. The proper standards can be maintained only if the students the university is required to deal with are – for the most part, at any rate – of university quality. If standards are not maintained somewhere the whole community is let down.

Leavis' letters thus throw light on the way he was concerned with and disinterestedly addressed himself to such issues as standards of university education, that were close to his heart. They also bring out his full command over the resources of critical idiom (innuendoes, asides, understatements and parentheses) which was equal to his powers of critical perception, his moral integrity and his sense of commitment, even when he was deeply involved in controversy.

9

Last Books

To be able to praise, it is not necessary to feel complete agreement.
T.S. Eliot

To judge poetry to be sincere doesn't amount to endorsing it.
F.R. Leavis

The Living Principle

In the last three years of his life Leavis brought out two books – *The Living Principle* (1975) and *Thought, Words and Creativity* (1976) – in which the vigour and vitality of his mind and thought as well as the creative resourcefulness and analytical quality of his use of language are as impressively present as in his previous books. Re-affirming his well-known convictions in new contexts and with a freshly-charged sense of commitment to the language as a discipline of thought, Leavis links them, in the first two sections of *The Living Principle* – 'Thought, Language and Objectivity' and 'Judgement and Analysis' – with his own practical exercises in judgement and analysis (where he is deliberately trying to preserve his teaching personality), reprinted here as ' "Thought" and Emotional Quality', 'Imagery and Movement', 'Reality and Sincerity', 'Prose', '*Antony and Cleopatra* and *All for Love*'. In the third section, '*Four Quartets*' – in some ways the most original part of the book – we are offered an elaborate and exhaustive comment on Eliot's poem which is the most extensive analytical comment Leavis ever wrote on a single work of poetry. The main thread binding this book is Leavis' response to creativity on two levels – the level of thought and the level of language. In 'Imagery and Movement', for instance, while discussing Shakespeare's use of English as that of a genius endowed with a 'marvellously quick and penetrating intelligence about life and human nature', Leavis compares the triumph of clarity and logic in Dryden's age with Shakespeare's power of apprehending and registering the subtleties and complexities of his thought, by pointing out that 'whatever was gained by the triumph of "clarity", logic and Descartes, the gain was paid for by an immeasurable loss'; that of 'cutting yourself off from most important capacities and potentialities of thought which of its nature is essentially heuristic and creative'. In

'Reality and Sincerity' – one of the best specimens of his close criticism of poetry – Leavis deals with Hardy's poem 'After a Journey' in which the poet's rare integrity is analysed in terms of his presentation of a specific fact and circumstance and sentiment – the death of his wife.

The book carries three epigraphs: one from Wittgenstein ('Give up literary criticism'); one from D.H. Lawrence – a note to 'The Crown', where, among other things, Lawrence talks about 'new shoots of life springing up and slowly bursting the foundations' and of how one must fight 'tooth and nail to defend the new shoots of life from being crushed out, and let them grow'; and the last from Leavis' own prelusive comments in 'Thought, Language and Objectivity' where he tells us that 'there's no redeeming the democratic mass university', and that 'nothing today is more important than to keep alive the idea of the university function – the essential function and what goes with it'.

The epigraphs throw light not only on the contents of the book, but also on the nature of the preoccupations which exercised Leavis' mind with a particular intensity and apprehensiveness during the last years of his life. In his Preface to the book he admits that 'it would be mere dream-indulgence to suppose that we might establish a university answering to the ideal implicit in my argument'. The menace of the change is seen to be both drastic and unavoidable – the menace represented by the world of 'triumphant modernity', the world of 'power-centres from which the quantity-addicted machinery of civilization is controlled, directed and exploited', the expansion of universities congested with 'telly and pin-table-addicted non-students'.

However, in spite of such a gloomy prospect, Leavis ardently believed in 'the living principle'. What this principle meant to him the whole of the book is devoted to defining as well as defining what 'to mean' means. Another point enforced by this book concerns 'intelligent thought about the nature of thought and the criteria of good thinking' which for Leavis are inseparable from intelligence about the nature of language itself. This entails a reformulation, in more analytical terms, of his old, familiar view of critical discipline as a discipline of intelligence, 'a training in delicacy of perception, in supple responsiveness, in the wariness of conceptual rigidity that goes with a Blakean addiction to the concrete and particular, and in readiness to take unforeseen significances and what is so unprecedented as to be new'.

In 'Thought, Language and Objectivity', the characteristically Leavisian concerns, educational as well as literary and critical, are discussed: 'English', a discipline 'sui generis – a discipline of intelligence'; his opposition to a 'new and triumphant academic institutionalism' and to 'student participation'; the need as he saw it for a 'creative centre of the educated public'; an attempt to define the nature of analysis and value-judgements in criticism as well as the way the day to day work of 'collaborative creation' includes the creating of language. All these themes are analysed in new contexts and in the light of such challenges as posed by the work of Bertrand Russell, Wittgenstein, Polanyi, Marjorie Grene, Professor Andreski (author of *Social Sciences as Sorcery*), and others. In the course of meeting these challenges, Leavis explains what constitutes 'the validity of a total inclusive judgement of a poem' and how it cannot be demonstrated:

> it is always possible in criticism to get beyond the mere assertion. The critical procedure is tactical; the critic, with his finger moving from this to that point in the text, aims at so ordering his particular judgements ('This is so, isn't it?') that, 'Yes' having in the succession of them almost inevitably come for answer, the rightness of the inclusive main judgement stands clear for the prompted recognition – it makes itself, needing no assertion.

Similarly, while vindicating the role of 'English' as a discipline of thought, he tells us how a great writer in the language

> belongs to the one collaboratively creative continuity. The discipline is not a matter of learning a deduced logic or an eclectic true philosophy, but rather of acquiring a delicate readiness of apprehension and a quasi-instinctive flexibility of response, these informed by the intuited 'living principle' – the principle implicit in the interplay between the living language and the creativity of individual genius.

Another preoccupation of Leavis' is the menace represented by the Americanisation of Britain – a menace which, since Leavis' death, has become increasingly inescapable on more than one front of English culture, civilisation and society in such a way that even he, with all his premonitions and apprehensions, would have been shocked.

Concerning what language means, how the linguisticians' attitude to language and that of a creative writer are fundamentally different, what words mean to him, and what a word *is* – Leavis argues that

> Linguisticians, finding it too much for them as yet, postpone dealing at all seriously with meaning. But language apart from meaning is not language. Wittgenstein, who didn't favour linguistics, knew that of course … it is plain that the study of the 'linguistic philosophy' doesn't in fact promote the insights into the nature of language that are most important (to anyone) and I am confirmed in my conviction that we must protect students of 'English' against the philosophic enthusiasts who prescribe seminars on Wittgenstein on them.

His own view of *a* language, meaning the English language – for, as he remarks, 'there is no such thing as language in general' – is that a language is more than a means of expression; it is the heuristic conquest won out of representative experience, the upshot or precipitate of immemorial living, and embodies values, distinctions, identifications, conclusions, promptings, cartographical hints and tested potentialities. It exemplifies the truth that life is growth and growth change, and the condition of these is continuity. It takes the individual being, the particularizing actuality of life, back to the dawn of human consciousness, and beyond, and does this in fostering the *ahnung* in him of what is not yet – the as yet unrealized, the achieved discovery of which demands creative effort.

In a passage like this Leavis' lifelong contact with and the way he critically 'possessed' the various masters and masterpieces of English literature, and the incomparable insight they afforded him into the nature of the language and his sense of history and tradition are fully borne out. The second part of *The Living Principle*, in fact, bears directly upon the question of the creativeness of the language as used by poets, prose-writers and dramatists. Dealing with the general subject of 'Judgement and Analysis', Leavis sub-divides what he has to say into five categories: ' "Thought" and Emotional Quality'; 'Imagery and Movement'; 'Reality and Sincerity'; 'Prose'; and *'Antony and Cleopatra* and *All for Love'*.

In ' "Thought" and Emotional Quality', Leavis takes up certain poems for comparison and contrast in order to appraise them in terms of the 'thought' and emotional quality embodied therein. The exercise amounts to what Leavis considers 'practical criticism' which implies 'a process of re-creation ... in response to the poet's words that any genuine and discussible reading of the poem must be'. Leavis compares Wordsworth's 'A Slumber did My Spirit Seal' and Tennyson's 'Break, Break, Break'. Even though Wordsworth wrote his poem because of something 'profoundly and involuntarily suffered', his experience has been so impersonalized that 'the effect, as much as that of "Proud Maisie", is one of bare and disinterested presentment'. In 'Break, Break, Break', the emotion, offered directly, 'seems to be "out there" on the page'. But even though behind Tennyson's poem there is 'a genuinely personal urgency', Wordsworth's poem is 'a securer kind of achievement'. A reader who cannot see that Tennyson's poem, with all its 'distinction and refinement', yields a satisfaction inferior to that represented by Wordsworth, cannot, according to Leavis, 'securely appreciate the highest possible poetic achievement at its true worth and is not likely to be at all strong or sure in the kind of judgement that discriminates between "Break, Break, Break" and "Heraclitus" '.

While examining the virtues and vices of 'metaphysical' poetry, Leavis demonstrates how an essential part of the strength of good metaphysical poetry turns out to be of the same order as the strength of all the most satisfying poetry: 'the conceitedness, the Metaphysicality, is the obtrusive accompaniment of an essential presence of "thought" such as we have in the best work of all great poets. It can be said in favour of the metaphysical habit that it favours such a presence'. The two poems Leavis uses as illustrations are some stanzas from Lionel Johnson's 'The Dark Angel', and a passage from Marvell's 'An Horation Ode upon Cromwell's Return from Ireland'. What is impressive about Johnson's poem is 'conditioned' by an absence of thought. It is poetry of the 'soul' where 'nothing has sharp definition and where effects of "profundity" and "intensity" depend upon a lulling mind'. As an example of a complete 'abeyance of the questioning mind' Leavis quotes the lines: 'Which are more still and great:/Those brows, or the dark skies?'. 'Taken as real questions, requiring answers', he tells us, 'they are merely ludicrous'. In fact, it is his own 'purpose' that Johnson is really concerned with, not Charles, who is merely 'an excuse, a cover and an opportunity'. Leavis quotes the penultimate stanza – 'King, tired in fires of woe!/Men hunger for thy grace:/And through the night I go,/Loving thy mournful face' – to explain what Johnson's 'own purpose' is – a comment that illustrates what is fundamentally constructive about Leavis' negative value judgement.

Marvell, on the other hand, was 'served' differently by the tradition of Horatian ode. For one thing, it is the nature of Marvell's ode 'not to be a product of strong personal emotion (there is no evidence in it that Marvell had any to control), but to be the poised formal expression of statesmanlike wisdom, surveying judicially the contemporary scene'. The attitudes and valuations it embodies seem to be 'wholly determined by the nature of what is seen and judged, and the expression of feeling to be secondary and merely incidental to just statement and presentment'. What is so significantly present in the ode is 'the contemplating, relating and appraising mind' – qualities by virtue of which Leavis regards the 'Horatian Ode', 'Proud Maisie' and 'A Slumber did My Spirit Seal' as vastly superior to Lionel Johnson, Tennyson and Shelley.

Leavis starts his essay on 'Imagery and Movement' by treating 'Image' and 'Imagery' as 'insidious terms' which have encouraged 'an immense deal of naive commentary' as well as 'confident reliance' on two closely related fallacies: (i) the too ready assumption that images are visual, and (ii) the conception of metaphor as essentially simile with the 'like' or 'as' left out. Leavis analyses the nature and implications of these fallacies, and takes up Macbeth's opening speech in scene VII of Act I as an example of what can be done creatively with the English language by Shakespeare. He considers the passage ('If it were done, when 'tis done, then 'twere well ... And falls on the other side') as superb dramatic poetry, creating 'the complex state of hesitant recoil, the magic weakness of self-knowledge, that Lady Macbeth, arriving at the close of the speech, precipitates into murder'. Through close analysis of individual lines and images, Leavis shows how the emphasis on Macbeth's recoil from the deed 'he nevertheless still contemplates is on the certainty of consequent disaster – disaster the more horrifying because it is the spiritual aspect of such "judgement here" that will have made worldly success impossible', and how 'this significant intentness on the deed he recoils from – the perverse self-contradiction that makes Macbeth's inner state a tragic theme – is wonderfully exposed to us in the speech, the total dramatic utterance'.

To appreciate the 'complex' tension that Macbeth himself analyses in his speech is, for Leavis, to appreciate how Shakespeare's poetry is 'the agent and vehicle of thought', and why the fact that he 'can't have first stated his thought explicitly, "clearly" and "logically" in prose, and then turned it into dramatic poetry doesn't make it any the less thought'. As to Shakespeare's relationship with the English language in 1600, with his 'marvellously quick' genius and his 'penetrating' intelligence about life and human nature, it was 'an ideal medium for the Shakespearean processes of thought', with its subtleties and complexities. If he had been born into Dryden's age, when 'logic' and 'clarity' had triumphed, Shakespeare could not have been Shakespeare and 'the modern world would have been without the proof that thought of this kind was possible. We should have lacked convincing evidence with which to enforce the judgement that neither Racine nor Stendhal represents the greatest kind of creative writer (I am assuming that Balzac is clearly not discussible as great in any way).'

As to the use of 'image' and 'imagery', Leavis regards it as 'distinctively Shakespeare's – a use he couldn't have developed in the later phase of the English language when "English grammar" and correctness had become firmly established'. That is why when Dr. Johnson notes how Shakespeare subordinated 'correctness' of expression to the 'series of ideas', he was not 'unequivocally' appreciating the advantages that the 'reckless Shakespearean genius', favoured by the cultural conditions of 1600, enjoyed in relation to 'obligatory "correctness" of observance of logic, grammar and decorum'. Commenting on Johnson's 'magnificent (and characteristic) passage' where he censures Shakespeare for not being able to express well 'an unwieldy sentiment' and for comprising it 'in words such as occur', Leavis in turn blames Johnson for not being able to see the relation between Shakespeare's 'untamed licentiousness in the use of the English language and the manifestation of creative genius'. And when Johnson praises Shakespeare for showing 'plainly, whether life or nature be his subject', that he has 'seen with his own eyes', so that 'the ignorant feel his representations to be just and the learned see that they are complete', Leavis points out that the virtue that Johnson praises 'involves more than he recognises – much more than his thought, conditioned by Augustan "correctness" is capable of grasping unequivocally'. The way Leavis criticises Johnson's criticism of Shakespeare is a vindication of his view of the 'inclusively' creative use of the English language of which Shakespeare is as much a master in English as Dante is in Italian. 'Correctness', 'rules', 'ideas', 'decorum' (which 'merged into morality' as Johnson conceived it),

'clarity', 'explicitness' and 'logical and grammatical statement' are virtues
by which Johnson and his age set much store. Nonetheless, they constituted the same kind of difficulty in the way of understanding
Shakespeare's use of English, as the cultural ethos represented by Locke
and Newton constituted for Blake in his way of asserting human creativity. Johnson, no doubt, admires the vividness and energy of Shakespeare's
English, but there is for Leavis a great deal more than that. There is 'a
power of bringing into thought a range of subtleties and profundities
central to human experience' that were beyond the range of the Augustan
ethos of the eighteenth century. Shakespeare forced upon his readers the
fact that language is essentially 'heuristic'; that in major creative writers
'it does unprecedented things, advances the frontiers of the known, and
discovers the new'. This is how Shakespeare achieved his 'miraculous
complexity', the analysis of which amounts in fact to analysis of 'matters
of complex verbal organization'. Hence metaphors, images and other local
effects cannot be treated as if their relation to the poem were 'at all like
that of plum cakes', rather than 'foci of a complex life'. Describing the
'evocative or representational felicity or vivacity' of a metaphor, Leavis
links it with the complexity of expression – a complexity that involves 'the
telescoping or focal coincidence in the mind of contrasting or discrepant
impressions or effects'. This gives the metaphor its life – a life that
'involves friction and tension – a sense of arrest – in some degree'. From
such an insight into the nature and working of metaphors, Leavis proceeds
to analyse their impact on poetry. 'Whenever in poetry', he tells us, 'we
come on places of especially striking "concreteness" – places where the
verse has such life and body that we hardly seem to be reading arrange-
ments of words – we may expect analysis to yield notable instances of the
co-presence in complex effects of the disparate, the conflicting or the
contrasting.'

In describing the nature and working of metaphors and images in
poetry, Leavis implicitly indicates the way his own mind as a critic and a
reader of poetry works, and how what he has called 'the black marks on
the page' are something more than black marks. Much of what he says in
'Judgement and Analysis' may, therefore, be considered as constituting
the theoretical basis of Leavis' criticism of poetry which goes a long way
towards explaining what he means when he observes that 'the reading
demanded by poetry is of a different kind from that demanded by philosophy', and that 'words in poetry invite us, not to "think about" and judge
but to "feel into" or "become" – to realize a complex experience that is given
in the words'.

Leavis' theoretical observations are invariably backed by practical demonstrations and a close scrutiny of the relevant texts – his own brand of
'practical criticism' which is essentially different from that of I.A. Richards
and William Empson. Thus, for instance, his evaluations of the well-
known passage of Tourneur ('Does the silkworm expend her yellow labours

.... To bet their valours for her?'), the Keatsian lines from 'Ode on Melancholy' ('Then glut thy sorrow on a morning rose,/Or on the rainbow of the salt sand-wave,/Or on the wealth of globèd peonies'), the three sonnets by Wordsworth, 'Calais Beach', 'Surprised by Joy – Impatient as the Wind' and 'Upon Westminster Bridge', Browning's 'Meeting at Night', the first two stanzas of A.E. Housman's 'Reveille' and Edward Thomas' 'Cock-Crow' – all illustrate not only his inimitable way of reading, analysing and judging poetry, but also the kind of poetry that appeals to him.

In the chapter 'Reality and Sincerity', Alexander Smith's poem 'Barbara', Emily Brontë's 'Cold in the Earth' and Hardy's 'After a Journey' are compared with a view to forming a relative value judgement concerning their individual worth interpretable in terms of their achieving varying degrees of reality and sincerity. Alexander Smith's poem is summarily dismissed as having all the vices that are to be 'feared' in his dealing with the theme of irreparable loss. The poem does not merely 'surrender' to temptation; it goes straight for 'a sentimental debauch, an emotional wallowing', and gives the impression of '*enjoying*' its pang. By contrast, Emily Brontë's poem, in spite of the 'emotional sweep of the movement', 'declamatory plangency' and 'dangerous temptations', has 'a controlling strength' in responding to the effect of 'passionate intensity', so that when the poet says 'Then did I check the tears of useless passion', it is 'more than said; it represents an active principle that informs the poem and is there along with the plangency. We have it in the movement, in the tough prose rationality, the stating matter-of-factness of good sense, that seems to play against the dangerous running swell.'

But an even superior achievement is Hardy's poem 'After a Journey'. Unlike 'Barbara' and 'Cold in the Earth' it is non-declamatory. There is a 'convincing intimate naturalness' about it, and the poem is 'self-communing' rather than 'conversational'. Absence of declamatory manner and tone suggests 'precisions of concrete realization, specificities, complexities' which give 'After a Journey' a great advantage 'in *reality*', so that it represents 'a profounder and completer sincerity'. Prompted by the opening lines of the second stanza of the poem, 'we are', Leavis notes, 'at first inclined to say that the journey has also been a journey through time. But an essential effect of the poem is to constate, with a sharp and full realization, that we *cannot* go back in time.' His comment on the last four lines of the poem ('Trust me, I mind not, though life lours,/The bringing me here; nay, bring me here again!/I am just the same as when/Our days were a joy, and our paths through flowers') interprets their ethos and meaning through what one might call a creative paraphrase where we see Leavis' critical prose at its most delicate and evocative. Not to take the significance of that 'Trust me, I mind not', we are told, is

> to have failed to respond to the complexity of the total attitude as well as to realize the rare kind of integrity the poem achieves. It is to miss

the suggestion of paradoxical insistence, the intensity of directed feeling and will, in 'Nay, bring me here again'. For what, in the bringing me here, he may be supposed to mind is not the arduousness, for an old man, of the long journey and the ramble by night. 'To bring me here', says Hardy, 'is to make me experience to the full the desolation and the pang – to give a sharp edge to the fact of time's derision. But I don't mind – I more than don't mind: bring me here again! I hold to life, even though life as a total fact lours. The *real* for me, the focus of my affirmation, is the remembered realest thing, though to remember vividly is at the same time, inescapably, to embrace the utter loss.'

Hardy's affirmation and his sense of the void, therefore, affect us 'as real presences', testifying to the poem's rare integrity and the way it is 'the sincerest tribute to the actual woman'. The phrase 'the stars close their shutters' gives 'the right defining touch' to Hardy's attitude towards the woman – to the spirit of his cult of memory manifest 'in the stars suggesting to him, and to us, as they disappear, not sublimities and the vault of heaven, but lamplit cottage windows – associations in key with his recollections of "forty years ago". The note is intimate – with the touch of humorous fancy, it is tenderly familiar and matter-of-fact. No alchemy of idealization, no suggestion of the transcendental, no nobly imaginative self-deceiving, attends on this devotion to the woman. It is the remembered as it was that Hardy is intent on.' It is a poem, Leavis observes, that 'we recognize to have come directly out of life .... And recognizing that, we recognize the rare quality of the man who can say with that truth "I am just the same", and the rare integrity that can so put the truth beyond question. It is a case in which we know from the art what the man was like; we can be sure, that is, what personal qualities we should have found to admire in Hardy if we could have known him' – something that Leavis could have said of Hopkins, but not of Eliot; of D.H. Lawrence, but not of Pound.

In 'Prose', the fourth section of 'Judgement and Analysis', while commenting on the differences – both in terms of style and in terms of the quality of thought expressed – between a prose passage from *Blackfriars* about the Oxford Movement and Herbert Read's own metaphor-free version of that passage (in *English Prose Style*), Leavis observes: 'In eliminating them [the metaphors] Read has eliminated the writer's insistent intention – his essential thought', inasmuch as 'the evaluative attitude, explicit enough in the metaphors of the original, is an essential component of the expressed thought'. The metaphors eliminated by Read have a vital relevance, as Leavis goes on to demonstrate, to the essential thought of the *Blackfriars* passage.

He also examines a passage from *The Tale of a Tub* where Swift's prose is seen to be more intellectual in the sense that 'it demands a greater alertness of the thinking-mind in the reader'. While commenting on the intellectual power, the nature of intelligence, and the 'astonishing play' of imagery in the Swiftian passage, Leavis refers to Swift's 'hatred of life, himself and the reader' and to the way he exploits it through his mastery of style, imagery and psychological insight which contribute to his intellectual power. This power is manifested in the way in which Swift makes the reader take 'the merciless impact of this hatred and expose the unwilling self to the communicated sense of life as insufferable and its own essential being as contemptible and hateful'. Another element in Swift's passage that holds the reader in 'an apprehensive fascination' and that makes his method work so 'unfailingly' is the paradoxical and menacing intensity, 'the paradox being the co-presence in himself of a response to the relaxed rational tone and a simultaneous tone of some insane energy of animus'. Both the intensity and the energy come out in the 'brutal' insistence of the imagery which cannot be separated from the discursive movement of the prose – 'the quasi-logical way in which it runs on as if this were a matter-of-fact exposition'.

The two other prose pieces Leavis examines are by Conrad (from *A Personal Record*) and Frederick Marrayat – one of the earliest influences on Conrad. The Marrayat passage is used as a foil to Conrad's prose qualities such as 'astonishing specificity', 'freedom from cliché, 'compelling concreteness', 'particularising force' and 'the evocation of concrete thisness'. Creative art itself is identified with an exercise 'in the achieving of precision' and, at the same time, in 'the achieving of complete sincerity'. For Leavis the very act of remembering is both creative and complex, entailing, as it does, 'the evocation of concrete thisness'. The 'disciplined' act of remembering must be 'selective, and, in its re-creativity, creative, as all our achieved apprehension of the real must be'. He then goes on to compare Conrad with Lawrence and Eliot, since for all three of them to write out of the present is to write 'out of a present that is with an immensely fuller realization on their part the present of the past than is represented even by the most cultivated contemporary speech'.

The last section of 'Judgement and Analysis' is '*Antony and Cleopatra* and *All for Love*'. Even though a critic like Bonamy Dobrée considers *All for Love* to be 'a proud and lovely masterpiece ... the fine flower of Dryden's genius', Leavis finds it impossible to make 'a serious and sustained comparison' between Shakespeare's play and Dryden's. The first twenty lines of *Antony and Cleopatra* demonstrate Shakespeare's superiority over Dryden – 'superiority in concreteness, variety and sensitiveness'. As illustration, Leavis chooses the two passages from Act II, scene ii, where Enobarbus is describing the barge Cleopatra sat in 'like a burnish'd throne' and compares them with two passages from *All for Love* (Act III). The comparison shows that Shakespeare's verse seems to 'enact its meaning, to do and to give rather than to talk about, whereas Dryden's is merely a descriptive eloquence'.

As to characters, too, while commenting on the lines '... and Antony,/En-throned i' the market-place, did sit alone,/Whistling to the air' Leavis points out how Dryden's Antony could not have sat in the market-place whistling to the air:

> his dignity wouldn't have permitted it. Or rather, to ask whether he could or not is to introduce a criterion of reality in the presence of which he doesn't exist. His Cleopatra couldn't have hopped in the public street, or anywhere. His tragic *personae* exist only in a world of stage-postures; decorum gone, everything is gone.

Shakespeare's characters, on the other hand, have a life corresponding to the life of the verse; 'the life in them is, in fact, the life of the verse'. This contrasts with Dryden's accomplished verse which lends itself to stage-de-livery, 'but it is hardly poetry. It is not poetry, in the sense that it is not the product of a realizing imagination working from within a deeply and minutely felt theme. Dryden is a highly skilled craftsman, working at his job from the outside.' But even when Dryden does use a simile or a metaphor it is a simile or a metaphor with the 'like' or the 'as' left out, and the structure of the verse remains always that of 'simple, illustrative, point by point correspondence'. One analogy may give way to another, and so again, but 'the shift is always clean and obvious; there is never any complexity, confusion or ambiguity. When there is development, it is simple, lucid and rational.' By comparison, Shakespeare's metaphors are, characteristically, 'less simple, as well as less tidy' than those of Dryden. As an example, Leavis quotes what Antony says about Octavia (Act III, Scene ii).

> Her tongue will not obey her heart, nor can
> Her heart inform her tongue – the swan's down-feather,
> That stands upon the swell at full of tide,
> And neither way inclines. –

as well as the footnote in the Arden edition which runs: 'It is not clear whether Octavia's heart is the swan's down-feather, swayed neither way on the full tide of emotion at parting with her brother to accompany her husband, or whether it is the *inaction* of heart and tongue, on the same occasion, which is elliptically compared to that of the feather.' Earlier on, in the essay 'Imagery and Movement', Leavis had observed apropos of this comment: ' "It is not clear" – it ought to be clear; that is the implication.' Here he tells us that Dryden would not have left it 'not clear'. If Shake-speare's passage is 'incomparably superior' to anything Dryden could have produced, it is, among other things, because a metaphor in Shakespeare is something 'more immediate, complex and organic than neat illustrative correspondence'.

From such critical and comparative exercises in evaluative judgement and the 'practical criticism' of various poems and passages of poetry and prose, Leavis, in the last section of the book, proceeds to deal with Eliot's *Four Quartets*. His exhaustive analytical commentary is a *tour-de-force* of exploratory and evaluative criticism of the poem and, not less, of the author himself. Leavis' sense of Eliot's greatness as a poet goes hand in hand with his severely limiting judgement of Eliot's thought and personality. Thus, while interpreting the thought behind the lines from *Burnt Norton* – 'But to what purpose/Disturbing the dust on a bowl of rose-leaves/I do not know' – Leavis regards it as something abstract and general, as different from actual thinking – 'the thinking quality and force of which relate essentially, in terms of the total significance, to its being impelled by a personal need and directed by an imperative personal concern'. But analysis of Eliot's thought is tied up with Leavis' critical evaluation of Eliot's use of language – a language which conveys with creative convincingness such abstract but poetically charged entities as 'a complexity of varying and cumulative evocation', 'a sure apprehension of what he can feel to be the ultimately real', the 'unreality, the unlivingness, of life in time' and 'the vibration of a yearning suffered in inescapable remoteness'.

And yet, for all his appreciation of Eliot's poetry and his creative use of language as a discipline of thought, Leavis found Eliot's evocation of a transcendent reality, something 'antithetically and excludingly non-human', far from appealing. He considered Eliot a prisoner of 'an inescapable self-contradiction', a 'divided man' who, as a result of his inner conflict, had accepted defeat. He found him lacking, therefore, in that profoundest and completest sincerity which characterises the work of the greatest writers. What comes out, in Leavis' dealings with Eliot's work and personality, is 'a limitation of self-knowledge that he [Eliot] can't transcend; a courage that he hasn't'.

The awareness of such limitations and the 'disabling inner contradictions' in Eliot made Leavis pay him the kind of tribute that only a critic of his calibre could have paid – the tribute of 'a profoundly convinced "No"'. He saw Eliot's devotion to his art marred by his 'frustrating and untenable conception of the spiritual', and the transcendental and spiritual kind of reality postulated by Eliot not only compelled Leavis' disagreement, but also sharpened his own powers of perception and strengthened *his* 'thought, conviction and resolution'.

Leavis' commentary on *Four Quartets*, thus, probes into the meaning of the words as well as into Eliot's thought and psychology. Through his close reading of individual lines and phrases he brings out the nature and mode of Eliot's thinking expressed through such 'ostensibly impersonal propositions' as: 'What might have been is an abstraction/Remaining a perpetual possibility/Only in a world of speculation.' One particular aspect of Eliot's concern is his exploration of experience – his own experience, to begin with

– through the creative resources of the language at his command. At times this exploration leads him into 'regions of the equivocal, and the delicacies of apprehension and divination', and makes him exploit the 'creativeness' of memory, and evokes the 'mélange of actual living experience'.

But at the back of such explorations, there is, especially in 'Little Gidding', 'the motive force of repulsion' which impelled Eliot to creativity. Leavis finds this paradox 'baffling' and the 'dominance' of repulsion to be a curious trait in Eliot. While commenting on the lines – 'Except for the point, the still point,/There would be no dance, and there is only the dance' – Leavis demonstrates how 'the insisted-on association of "dance" with the "still point" is essential to the significance of the "pattern" and to the "release" it brings'. Both the sense of pattern and the sense of release appertain to Eliot's spiritual reality. But for a reader and a critic like Leavis, Eliot's notion of reality leaves many questions unanswered – questions to which, he remarks, we ought, ultimately, to find answers. For example, what is the relation between 'the still point' and 'the dance' (or 'pattern')? Leavis deals with this question in terms of Eliot's 'preoccupation with establishing an apprehension of, and so an assured relation with, eternal reality'. But this itself leads to a contradiction insofar as 'the ultimately really real that Eliot seeks in *Four Quartets* is eternal reality, and *that* he can do little, directly, to characterize'. And yet, in order to achieve the unachievable, as it were, Eliot uses the everyday physical world as a 'springy *pied-à-terre* for the quick inevitable glide into the spiritual realm', the realm in which 'the expectations sorting with common-sense matter-of-fact are left behind'. Creative suggestion and 'analogical pregnancies' are seen to be part of the Eliotic process of exploring the spiritual reality and creating the concept of eternity. However, neither Eliot's concept of spiritual reality nor his concept of eternity nor his attitude to time, convinces or appeals to Leavis for whom 'an attitude towards time is an attitude towards life'. Hence his adverse view of Eliot's attitude to time and to reality.

In a certain way, therefore, one can say that in Leavis' commentary on *Four Quartets*, what is under scrutiny is not only what Eliot believes and is, but also what Leavis *himself* believes and is. In this respect Leavis' criticism of Eliot is 'personal' and *has* 'an axe to grind', as is borne out by his comment on what seems to him to come from 'the heart of the poem – from, that is, the essential Eliot himself ':

> Go, go, go, said the bird: human kind
> Cannot bear very much reality.

This, according to Leavis, implies a concept of reality and a 'perverse' judgement of human kind that he cannot but repudiate. It also implies 'a suggestion of failure on the part of human kind, the paradox being that of *cannot but ought*'. Of such a comment too, one can, paraphrasing Leavis, say that it comes from the heart of Leavis' criticism – from, that is, the essential Leavis himself. And so does his distaste for Eliot's opposing of consciousness to flesh – of spirit to body – for his preoccupation with eternity, and for the attitude it seems to entail towards time. Thus, more than any other poem of modern times, it is *Four Quartets* that raises for Leavis the questions: how must reality be conceived and what is the nature of the human situation? It raises them in such a way as to compel one to 'determine and verify one's own ultimate beliefs'. That is why Leavis has no hesitation in asserting that his answers to those questions are not Eliot's, and he goes on to elaborate the difference between himself and Eliot in terms of what any poem in question means to the poet and what it means to the reader:

> But the difference between me and Eliot insists on itself immediately as immense. The poem, the real poem as opposed to the black marks on the page, exists, I should say, in the third realm, which is spiritual. And when I say 'spiritual' I am not thinking of spirit (or mind or 'consciousness') as something that is to be set over against body as its antithesis. The minds that meet in the poem are the minds of persons who have tongues and vocal organs together with the bodies these imply. But for the fact that minds are the minds of bodies there could have been no poem – there could have been no meaning and no communication. When I say that the poem, the real and living poem, is 'there' between us I think of it as the type of that collaboratively created and sustained reality, the human world, without which there could have been no significance, and no spiritual problem to be explored.

As for the way the poem (*Four Quartets*) relates to time, Leavis again takes issue with Eliot for suggesting that it represents a liberation from 'the enchainment of past and future'; in other words, an escape from time. Far from being an escape from time, however, the poem, insofar as it is a manifestation of language, is part of its 'immemorial living process ... exemplifying the essential part time has had, and has, in the life that, having become conscious, capable of responsibility and given to thinking, inquires into its own meaning'. In postulating that those who are alive have only one aim – i.e. to experience the moment which is 'in and out of time', and to be 'conscious' which is 'not to be in time' – Eliot merely insists on 'the unreality, the unlivingness' of life in time. How could, Leavis asks, spiritual reality, for the apprehending of which Eliot uses the word conscious, '*be* a reality for us, or anything but a conventionally empty phrase, unless apprehended out of life, in which we are, and in terms of our human livingness?'

Leavis' critique of the poetry of *Four Quartets*, thus, inevitably turns into a critique of the substance and structure of Eliot's thought as well as

of the logic behind that thought, which often appears to be illusory. And
the same may be said of the succession of the 'discursively stated paradoxes' such as 'the end precedes the beginning/And the end and the
beginning were always there/Before the beginning and after the end./And
all is always now'. With a strikingly firm analytical grip on the concrete,
Leavis describes the illusory nature of such successions.

> A local and limited intensity of thought again and again there
> certainly is; but the subtly marshalled complexity of movement that
> offers to have enclosed, and presented for our contemplation, an
> unstable transcendent reality is marshalled, not by the promptings
> of a supremely apprehensive and confident *ahnung*, but merely by an
> insistent intention, the intensity of which is the intensity of the poet's
> need.

As to the line 'And all is always now', he tells us how

> The explicitness of this is spectral; the air of meaning something, and
> something supremely important, is merely an air. All the discredit-
> ing of clock-time and common sense that Eliot's peculiar poetic
> genius has achieved, and all the creative play with memory, have,
> between them, done nothing to make the spectral anything but a
> personal plight disguised – and betrayed.

Leavis' assessment of Eliot's art and Eliot's personality is, to some extent,
conditioned by Eliot's dictum that 'the more perfect the artist, the more
completely separate in him will be the man who suffers and the mind
which creates'. As a general notion Leavis does not accept it, but it might
well have been true of Eliot himself, whose technique not only lacks logic
and demonstrative cogency, but is not the kind of technique that means
sincerity. Hence Leavis calls Eliot's genius paradoxical, insofar as it was
the genius of a major poet who had 'disabling contradictions to struggle
against'. His achievement, therefore, brings out both 'the unquestionable-
ness of the genius and the frustrations that life suffered in him'. The
co-presence of these two elements makes Eliot's 'involuntary testimony
challenging in a highly significant way', inasmuch as the 'consideration of
the plight his poetry reveals sharpens our understanding of our civilization'.

And yet what Eliot asserts about his spiritual quest is, for Leavis, 'worth
little', his 'painfully developed or enforced offer of apprehension' is illusory,
and the real to be apprehended is 'nothing'. Commenting on what he calls
the 'magnificent piece of Eliotic poetry' (in the third section of 'East
Coker'), and especially on the lines 'And you see behind every face the
mental emptiness deepen/Leaving only the growing terror of nothing to
think about', Leavis observes: 'The terror of nothingness ... is Eliot's own;

he brings it from the funeral where "there is no one to bury" ... it brings out a distinctive trait of Eliot's: his inner conflict, with the accompanying insecurity, entails an uncertainty, a limitedness and a lack of imaginative penetration in his awareness of other people. It is an aspect of the limitedness of his sense of the human world.' That is why 'East Coker' is much more personal than 'Burnt Norton' – personal like *The Waste Land* which depicts not the 'waste land' of western man, but 'the peculiar personal "waste land" of T.S. Eliot, who (inevitably, one may say) assumed it to be, in its significance, representatively human'. Still *Four Quartets* has for Leavis, and in a much greater degree than *The Waste Land* or 'The Hollow Men', 'a rare kind of value', providing us, as it does, 'with an incomparable study of what, in its most serious use, is meant by "sincerity" – a word we cannot do without'. But judging poetry to be sincere does not mean for Leavis endorsing it. That is why, while commenting on the passage from the fifth section of 'East Coker' –

And what there is to conquer
By strength and submission, has already been discovered
Once or twice, or several times, by men whom one cannot hope
To emulate – but there is no competition –
There is only the fight to recover what has been lost
And found and lost again and again: and now, under conditions
That seem unpropitious. –

Leavis refers to the 'completely anti-Blakean' nature of Eliot's sense of the human relation to that reality of which 'human kind cannot bear very much'. But such a relation either to reality or to men whom 'one cannot hope to emulate' is 'a non-relation'. For, even if humanity has depended and depends on such men, their genius itself cannot but depend on their humanity, since in the exercise of their genius, they are dependent on 'collaboratively creative human continuity' exemplified by Eliot's own dependence on the English language. Hence, so far as Leavis is concerned, both what Eliot vindicates as the 'spiritual' and his notion of reality amount to no more than 'a vacuum'.

However, he distinguishes Eliot's conception of reality as such, and 'the irresistible realness of the evoked world'; as, for instance, in the first movement of 'The Dry Salvages' where Eliot is concerned with the essential human condition. But even here, the 'basic creative drive' in Eliot is still desperation. The second movement of 'The Dry Salvages' has for its theme 'the goallessness', and for its drive the 'obsessed recoil' from it. And yet, for all his self-contradiction, his equivocations, his sense of deprivation, his hunger, Eliot's desperation is 'the desperation of the sophisticated', since Eliot is, according to Leavis, even more sophisticated than Yeats.

Coming to the third movement of 'The Dry Salvages', where Krishna, with his admonition to Arjuna on the field of battle, is brought in, Leavis again takes Eliot to task for what he says in the lines 'Consider the future/And the past with an equal mind' and 'the moment which is not of action or inaction'. Far from thinking his own thought, however, Eliot seems to be merely transcribing poetically in these lines what he found in *The Bhagavad-Gita*, and which, far from being an example of 'not easily intelligible subtlety' is, in Leavis' own words, a 'profound impersonal constatation of indisputable truth'. In fact, together with a given Christian tradition to which Eliot's convictions and his concept of reality belong, there is also Indian philosophy, and especially *The Bhagavad-Gita* which contributed in no small measure to the formation of Eliot's religious beliefs and to his moral and philosophical thought and sensibility. For instance, the occupation, as Leavis sees it, of Eliot's saint – his 'rigorous self-confinement, the identity's self-reduction to purely passive receptivity' and his realising, in his own person, both 'the abject nullity of human kind' and 'the pure otherness' in his conception of the supreme 'Real' – is also the occupation or one of the occupations of the perfect Yogi as preached in *The Bhagavad-Gita* and in other classics of Indian philosophy with which Eliot was familiar. Leavis' antipathy to Eliot's view of the supreme Real, and implicitly to the Indian philosophical tradition, is at least partly due to the fact that he sees in Eliot's conception of 'the pure otherness' an antithesis to the real in human terms, to 'the irresistible realness of ... world' that Eliot himself evokes in *Four Quartets*.

As to Leavis' charge against Eliot – 'his inescapable dividedness' which amounts to 'an incapacitating malady' and his capacity for deception and evasion – it can, in a way, be seen as a blessing in disguise, in so far as it gives his poetry 'a penetration, a subtlety and a memorableness in relation to very important regions of human experience', even though his limitations and disabilities prevent him from achieving what Leavis calls 'a completeness and clarity of insight into himself'.

'Little Gidding', Leavis finds on the whole poetically inferior, with the exception of the 'terza rima' passage where Eliot is seen to be as 'unquestionably major' as anywhere in his *oeuvre*. What impresses Leavis is the vivid precision with which the sinister reality of bombed London is evoked; the organic complexity of the passage; the uncanny silence foreboding destruction and death. But it is not the mode of evocation of the real as such, or the metaphorical life and the organic complexity of the Dantesque narrative passage that alone matter; it is also, and above all the evocation, 'without the usual evasiveness', of the reality of what Eliot himself is. If, by making the 'supremely Real a vacuum', Eliot has committed himself 'to a frustrating self-contradiction as a man is committed to prison', in this 'magnificent' passage, he comes near to escaping. It is too late for Eliot, Leavis argues, to tell himself that, for all the paradoxes of his profound self-contradiction, 'he has always been committed to creativity, and creativity belongs, in terms of the Blakean distinction, to the identity. But he

knows now that he has a desperate need to overcome shame; he cannot, in
the Dantescan moment of the "All Clear", *not* know that.' While describing
the last of 'the gifts reserved for age', Eliot himself refers to the sense of
shame thus:

> ... the rending pain of re-enactment
> Of all that you have done, and been; the shame
> Of motives late revealed, and the awareness
> Of things ill done and done to others' harm
> Which once you took for exercise of virtue.

Here, in its diagnostic probing and merciless finality, is Leavis' conclusive
comment:

> But there will be no permanent escape from prison; the unequivocal
> recognition of motives late revealed and of things ill done and done
> to others' harm won't be maintained. Human kind cannot bear very
> much burning shame, and the exercise of Eliot's genius has entailed
> the intensive practice of a subtlety that makes the self-recognition
> required of him peculiarly difficult.

The 'burning shame' itself is not felt as burning, or as shame at all. It is not,
Leavis tells us, 'one of the "fires" sternly confronted as possibilities in IV':

> The only hope, or else despair
> Lies in the choice of pyre and pyre –
> To be redeemed from fire by fire.

   Although Eliot's poetry in general, and *Four Quartets* in particular,
rendered a great service to life and humanity by exposing 'the disastrous-
ness of today's triumphant philistinism', his solution in terms of humility,
renunciation and expiation is not, according to Leavis, the answer. And
yet if *Four Quartets* repays 'a close and sympathetic study', it is because
'the defeated genius *is* a genius, and the creative power is inseparable from
the significance of the defeat'. Eliot may have been a divided man – and
Leavis' recurrent insistence on that datum is crucial to his criticism of
Eliot – but his undertaking in *Four Quartets* and what it represents and
achieves, are something to which 'no undivided man could have lent
himself'.

Thought, Words and Creativity

That Lawrence, together with Eliot, should have been the central force
behind Leavis' writings as well as behind his own development as a critic
is borne out by the fact that on no other modern writers has he written so

often and with such a sense of commitment. But it was Lawrence – not Eliot – who commanded his unqualified moral esteem as well as critical admiration, so much so that having written *D.H. Lawrence: Novelist* (1955) – one of his best books – he felt the need to write another: *Thought, Words and Creativity: Art and Thought in Lawrence* (1976). In both books *The Plumed Serpent*, *Women in Love*, 'The Captain's Doll' and *The Rainbow* are accorded pride of place as being peculiarly illustrative of Lawrence's genius. Leavis had obviously been re-reading these books and pondering on their significance, in terms both of Lawrence's art and thought, and of the way they interacted, especially in dealing with the 'frightening' problems of modern civilisation. In *Thought, Words and Creativity*, while analysing that thought, there is no attempt on Leavis' part to be exhaustive – something that would 'exhaust and bore the reader', and that, whether one agrees with him or not, one can never say of Leavis. Moreover, his analytical exposition of Lawrence's thought and his evaluation of it is reinforced by his own preoccupation with 'the confident materialism of a technologico-Benthamite civilization' and the 'spiritual philistinism' of our times which was also Matthew Arnold's and Lawrence's. Thus, in the last book published a couple of years before his death, Leavis' role as a critic of literature clearly becomes indistinguishable from his role as a critic of the problems of the civilisation and society of his time and their relation to 'art, being and culture'. What the book purports to do, as Leavis himself indicated in the blurb he was requested by Ian Parsons to suggest, is 'to illustrate and reinforce the implicit argument – the essential logic and intention – of *The Living Principle*'. The book carries three epigraphs: one from Ortega Y Gasset ('It is not the fact of judging rightly or wrongly – truth is not within our research – but the lack of scruple which makes them omit the elementary requirements for right judgement'); one from P.T. Bauer ('Such a result is the logical outcome of Professor Myrdal's conception of man and society. By decrying cultural, ethnic, religious and economic differences, and unceasingly inveighing against discrimination, he seeks to build a society which is profoundly dehumanized'); and one from D.H. Lawrence ('Man or woman, each is a flow, a flowing life, and without one another, we can't flow, just as a river cannot flow without banks. A woman is one bank of the river of my life, and the world is the other').

In the first chapter, 'Thought, Words and Creativity', while reiterating his dismissal of Eliot's view of Lawrence as one 'incapable of what is ordinarily called thinking' and ignorant in the sense that 'he was unaware of how much he did not know', Leavis sets out to assess how Lawrence's thought, in its originality, is inseparable from his art. That is why its impact is as strong in *Women in Love* as in *Psychoanalysis and the Unconscious*, since both the works derive from the one vital intelligence and the one achieved wholeness of individual being. Quoting Lawrence to the effect that 'it was the greatest pity in the world, when philosophy and fiction got split like a nagging married couple, with Aristotle and Thomas Aquinas and that beastly Kant', and the novel 'went sloppy, and philosophy went abstract-dry', Leavis demonstrates how in Lawrence's work, and particularly in these two novels, they 'come together again'. For, in spite of his distaste for 'the kind of intellectuality that starts, as so much philosophical writing does, from a mathematico-logical assumption about the criteria of valid thought', Lawrence brilliantly succeeded in integrating philosophy and fiction in his novels. That is why in defining and characterising the hall-mark of his art Leavis repeatedly uses the word 'thought'. And creative writing being in question, analysis of Lawrence's thought inevitably leads to analysis of his language and of the underlying meaning. That he wrote in English, a language 'waiting quick and ready for him', was an additional boon for Lawrence, enabling him to think and communicate his thought creatively.

In analysing and evaluating Lawrence's thought – 'thought, lived and living thought – for there is nothing else to resort to' – Leavis achieves his own thinking – the thinking of one who calls himself 'an anti-philosopher'. With 'the embracing organic totality of Lawrence's thought' in mind, Leavis compares Lawrence with Blake, since for both of them 'the notion of thought as something apart from the creative writer's creativity' was something meaningless. Hence Lawrence's distaste for 'the kind of intellectuality that starts, as so much philosophical writing does, from a mathematico-logical assumption about the criteria of valid thought'. The nature of Lawrence's thought and how it merges with his criticism of life as well as with his criticism of the civilisation of his time – and for Leavis 'the civilization he diagnosed is ours' – is a theme ubiquitously tackled in *Thought, Words and Creativity*. Here are some of Lawrence's key thoughts analytically commented on by Leavis. 'It's the hardest thing in the world', says Birkin, for instance, 'to act spontaneously on one's impulses – and it's the only gentlemanly thing to do – provided you're fit to do so.' 'The world of art', remarks Ursula, 'is only the truth about the real world, that's all.' And Hannele: 'You could call it an illusion if you liked. But an illusion which is a real experience is worth having. Perhaps this disillusion of life was falser than brief moments of real illusion.' And Alexander: 'If a woman loves you, she'll make a doll out of you. She'll never be satisfied till she's made your doll. And when she's got your doll, that's all she wants. And that's what love means.' And then there are Lawrence's own dicta: 'At the maximum of our imagination we are religious'; 'Nothing is important but life', 'Art-speech' is the only speech and so on.

Such thoughts – and they are applicable to and present in Lawrence's work as a whole, so that what Leavis says of 'The Captain's Doll' ('The tale itself *is* the thought') may be said of all his great novels and tales – condition as well as inspire Leavis' own views, moral and philosophical as well as critical. His re-reading of *The Plumed Serpent*, *Women in Love*, 'The Captain's Doll' and *The Rainbow* reinforces and reconfirms his past

critical reactions and judgements now reformulated within a new context
and in terms of his present preoccupations. For instance, he tells us of *The
Plumed Serpent* – 'a novel by a great novelist' – that it contains 'abundant
evidence of the great writer who wrote it; and in the course of my recent
re-readings I have filled a large part of a notebook with felicities of thought
– formulations that belong distinctively to a novelist's creativity and that
one would wish to have ready in one's mind to use'. However, notwith-
standing this, he found *The Plumed Serpent* unsatisfactory.

In *Women in Love*, on the other hand, Lawrence's creativity, 'like that
of all great writers', manifests itself 'in new shades of suggestion, new
felicities of force, got out of the common language – in (we feel) an inspired
way, rather than by calculating intention'. Leavis quotes relevant passages to illustrate this as well to bring out the 'unity', the 'coherent organic
and comprehensive totality' of Lawrence's thought – concerned, among
other things, with the relation of art to life, or the place of art *in* life. Both
what the novel sets out to do and the creatively realised thought behind it
are 'inexhaustibly complex and pregnant'. Part of that complexity is
Lawrence's treatment of, and Leavis' diagnostic comment on, Thomas
Crich's religion – the religion of compassion. For Lawrence, such a religion
'ignored, and in ignoring, outraged something that has its part in any truly
basic, any profound and lastingly satisfying attitude in the face of cosmos'.
To explain what this something was, Leavis quotes two passages where
'thought and art are triumphantly one in the exposure of Thomas Crich's
"philanthropy" as a dominant mode of egoism in him, a self-centred
indulgence belonging to the enclosed ego'. His egoism and will are 'revealed as such in the manner, rendered dramatically, of his clinging to life
when plainly dying'; and Lawrence's mastery of his 'art-as-thought is
manifested in the impossibility of separating what is itself expository
Laurentian comment from the relevant directly dramatic presentment –
about the impossibility of fixing imaginatively a line between them'.

When Birkin asks Gerald 'Then wherein does life centre for you?' (if not
in 'the love between you and a woman') – and Gerald answers 'I don't know
– that's what I want somebody to tell me. As far as I can make out, it
doesn't centre at all. It is artificially held *together* by the social mechanism', Leavis considers the answer to be 'still a modern answer – the real
and unusually intelligent modern answer', and emphasises 'the rightness
and supreme importance of the way Lawrence associates – rather, makes
inseparably one – the question, or problem, "What ultimately for?" and the
problem of love; or rather the problem of finding the right answers, the
humanly most satisfying answers, to serious self-questioning about the
relation between individual women and individual men'. Birkin and Ursula, as a pair, are played against Gerald and Gudrun in 'the total thought'
of *Women in Love* – the thought that 'completes itself in Gerald's death in
the snow-world'. Leavis' comment on Ursula's demand for love – because
only love can justify marriage – is indicative of a suggestive fusion in his

criticism between critical and psychological insight and moral perception and certitude which he brings to bear on his 'reading' of Lawrence's masterpiece. Only love, real love, can justify marriage, he tells us, 'but, there being no such thing as "perfect love", the essential marriage-understanding is that the relationship between the two individual beings shall be permanent, transcending change'. Such a realisation on Ursula's part makes her different from Gudrun: Ursula who had for husband 'a man whose individual life was open to the deep source, to the unknown, and who had his part in the creativity that kept civilization rooted and changing – that is alive. But he couldn't have been that without her' – a comment the veracity of which is rooted in a moral conviction which Leavis implicitly shares with Lawrence.

In the chapter on 'The Captain's Doll' – an extraordinarily subtle and illuminatingly 'personal' reading of the work – Lawrence's importance as a novelist is measured also in terms of his importance to our civilisation which 'desperately lacks the thought it has lost the power even to recognise *as* thought – the thought that entails the creative writer's kind of creativity' and that cannot be abstracted from its creatively charged context.

Leavis quotes the various bits of the dialogue between the Captain and Hannele, with his own critical and elucidatory comments thrown in between. 'The friction between them', he tells us, 'and their manner of conveying it imply that they matter to one another as profoundly as a man and a woman can. They are intimate with a reality far more real than the intimacy of a pair of lovers intoxicated with the passion of adoring love. The running altercation between them is that of a man and a woman who essentially *want* to justify their feeling that, between them, they have the qualities that might go to form a permanent union of the right kind. The trouble of course is that they differ as to what the right kind is.' Both Hannele's demand for 'love on equal terms' and the doll Leavis interprets to be 'expressions of the female ego: the flatteringness of the doll and the plausibility of the demand are specious; they cover resentment at the male strength that went with the mystery in Alexander – the profound vital maleness that Hannele, in her complex reaction, so admired in him and that made her at the root of herself, for all his disconcertingness, trust him as she did'. While writing in this vein, so closely interfused is his own thinking with Lawrence's, Leavis at times gives the impression of writing parts of the novel himself. And the conclusion of his creatively 'personal' commentary on the dialogue between Hannele and Alexander is at once Laurentian and Leavisian:

> She came (but pulled up) to the brink of marrying the Herr Regierungsrat because his way of kissing her had made her feel 'like a queen in exile'. But when the Captain reappears her profounder being at once decides for *him* .... The friction and running altercation

confirm in him the lesson of the 'love'-marriage with the little lady; it is for the man in especial to cultivate the singleness and to devote himself to some creative purpose that the deeper, the non-ego promptings of his individuality impel him to, or there will be no prosperous final union.

10

On Critics and Criticism

I *am* damned critical – for it's the only thing to be, and all else is
damned humbug.

Henry James

It's only when a few men who know, get together and *disagree* that any
sort of criticism is born.

Ezra Pound

Since as early as 1959-60 Leavis had been thinking of writing and finishing one particular book more than any other. It was provisionally called
The Function of Criticism, and was to include his essays on Johnson,
Coleridge, Matthew Arnold, Henry James, D.H. Lawrence and T.S. Eliot
as critics. He was to add a couple of chapters 'making it really a book –
quintessential, concentrated, presenting an Idea, and (in my way) not an
abstract one'. In fact, it was to be a book, and not a collection of essays.

Such a book, however, was never achieved, and all we have are his
separate essays on these critics in which, to use Eliot's phrase, he is
criticising the critic from the point of view both of the intrinsic worth of
their criticism and of its relevance today. Some of these essays were
originally published in *Scrutiny* and later included in Leavis' books.
'Johnson as a Critic', 'Coleridge in Criticism' and 'Arnold as a Critic'
appeared in *Scrutiny* (vols. XII, IX and VII respectively); 'T.S. Eliot as
Critic' appeared in *Commentary*, and 'James as Critic' was published as
Introduction to *Henry James: Selected Literary Criticism*, edited by Morris
Shapira, in 1957. The Johnson and Eliot essays are now to be found in
'Anna Karenina' and Other Essays; and the Coleridge, Arnold and James
essays in *The Critic as Anti-Philosopher* (1982).

Leavis brought to bear upon his examination of critics and criticism the
same spirit of disinterested scrutiny and evaluation as informed his
treatment of creative writers. Being at once more searching and more
forthright than Eliot, if he values Johnson more than Dryden, it is because
Johnson's critical writings are living literature the way Dryden's (*pace*
T.S. Eliot) are not: 'they compel, and they repay, a real and disinterested
reading, that full attention of the judging mind which is so different an
affair from a familiar kind of homage'.

For Leavis, Johnson's importance as a critic does not lie in what he says about the particular authors with which he is dealing; nor in any instruction to be derived from his critical thinking. It lies in the vigour and weight of Johnson's writings – 'the vigour that comes from a powerful mind and a profoundly serious nature, and the weight that seems to be a matter of bringing to bear at every point the ordered experience of a lifetime'. Leavis examines Johnson's limitations in order to offset them against what is both valid and original in his criticism. For instance, while commenting on his 'defective ear', he goes on to show how it was the product of a training in a positive taste. But Johnson's limitations as a critic of Shakespeare are more disabling and more revealing; for instance, 'his radically undramatic habit' and 'his bondage to moralistic fallacy' which makes him censure Shakespeare's indifference to poetic justice and Shakespeare's general carelessness about the duty to instruct. Such limitations, in Leavis' view, prevent Johnson from appreciating the poetry, as a result of which he cannot appreciate Shakespeare's dramatic organisation. He cannot appreciate 'the ways in which not only Shakespeare's drama but all works of art act their moral judgements. For Johnson a thing is stated, or it isn't there.'

Another limitation in Johnson as a critic of Shakespeare is the fact that his mind and sensibility were formed in and through a language which was utterly unlike Shakespeare's. In commenting on this limitation, and all that it implies, Leavis brings out his own attitude to Shakespeare's art and poetry, so that his diagnosis of Johnson's limitations, with their 'positive correlations', becomes, to some extent, a diagnosis of Leavis' own critical tenets, criteria and attitudes.

But when it comes to the eighteenth-century poetry, Leavis finds Johnson a better critic than Arnold; being himself trained 'in so positive a tradition' as Arnold was not. Johnson's 'rational vigour', coupled with his 'constant and uncompromising' recourse to experience, which is so 'subversive of Neo-classic authority', accounts for the fact that his criticism does 'the best that criticism can do before Coleridge'.

In spite of his 'rarely gifted mind', Leavis finds Coleridge's 'producible achievement ... disappointingly incommensurate'. And for all his interest in theoretical philosophy of art, his criticism remains at a level where it is not likely to improve one's 'capacity and equipment for dealing critically with works of literature'. His very prestige owes a great deal to 'the transcendental aura' and his being accepted as a master of theoretical criticism is largely due to 'an awed vagueness' concerning his philosophy. Even his interest in metaphysics, poetry and facts of mind – his 'darling studies', as he called them – amounts, in terms of literary criticism, to no more than 'an impressive array of characteristic utterances and formulas'. These, no doubt, demonstrate Coleridge's qualifications for a great achievement in criticism. But while the qualifications are obvious, the achievement itself, as such, 'isn't readily sized up'. His case, like Dryden's, proves once again that 'a critic may have an important place in history and

yet not be very interesting in his writings'. Leavis finds the Fancy-Imagi-
nation contrast in Coleridge is useful only insofar as it calls attention to
'the organic complexities of verbal life, metaphorical and other', as well as
illustrating Coleridge's gift for critical analysis and his capacity for 'a kind
of sensitive analytic penetration such as will hardly be found in any other
critic'. Even his Shakespeare criticism is not so much achievement as
evidence of 'a critical endowment that *ought* to have achieved something
remarkable'. The two chapters on Wordsworth in *Biographia Literaria*, on
the other hand, are 'a classical document' at least partly for historical
reasons, because 'Coleridge on Wordsworth is Coleridge on Wordsworth,
and not because of achieved criticism of high order contained in them'.
While analysing the unsatisfactory nature of *Biographia Literaria* – 'the
disorderliness, the lack of all organisation or sustained development' –
Leavis analyses Coleridge's own unsatisfactoriness: his failure, even in
the best places, 'to bring his thought to a sharp edge' and his being 'content
with easy expression'. Expression, says Leavis, 'came, in fact, too easily to
him; for a man of his deep constitutional disinclination to brace himself to
sustained work at any given undertaking, his articulateness was fatal. He
could go down to the lecture-hall at the last minute with a marked copy of
Shakespeare and talk – talk much as he talked anywhere and at any time.'

It is, however, Chapter XV of *Biographia Literaria* that shows Coleridge
at his best – Coleridge who had devoted 'his finest powers of sensibility
and intelligence to the poetry of his own language'. Leavis quotes the
passage dealing with 'Venus and Adonis' as an example of 'a fine piece of
practical criticism' – there being nowhere in Coleridge 'anything more
impressively to be found than that'.

Nevertheless, Leavis draws the 'depressing' conclusion that Coleridge's
currency as an academic classic is 'something of a scandal', whatever plea
I.A. Richards, in *Coleridge on Imagination*, might make for recognition of
him as a critic and an original thinker. And though he was very much more
brilliantly gifted than Arnold, 'nothing of his deserves the classical status
of Arnold's best work'.

And yet, while examining even Arnold, though he admires him for his
plea for critical intelligence and critical standards, Leavis finds 'critical
justice towards him oddly difficult to arrive at'. In dealing with him, he
has Eliot's assessment of Arnold, especially in *The Use of Poetry and the
Use of Criticism*, in the background. It is at least partly through his
disagreement with Eliot that he makes his point, bringing out Arnold's
validity and relevance as a critic and his right to be regarded as a great
critic – 'an extraordinarily distinguished mind in complete possession of
its purpose and pursuing it with easy mastery'. Whatever Arnold's limitations – of which Leavis is no less conscious than Eliot – he finds Arnold's
critical writing, as that of no other English critic before him, to be
'compellingly alive', and Arnold himself 'more of a critic than the Sainte-

Beuve to whom he so deferred' or than Dryden who is read, if at all, only
because of his place in literary history.

As regards Eliot's charge that Arnold was apt to think of the greatness
of poetry rather than of its genuineness, and that the notion 'art for art's
sake' derived from Arnold's 'criticism of life', Leavis points out that

> the evaluation of poetry as 'criticism of life' is inseparable from its
> evaluation as poetry; that the moral judgement that concerns us as
> critics must be at the same time a delicately relevant response of
> sensibility; that, in short, we cannot separate the consideration of
> 'greatness' from the consideration of 'genuineness'.

While assessing Arnold's position as a critic, Leavis, in a way, outlines
his own which, in some fundamental respects, was similar to Arnold's.
Instead of the 'gift for consistency or for definition', in which Eliot found
Arnold lacking, he has, according to Leavis,

> certain positive virtues; tact and delicacy, a habit of keeping in
> sensitive touch with the concrete, and an accompanying gift for
> implicit definition – virtues that prove adequate to the sure and easy
> management of a sustained argument and are, as we see them in
> Arnold, essentially those of a literary critic.

'The Function of Criticism at the Present Time' and 'The Literary
Influence of Academies' are for Leavis 'classical presentment of their
themes' and show Arnold 'at his strongest', with their 'memorable formulations of classical rightness'. Formulations such as 'a very small circle ...
resolutely doing its own work', 'deference to a standard higher than one's
own habitual standard in intellectual matters', a 'centre of intelligence and
urbane spirit', or 'a force of cultivated opinion' for a critic to appeal to,
anticipate Leavis' own concern with minority culture, educated public and
standards of criticism. And yet even these essays, in the absence of 'any
very taut or subtle development of an argument or any rigour of definition',
are no more than higher pamphleteering, although such a pamphleteering
'has lost little of its force and relevance with the passage of time'. But
where Arnold manifests his 'notable qualifications in criticism' is in his
judgement on the Romantics as well as in the essay 'The Study of Poetry'.
Leavis claims classical status for this essay because it performs what it
undertakes to do 'so consummately' and with 'vigorously independent
intelligence'. He, like Eliot, has no use for Arnold as a theological or
philosophical thinker, but he finds his best work to be that of a literary
critic, even when it is not literary criticism. It comes 'from an intelligence
that, even if not trained to some kinds of rigour, had its own discipline; an
intelligence that is informed by a mature and delicate sense of the humane
values and can manifest itself directly as a fine sensibility'. Discipline,

intelligence and sensibility – these are words that would aptly characterise the ethos of Leavis' own criticism, and that Leavis himself will use
frequently.

In commenting on the best-known tag from 'The Study of Poetry'
('criticism of life'), Leavis does not so much defend Arnold as clarify what
he really intended. He intended, not to define poetry, but, 'while insisting
(a main concern of the essay) that there are different degrees of importance in poetry, to remind us of the nature of the criteria by which
comparative judgements are made'. Similarly, while commenting on Arnold's critical tip, the 'touchstone', Leavis elucidates the intent behind it;
namely, that of 'mobilizing our sensibility ... focusing our relevant experience in a sensitive point ... reminding us vividly of what the best is like'.
In 'The Study of Poetry', if Arnold speaks with 'economy and authority', it
is because his critical position is 'firmly based', because he knows what he
is setting out to do, and because he is 'master of the appropriate method',
with his habit of 'keeping in sensitive touch with the concrete, and an
accompanying gift for implicit definition'.

Of the value of the other essays by Arnold Leavis is sceptical in varying
degrees. The 'Gray' dates most of all and 'dates in the most damaging
sense'; neither the 'Keats' nor the 'Shelley' 'makes any show of being a
model critique of poetry', even though 'the rarely gifted literary critic is
apparent in them'. On Keats, Leavis finds Arnold 'extraordinarily just, in
appreciation both of the achievement and of the potentiality'. The
'Wordsworth', with all its limitations, is rated to be a 'distinguished
personal estimate', with its 'salutary firmness about the "philosophy" '.
Leavis also underlines the importance of Arnold's 'relative valuation' of
the great Romantics: Wordsworth first, then Byron '(and for the right
reasons)', then Keats and, last, Shelley, a valuation which, 'in its inde-
pendence and its soundness', is 'a more remarkable critical achievement
than we easily recognize today'. In the essay 'On Translating Homer', too,
the actual achievement in terms of producible criticism may not be very
impressive, but, Leavis observes, 'we had better inquire where a more
impressive is to be found'.

After Arnold, the critics that mattered most to Leavis are Henry James,
D.H. Lawrence and Eliot. For Leavis, Henry James' standing as a critic is
tied up with his creative achievement as a novelist. However, he does not
set much store by James' *Prefaces*. It is not only that it requires a great
effort to read them, but the effort itself is not rewarding. 'Those academics', Leavis tells us, 'who take seriously the suggestion that it is the
novelist's *vade mecum* will indeed be drawing from it an academicism'
which means 'a misdirection and ... a corvée'. Nevertheless Leavis accords
James a high place among the classical critics, not only because of his
distinguished critical intelligence regarding his own art, but also because
he handled the theme of morality and art, refuted Aestheticism, challenged the Flaubertian exaltation of art and conveyed 'his charged sense

that the creativity of art is the creativity of life – that the creative impulse *is* life, and could be nothing else'.

But James is seen at his best as a critic in his dealings with Maupassant, Flaubert and Balzac. If Leavis finds James' evaluation of Flaubert 'sympathetic, grateful, admiring, full of piety, but inexorable in its limiting judgement', it is because of 'the close relevance, the essential economy, the combined trenchancy and suppleness, the sensitiveness and the penetration' that characterise it – qualities that Leavis himself aspired to in his criticism, and, to a large degree, achieved.

Underlying James' criticism throughout, Leavis notes that sense of the human significance of art as well as of the inevitable relevance of moral judgement to art which is so central to his own criticism. For James as well as for Leavis, 'there is no eliminating and no escaping the appeal to life, however one may suppose oneself to believe (as Flaubert did) in the ultimateness or self-sufficiency of art'. That is why, apropos of *Madame Bovary*, Leavis could well say that 'the default of intelligence in the artist as artist *is* a default of intelligence about life' – a neat refutation not only of Flaubert's aestheticism, but also of art as conceived by a cynic-sensualist like Maupassant, with its 'sadly limited range of interests', and leaving so much of life out. But for James, as for Leavis himself, 'the work that commands the reader's most deeply engaged, the critic's most serious, attention asks at a deep level: "what, at bottom, do men live *for*?" '

In Balzac's case, too, what James admires – 'the portentous energy, industry and courage of its creator, and the degree of success he has achieved' – is 'the antithesis of himself'; since, for all its populousness, Balzac's world appears to James as being 'dauntingly empty'. He may have been impressed by Balzac's 'extraordinary scale and his terrible completeness', qualities which made him appear to be 'the largest, weightiest presence' among the novelists; but in Balzac's world there is hardly that 'life' which provides the themes and materials for James' art. No wonder, for all his admiration of the French novel, and the stimulus he received from it, – his 'Parisian initiation' as Leavis calls it, – James decided to turn to and settle in the country of George Eliot. 'My last layers of resistance to a long-encroaching weariness and satiety with the French mind and its utterances', Leavis quotes James as saying, 'has fallen from me like a garment. I have done with 'em, forever, and am turning English all over. I desire only to feed on English life and the contact of English minds.' For Leavis this was 'a mature conscious realization of what was (for James) fact and necessity', because he knew, while being 'not the less committed to go on developing his own post-Flaubertian conscience of the *atelier*', that his real company was, not Flaubert's associates and disciples, but George Eliot, Hawthorne, Dickens and Jane Austen. In dealing with the French novel Henry James was confronted with the antithesis not only between Life and Art, but also between Life and Morality – an antithesis that is also reflected in his criticism.

In Lawrence, on the other hand – both in his novels and in his criticism – such an antithesis had no place and no relevance. The keynote in his writings is 'Life'. But 'life', observes Leavis, 'is a large term – too large to be of much use in criticism'. And yet it is a term that neither Lawrence nor Leavis could do without. Response to art in Lawrence means a response to life, and so does a response to 'the black marks on the page' in Leavis. In 'Genius as critic', a review-article on *Phoenix* (now in *Valuation in Criticism and Other Essays*) which he regards as 'the finest body of criticism in existence', Leavis discussed Lawrence's merits and qualities as a critic, and his appreciation of those qualities underlined (by implication) what he himself most prized in a critic. In fact, Leavis' own development as a critic, after the initial stages in which I.A. Richards, Middleton Murry and above all T.S Eliot influenced him in varying degrees, was profoundly influenced by Lawrence's critical no less than by his creative writings. Had he been able to read *Phoenix* (1936) earlier, Leavis tells us, 'what a difference it would have made to me as an undergraduate!' He not only found Lawrence's criticism 'subtle, penetrating and individual', but also took to heart what, in his essay on John Galsworthy, Lawrence had to say about the nature of an ideal critic. 'Alive in every fibre' – for Leavis, to read Lawrence's criticism, amounts to having 'that phrase charged with meaning'. For though what Lawrence says about the nature and qualification of a critic 'in its un-Eliotic freedom of utterance, may sound a little naive', 'there is unmistakably in evidence the vital and sure intelligence of the actual phoenix, the rare being who is alive in every fibre and has the centrality and easy swiftness of genius. The naivety is that habit of complete honesty which it has never occurred to him to suspect that he can't afford.'

For Leavis, all these qualities in Lawrence – creative, critical and moral – spring from the same source: 'a deep centre' – which so conspicuously distinguishes him 'from our versatile pundits of the Sunday papers!' It is from this centre that Lawrence did all his thinking. For, even though he disclaimed any philosophical bent of mind or aptitude, Lawrence was 'a most powerful original thinker who always was preoccupied with fundamentals'. Such a preoccupation is impressively present even in his occasional work. Hence the term 'moral' has a special context and a particular force and relevance in Lawrence and makes his critical thought 'immensely more subtle and deep-going than Arnold's, the other great critic who challenged a basic critical function for the word "moral" '.

In Eliot's case, on the other hand, there is not the same kind of kinship or correspondence between his creative work and his criticism. Leavis admired, and to some extent was influenced by, Eliot's earlier criticism, but he had serious reservations about his later criticism. The earlier criticism was 'remarkable for its directness, its concentrated purity of interest, its intense and rigorous concern to convey the essential perception and the bearing of this as realized by the critic'. It influenced Leavis' own development as a critic, helping him form his view on literary criticism as 'a special discipline of intelligence'. He singled out 'Tradition and the Individual Talent' as being pre-eminently the essay on which Eliot's reputation as a thinker, with a disciplined intelligence, 'capable of vigorous, penetrating and sustained thought' depends. And yet, even in this essay, there are 'ambiguities', 'logical inconsequences', 'pseudo-precisions', 'fallaciousness', together with 'the aplomb of ... equivocations and ... specious cogency'. As an example, Leavis quotes what Eliot has to say about Keats' 'Ode to the Nightingale', namely, that it contains a number of feelings which have nothing to do with the nightingale, but which the nightingale, 'partly because of its attractive name, and partly because of its reputation served to bring together', and comments:

> As if there were not something else, more important, to be said about the relation of the Ode to the life, the living form from which it derived the creative impulsion; derived something without full recognition of which there can be no intelligent appreciation of the 'artistic process' of the art.

But when Eliot brought out *After Strange Gods*, Leavis considered the book 'painfully bad – disablingly inadequate, often irrelevant and sometimes disingenuous'. In his later criticism Eliot's increasingly religious preoccupation went hand in hand with less and less 'discipline of thought and emotion, less purity of interest, less power of sustained devotion and less courage than before'. In fact, after *For Lancelot Andrewes*, Leavis notes as a rule, less 'nervousness' and more 'hesitation and diffidence' in Eliot's criticism as well as 'a radical uncertainty about his intention and its validity'. All these features paraded themselves at times under the cloak of 'haughty humility', so different from what Leavis considers to be the essential qualifications of a real critic: unequivocal forthrightness with which he thinks and feels about literature; and 'a sure rightness' of judgement as well as a serious view of the relation between literature and life.

Among the specific faults Leavis finds with Eliot's criticism are overvaluation of Dryden, at the expense of 'the incomparably greater Pope', failure to attempt 'any radical valuation of the Jacobeans', endorsement of the traditional valuations, taking Wyndham Lewis, Henry Miller and Lawrence Durrell seriously, considering Joyce's *Work in Progress* important and appreciation of Landor due to the quality of 'impersonality' in him, whereas for Leavis Landor's impersonality stands up empty – 'impersonal because there is nothing there'.

Leavis also challenges other critical pronouncements of Eliot's – such as his considering *Coriolanus* and *Antony and Cleopatra* as constituting Shakespeare's 'most assured artistic success'; and his evaluations of *The*

Cenci as the greatest of the verse-plays by nineteenth-century poets; of Dryden's *The Hind and the Panther* as a great poem and of Dryden himself as one of the three greatest critics of poetry in English literature (the other two being Samuel Johnson and Coleridge). Such an evaluation constitutes for Leavis 'a portent of conventionality', whereas Eliot's discussion of Kipling's verse or his taking Auden and Spender as distinguished poets, is 'hardly credible'. Leavis finds Eliot's value-judgements in general 'weak', and ascribes that weakness to 'some radical inner condition' which prevents him from being aware of 'the profounder, the essential criticisms which *Family Reunion* and *The Cocktail Party* invite' and which express 'one's sharpened sense of the importance of literature, and therefore of the relation of literature to life'.

Apart from Leavis' critical assessments of the major critics from Johnson to Eliot, his various pronouncements on, or agreements or disagreements with, other critics' views form an important part of his critical heritage. Academic critics or criticism usually meant very little to Leavis and he did not mince words in dealing with them. Thus, for instance, he found 'not a paragraph of criticism in all the six volumes of Oliver Elton's *Survey of English Literature*'; considered Lionel Trilling's book *Matthew Arnold* 'disappointing' for its lack of 'any notable vigour of first-hand thinking'; I.A. Richards' *Coleridge on Imagination* 'full of irresponsible generalities, bright ideas and uncritical tips'; and Herbert J.C. Grierson and J.C. Smith's *Critical History of English Poetry* containing 'all the fallacies and the substitutes for thought from which the student should be emancipated in his first term', as he should be from René Wellek and Austin Warren's *Theory of Literature*.

The only training worth having for a critic is that which enables him to discriminate critically, and which is not the same thing as 'a vast and deadening acquisition of names, titles, dates, externalities of information, and sedative permissibilities of quasi-critical comment'. Such a training would not, by its very nature, be of a restrictively specialised kind, but would take into consideration both the non-literary and the literary influences, see what these influences are worth, and discover, for instance, that 'the unconscious and the subconscious didn't wait for Freud to let them into literature'; that Metaphysical poetry has for an essential part of its strength something that is 'of the same order as the strength of all the most satisfying poetry'; and that 'the conceitedness, the Metaphysicality, is the obtrusive accompaniment of an essential presence of "thought" such as we have in the best work of all great poets'. Awareness of this 'essential presence of "thought" ' is an indispensable ingredient in one's critical response to 'the black marks on the page', which is not exclusively concerned with those marks (i.e. words) as such; nor are words merely 'words'.

Leavis' own use of language as a critic is invariably characterised by analytical subtlety, moral conviction and intellectual depth; as, for example, in the following sentence concerning Swift:

The dispassionate, matter-of-fact tone induces a feeling and a motion of assent, while the burden, at the same time, compels the feelings appropriate to rejection, and in the contrast – the tension – a remarkably disturbing energy is generated.

It is by virtue of such analytical grasp and acumen as displayed in this sentence, that one can claim for Leavis' own criticism in general what he claims for *Scrutiny*; namely that it offers 'an incomparable literary history of the period' and, at the same time, 'a major revaluation of the past of English literature'. His criticism of other critics is an essential part of that history and that revaluation.

11

The Final Fifteen Years

When one is alive one *is* alive, and goes on fighting.

F.R. Leavis

Though averse to writing his autobiography as, on more than one occasion, he was approached to do by various publishers including his own, Leavis occasionally furnished glimpses of an autobiographical nature in his writings as well as in his correspondence. What he said there goes further towards explaining the drives and pressures, aims and ideals, battles won and lost in his life than any autobiography as such could have done. Some of his epistolary comments bring out his personality as well as the sense of his own achievement and its relevance to the thought and culture of his age. They also offer curt and pointed assessments of contemporary writers, thinkers and academics.

My own correspondence with Leavis started in 1963 just after he had given his widely publicised lecture on 'Two Cultures? The Significance of C.P. Snow'. At that time I was lecturing in English at Bocconi University, Milan, Italy, and had followed the controversy aroused by that lecture which received press coverage also in Italy. I thought of making the text of Leavis' lecture available in Italian. And so, during my visit to London, I wrote to Leavis, whom I had never met before, asking if I could call on him. 'You would find me,' he wrote back promptly, 'in lecture Room E on Saturday, 27 April at 12 noon. The Porter in the Porter's Lodge would tell you where E is.' This was the beginning of our association, which was to last till the end of his life.

In that year I also sent him a copy of my letter to *The Times* in which I had challenged some of the points Barbara Reynolds had made in her article on Croce (3 October 1963), which was part of a series of articles called 'Critics Who Have Influenced Taste' that *The Times* used to publish every Thursday in the early sixties. Barbara Reynolds' argument was that after Croce, one was either a Crocean or a non-Crocean. In my letter which was not published, I pointed out that so far as the most important and influential English critics were concerned – Eliot, Leavis, Richards and Empson – Croce's thought and criticism had little or no relevance. I sent a copy of my letter to each of the four critics.

Only Eliot and Leavis answered by letter and corroborated what I had said. Leavis' reply was as follows:

> It's a quite simple matter to comment on your note. You seem to me to be right. Croce's name, of course, was in the modish currency in the 1920's; we were all prepared to be told that 'art is expression'; but Croce's aesthetic – Croce's 'influence' – made no difference at all in literary criticism or on taste.
>
> There is nothing else I need to say – or could say – so blank is my memory in respect of any Crocean influence.
>
> This is hardly worth quoting, but I shouldn't at all mind going on record as having said it.

Some months later, in another letter, Leavis drew my attention to a critique of Croce by James Smith that had appeared in one of the early volumes of *Scrutiny* and pointed out that *The Foundations of Aesthetics* by C.K. Ogden, I.A. Richards and James Wood (ca. 1925) contained a 'brief dismissal of Croce', adding that 'I.A.R. and Ogden, of course, represent the Benthamite tradition'. Leavis himself, however, did not claim to be an Italian expert. 'I doubt', he observed, 'whether my Italian is good enough. The ambition to work (and keep) it up lapsed decades ago in the inexorable rigour of life.' And in another letter he added: 'As you know, I haven't claimed to be qualified in Italian, I did work hard in order to be able to read *out* Italian poetry. I learnt some Leopardi by heart, using (I remember) the Bickersteth text-and-translation volume. I know a great deal of Dante by heart.'

In the early 1960s, besides his retirement from Cambridge, his subsequent resignation from his Downing fellowship in protest against the way the 'English School' he had built up at Downing was going to be drastically changed under a new director, and his appointment to the Visiting Professorship at York University, the most important event in Leavis' life was his Richmond lecture 'Two Cultures? The Significance of C.P. Snow' and the controversy it aroused. As a contribution to the controversy Aldous Huxley brought out what was going to be his last book – *Literarism and Scientism* – of which Leavis had this to say: 'Huxley's book seemed to me a non-disinterested piece of bookmaking. Not that he was ever much of a mind. Nevertheless, even tho' living in the region of Hollywood, he ought to have known what was at issue.'

Later on, in another letter, Leavis said that 'there was no overt reaction [to his "Two Cultures?"] in England, but abuse. I had, however, much private assurance of approval: "Thank God, some one has said it, at last." (From many scientists too). And though I got nothing but abuse, my lecture did the work: every reviewer of Snow now takes care to make plain that he doesn't suppose Snow matters. But there was *no debate at all*. The muddle of thought continues; still talk of "two cultures", tho' my point is that there *is* only one.' In the same letter, Leavis referred to his York appointment: 'I shall not desert Cambridge, but go to York for 3 days a week. Lord James, the Vice-Chancellor, and Harwood, Chancellor, are anxious to make York a real university. I shall take care not to miss my meeting of the Faculty Board at Cambridge, where I am needed, to keep the ward-bosses in check. The battle goes on. I've had my name removed from the books of Downing College. A great defeat there.'

While translating 'Two Cultures?' into Italian – it was published in the Milanese periodical *Il Verri* (1964) – I got the idea of translating a representative selection of Leavis' critical essays into Italian and sent a preliminary list of contents to Leavis for his comments. Naturally, he wrote,

> I look with benevolent interest upon the project for a book of essays. My mind had been exercised a great deal on the supposed list of contents, but the upshot is that I feel I had better refrain from interference: the appropriate criteria are more in your possession than in mine. I think that the nearly 30-year-old Forster essay implies (at least) a higher valuation than I think justified, and, actually, I discouraged the inclusion of it in the 'World Classics' volume *English Critical Essays: XXth Century*. I should have preferred the inclusion in the projected volume of something on Dickens (on whom I have pioneered); say the essay on *Dombey and Son* that appeared in the *Sewanee Review*, Spring 1962. But I see that, from your point of view, there may be strong reason for putting the Forster essay in. (At the first opportunity – EMF is still alive – I shall express my view that he has been preposterously overvalued).

The reason why, in spite of Leavis' reservations, I included the Forster essay in the volume – *Da Swift a Pound: saggi critici di F.R. Leavis* (Einaudi: Turin, 1973) – was that Forster was well-known in Italy, and Leavis' essay on *A Passage to India* was the most illuminating and authoritative available at that time on that novel. Moreover, Leavis' book on Dickens, which contained the essay on *Dombey and Son*, had not yet come out when I made my selection, and the idea governing the selection was that of including only those essays that had already been published in books.

Some months later I also sent Leavis the draft of my introduction to the selection of his essays. He suggested some changes, and questioned my statement about Eliot's influence on him. 'At the close of your opening paragraph,' he wrote (1 September 1965),

> You might, I think, intimate that Eliot's was a decisive influence, but that my debt to him was a matter of my having been made to say 'No!': e.g. I myself should say that (see TSE's 'Tradition and the

Individual Talent') there is *never* a separation between the man who
suffers and the mind that creates. He made me see that 'impersonality' is an important idea, but that his account won't do. Positively, I
owe much more to D.H. Lawrence's criticism; that should be said
somewhere.

And a couple of months later, while commenting on the draft of my longer
essay on him that was to appear in *English Miscellany* (Rome, 1966) and
that was later on to serve as an introduction to my Swedish selection of his
critical essays – *Essäyer av F.R. Leavis* (utval och indledning av G. Singh,
Bo Cavefors: Malmö, 1966) – Leavis referred to my quoting from *The Great
Tradition* to the effect that Dickens' was a genius of an entertainer. 'That
note,' he said, 'you quote from *The Great Tradition* (an addendum to a
hasty appendix) doesn't represent my estimate of Dickens. It was absurd
enough at any time – self-contradictory. I had already stated that on
re-reading of the Dickens oeuvre that led me to the view: it *was Dickens
who created the modern novel – Dombey and Son, Hard Times, Little
Dorrit, Great Expectations.*' Even after his retirement from Cambridge,
various kinds of pressure continued to be the driving force behind Leavis'
work and thought. 'I've been,' he wrote to me in the same letter,

> unspeakably rushed all the summer (& before); always panically
> straining in the face of imminent 'deadlines'. Two publishers (other
> than Chatto's – themselves aggrieved) have insistent claims on me.
> I had moral obligations to certain distinguished but unfortunate
> younger men. I had an exacting 'military' situation to keep me alert
> on the Cambridge front. I had the Finnish trip come near – and no
> lectures ready. I had the prospect of York behind that. I was fighting
> all the while for time (& peace) in which to do the urgent things that
> required concentration. Correspondence snowed in all the while.

When my Italian translation of 'Two Cultures?' was published, and my
article on Leavis – 'Better History and Better Criticism: the Significance
of F.R. Leavis' – appeared in Mario Praz's *English Miscellany*, I sent him
the offprints, together with a copy of the Swedish periodical *Horizon* in
which another article of mine had appeared. He wrote to thank me, adding:
'I should be grateful for 3 copies of the *Miscellany* – if you can without
bother let me have them. The *Horizon* came. Again – many thanks. The
trouble is I've been too unremittingly driven to reply. I've no secretary, and
I'm badly exposed. Consequence of having lived an outlaw.'
Retirement from Cambridge, therefore, meant no slackening of activity
for Leavis. For besides commuting between Cambridge and York, he was
also giving public lectures at various universities in Britain as well as
abroad. In 1964 he gave the Chichele lectures at Oxford on Dickens; in
1965 he and his wife went to Finland on a British Council lecture tour; in

1966 he came to Belfast to give a Yeats centenary lecture; and there was the American pressure to visit America.

No, there will be no relaxing this summer. It's a tense time, there's an appalling amount to be done, and I should have resisted the American pressure again if that had been really possible. There will be much wear and tear on this brief visit, and I don't want the kind of reception I'm promised. Far from it.

But in spite of multiple pressures and commitments – which included preparation of the Clark lectures he was invited to give at Cambridge in the Lent term – Leavis managed to comment on and offer suggestions regarding my selection of his critical essays every time I approached him. For instance, I was not sure whether to include his Wordsworth or his Keats essay from *Revaluation*. I thought – and still think – the Wordsworth essay, together with the essay on Shelley (which was to be included), to be the most original and characteristic in *Revaluation*. However, I knew that Wordsworth's standing in the eyes of the Italians could never be so high as that of a 'romantic' poet like Keats or Byron. So I let Leavis' preference clinch the matter. 'As for your inquiry,' he wrote,

I'll answer with a genuinely modest question rather than a suggestion. Wouldn't there be more point in the Keats than in the Wordsworth? This is only a question: you know the public and the situation in view. But – is any considerable public going to be interested in Wordsworth? True, he's very *English*. But Keats in his way is too, and he, while transcending aestheticism, does essentially bring up the familiar (to the Continent) themes of beauty and Aestheticism. I do, however, leave it to you.

The beginning of 1967 saw the Clark lectures delivered in the Lent term. Still there was, for Leavis, a tremendous amount of work and a great deal of pressure and struggle in his everyday life. 'I shall be fighting for life. I am a distance runner who means to win, but know there's a spring to come.' When my Swedish volume of his essays came out, I sent him a copy. He wrote back thanking me, but added:

I wish they hadn't used that odious cover design – meant to be taken for me. It must be based on the illicit cartoon *The Spectator* inserted in my Snow lecture – to pair with one of Snow. The idea was to present me as an insufferable sneering Intellectual: *The Spectator* wanted to placate Snowmen (i.e. the Literary World). I told the editor my opinion of the whole manoeuvre, and I should be grateful if you would tell the Swedish publisher that I am full of resentment. I'm now that for Scandinavia.

With the Clark lectures – 'my being asked to give the Clark lectures', he wrote to me, 'was something in the nature of a revolution in academic attitude' – and the Chichele lectures at Oxford behind him, capped with an honorary D.Litt. from Leeds University (1965), the lecture tours in Finland and in the United States still to come, the echoes of the controversial 'Two Cultures?' still lingering, and with various lecturing commitments at various universities, Leavis had by now become a celebrity even outside the academic world. Moreover his fame, especially after 'Two Cultures?', was not confined to his achievement as a literary critic. In view of all this, I approached Leavis, asking him if he would countenance the idea of a *Festschrift* in his honour. I was pleasantly surprised to get a reply which was not one of outright rejection. 'As for the question of a Festschrift,' he wrote,

> that is a delicate matter. I had the strongest reasons for nipping in the bud the project you refer to, but it's just possible that what you have in mind escapes the objections that were then decisive: a contemptible tradition that couldn't in the eyes of the intelligent and disinterested, do me *honour* and all kinds of undesirable people climbing on to the bandwagon ... Perhaps you could let me know who are being thought of as possible contributors? ... Is there any possibility of publication by the Cambridge University Press? – I ask because I don't think I should countenance a volume coming from Chatto and Windus – my own publisher.

But when Leavis got my list of the people I was thinking of inviting to contribute to the *Festschrift*, he, not altogether unexpectedly, withdrew his assent. 'You mustn't take it ill,' he wrote,

> when I say that (as I expected it would) my objection holds ... The reasons for which I turned down the earlier plan for a *Festschrift* apply again. Some of the people you list don't love me at all, and, of those, a number would decline. But it's those who would *accept* who frighten me. A *Festschrift* is in general a bandwagon – and is known to be: most of the people who climb on are people one (*this* one) would rather not have his causes associated with. *That* sums up my reasons: such a demonstration as you sketch wouldn't advance the causes I lived and fought for. True friends would feel: 'At last *he* has compromised.'

This letter was accompanied by the text of the Introduction Leavis had written for the volume of the selection of his essays I had translated into Italian for Einaudi. The text, so far unpublished in English, is as follows:

The pieces chosen by the Editor of this Selection from my work were

written at various times during a third of a century – the period that
separates the earliest from the latest. Inevitably those years didn't
pass without some change in the critic: it is possible, I suppose, that
the reader will feel that there have been developments in approach,
style and procedure. I myself will comment only on the differences of
tone and emphasis that would be found by anyone who compared my
earlier and my later treatment of certain writers.

Three and a half decades have made a great change in the recognized standing of Yeats. He was well-known when I was a child,
having been publishing poetry for some years before I was born.
There had, however, been no reason for acclaiming him as a major
poet before the volume called *The Tower* came out (1928 – the London
edition). That volume, at any rate, brought a new conviction to me,
and prompted me to write my account of his development out of
Victorian romanticism, and to insist on his new importance as a
companion modern poet to T.S. Eliot. As far as I know, the brief
critique of *New Bearings in English Poetry* was the first to present
him in this light; at least, I had found nothing helpful in the commentaries of earlier critics. I myself was disappointed by the poetry that
Yeats wrote in the remainder of his life but he was, of course, when
The Tower appeared, already near sixty. But, although my critique
seemed to have a decisive influence, I remained an isolated voice. For
the recognition of Yeats as a great modern poet took hold rapidly, my
disappointment was not generally shared, and a cult was established
in the universities of England and America; Yeats was awarded a
Nobel prize.

The cult, especially as it was maintained in the universities,
entailed a reverent and intensive preoccupation with his prose writings, with his esoteric disquisitions and his various symbolic sys-
tematizations. I myself, in a Centenary lecture I was invited to give
in Northern Ireland last year, expressed my view that those who
appreciated his truly remarkable poetic achievement ought to be able
to tell themselves that life was given them for other purposes than to
spend it on Yeats' esoteric lucubrations, which may have been in
some curious way necessary to Yeats, but were a nuisance from the
point of view of a genuine admirer of the poetry. I said also that I
judged his major poetry to be a very small proportion of his poetic
oeuvre, and that Eliot seemed to me decidedly the greater poet.

When I wrote about Eliot in *New Bearings* it was the Eliot of the
nineteen-twenties. If I now think that we who at that time acclaimed
The Waste Land attributed to it a status as an achieved organic work
that it doesn't really justify (impressive as it was, and important as
it remains historically), that is largely a consequence of the changed
sense of Eliot the poet that his later work has compelled on me. It is
a sense that leads me to lay much less emphasis on *The Waste Land*

than it was natural to lay on it in the nineteen-twenties: Eliot's achievement is so immensely impressive, and calls for terms of appreciation that one could not have anticipated in those days. The development (to suggest the graph that now seems to me most helpful) from *The Portrait of a Lady* through *La figlia che piange*, *The Hollow Men*, *Ash-Wednesday* – the opening poem of which was entitled 'Perch'io non spero' when I just read it by itself in the Parisian publication *Commerce* – to *Four Quartets*, is so astonishing and cogent, and, in its logic and its unpredictableness, of such a kind, that I find myself thinking of the whole Eliotic corpus as one great poetic work. Pound, who knew and influenced both Eliot and Yeats, was himself a decidedly lesser poet than either of them. Since I wrote the chapter on him in *New Bearings* he has written many more Cantos. I see no reason, however, to alter what I wrote about him all those years ago. And I take the opportunity to record that Eliot, who had spoken so highly of the *Cantos* in the Preface to his *Selected Poems of Ezra Pound* (1928), wrote to me in the last year of his life to say that he had just read the Postscript to the later edition of *New Bearings* and would like me to know that he now agreed with me about the *Cantos*.

The essay that now seems to me to convey an indefensibly high estimate of its subject is that on E.M. Forster. It is true that in that essay I have made some drastically limiting and qualifying judgements. But at the same time I imply that Forster demands, and repays, a more serious consideration as a novelist than I would claim for him today. I don't, for that reason, regret having written it, or think it discredible: it 'dates' in a way in which some of one's work *ought* to date. Forster in the nineteen-thirties, the decade of triumphant Fascism and Nazism, was a voice of liberal civilization and humane tradition, and I can see today that my essay expresses an accordantly hesitant and incomplete judgement. It had, I believe, some influence. There is the more reason now for my saying brutally that to talk of Forster as a *great* novelist, or writer of any kind, is ridiculous, and that the estimate – a generally current one – represented by Trilling's book on him is mere inert academicism.

As for my lecture on Snow, that, in a sense, is 'dated' too; for, though so brief a time has passed since I gave it, not even *New Statesman*, the left-wing intellectual weekly of which Snow is – or was – on the board of directors, cares to be suspected of taking him seriously as a distinguished mind. So decided can it be to state aloud, in full publicity, the unanswerable and obvious truth that the Emperor is naked.

Actually, of course, Snow himself was only incidental to my theme, which remains as important as any the world has to face: the blind, reductive, anti-human automatism of our technologico-Benthamite civilization – the civilization in which material productivity and a 'rising standard of living' pass as ultimate human ends, and a terrifying spiritual Philistinism prevails.

If 1967 was in many ways a particularly active, eventful and momentous year for Leavis, it also proved to be important for Q.D. Leavis. It saw a second reprint (the first having appeared in 1950) of *Fiction and the Reading Public* of which Leavis, in a letter (October 1967), evaluated the importance in terms of its relevance to his own work and to the work of *Scrutiny*. More than a book of criticism, he said,

> it was – it inaugurated – a new kind of study; it was a pioneer work, and has since its publication been recognised as such in all the American universities ('required reading'). Smothered in England by academic jealousy, and by the hostility of the literary and academic worlds to me and *Scrutiny*, it has only just, after about 35 years, been reprinted. We could have done with the royalties – we were nearly starved out .... *Fiction and the Reading Public* was basic for *Scrutiny*, being the kind of *sociological* work that only a distinguished critic could have produced – i.e. *real* scholarship and research. It provided that analytic (and documented) realization of the cultural situation which gave us (in *Scrutiny*) our strong consciousness of aims and methods. *Culture and Environment* was merely a by-product: I (who wrote it) had merely to put together material that my wife found left over from her files.
>
> My wife is a critic of the novel – the finest and most authoritative writing in English. *Scrutiny* was essentially a product of our collaborative work (the two of us). Our drawing-room was the centre from which the English-speaking world was permeated (*via* the schools and universities). That is why we are hated (see Holroyd's biography of Lytton Strachey and the reviews of it) .... The wholly new conception of Jane Austen's art and achievement (see English Tripos papers of 30 years back) was argued, enforced and made current by my wife's work in *Scrutiny*.

Leavis distinguished his wife's criticism of Jane Austen from that of another *Scrutiny* collaborator – D.W. Harding – which he described, in the same letter, as being 'in a bad sense a psychologist's: i.e. it assumes naively that manifestations, in the novels, of literary convention and social convention (he being ignorant of the period conventions) are to be interpreted and explained as psychological evidence'.

My selection of Leavis' critical essays, for which he had written the Introduction, came out in 1973. There had to be a change of publisher (originally Il Saggiatore of Milan; eventually Einaudi of Turin) which meant considerable delay. However, during this time I brought out another and smaller selection in my Italian translation of Leavis' more explicitly polemical essays for the series called 'Dissensi' published by De Donato of Bari. When I sent my choice of contents to Leavis, he agreed with my inclusion of 'Eliot as Critic' as being 'the most suitable essay'. However, instead of 'What's Wrong with Criticism', which I had intended to include, but which Leavis thought 'belonged to too far back in history (the names etc.)', he suggested 'Keynes, Spender and Currency Values' as being 'more to the point'. Another item I had suggested was his polemical exchanges with Bateson; but Leavis wondered if they were not 'a bit too difficult for the Italian reader,' and added:

> But if you think otherwise my first piece 'The Responsible Critic, or the Function of Criticism at any time' seems to me the best for use: the analysis of Marvell's poem is one of the best things I've done – but isn't it asking a lot of the Italian reader? And the *poem* – what would be done about that? The other piece in that bout with Bateson needs the content of the *whole* exchange (which actually is to appear in the forthcoming C.U.P. Selection).
>
> ? Possible? – My review of Harry T. Moore's Lawrence letters (*Sewanee Review*, Winter 1963): it's reprinted in the forthcoming *'Anna Karenina' and Other Essays*.

In the following letter, Leavis agreed with my inclusion of 'Joyce and the Revolution of the Word' – 'if you find that suitable' – and 'The American-ness of American Literature' – 'never reprinted – but one of my best things'. As to my suggestion to include 'Scrutiny: A Retrospect', Leavis agreed, adding: 'Could you extract from it??? – I've no time to look it up and consider its length.' He also made two other suggestions: 'The Literary Mind' and 'Under Which King, Bezonian?' (both from *Scrutiny* Vol. I, 1 and Vol. I, 3, respectively). I chose the second and used it for the general title of the volume – *Sotto che re, briccone?* – which appeared in 1969, and which included, together with that essay, 'Eliot as Critic', 'Joyce and the Revolution of the Word', 'The Americanness of American Literature' and 'Keynes, Spender and Currency Values'.

Before the end of 1967, Leavis' *'Anna Karenina' and Other Essays* had come out and it was, as was to be expected, widely but, on the whole, adversely reviewed. One such review was by John Gross in the *Observer* which prompted me to write a letter of protest which was not published. Leavis, to whom I had sent a copy of my letter to the *Observer*, commented:

> Your effort wasn't wasted: these things tell. I *know* of a number of letters, not printed – one to the *Listener* from a moral scientist at Cambridge. But the whole of that hard-solid literary world is aware – and frightened. They talk of the 'shoals of letters' that 'avalanche

in' from Leavis' 'followers' whenever I'm 'adversely reviewed'. They feel the 'real' world is hostile!

I've never printed a word about John Gross or Donald Davie or Raymond Williams or George Watson or .... The Literary Editor of the *Observer* sent the book to Gross *in order* to get that kind of review.

As for Eliot, he was profoundly ashamed, but couldn't find the courage, or the will to it, because he resented my existence, – and was ashamed of himself for that. And there you have a datum about the 'pressure' in the 'vessel' out of which his poetry came ('Tradition and the Individual Talent').

He wrote to me (after 15 years' silence) not long before his death, saying nothing to the point, but betraying that I was on his conscience. The poetic evidence is there in the post-air-raid section of *Little Gidding*, which includes things he said to me (about growing old) – in my house – at the time of the composing.

Also

> the rending pain of re-enactment the shame
> Of motives late revealed, and the awareness
> Of things ill done or done to others' harm
> Which once you took for exercise of virtue.
> The fools' approval stings ...

But he went on doing them. Sad.

The year 1968 started with the publication of the two-volume *Selections from 'Scrutiny'*. 'It's off my hands,' he wrote (6 January 1968) 'which are still more than full'. Independently of the two-volume *Selections from 'Scrutiny'* – and before they actually came out – I was myself contemplating a one-volume selection from *Scrutiny* in Italian translation and had corresponded with Leavis about the possible inclusions. His replies and comments were both helpful and revealing. When I submitted the list of my proposed contents – which included contributions to *Scrutiny* from the Leavises, D.W. Harding, D.J. Enright, L.C. Knights, H.C. Mason, John Speirs, Derek Traversi, Martin Turnell and James Smith – the only item he queried was Mason's article. 'I don't think,' he wrote,

> that it, or indeed anything of his, is good enough. We used him because of his languages and his journalistic facility, which could be kept, or raised, to a reasonably intelligent *informational* level which was in close touch with the conversation in my drawing-room .... Re-reading confirms my sense that he says, critically, very little – in a lot of words. His useful function was to put our readers on to what was coming out. Plausibly glib and superficially intelligent.

James Smith – 'at his best he is very good, e.g. the Mallarmé,' – and

Q.D. Leavis' Henry James essay ('Henry James: Short Stories'), Leavis thought should go in, being 'one of her best (and for the cosmopolitan-cultured Italian reader very useful), and the Santayana "George Santayana as a Critic" should not; it was gifted higher journalism, written in haste to fill up a gap, and neither she nor I would now stand by that praise of Santayana on Dickens'.

I had asked Leavis' advice as to the choice between Traversi's essay on *Coriolanus* or *The Tempest*. Leavis replied to the effect that he himself found it hard to decide and suggested that I might, in asking permission, ask Traversi to decide. As to Enright, Leavis said, 'he has good solid virtues, but doesn't represent the decisive *Scrutiny* criticism. That is, I don't think you could find anything of his more deserving to be selected – and, on literature equally foreign to the Italian reader as to the English, the *Faust I* is deserving.' Of Martin Turnell, Leavis said: 'I'm obliged to say that I don't like Turnell, and didn't, but he was worth our publishing on French literature, where there was so little help. I think the Proust would be a good choice. If anything further occurs to me to suggest in the next few days, I will write.'

In June, Leavis and his wife paid a lecturing visit to Holland (Amsterdam and Nijmegen) and on his return he corresponded with the British Council regarding his proposed lecturing visit to Italy. The British Council headquarters in London had written to inquire if he was disposed to go to Italy in September. 'I replied,' wrote Leavis (5 June 1968), 'that there was no question of my going in September, and that I shouldn't think of going without my wife – adding that we should be free next May and June. The B.C. rejoinder was characteristic: they couldn't help in respect of my wife "unless she was prepared to lecture" – implying that that was very improbable. Actually, of course, she is very much better known and more distinguished than most of the lecturers the B.C. sends out.' The following year both he and his wife were invited by the British Council to lecture in Italy.

A couple of months later, in connection with the election for the Chair of Poetry at Oxford, Hugh Trevor-Roper had written in the *Spectator* proposing Leavis' name as a candidate. I wrote a letter to the *Spectator* applauding Trevor-Roper's suggestion. My letter was published and Leavis wrote to me (4 October 1968) to say that

> Trevor-Roper, no doubt (I don't know him) will be gratified by your letter in *The Spectator*. His 'casual' formulation seemed to me tactical – as did his whole article. He wanted to get my name into circulation – but can hardly have hoped to put me in the chair. He does, along with others, hope (I think) to make Oxford reflect on the discreditable fatuity of the now traditional kind of circusing. It would in any case not have done to mention me otherwise than 'casually', I not having been approached. I don't think anyone has the nerve to approach me.

You've underlined Trevor-Roper's intended moral. It *was* Arnold's Chair.

In the same month, a letter from Leavis appeared in *The Times*. 'The War against enlightenment goes on', he wrote to me (12 October 1968). 'As before, my letter enrolled pleasing private demonstrations – including a letter from the Warden of All Souls (where Mr. Quintin Hogg and other Tory chiefs dine)'.

Sometime in November I was sent a copy of an informative-cum-evaluative article on Leavis that had appeared in Italy. I passed a copy of this to Leavis who commented on it in his letter of 21 November 1968, saying that he found the Italian article

> very interesting – very representative of the British literary world (for quite clearly the writer had picked up his account of me there – or from travelling delegates British Council sends.
>
> As such it's encouraging – I'm thinking of the evidence that (*malgrado* ...) I've survived and that my work is recognized to be unignorable. That the recognition comes from the enemy shouts at one in the explicit assumption of the *mafia* and my arrogance and brutality and dogmatic 'authority' (why not expose a Snow without being cruel to him – or a Bateson – or a Tillyard?) This last name recalls that I smiled, not too wryly, at the reference to my university having placed me 'in pensione' – If we had to live on my academic pension my wife and I should be in straits. As it is, having launched our children, we at last haven't to worry, because all my books (again *malgrado* ...) go on selling – increasingly as Dr. L. becomes more and more 'legendary'.

By the beginning of January 1969, the Leavises' lecture tour in Italy had been fixed. They were both to lecture at Milan, Padua, Bologna, Rome and Naples. *Lectures in America*, too, was to come out at the end of January, after 'a tormenting battle to deal with between Harvard and Cornell about publishing our lectures – which we really want neither to publish'. The Cheltenham Festival lecture Leavis gave in October the previous year was to appear at the beginning of February in the *Massachusetts Review*. 'I'm desperately busy', Leavis wrote (19 January 1969), 'commuting with York starts on Tuesday, I go to Leeds on Thursday, and to Wales *via* Newcastle a week later: for Wales some difficult preparing to be done .... The proofs of my Clark lectures *English Literature in Our Time and the University* may arrive at any time'. Such a busy schedule may at times have tired Leavis physically, but was a spur to his thought, the driving force behind his apparently inexhaustible intellectual energy and his combative spirit. 'I'm unspeakably driven', 'I'm almost in a panic of haste,' 'I badly need opportunities to feel relaxed,' 'I'm working against time myself, with too much on my mind,' 'I'm driven nearly crazy by appointments, deadlines, correspondence,' 'I seem to have little spare time – or freshness; one way or another I am kept busy' – Leavis' letters to me are studded with such phrases. And yet it is precisely this rhythm and tenor of life that made him, almost till the very end, feel himself to be really fulfilled. And this in spite of his problems with his digestion – 'very difficult away from home (and a problem even there)' – and his badly needing 'a spell of relaxed regularity – which I seem unlikely to get' (26 May 1967). He kept fighting for time for what he called 'my living interests' (11 April 1968): 'I want to get my books written – some of them while I'm still in my seventies.'

His commitment to the books he wanted to write and his fighting for time to be able to do so, together with his lecturing engagements which entailed travelling away from home as well as 'an infuriating load of correspondence to shift' did not, however, prevent him from dipping, whenever possible, into such weeklies as the *Spectator*, the *Listener*, *The New Statesman* and the *Times Literary Supplement*, for all his well-aired reservations about them. 'A glance over one of the *TLS* lying about unread', Leavis wrote to me (28 February 1969),

> brought home to me that you yourself had written a letter to that organ about a pronouncement of Empson's.
> Swinburne presents some interesting critical challenges: i) What is the difference between his 'live' poetry, and the almost automatic stuff which occupies so much of his Collected Volumes? ii) What analytic account can one give of the difference between Swinburne and Shelley? iii) What in particular would Lawrence have said about A.C.S.'s genius? My generation suffered from the spell.

When the Leavises' Italian trip had been completely finalised – they were going to be in Milan from 18 to 20 April, with Leavis giving two talks (one on Yeats at the British Council, and one on Eliot in the Catholic University) and Mrs Leavis speaking on Jane Austen at the State University in Milan – I asked if they would like to meet Montale and also if they would care to go to an opera.

'We would, of course, be delighted to meet Montale', wrote Leavis (3 March 1969) and 'the suggestion of an evening at the opera is very welcome. My wife (who has much relevant early experience of opera) would prefer *Don Carlos*, but, since convenience or limited possibility may determine, says she would be happy to be present at either' (24 March 1969) – the other opera also being, I do not now remember which, by Verdi. As to the suggestion, from the head of the British Council in Milan, of a relatively distant excursion, Leavis declined it, saying, as he wrote to me, 'that we would undoubtedly be very tired by the time we get to Milan' – which was the last lap of their Italian journey before flying back to London, and should react badly to further travel, especially by road. Neither of us is a good car passenger, and my wife has been having a lot of sinus trouble, which in her is a sign of more than her usual sensitiveness. We think it would be better to drift, in a relaxed and non-exacting way, seeing Milan – better, that is, than being committed to an excursion. We may be tired. I myself never break down, but the nutrition problem will be very difficult in Italy: I've been an acute dyspeptic for more than half-a-century, and at York live on the breakfast-provision I take with me there. I hope there will be some sunshine to keep me going in Italy. I am so fit (an old distance runner) that people find it hard to credit my disability, but it is remorseless ... I am trying to prepare something suitable for lecturing in Italy. Very difficult.

One cause of this diffidence was Leavis' awareness, as he wrote (24 February 1969), that his 'normal' lectures were 'considered (I gather) taxing to follow, and it wouldn't be suitable to offer any *Italian* audience one of them.' He prepared 'two simplified scripts' on Yeats and Eliot and was going to devote a large proportion of his time to actual poems. And so far as the Eliot lecture was concerned, he incorporated, as he informed me (6 April 1969), 'in my desperate haste,' a great deal from his Cheltenham address (published in *Massachusetts Review*). Nevertheless the Italian lecture is 'quite different (it won't be published except in Italian)' and added: 'These occasions ("All his attempts were occasional" – Johnson on Dryden) help me to arrive, in sum, at a fair treatment of T.S. Eliot's complexity.'

The Leavises were pleased with their Italian visit and with the people they met – Eugenio Montale, Vittorio Sereni and Sergio Solmi in Milan, Mario Praz and their old *Scrutiny* collaborator Derek Traversi in Rome, Elio Chinol in Padua – except one: an Englishman, public school and Oxford, they thought, whom they came across in Bologna and whose bureaucratic officialdom, punctiliousness and cold and correct manners irksomely contrasted with the genuine warmth and cordiality of the Italians who came to listen to them. On their return to England, Leavis wrote me to say (23 April 1969) how 'Italy from our point of view (even taking account of the Bologna Englishman) was a great success. My wife, not easily pleased, is delighted. We are very grateful to you for your part.'

In the meantime Leavis had agreed to be, during the first term of the academic year 1969-70, a visiting professor at Wales University, and was going to commute weekly from Cambridge (alternately) with Aberystwyth and Bangor. This was followed by a visiting Churchill Professorship at Bristol for a month after Christmas and then he was to resume for the remainder of the term his weekly visits to York. 'This Christmas vacation', he wrote to me (11 December 1969),

will be a busy one: I have things to prepare for Bristol, and I am
finishing my part of a book that my wife and I have nearly completed
for the centenary year. This commuting entails more than might
appear at first sight. I had, for instance, to travel from Bangor to
Cardiff 'on my way' home in order to give an Open Lecture – the most
taxing kind of performance. Moreover, I called and performed twice
at Oxford – and I shall have to, twice, 'on my way' from Bristol. I
resist the more local invitations as far as I can, but can't escape all –
Bristol is very much a centre.

Though 75 years of age, Leavis took all this in his stride both for the
sake of his commitment to the causes he had lived and fought for, and
because, in the course of these commutings and associated visits, he had
come to realise that he had 'a great deal of support in the country – which
explains the intensity of the hatred directed at me in the weeklies and the
Sunday papers. Some very important and responsible people have come to
realize that I alone can be counted to say – and say in public – the things
that need to be said about the Robbinses, Annans, Crossmans, and the
Enlightened in general.' And in a postscript he added: 'It was Lord Butler,
Master of Trinity, and not an academic, to whom I owed the invitation to
give the Clark lectures (a Trinity foundation).'

But all this made no difference to the kind of reviews his later books
('*Anna Karenina' and Other Essays* and *Lectures in America*) got: 'too
stupid to argue with and full of the kind of hatred which is a tribute.' As
an example, he listed Graham Hough's *New Statesman* review: 'the most
impudently and openly a gesture of spite. It has always been like that –
and yet all my books go on selling (otherwise my wife and I should have
virtually nothing to live on).'

To Leavis' lecturing and visiting commitments at the beginning of 1970,
which also saw the publication of his and his wife's book *Dickens the
Novelist*, was added the pressure and preoccupation due to his wife's
illness, as a result of which he cancelled a second projected trip to Italy in
April 1970. 'I had left her reluctantly a week ago yesterday to go to York,'
he wrote (10 March 1970), 'taking the doctor's judgement that she was
recovering from an after-flu sequela. I found her worse and very weak on
Thursday evening. My daughter has been here over the week-end, and the
doctor brought a consultant this afternoon. Upshot: she's to go to hospital
for tests etc. No more York this term.' About a month later he wrote again
(20 April 1970):

Your letter arrives luckily: I've just, this afternoon, learnt that I may
fetch my wife home from hospital tomorrow. It is scientifically a very
distinguished place, and the team of doctors, with their laboratories,
etc., to hand, saved her life, which was long in doubt. She will
continue to need a great deal of medical and other care, but they

agree that she is better now at home: hospital conditions (*not* the science) were militating against her recovery. It remains to be seen how far there are lasting effects of the illness. She will not be allowed to teach this coming year, but her mind is very active, and she will undoubtedly write.

I shall see her this evening and will tell her of your inquiry. P.S. She suggested some time ago that I should send you a copy of the forthcoming TLS which prints a sermon I preached at Bristol with the Vice-Chancellor in the Chair.

It was in connection with the publication of this 'sermon' that Geoffrey Grigson wrote a letter to the *Times Literary Supplement* complaining about Leavis' obscure and incomprehensible English and his convoluted syntax and wondering what his students could make of it and how they could really be said to have been educated by him. I protested against Grigson's comment in a letter that appeared in the *Times Literary Supplement*, concerning which Leavis wrote (14 May 1970):

Grigson's fatuously nasty letter – he has been doing it for 40 years, and I take no notice, which reduces him to transports of rage – is an expression of pure spite: I've given him no grounds, except to *be* what he feels as a menace to his self-esteem, so that his hatred amounts to a flattering tribute. ... What's in a way significant is that the Editor (who must know him) thought him worth printing – in order to please him and Co. and demonstrate TLS impartiality (which doesn't exist) ....

As for my bad style, that's not Grigson's invention; it's orthodoxy among the boys of the London literary world. The late Blessed Edith Sitwell wrote defending Snow: 'Dr. Leavis attacks Charles because *Charles* writes good English.' In my robust complacency, I'm not troubled. How can I *not* know that I'm a creative writer at any rate in the sense that I'm one of those who maintain the language, (as T.S. Eliot said of the poets).

At the end of June 1970 Leavis travelled to Aberdeen 'to make a brief and strenuous appearance', as he put it (21 June 1970), 'for one of those honorary degrees' – having already received one from York and one from Leeds. There were also other lectures, like the one he had delivered at Bristol 'asking to be delivered' and 'the unwritten books – the abandonment of which is *not* a price I could pay for being known for a year or two as the "greatest living Englishman", (I've actually heard that phrase).'

Meanwhile his wife, who had come back from hospital, was 'moving slowly towards normality ... the doctors are watching, among other consequences of her illness, her heart condition very sedulously. We – myself,

my daughter and my younger son – have arranged to take her to Bath for
a fortnight in July.'

When the new academic year 1970-71 started, Leavis resumed his visits
to York where, at the end of October, he gave a public lecture – on
'Pluralism, Compassion and Social Hope'. He sent the text to the *Times
Literary Supplement* but they turned it down. 'I posted it Thursday
evening and it came back for Saturday breakfast. It's evident that there
has been a formidable demonstration in the cultural background of the
TLS' (November 1970) – it was published in the *Human World*, and
subsequently included in *Nor Shall My Sword*.

On 29 March 1971, Leavis wrote to me to say that he had received a
letter from the editor of *Nuova Antologia* – the oldest Italian periodical
with a classical standing (it was founded in the last century and is an
institution in itself) – requesting him to contribute to a special number
they were bringing out in honour of Montale on the occasion of his
seventy-fifth birthday:

> My first response was to laugh at the impossibility: not only have I
> never written Italian, I know my Italian isn't good enough to make
> me a real critic in respect of Montale – whom I can see to have a most
> delicate command of tone and the (written) speaking voice. But then
> I liked *Xenia* so much, and like Montale himself (he is so unlike the
> late T.S. Eliot) – and (yes) his book (*Satura*) has come, inscribed 'in
> friendship' to me. To put it bluntly and boldly, I'm wondering
> whether I couldn't write 3 or 4 pages on *Xenia* – using your tip *re*
> Hardy. Pointing out the reasons for that tip, I go on to consider the
> essential differences. Montale is as direct and openly personal as
> Hardy, as un-Eliotic in that (and what did Eliot know of 'love' in any
> sense?); but he's immensely more sophisticated and intellectual –
> and he's witty! What I shall aim at would be unstupid enough to
> please Montale. He is *truly* 'impersonal'. No funk.
>
> But then the *Nuova Antologia* seems to expect something in
> Italian and I couldn't supply that. I should have to ask you if you
> would translate my brevity.

I wrote to Leavis to say that I would be delighted to do so. He then replied
to the Editor of *Nuova Antologia* accepting the invitation, but wrote to me
to explain what he felt his difficulty to be:

> My difficulty re Montale isn't lack of conviction, but that I'm not
> qualified. The fact that in the postwar 1920's I gave up doing Olympic
> times along the Ely road at midnight – a cure for desperate insomnia
> (which it wasn't), and took to standing till tired into a daze learning
> some text – often Dante or Leopardi – that rested on my swivel
> mirror. I am, however, convinced about *Xenia*, and hope to say

something that looks intelligent about the differentia that distinguished him (Montale) from Hardy – a useful comparison that goes
to the centre of Montale as *Xenia* gives him.

   Of course I propose to go on cultivating Montale and should be
grateful for the chance to see your translations. Such help, for one
thing, enables me to concentrate on the rhythm, the 'thisness' in
general, of the Italian.

But Leavis' sense of the difficulty and his diffidence concerning Montale
were not to be easily dispelled, and were made worse by the fact of his
being, as usual, 'too hard-driven'. As he wrote to me (26 April 1971),

   but for my sense of the Higher Obligation – my respect for him
   (Montale), that is – I shouldn't have committed myself: I fight a
   running battle against urgings and invitations. I go to York tomorrow, and shall be taking seminars on Blake, Wordsworth and Paul
   Valéry, but haven't even sorted out my books, still less prepared. I've
   had an unexpected burden correcting the 2nd edition of the Dickens
   book, in which the printers had made new and inexcusable mistakes,
   so that the whole had to be carefully read ... What I really wanted to
   do was to get the Introduction written to my Richmond and post-
   Richmond 'Public Lectures', which – under the title *Nor shall my
   sword* – make a book (for the autumn?). I hope to get the few pages
   on Montale done in the next couple of weeks or so.

In fact, on Friday 4 June 1971, he wrote to me again, saying he had not
forgotten his obligation regarding Montale, but that he had been

   fighting – with a bad conscience (ought to have been so desperately
   optimistic and said 'Yes'?) – to make a space in which to squeeze out
   my commentary on *Xenia* (which I know by heart). It seems a losing
   battle. But last Thursday (having got up at 4 a.m.) I succeeded in
   making up the packet that contained my series of Peter-the-hermit
   public lectures long awaited by Chatto & Windus (*Nor shall my
   sword* ...). I ran down to the Post Office, ran back, and finished my
   packing for York – my taxi came at 10.30.
   I have resolved to postpone finishing the introduction to the new
   book and devote this week-end to Montale. And I shall. I can only do
   what I *can* do – and I am no journalist.

I received his Montale critique soon after that which he called (7 June
1971) 'my attempt to honour my promise to Montale', and added:

   For what it's worth (and heaven knows I am not in a state to judge,
   but am certainly not cheerful about it). I couldn't have written it if I

hadn't done much reading of, and thinking about Xenia: I had something to say. I am still facing a battle with time; there's the introduction to my collected Sermons to finish etc etc ...

I ought never to have said Yes to *Nuova Antologia*, I have been so
steadily overcommitted. And now I see that No. 3 *The Human World*
thinks I ought very soon to have produced a book on *Four Quartets*.
It doesn't seem to understand that I have a *number* of books in my
mind but that *my* books aren't written easily.

In his *Xenia* critique Leavis had quoted just the first line from Hardy's
'After a Journey' while referring to the poem as a whole. I wrote to ask if
he wanted me to translate Hardy's poem in its entirety. He promptly
replied (9 June 1971):

I hadn't meant to quote anything but the first line of 'After a Journey'.
After some hesitation it struck me that, after all, I was quoting very
little of Montale himself, and that where Hardy was in question, all
that was needed was some particularity of reference for such readers
as could, and would, look up the English text. And that first line does
illustrate the un-Montalesque nature of Hardy's diction.

When Leavis' Montale critique appeared in *Nuova Antologia*, both he
and Montale were pleased. Montale sent him – Leavis told me in his letter
(8 October 1971) – 'a very agreeable card – most of which I managed to
make out'. And Leavis himself observed:

I have been repaid by the pleasure of doing what I found I *could* do
with conviction. I also enjoyed the modest reflection that I could say
critically, with central relevance, about *Xenia* what I don't suppose
anyone else could. I let down, I think, neither Montale nor myself.
There is, further, this consideration: the literary world (i.e. Snowmen, Grigsons and Co.) have agreed that I am narrowly provincial,
and anything that tends to make that axiom (from them!) look silly
is an advantage – I am thinking about my causes. After all, I'm a
better European than Mr. Heath, for I believe in something real, and
am the basic anti-Americanizer.

Leavis had already started working on *Four Quartets* under the title
'Eliot and the Human World' – part of his projected Eliot book – but he had
to interrupt that work in order to give a lecture on Blake at Bristol in
mid-November. 'To get anything worth saying said about Blake in an hour
is a formidable undertaking. But the effort will help me.'

With all these commitments in hand, it was impossible for Leavis to
accept my invitation to give a lecture at Belfast during the Michaelmas

term, or at some later date. He provisionally suggested 10 May 1972, and, as for the subject, wrote (14 October 1971):

An idea I'm toying with is that of demonstrating, with observations and illustrations, my views about the reading out of poetry: certain Eliot poems, some Shakespeare passages (how I hate actors – being myself histrionic – in a way), and the other things I would specify beforehand. Perhaps commitment to a given subject would wait for a bit. I go to Oxford tomorrow. And have to decide pretty soon whether I will go to Spain in March.

Together with his work on Blake and Eliot, Leavis was also working on his 'Memories of Wittgenstein' which the *Human World* had announced was going to appear there; and, Leavis wrote (5 November 1971), 'if they (as they will) print that they ought also to have, not long after, my reflections (i.e. "warning" and "dissociation") on the cult of Wittgenstein in English Schools'.

But while his own hands were full – 'I have too much on hand' (14 October 1971) – he was happy to know that his wife too, in spite of her illness, was carrying on '*her* literary work with rather frightening pertinacity. I've no doubt that there will be a new book of great distinction which the boys of the Literary World will blackguard, pillage and plagiarize – *comme d'habitude*. I'm getting back to *Four Quartets* from Blake.'

Of all the pressures now – and he had lived all his life 'steadily under great pressure' – that of getting his books written was, together with his concern for his wife's illness, the most urgent. Referring to a cheque from a foreign publisher, which he had mislaid and to his being ashamed of his unbusinesslike habits which made it impossible for him to affirm categorically whether he had received it or not, Leavis explained (29 November 1971):

You see, in the ordinary way I assume that all foreign payments come *via* Chatto and Windus (or the C.U.P.). Great wads of statements come to me from both concerns, and I'm always too hurried to establish what exactly comes under 'foreign'. I bundle my 'documents' along to my bank, which does my Income Tax return. As I get older, and feel more urgently that I must get my books written, it becomes more impossible than ever to spend myself being businesslike – I'm *not*, after all, ashamed. I know what I'm alive for.

The books he wanted to write certainly did not include what he had once again been approached to consider writing – namely, a memoir to be written both by him and his wife. There were indeed few decisions about which Leavis was so categorically firm and unyielding as that of not undertaking such a task nor countenancing that others should do so, as he explained to me in his letter (8 December 1971):

> I have to protect her [Q.D. Leavis] against all emotional intensities she can be spared ... I should have to go in for specificities about persons – Tillyard, I.A. Richards, E.M. Forster, Eliot, L.C. Knights, Hough & Co. – that aren't possible for me. I don't feel intense resentment, and in any case there would be no profit for the causes I care about. I could do it all in a novel – but at my age I've other things to do (and my wife would read the novel).
>
> My wife is different from me: she would recoil both from the full explicitnesses and from the evasions and repressions. If (hardly likely) she agreed at the start, she would find the problems multiplying. And if one could suppose the book written and published, the meannesses of the reviews would infuriate and wound her. Our part in the process of the writing would mean a horrible time for me: I should be under constant strain, and I should be *responsible* (I'm thinking of my wife). The life-long discrimination against her continues still. She knows, in a way, that we have won – we have not been suppressed; and deep down she has satisfaction in that. The actual record of the truth in print wouldn't bring satisfaction proportionate to the pain and the mischief (her heart was permanently damaged by last year's illness).
>
> I myself am not phlegmatic – but I have been in the country (so to speak) four hundred years. And, after all, not every Englishman is phlegmatic. Also, I'm an old – physically not old – distance-runner; 'in everything', I was told at school by the Games Master (mortally wounded at Loos in 1915).
>
> What I look for, so far as my wife is concerned, is some intelligent critical recognition. That is what she needs.

In the meantime, pressures upon him kept getting worse as he grew older. 'Not,' he wrote (14 December 1971),

> that my powers are failing, but that the 'creative' impulsion develops; the themes take shape and one thing leads to another. And of course I feel some urgency about getting my books written. There is the further consideration that I care very much about the issues that are concerned, and each new book co-operates with the other. This sounds self-important, but while one is alive, the world being what it is, and I being *not* Eliotic ... *Puritano frenetico*.

In 1972 *Nor Shall My Sword* came out. Leavis paid a flying visit to Spain in March in order to lecture at Bilbao University. In May he came to Belfast and lectured on 'Reading Out Poetry'.

In the meantime I had sent Leavis the draft of the Introduction I had written for my selection of his essays that Einaudi of Turin were bringing out. He read it and made some suggestions. For instance, while referring to *The Great Tradition*, I had pointed out that Jane Austen together with George Eliot, Dickens, Henry James and Conrad, constituted 'the great tradition' of the English novel for Leavis and that his critical and evaluative judgements on them had a revolutionary impact on the criticism of the novel in general. He suggested that I should leave out Jane Austen, observing:

> Of course, I don't myself leave her unmentioned, but I've devoted no critique to her. It's a delicate matter for me, since my wife ... wrote the (wholly original) classical criticism, which, in indignation, she has refused to publish in book form.

He also queried what appeared to him to be my 'implicit valuation' of I.A. Richards:

> He *has* a place in history – conditioned by his reckless self-contradiction and the nullity of the academic mind re literature. He stood for pseudo-science; e.g., the *quantitative* theory of value .... My own testimony is that he performed a valuable service in *The Principles* by waking us up out of a world of academic nullity by commonsense jogs – e.g. in the chapter summarizing Coleridge on rhythm and metre. But *Practical Criticism* is misnamed; Richards had *no* judgement (he got his tips from Forbes), and does no analysis, and in three or four of his chosen examples prompts wrongly. He is now in England a great and bad (Progressivist-philistine-mechanist) influence in Education Departments. An arch-enemy of Coleridge (being the great neo-Benthamite) and of my work. A pure Americanizer.

And in commenting on my references to his criticism of Hopkins, Leavis summed up Hopkins as 'the greatest technical inventor among Victorian poets', a poet 'who alone among the Victorian poets triumphs over the romantic tradition'.

In the same letter he also outlined what was going to be included in his forthcoming lecture at Belfast on 'Reading Out Poetry':

> As for my programme for May 10th I can't be definitive yet (or, possibly ever). But, having just read out successfully (at York University) all *Ash-Wednesday*, I realize how good, in its diversity, that work is. I should *start* with Shakespeare: The 'It is the cause' speech and Othello's last ('Soft you'); *Antony and Cleopatra*: 'The barge she sat in' and what *All for Love* does with it; then T.S. Eliot; possibly 11-15 of *The Wreck of the Deutschland* and a sonnet or two.

Though his lecture was eventually to include all this and something more – passages from *The Dunciad* and Hardy's poem 'After a Journey' – he remained uncertain till the very end as to what he was going to read out. Or, as he pointed out in a letter (29 April), he was still not 'absolutely definitive'.

> There are problems, and I've had little time or mind to spare for them. When I threw out my 'subject' I did so out of the habit of one who does much informal talking to limited audiences of people who know me and expect that. The formal circumstances and possibly large audience make an essential difference: I can't appear as offering a recital – haphazard, except as chosen by me. There must be something of a theme as introduction, frame and excuse. I've realized this in thinking about the event. I think I have now done the greater part of the necessary preparation (whatever the quality!).
>
> Giving myself a *direction* in some preliminary considerations, I have attached these to the first two poems in *Ash-Wednesday*; ... I shall go on to particular aspects of Shakespearian verse (I can make it an obvious critical sequence), confining myself to two passages from *Othello* ...
>
> Relation to Shakespeare (and the difference from T.S. Eliot) takes me to Hopkins ... Then to balance the distinction of *kinds* of verse, I want to read, of *The Dunciad*, Book IV, the first 16 lines and the last 30 ...
>
> How long all this will take I can't with confidence guess. But I should be morally licensed, if practical considerations left it reasonable, to read 'After a Journey'.

Leavis came to Belfast on the afternoon of 9 May, gave the lecture the following day and left for London the day after. The lecture, like the one on Yeats some six years earlier, was a tremendous success. The venue had to be shifted at the last minute to Whitla Hall with the largest seating capacity in the university, to accommodate a much larger audience than had been expected. In introducing Leavis to the audience, Dr. (now Sir) Arthur Vick, the then Vice-Chancellor of Queen's, recalled how, as a young lecturer in Physics at University College, London, he used to borrow copies of *Scrutiny* from friends long before Leavis had acquired the name of distinction he was to do in later years, and long before Dr. Vick came to know about Leavis' 'wide and lasting influence'. The lecture lasted well over an hour during which Leavis read out, in his incomparably and inimitably effective way, and with 'subtle shifts of tone, inflection and attack', the various poems and passages, accompanying his readings with critical comments on what was read out and also on the way poetry is generally read out, especially by actors. Thus Leavis' recitation of the poems turned out to be an exercise in close critical interpretation. At the outset of his lecture he asserted his belief that 'the mere reader of poetry who doesn't do a great deal of full reading out won't be able to read out in imagination', and that one's way of reading out poetry determines and is determined by one's critical awareness of and response not merely to 'the black marks on the page', but also to the rhythm, cadence and intonation which enact for him the subtlety and delicacy of the poet's thought and feeling. No wonder Leavis could say that where poems he cares about are concerned, he did not, as a rule, like other people's interpretations; did not, that is, like their way of reading out poetry.

After the lecture Leavis came to my room and although quite exhausted, he agreed, after taking a rest, to read out, at my request, that poem of Pound's he admired so much and on which he had written with such critical authority and acumen in *New Bearings in English Poetry* – *Hugh Selwyn Mauberley*. He read out the whole sequence – putting in some comments, in between his reading of one section and another, regarding Pound's superb mastery over the spoken idiom and cadence. His recital of the poem that evening brought out, charged with inescapable force, the meaning of what he had written almost half a century earlier, concerning Pound's verse which he found

> extraordinarily subtle, and its subtlety is the subtlety of the sensibility it expresses. No one would think here of distinguishing the way of saying from the thing said ... The rhythms, in their apparent looseness and carelessness, are marvels of subtlety .... What looks like the free run of contemporary speech achieves effects of a greater precision than can be found very often in *The Oxford Book* .... The movement is extraordinarily varied, and the tempo and modulation are exquisitely controlled.

On his return to Cambridge, Leavis wrote to say that he had had a comfortable flight to Heathrow and that he had found a circular ('in duplicate – one for Dr. Q.D.L.') of which he sent me a copy. It was a Cambridge Faculty of English Joint Academic Committee circular describing the meeting that had taken place on 1 March 1972 at which Professor L.C. Knights and other members of the Faculty of English were present. They discussed the subject of Practical Criticism and the circular reported it as follows:

> *Practical Criticism*. Professor Knights spoke to his paper (FB.72.7), and requested the views of the JAC on whether his assessment of the present situation was correct; if so, what were the reasons for a decline in enthusiasm for Practical Criticism, and what remedies might there be?
>
> A discussion took place in which the following points were made. Practical Criticism seems to have become an end in itself, whereas

close reading, which it is designed to encourage, should lead to a further end. Professor Knights was right in thinking that a problem had arisen, but classes and lectures, arranged centrally, by the Faculty, might provide a necessary new stimulus. Such stimulus is better provided in small groups. The present fault might be rather with the examination system than in Practical Criticism itself:

More exciting questions and passages might be chosen; and again most people found it more valuable to think about passages and poems for a longer period and in their own time, than to do so in exam conditions. The need for close reading was not being challenged, but the formal test of its proficiency through the Practical Criticism exam has become entangled with the specific views about authors of F.R. Leavis; in such conditions it has come to seem like merely assuming an orthodoxy, playing a game. Again, if people have rigid ideas in their minds as to which are *the* major, and the minor, English authors, Practical Criticism may come to seem like a hollow exercise.

Commenting on the circular, Leavis, in his letter to me (13 May 1972), observed:

Who, seeing the document, would guess that I have been 'retired' for a decade, and, before that, didn't (officially) *exist* as an intellectual force? ('Leavis' importance is zero' – G. Watson in the press, *Sunday Times*).

What interests me is that Professor Knights has in his Christian way sanctioned as normal the assumptions about and attitude towards me and my life's work clearly implied as current and decent in that brief J.A.C. summary.

There is no excuse for not *knowing* that Criticism (Practical = 'in practice' for me) fosters responsibility, and of its essential nature, as I have again and again insisted, explicitly and in practice, can't aim at 'rigid' values: I, like Polanyi, am dedicated to the exorcising of the Cartesian ghost. It's curious that Practical Criticism should not have been entangled with L.C.Knights' or Hough's or anyone else's 'specific views' as to which authors are major and which minor. And it's revealing that Knights permitted my name to figure in the 'report' in that way.

Leavis also wrote to the Vice-Chancellor of Queen's (14 May 1972) to thank him for what he had done to make his visit to Belfast a pleasurable experience:

I take the opportunity to express the pleasure with which I look back on my visit to Belfast. It had been, I won't deny, with an effort that I braced myself to the enterprise: I had been too long on the stretch and, moreover, wasn't at all sure that my throat would hold out – it hadn't fully recovered from an incapacity incurred in the rigours of a frustrated attempt to get to Bilbao a month ago. Since then I had actually been to Bilbao and several times to York.

I shouldn't involve myself in these things, if I didn't find them, for myself, disproportionately profitable, and I should like to say now that the visit to Belfast was very far from an exception. For that I owe a debt of gratitude to the Queen's University as a whole, but I know how great a special indebtedness that entails to yourself and Singh ...

I don't underrate the odds against us, but I am always – it's 'the university' as I conceive it that I'm thinking of – truly grateful to be confirmed in my conviction that we mustn't think of the battle as lost.

A fresh confirmation of what such a conviction meant in practice came in the form of Leavis' new book, *Nor Shall My Sword*, which was widely reviewed, although the reviews were, predictably, for the most part provocative and misrepresentative, not so much offering a disinterested appraisal of the themes and ethos of the book, as giving vent to the familiar stereotyped criticism of Leavis. The reviewer in *The Times* (13 July 1972), for instance, found the 'central difficulty' in dealing with Leavis' book to lie in his 'ultimately unacceptable language', meaning that it was not the language of such experts on cultural topics as Aldous Huxley, C.P. Snow, Lord Annan and Lionel Trilling, which was more congenial to the reviewer, even though she largely agreed with what Leavis had to say on cultural topics. Another criticism levelled against Leavis was that 'his stringency, his criticism of life have not led to any great creative energy or vitality in English schools, let alone in imaginative writing', as if Samuel Johnson's, Coleridge's, or Arnold's criticism of life had done so.

The *Times Literary Supplement* reviewer (21 July 1972), on the other hand, based his review largely on the supposed relevance of certain questions he posited and their implied answers, to the book under review. 'What did our most creative living minds actually study?', 'Has English literature as long a continuity as the study of the classics, or mathematics, or geography, or medicine, or anthropology?', 'Are its teachers obviously wiser and more mature than others?' Through such questions the reviewer tried to deal with or rather dispose of Leavis' concern regarding the English literary tradition, literary and cultural continuity, literary study as a training of intelligence and sensibility, as different from what he calls 'a confident "finish", the sense of adequacy, the poised and undeveloping quasi-maturity' which is inculcated by the study of the classics. The *Spectator* review, for its part, pontificated to the effect that 'If Blake failed in that enterprise, Dr. Leavis cannot hope to succeed,' adding: 'but something may still be achieved by his unsleeping sword', though he did not specify what. Instead, through a series of thinly veiled innuendoes, he set out to put in proper perspective, as it were, Leavis' whole career as a critic. 'Eliot was established as a key figure several years before Dr. Leavis published *New Bearings in English Poetry*', we are told, but not in what way or through the work and interpretation of which critic or critics. Similarly, we are told that 'there was a lot of critical money on Lawrence before Dr. Leavis backed him', but not a single example is given. And even when the reviewer defends others against Leavis' 'offensive tone', his 'gratuitously insulting tone', he gives us no more concrete or convincing example than Leavis' referring to Richard Wollheim as 'Professor Wollheim, who is a philosopher.'

Even the *Listener* review which, on the surface, seemed to do more justice to the book and to its author, could not help distorting Leavis' views, or attributing to him what his own writings would scarcely warrant. For instance, we are told that for Leavis 'nothing seems admirable until it is over' or that 'only the literature of the past can help us to live', which not only ignores the fact that the bulk of Leavis' writings is about modern literature (Yeats, Pound, Eliot, Lawrence, Joyce), but also flies in the face of Leavis' conviction that 'to initiate into the idea of living tradition except in relation to the present is hardly possible', that 'an addiction to literature that does not go with an interest in the literature of today, and some measure of intelligence about it, goes with the academic idea of tradition – traditionalism that is, in the bad sense'; and that 'a lack of interest in the present meant usually an incapacity for any real interest – the kind of interest that understands the meaning of "technique" – in literature at all.'

Leavis himself did not send any corrective rebuttals to these reviews, but on another matter he wrote a personal letter to Mr. Arthur Crook, the then editor of the *Times Literary Supplement*. On 3 November 1972 the *Times Literary Supplement* had published a review of *Sessanta posizioni* by Alberto Arbasino, Italian novelist and journalist, in which the reviewer set out to rectify Arbasino's errors, but in doing so he himself committed some. For instance, he said that Leavis 'has received the single honour previously only accorded to Samuel Johnson and Matthew Arnold, of always being referred to as "Doctor" ' and added, with pretentious knowledgeableness, that in Leavis' case 'the tag is unfortunately only too often used ironically rather than as a mark of distinction'. I wrote a letter to the editor of the *Times Literary Supplement*, protesting against such a misrepresentation.

The reason Samuel Johnson was referred to as 'Doctor' is partly because he had an honorary LL.D. conferred upon him by Oxford – honorary degrees have been before and after conferred by Oxford and Cambridge on lesser mortals than Dr. Johnson and Matthew Arnold – and partly because, at least in spoken English, it avoids confusion between Samuel Johnson's and Ben Jonson's names. As to Matthew Arnold, Signor Arbasino has obviously mistaken him for his father

Dr. Thomas Arnold who was a Doctor of Divinity. Although Matthew Arnold was himself in his later life awarded a D.C.L. by Oxford and an LL.D. by Edinburgh, he never allowed himself to be called Dr. Arnold; nor has he ever been referred to as such in literary history and criticism.

Lastly, Dr. Leavis. The use of 'Doctor' in his case indicates – no more and no less – the fact that he earned a Ph.D. in English literature from Cambridge in 1924, although in the last few years honorary degrees have also been conferred upon him by other universities. Hence there is nothing ironical in Leavis' being referred to as 'Doctor'. However ironical or laudatory your intent might be, you cannot in this country call a person a Doctor unless he has a doctorate or unless he holds a degree in medicine or divinity. Perhaps your reviewer as well as Signor Arbasino was thinking of Italy where titles are used with a certain degree of flexibility.

The *Times Literary Supplement* did not publish my letter, but I sent a copy of it to Leavis. He wrote to me (19 November 1972) to say that both he and his wife found my letter 'admirable' and that he was going to write a personal letter to the editor. Q.D. Leavis wrote (20 November 1972) separately to say that she was 'very touched' by the letter and referred to the *Times Literary Supplement's*

becoming increasingly scandalous in its deliberate and continuous anti-Leavis campaign. I was particularly disgusted by their long article on literary criticism in our time in the last number (Nov. 17) by Peter Porter, where the omission of *Scrutiny* and F.R.L. was so noticeable. This tradition goes back before the editorship of Crook to the reign of Pryce-Jones and of Charles Morgan before that (who wouldn't even allow our books to be reviewed, or mentioned except adversely) ... What saddens me is the cowardliness of so many of my husband's eminent old pupils who owe everything to him and for whom he often made sacrifices, but whose first instinct on achieving a position in the academic or journalistic world has been to drop us and take the popular line, sometimes while trying at the same time to keep a foot in our door to assure themselves that they have a good conscience. Human nature in the world of Eng. Lit. is very base I'm afraid, but even so you'd think that they'd have some shame about a concerted and perpetual attack of scurrilous misrepresentation and insult against a man in his seventy-eighth year who has done so much for literary studies and education and got so little out of it for himself.

A few days later, Leavis himself wrote to the editor of the *Times Literary Supplement*:

Dear Mr Crook,

After volunteering, in a telephone call earlier in the year, that you
knew I had had reason in Pryce-Jones's time for charging the *TLS*
with sustained and calculating discrimination against me, you expressed surprise at my insistence that there had been no change for
the better. I will, then, call to your notice a representative proof that,
if you really felt surprise, I am fully justified in calling *that* surpris-
ing. I have just received from Prof. Singh of Belfast a copy of a letter
for publication which you have not printed. He has never been in any
way a Cambridge man and he is not a pupil of mine: he is Head of the
Italian Department of the Queen's University, Belfast. His letter
regarded the review of Arbasino's book, and corrected unanswerably
a cannily injurious suggestion made, gratuitously, by the reviewer at
my expense.

Please don't reply that you can't find room for all the letters you
receive: that would be too patently impudent to be discreet. You will
recall that you had no hesitation in printing a letter from your
Geoffrey Grigson written merely, and with unconcealed gratuitousness (passed by you, no doubt, as public spirit), in order to express
his animus against me – who certainly have not by any offence
against him earned it – in a way significantly identical with your
reviewer's: by, that is, offering to make damaging play with the
'Doctor' that, in established habit, has attached itself to my name.
You had no excuse for printing Grigson's letter, and you were edito-
rially obligated to print Professor Singh's which you suppressed. But
Grigson is one of the boys: he can be sure you will print him – you
enlist him, indeed, for payment, and he knows that you won't edit out
of his space-filling the dragged-in sneer at me.

You will hardly tell me that Grigson is notorious, and that that
kind of thing doesn't do me the harm it is meant to. It is I who tell
you that. What, with so much like it, it does is to call more than
usually wide and marked attention to the anti-Leavis critical bias so
grossly apparent in the *TLS* and make even occasional and remotely
domiciled readers realize that the impudent treatment you meted out
to my wife's and my book on Dickens in the centenary year (and to
me, before it appeared, in a revealing fatuous article) was anti-criti-
cal policy you were committed to.

It's of no use replying to those (they are many) who comment
adversely on such treatment that the book deserved no better – for
the book was not eliminated (though the *TLS* policy impedes recognition). Of course, you had the approval of the coterie, and that is
obviously what matters to you. All the same, the coterie-control is
recognized in the universities, even among the inert and cynical –

and recognized increasingly for what it is: inimical to critical, and so to creative, life.

This statement, made responsibly out of wide experience, won't impress you, though, to my knowledge, you have received in your time many letters for publication which you have suppressed for the same reason as you have suppressed Professor Singh's: their having point and force that should have been decisive for you, and would therefore have offended your friends.

I don't expect you to be seriously troubled by the assurance that this letter, together with Professor Singh's, will be widely read at more than one university. You know, at any rate, why I won't let myself to be supposed to respect the *TLS*, or to regard it as anything but an enemy of what I stand for.

Mr. Crook's reply (5 December 1972), of which Leavis sent me a copy but which cannot be quoted, assured Leavis that had he himself written a letter on this particular subject, he was reasonably confident it would have been published, provided it was not libellous. Leavis 'rejoined', as he wrote to me (12 December 1972), by sending Mr. Crook a copy of *Virtue in our Time*

– the prolonged exchange of letters I had with Alan Pryce-Jones twenty years ago (there are two bound copies in the London Library – as Crook probably knows) ... Crook very likely won't sanction public use of his impudent reply, but I can't be stopped from printing my letter to him. I've an idea that it (and yours) might go with *Virtue* to form an addendum to a collection of my letters to the press that Tasker has my permission to assemble. I'm very interested in your other letter – that to the T.H.E.S. Too busy at the moment to comment.

Leavis' letter to Mr. Crook was not included in *Letters in Criticism*, which appeared in 1974.

The year 1973 found Leavis busy writing his new book (*The Living Principle*). In a letter he explained to me the sort of problem he had to deal with in the course of writing it:

Since my work has begun to get attention from philosophers I must ponder how much it would pay to dispose of them explicitly (e.g. the Wittgensteinians and Popperians) in the course of the new book – though I don't think philosophers are intelligent enough as a rule to repay the refuting them. The pondering entails the expenditure of thinking-time: my God! what linguistic gratuitousness the Wittgensteinians commit, and what naiveté they exhibit! In any case, I've confirmed my worst suspicions: that is something useful.

At this time he also received from Montale a new book of his poems, *Diario del '71 e del '72*, and when I visited him during the Easter vacation he wrote Montale a personal letter to thank him for the book:

Dear Montale,

I am not, in this informality of address, taking a liberty, but recognizing a fact: that your status as a great poet is so clear that one thinks of you, by the bare name. Also I like to feel that I know you in a personal way; I can't read your poetry without feeling *that*. Many thanks for the inscribed copy of *Diario del '71 e del '72* that Singh has left on his way back to Belfast. I have compelling anticipations in regard to the contents, but up till now have been able only to dip. My enemies stress my narrowness, but in spite of that I find my field of active interest continually expanding. I am not, for instance, a philosopher, and I have found most philosophers, in the pejorative sense, academic. Wittgenstein, who was my friend forty years ago, wasn't to be dismissed as that, but of late our very ignorant and stupid higher journalists have taken to associating me with him in a knowing way, though I had a basic antipathy to what he stood for. So I am faced with having to state and justify – marginally to a work centred in literary-critical thought – that antipathy. I must do it, dauntingly to philosophers, without the impossible expenditure of time and energy that would be incurred by attempting to do it in a 'philosophical' way. I must do it 'finally' but not thoroughly.

Finishing my new book was exacting enough in any case, without the undertaking to dispose of the Wittgensteinians, who call the philosophy they are interested in 'linguistic'. Actually they are naively fatuous about language: no exceptions to my offensive generalization, 'philosophers are always weak on language'. I shan't then have spare energy to *earn* my enjoyment of *Diario* for some time.

My wife joins in remembrances,
                              Yours sincerely,
                              F.R. Leavis

In the second week of May Leavis came to Belfast again to take a couple of seminars in my department on Dante and the English poets (Keats, Shelley and Eliot). A week before visiting Belfast he wrote to me to say (3 May 1973) that, on the occasion of its Golden Jubilee celebrations, Delhi University was going to award him a D.Litt. and had cabled to ask him if he was to go out and take it in person.

I replied at once by air-mail to the effect that I shouldn't think of declining such an honour from Delhi, but that it was impossible for me to go there for May 15. Since then the British Council has tried to 'persuade' me, but actually persuasion couldn't overcome near-impossibility. Today I got an air-mail letter from the Vice-Chancellor. I've answered *non possum* by cable, but I haven't revoked the acceptance. So it stands.

Some weeks after having come to take the seminars in my department, Leavis returned to Belfast again – this time to receive an honorary degree of D.Litt. from Queen's on 6 July. It was at this time that the IRA had issued a threat to bomb Belfast airport. Leavis himself was not perturbed, but he wrote to me to say (9 June 1973), that his wife 'having heard of IRA intentions *re* airport, is, I think, worrying at the thought of danger to me. Is there anything I can say with a view to assuaging her fears regarding new menaces?' I wrote back at once to say that, as far as one could humanly foresee, there was no greater danger to him in coming to Belfast now than there had been during his last two visits (May 1972 and May 1973) and that, in spite of or rather because of the IRA warning, Belfast airport was even safer than any other British airport – an answer which seems to have reassured Mrs. Leavis.

After taking his honorary degree Leavis returned to Cambridge, and wrote back to report his safe arrival, adding (8 July 1973):

It was from my point of view an extremely felicitous visit to Belfast. I won't pretend to like the public exposure necessarily involved, but that was very much more than compensated by the accompaniments – the multitudinous reminder of the human kindliness of ordinary people (in spite of the strains they suffer in Belfast), and the talk with a dozen or so human individuals who reassure one in relation to the potential community one *must* hope and work for. I feel this need desperately after terminals, flights, the Heathrow blight and the underground. Everyone I needed to address me was 'nice', but, my God! the civilization that has flypapered them, and is working its way down to the root and the seed.

   Vick is a good and intelligent man – two adjectives for the central quality in him.

On 12 July, Leavis wrote again to say that he had declined, 'in the face of pertinacious pressure, the invitation to be present the following Saturday (Fête Nationale) at a dinner at Peterhouse in honour of Sir Geoffrey Keynes. Not because (though it is) my 78th birthday: I recoil from the thought of meeting the bevy of Blake authorities. They haven't been very useful to Mark Roberts [Emeritus Professor of English, Keele University] – or to anyone (I mean, critically).'

Leavis was still working on his new book of which, he wrote (23 November 1973), 'only the last of the three parts is devoted to *Four Quartets*. I'm calling it: *The Living Principle: 'English' as a Discipline of*

Thought and giving as lectures at York the first part in three instalments: "Thought, Language and Objectivity".' The part devoted to Eliot was the longest of the three parts, described in a letter (21 September 1974), as 'an analytico-interpretative commentary to *Four Quartets*. To pay it that amount of attention is to pay it a great tribute, however qualified.' Leavis continued visiting York for lectures and seminars throughout 1974, 1975 and 1976. Before *The Living Principle* actually came out, Chatto had already received Leavis' subsequent and last book *Thought, Words and Creativity*. In 1976 *Universities Quarterly* brought out a special number dedicated to F.R. Leavis which included Michael Tanner's review of *The Living Principle*. In a successive issue the *Universities Quarterly* published Leavis' comment on Michael Tanner's contribution. 'He was,' said Leavis (15 January, 1976), 'flattering, but suffered (as I did) from a philosopher's misconceptions. I couldn't elucidate my intention in *The Living Principle* without taking space. My commentary cost me some exhausting thought. But that, I felt, pushed the frontier forward.'

Anything in the nature of a challenge to his powers of critical thought and analysis, however exhausting, Leavis found stimulating in spite of his age. For instance, on 5 November 1976, he wrote to say that he wouldn't be commuting to York in the Lent Term. 'At present I am concentrating on next Wednesday's seminar which is on an intrinsically very difficult theme – very profitable to me.'

The year closed with the publication of what was to be his last book to appear in his lifetime – the second book on Lawrence (*Thought, Words and Creativity: Art and Thought in D.H. Lawrence*) – and the year 1977 found him, as he wrote to me (22 April 1977) – the last letter I received from him – 'just finishing for my new book a critique of an unprecedented kind which I should like to think would be attended to.' This new book of which the critique was to be part was unfinished before Leavis was taken ill. Selected material from it and from what he had been writing in his last active months appeared in the first and second posthumously published volumes of his essays: *The Critic as Anti-Philosopher* (Chatto & Windus, 1981) and *Valuation in Criticism and Other Essays* (Cambridge University Press, 1986), both edited by me.

In 1975 *The Times*, the BBC, and the *Spectator* all marked Leavis' eightieth birthday with some token of recognition. *The Times Profile* of F.R. Leavis by Victoria Brittain, subtitled 'Half a Century of Arousing Academic Enmity' (17 February 1975), paid tribute to him, as 'teacher of English literature, critic of English society, ... the educator and moralist extraordinary and the fierce guardian of our civilization who has been loved, hated and embattled throughout his career'. 'It's hard to imagine, when you meet Leavis', the profile-writer concluded, 'that a man of such old-fashioned politeness, modesty, scrupulous attentiveness and candour should have come in for so much venom from the academic establishment.' And she reported what Leavis told her by way of explaining such enmity:

'It is the nature of English that it has no rigorous tests of excellence – being at the other end of the scale from mathematics. In English there are no tests. The mediocre coagulate and hang together to keep people of vision off the appointments board.'

Just a few months before his death Leavis' name was included in the New Year's Honours List: he was made, together with Jack Jones, a Companion of Honour. *The Times*, in its editorial, hailed the honour by observing that 'it would be hard to find another pair who had trodden two such different paths to two such different kinds of recognition, having only the pugnacity, their measure of influence, and their deserts in common'. Speaking largely of Leavis, the editorial indicated that it was 'a belated honour', and that 'he would not be Dr Leavis if he did not find some extra satisfaction in spotting in his CH an implied rebuke by the establishment proper of the petty establishment in Cambridge'. In determining 'the true measure of his contribution', in spite of his 'infuriating' methods of controversy, the editorial referred to Leavis' influence before, during and after the Second World War as operating on two levels: 'dissemination of a new form of academic literary criticism' and 'promoting a revolution in taste, a new sensibility' through his 'original reappraisals of lasting importance'. Leavis' characteristic combination of 'exaltation and rigour', the editorial concluded, 'is falling out of fashion again, though Dr Leavis has continued to preach it as fiercely as ever. He is most happily honoured for it.'

Commenting on *The Times* leader, Mr. Geoffrey Robinson, Labour M.P. for Coventry, North West, also pointed out 'the belatedness' of Leavis' honour, a sort of 'disrespect to the man and an inextinguishable blot on the working of the honours system'. And he added: 'But it is to the Prime Minister's credit that justice has finally been done. For Dr Leavis and Lord Keynes must rank as the two great pedagogues of the century.'

There were also many letters of congratulations from individuals – Vice-Chancellors, academics, men of letters and politicians. Denis Healey wrote to say how glad he was at the honour conferred on Leavis, and he added: 'You have been a great influence on my thinking and writing ever since I first began reading *Scrutiny* in the early Thirties. I imagine there must be thousands of others you have never met who would say the same.' Lord Shackleton too wrote to say that 'although we have never met, I have been an admirer, if I may say so, of your work for many years. It is a most appropriate honour even though it is overdue.' In her congratulations Shirley Williams observed how pleased she was to see his name in the New Year's Honours List – 'a well-deserved recognition of your work'. 'I do not believe', wrote Lord Goodman, 'that during my sojourn at Downing we ever met but it has given me great pleasure to read of your honour and as a most undeserving member of the same Order I send you my warmest congratulations.' In the world of letters, and considering the relationship between the two, the most significant letter was from I.A. Richards: 'Warm companion's felicitations! You should have had them long before this, but we have been away in Spain and Magdalene between Christmas and the Lent term seems to hibernate as regards letters.' Among *Scrutiny* contributors and editors the only person to write to congratulate Leavis was D.W. Harding. 'You will be overwhelmed', Harding wrote, 'with congratulations and this note needs no reply. But I do want to say how immensely glad I am. I hope it has been a pleasure to you and Queenie. Belated acknowledgement is all too familiar to you but there is generosity in accepting it – and the appointment gives real satisfaction to those who admire you and know how much we owe to you.'

Lord Eric James, the then Vice-Chancellor of York University, where Leavis had been Visiting Professor since his retirement, wrote to say that it was

> immensely encouraging that the system which produces these things does sometimes produce an answer so completely *right* as this. For who deserves honour more than the creative critic who has helped so many to recognise and appreciate the best, and not only that, but the great teacher who has affected the teaching of English not only in universities but in schools so that it is becoming a genuine cultural force? That this has at last been so strikingly recognised is something that really does illuminate the beginning of a New Year for all the many people who are grateful to you.

Lord Boyle, Vice-Chancellor of Leeds University, also congratulated Leavis:

> this surely is one of those awards – perhaps one of the few – whose currency has been maintained in coinage not a whit debased. Certainly there can never have been a worthier recipient.
>
> The twenty volumes of *Scrutiny*, happily reprinted before the 'great inflation', would alone have satisfied most men as an *oeuvre*, and the expression of your belief in the University as a creative centre of civilisation. But you have gone on still further – I'm thinking especially of your essay on *Little Dorrit*, your magnificent exposition of the *Four Quartets*, and – not least – those years at York University which I hope gave you at least a fraction of the pleasure and satisfaction they gave Eric James.

Derek Bower, Master of Emmanuel College, Cambridge, where Leavis studied and later on lectured and supervised, congratulated Leavis on behalf of the College, and noted that for him there was

> extra pleasure in writing because it is so outstanding an award to one of the very few literary critics of the 20th century who had always kept his nerve about the value of the study of literature. I am sure I

do not exaggerate when I say that many thousands of people throughout the country will feel real pleasure at the award.

Henry Gifford, formerly Professor of English at Bristol University, where Leavis had been Churchill Professor for a term and where he had also given some public lectures, including the Wordsworth Birth Centenary Lecture, referred to 'this long delayed recognition' and told Q.D. Leavis that

> Ten years or more ago it would have heartened him in the efforts he was then making to round off his work. But I'm sure you are both glad of it – although honours from the state count for little when set against the achievement itself. Such work needs no validation from outside.

Among Leavis' former pupils who wrote to convey their sense of gratification for the award, two representative examples may be cited: one from a headmaster and one from a retired Civil Servant. Mr Robin Williams, Headmaster of Walton High School, Nelson, Lancs., wrote to say:

> You will have forgotten me. I was at Downing from 1952-55 and you were to distinguish me from another by the term 'The Northern Williams'. What little I understand of education I chiefly owe to yourself.

Mr Patrick Harrison, formerly in the Civil Service, congratulated Leavis while dwelling on the particular distinction and privilege the Companionship enjoys:

> From my days as a private secretary in the Civil Service I seem to remember a note about the Companionship to the effect that it was an honour of special distinction to be reserved for those for whom a knighthood was inappropriate or too commonplace. How right for you!
>
> It may sometimes have caused you regret that some of your pupils strayed, as I have done, into wildernesses far from the influence of English Literature. You should know, for myself at least – and it might be true for many another of us and it is this which gives the news its real point – that in the unending struggle to think and behave well I owe you more than anyone else alive.

Some four months after the award of the CH Leavis died, on 14 April 1978. His death was reported in *The Times*, the *Guardian* and the *Daily Telegraph*, each of which published long obituaries and critical appraisals. The most comprehensive and well-balanced was in *The Times*. It summed

up Leavis' achievements as a critic – 'the most controversial literary critic
of his time' – and their revolutionary impact on the concept and practice
of literary criticism. *The Times* described Leavis' methods of critical
scrutiny and evaluation as superseding 'the narrative type of literary
history, the older mode of Legouis, Oliver Elton and Saintsbury', and went
on to say how

> By his studies of great literary figures of the interwar years – Eliot,
> Pound and Joyce, but above all, D.H. Lawrence – and by his attacks
> upon what he judged anaemic, shoddy or pernicious – Georgian
> poetry, the works of Arnold Bennett, popular journalism and mass
> media – Leavis sharpened the contours of taste and judgement. In
> tracing the main lines of English poetry through Donne to Pope, and
> Johnson, through Blake to Hopkins and Eliot, or marking more
> stringently the 'great tradition' of the novelist in five novelists he
> displayed his fine responsiveness and powers of literary 'placing'.

Scrutiny was described as 'Leavis' greatest contribution to English letters',
the Downing School of English as 'a highly individual and personal creation', and Leavis' literary judgements as being 'at once highly specific and,
while in form tentative, yet delivered with great natural authority', as a
result of which he became 'a symbolic figure both nationally and wherever
English is taught – in America, India, Australia'. And *The Times* obituary
concluded by pinpointing the essential trait of Leavis' personality and the
nature and extent of his influence:

> A certain Spartan frugality and fine intensity of living marked him
> with a mixture of vitality and asceticism; something at once very
> fragile and very wiry in his slight figure, but above all the flame-like
> nimbleness of his speech and glance, compelled attention. While to
> some he seemed a rare talent grown painfully awry, to others he
> assumed almost Socratic powers. His influence extended far beyond
> the boundaries of the subject to which he confined himself.

Spontaneous expressions of esteem, indebtedness and admiration accompanied letters of condolence Q.D. Leavis received from many people.
One of the first to send his condolences was G. Wilson Knight – in which
he, like others, linked the names of husband and wife in recognition of
their lifelong collaboration and of what they had achieved together.

Professor (now Lord) Brian Morris of Sheffield University, and formerly
of the University of York where he had worked with Leavis from 1964 to
1970, wrote to Q.D. Leavis to say that Leavis had left them

> in no doubt that his work and his achievement would have been
> impossible without you. He often mentioned the quite inestimable

contribution you had always made to his thinking and his critical judgements, in addition to your own work, and said that we all owed far more than we would ever know to your scholarship and your acumen. I would just like you to know that there are those of us who appreciate, and are deeply grateful for all that the two of you, together, have done for English studies.

Lord James, under whose Vice-Chancellorship Leavis had been a Visiting Professor at York University, wrote to say, among other things, that

> Frank was one of the very few unquestionably great men that I have known. I suppose I felt a particular respect for him because he was a supreme exponent of my own profession – that of the teacher. He was also the clearest voice on the other thing I cared about – making the universities a centre for sweetness and light. Ever since I read your own *Fiction and the Reading Public* at Oxford, the Leavises have been one of the major formative influences on my thinking – as it has been on many hundreds of others all over the world. For example, at Peshawar on the North West Frontier I was listened to with something like awe because I knew you both. He really has a memorial more lasting than any other could be – the fact that countless men and women think more clearly and care more deeply for excellence and truth because he lived.
>
> It is one of the proudest and happiest things in my life that York had the privilege of the presence of you both, and that you found something congenial there.

Another Vice-Chancellor, Lord Edward Boyle of Leeds University, also mingled the expression of his condolences with a tribute to Leavis:

> Dr. Leavis once wrote that the kind of poet who matters is 'at the most conscious point of the (human) race in his time'; those words were also true of *himself*, and that is why he was so great a man.
>
> He raised the whole standard of literary criticism in this country, and he enlarged, for countless pupils, their sense of the possibilities of life.
>
> I only hope there will never be lack of men and women who give *his* writings the same attention that he bestowed on those poets and novelists so uniquely well. He fought hard, and did not shrink from personal controversy, precisely because he was absolutely committed – heart and soul – to those overriding *impersonal* causes of civilization and tradition.
>
> I have always felt amazed that it should have fallen to me to speak when *we* were both awarded honorary degrees here, and it truly was one of the most memorable occasions of my life.

The letter from Alan G. Hull, Vice-Chancellor of Cambridge, was, by comparison, formal and succinct: 'Please accept', he wrote to Q.D. Leavis, 'my deepest sympathies on the most sad loss of your highly esteemed husband'. There were, however, other letters from Cambridge dons and scholars with more specific references to Leavis' achievement, to the impact he had made on the teaching of English and to what he stood for. John Stevens, Chairman, Faculty Board of English, Cambridge, wrote on his own behalf and on that of many members of the English Faculty, to express their admiration and gratitude for Leavis' work. Alluding to 'many personal memories of FRL, dating especially from the days, long ago, when he invited me to supervise his Downing freshmen in medieval literature', Mr. Stevens observed: 'But the debt of my generation to FRL's dedicated life and work is hardly to be measured in personal terms. For many of us what he did, and stood for, forms a bastion in our literary experiences and one for which we shall never cease to be grateful.' Although 'hardly more than briefly acquainted with him in any direct way', H.C. Prynne of Churchill College wrote to say that through Leavis' work 'I have known and admired his profound creative energy for many years. It is perhaps fruitless to look for much gratitude in relation to such a tellingly exemplary career; but there is wide-spread and deep-rooted indebtedness which cannot be ignored, and for myself I feel thankful for that in a quite specific and personal sense.'

Letters of condolence came from the 'English' Schools and education faculties in other Universities as well. Professor Philip Brockbank who had been instrumental in getting Leavis to accept the Visiting Professorship at York wrote to attest to 'the University's great debt and obligation' during 'the crucially important last phase of his work'. There are many here, wrote Brockbank,

> who feel a vivid sense of loss, which will for some be attended by a renewed sense of what he stood and stands for. The porters and domestic staff too speak of him with great respect and affection and were eager to contribute, had it seemed appropriate, flowers and formal remembrances. F.R.'s concern with everyday humanity was not theoretical.

Professor Henry Gifford wrote of the great privilege and happiness it was to have Leavis at Bristol as Churchill Professor. 'The entire dedication of his mind to the work', he said,

> did not surprise me, though in a man of his age it was moving and inspiring. What I had been less prepared for was the friendship he offered, and the warmth of his response to Bristol and to ourselves .... All of us have learned immeasurably from him, most of all

perhaps an attitude summed up in the final words about poetry in *New Bearings*: 'Those who care about it can only go on caring.'

Professor William Walsh, who had studied under Leavis, published a book on him soon after his death, and had taken part in the BBC tribute to Leavis on the occasion of his eightieth birthday, referred to 'the great loss sustained by English life and letters' in the death of Leavis. René Wellek with whom Leavis had had an exchange of views in the fifties about the relation of philosophy to poetry and to literary criticism, which elicited Leavis' celebrated essay 'Philosophy and Criticism' (*The Common Pursuit*) said: 'I shall never cease to admire him for his courage, integrity and insight in spite of disagreements which are inevitable given my different background, training and experience.'

Some people came to know Leavis during his visits to various universities, especially after his retirement from Cambridge. 'We remember with pleasure and gratitude', wrote Mr. Desmond Slay, Head of the English Department, The University College of Wales, Aberystwyth, 'the period when, some eight years ago ... your husband held at Aberystwyth a University of Wales Visiting Professorial Fellowship. The lectures and seminars he gave us during his visits then, like his many writings, were an inspiration.' Mr. James Ogden, another member from the same department, wrote to say that he owed to Leavis the better part of his intellectual life and assured Mrs. Leavis that 'there are many people unknown to you, who will be trying to carry on his work and yours'. The Principal of the University College of Swansea – Professor Robert W. Steel – quoted by way of endorsement what the *Guardian* had said about Leavis in its obituary: 'possibly the finest English literary critic and teacher of the century.' Professor Alun R. Jones of the University College of North Wales wrote to say that his department was 'honoured to be associated with him while he was Professorial Fellow in this department; we came not only to admire him, but to develop a personal affection for him'. Dr McDemslie of the English Department, University of Edinburgh, while sharing Mrs. Leavis' grief, said that 'While misrepresentation has, in obituaries, pursued F.R. Leavis beyond the grave, be assured that those who knew him and learnt from him, however briefly, recognize this.' Professor A. Wigham Price, Head of the English Department, Durham University, who had been Leavis' student, wrote to attest how much Leavis had given him when, around 1936, he joined his 'Appreciation and Analysis' course, 'as he led us into the heart of poem after poem'; and added:

Youth is naturally self-centred. It is only as you come to the age of retirement (as I have) that you look back over the years, decide who the (few) people were who *really* gave you something precious in your youth, and wish you had been more appreciative at the time. It is, alas, now too late to thank *him*; but it is not too late to share with *you*

my deep sense of gratitude, typical (I'm sure) of hundreds of others.
His approach to the task, his rigorous standards, his general concern,
have become part of us. It was a privilege to have sat at his feet.

Perhaps the longest letter Q.D. Leavis received was from Peter Green-
ham of the Royal Academy of Arts, who had painted him some sixteen
years earlier – a letter in which he recalls in a detailed and vividly
evocative way the various traits of Leavis' personality, his temperament
and his habits as observed by a painter. 'I could never forget', he told Mrs.
Leavis,

I had painted your husband – was it sixteen years ago? Very little
time goes by but I think of him and the intense pleasure I had from
our meetings. I always think of him moving lightly and quickly.
There were so many things that my first sketches don't show, his
courtesy, his quickness, the sweetness of his smile as well as the
fierceness and nobility of his eyes, that the reason I did not send them
to you was that I didn't think they were good enough to do him justice.
There was no moment when I thought to myself 'I won't send them'.
It is simply that the more I looked at them the less I thought they
would do.
  I can remember so much of what happened when I painted him:
his walking with me one day to the shops when I had run out of white
paint; the visit of an American to the hall where we worked; the stray
Alsatian which used to roam the garden, which Dr. Leavis fed; the
afternoon when the butler asked us to tea and your husband begged
me to eat the jam toasts in case the butler should think his hospitality
slighted; his telling me I didn't when I said I liked the novels of
Arnold Bennett: well, anyway (I stuck it out) some of them; well,
there was a time when I thought I did. And in the afternoon he
brought a book and read to me what Henry James said about *Clay-
hanger*. I was tremendously grateful to him for 'he was a nice man',
for it's that that seems to count in Bennett's books, after all.
  I can see him now as clearly as if it were yesterday afternoon:
sitting on a bench by a long table in the hall, never restless yet both
calm and tense: suddenly silent for a while, then perhaps very quietly
speaking a poem of Hardy's ('After a Journey'), then listening while
I said I always wanted to like Kipling, but was always dashed when
I read him. I said a number of silly things and in those days smoked
without stopping, yet he never showed the slightest impatience: not
even when I told him I liked one brush better than the others though
it was nearly worn down, and that I had been to the cinema two or
three evenings running (he said Wittgenstein did the same!). The
strongest impression is of being in the presence of genius and of a
man so unworldly as to be almost of a different race from other men:

as Lawrence seemed to be: and he shared with Lawrence the shabbi-
est obituaries of our time, I think.

In the two last remaining years of her life her husband's death gave a
new perspective to Q.D. Leavis' own thinking, and a poignant meaning to
her recollection of his life, work and personality. What she always thought
of him, from the day she fell in love with him as an undergraduate,
acquired an added significance and impinged upon her with a particular
force. If, in his earlier years with her, he reminded her of the cock's crow
in Melville's tale *Cock-a-Doodle-Do*, 'full of pluck, full of fun, full of glee. It
plainly says Never say die!', in his later years she came to see him in the
terms he himself had applied to Hopkins in his lecture: 'a man of high
intelligence, fine human perception, irresistible charm and complete integrity' – a quote she had copied in her notebook.

Another quote she had copied – a quote the spirit of which she herself
fully shared – is from a letter from John Speirs, the one *Scrutiny* collaborator who remained close to the Leavises till the very end, and to whom,
after Leavis' death, she had sent a photograph of Robert Austin's charcoal
drawing of Leavis at the age of thirty-nine (now in the National Portrait
Gallery, London). 'It brings him back to me', wrote Speirs, linking his
impressions of his first and his last meeting with Leavis,

> as he was in those earlier years. I never forgot my first meeting with
> him in his room (at Emmanuel), his wonderful vividness and how in
> a few minutes he put me in living touch with the reality of the
> contemporary literature for the first time. Yes, that last meeting with
> him too, is as unforgettable. It was in a strange way also a happy
> moment – the smile that lit up his eyes as he recognized me and
> pronounced my name. In general the sadness of his own life becomes
> unbearable when one begins to think about it, but there are those
> wonderful 'creative memories' as I often remember Frank himself
> once called them. It must, in spite of your sorrow, also be a high
> satisfaction to you to think of your great creative achievement to-
> gether through all those years and lifetime of creativeness together
> – such a great achievement and that is now *permanently* there.

12

Posthumous Publications

> I think of myself as an anti-philosopher, which is what a literary critic
> ought to be – and every intelligent reader of creative literature is a
> literary critic.
>
> F.R. Leavis

The Critic as Anti-Philosopher

After Leavis' death, one of the tasks Q.D. Leavis was confronted with was
that of preparing a selection of his hitherto uncollected essays in book
form, together with her memoir of him. She wrote to me, giving me a list
of what she was going to include, and asked if there were other items I
might suggest. After her death, the task of editing and bringing out this
volume fell to me. The selection, including all she had intended to publish
as well as some other items I chose, came out with Chatto in 1981, with
the title *The Critic as Anti-Philosopher*. The title reflected the position
Leavis had consistently maintained since he wrote that well-known essay
'Philosophy and Literary Criticism' (*The Common Pursuit*) in which, while
defending himself against René Wellek's criticism of *Revaluation*, he had
outlined what he considered to be the fundamental differences between a
philosopher's approach to a literary text and that of a literary critic whom
he identified with 'a whole critic'.

This volume was intended by Q.D. Leavis as the third of a trilogy, of
which the other two – *The Living Principle* (1975) and *Thought, Words and
Creativity* (1976) – had come out in Leavis' lifetime. The first two essays
in the volume, 'Justifying One's Evaluation of Blake' and 'Wordsworth:
The Creative Conditions', and the last two, ' "Believing in" the University'
and 'Mutually Necessary', as well as 'Memories of Wittgenstein' and
'Eugenio Montale', are part of Leavis' last writings; the other essays are
older – some had been published in *Scrutiny* or in other periodicals, while
some are introductions or contributions to books.

Leavis' latest essays reflect his continuing interest in the problems and
predicaments of contemporary civilisation, as well as in the nature of
thought and art-speech in the non-philosophical sense, and how they affect
creative writing. Motivating this interest was, as he put it, 'my very
painful concern – Lord help me! – ... for the re-establishment of an

educated reading public, so that there might again be a living literature continuing what is now "classical", and major creativity might again have some influence on civilization'. It was, of course, by no means a new concern; but during the last years of his life it preoccupied him to an almost obsessive degree, as he contemplated the changes and developments around him.

Another preoccupation of his was the definition of the nature of thought and language, which he regarded as inseparable from his concern with the problem of creating a new educated public. 'It is an urgent matter,' he jotted down in his notes, 'to achieve articulate thought about meaning, value and art-speech in a civilization whose philistine commonsense has lost any sense of the difference between life and electricity.' But the nature of this problem and the way he set about resolving it were, as he cogently argued in the essay 'Mutually Necessary', 'most decidedly *not* philosophical'; nor were the criteria that governed his thinking the criteria of a philosopher. What Leavis calls 'my "anti-philosophical" mode of thought' is seen in its application in all the essays included in this volume, though dealt with more specifically in 'Mutually Necessary'.

The very title of this volume emerges from Leavis' comments as he was planning it, comments that may be taken as so many headings or aspects under which he was to characterise – as he does in the essay included in this volume – the nature of thought as it should interest a literary critic and his own position vis-à-vis that thought: 'Language and Anti-Philosophic Thought', 'Thought and Art-Speech' or 'Art-Speech as Thought', 'Rightness, Precision and Belief: Thought and Impersonality', 'Discrepant Thought-Modes and Dual Word-Values', 'Individuality as Transcendent Thereness of Life'.

In the first two books of the trilogy, T.S. Eliot and D.H. Lawrence were the centre of Leavis' critical – and creative – thought; in the last, along with Blake, it was going to be Wordsworth who, Leavis wrote down in his notes, 'affects us as a creative force of life', as the 'growing tip of life' and as 'robustly individualized as a human being can be'. And even though Wordsworth is 'of the acclaimed poets the neglected one', he is peculiarly qualified to speak to our 'present sick civilization'. If Eliot demonstrated in this century 'how formidable poetry can be as thought', in the last century it was Wordsworth – 'the poet of genius capable of creating reality' – who did so.

The last public lecture Q.D. Leavis had given and seen published in her lifetime was entitled 'The Englishness of the English Novel'. If Leavis were to have given a lecture on 'The Englishness of English Poetry' (hardly a Leavisian title, I should have thought, until I recalled his essay on 'The Americanness of American Literature') Wordsworth would surely have figured in it as a key name or, to use a Poundian phrase, a key 'exhibit,' just as Jane Austen, George Eliot, and Charles Dickens figure in Q.D. Leavis' lecture. However, if only non-dramatic poetry were in question, he would be perhaps *the* key figure. Of course Leavis did not write on Wordsworth as much or as often as he did on Lawrence or Eliot; nor did he, in matters relating strictly to form, technique, and style, consider Wordsworth as important, or, at least, as interesting as, say, Donne, Pope, or Hopkins. And insofar as he responded to the mystical, the religious, or the visionary in poetry, he valued Blake more than Wordsworth or Eliot.

Yet Wordsworth's poetry at its best meant a great deal to Leavis. What it meant is as difficult to pinpoint or illustrate as it is to give, in Leavis' own words, 'a satisfying account of Wordsworth's greatness.' He responded to it, with the utmost powers of perception, analysis, and judgement at his command; and he wrote about it with an unusual degree of sympathy and inwardness. In fact, there is no major poet other than Shakespeare about whom Leavis had fewer critical reservations than Wordsworth. The earlier essay of his from *Revaluation* (1936) – the weightiest and the most original in the volume – is a landmark in Wordsworth criticism, and more significant than any other single piece of Wordsworth criticism since Arnold's essay, not excepting even James Smith's *Scrutiny* essay which Leavis himself admired.

After *Revaluation* Leavis' critical interest shifted to and was mostly focused on T.S. Eliot and D.H. Lawrence; but in later years he returned to Wordsworth. He gave seminars on him at York University, and delivered the 'Wordsworth Bicentenary Lecture' at Bristol University, and in the last two years of his life, whatever he was engaged in writing was directly or indirectly connected with Wordsworth, whom he came to see both as a corrective and as a supplement to Eliot – and not least so because like Eliot, Wordsworth, too, had altered expression.

In the 'Bicentenary Lecture', while discussing the creative conditions which made Wordsworth possible, Leavis set out to account for the greatness of a poet who was 'in the nineteenth century, and still in my childhood, a very important influence – such an influence as only a great poet could be'. In doing so he reformulated his own approach to Wordsworth's poetry, contrasting it with what he considered to be the 'inert concurrence in conventional valuations and reputations' that Wordsworth criticism – past and present – amounted to for Leavis.

In his earlier essay (in *Revaluation*) Leavis had confined Wordsworth's decisive creativity – his innovating power and the nature of his originality – to a very limited phase of his life, and had singled out the story of Margaret – 'The Ruined Cottage' – as a poem that more than any other single poem by Wordsworth vindicates his importance and originality as a poet. In his 'Bicentenary Lecture', he examines that poem again. Quoting from 'Peter Bell the Third,' where Shelley 'turns the intensity of his interest and critical intelligence on Wordsworth', registering, among other things, 'his perception of the differences between himself and Wordsworth', Leavis considers some of Shelley's remarks a real tribute to

Wordsworth's genius – a tribute that helps him define and pinpoint his own critical response to Wordsworth's poetry.

According to Shelley, Wordsworth 'had a mind which was somehow/At once circumference and centre/Of all he might or feel or know', had 'as much imagination as a pint-pot', and was a 'kind of moral eunuch'. And yet, Shelley noted, 'his was an individual mind,/And new created all he saw/In a new manner', and that language in his hand was 'like clay while he was yet a potter' – a tribute 'the more impressive for being accompanied by severe adverse and limiting judgements'. If Leavis finds Shelley's criticism which he implicitly endorses stimulating, it is because it brings out the differences between Shelley and Wordsworth which Leavis comments on as follows:

> Wordsworth seems static; poised above his own centre, contemplating; Shelley always moving headlong – eagerly, breathlessly, committed to pursuing his centre of gravity lest he should fall on his face ... Shelley always seems to *have* a temperature – the effect is given by the pervasiveness in his verse of erotic suggestion, overt or explicit.

No wonder Shelley finds Wordsworth cold, frigid and devoid of suggestions 'of embracing, caressing, fondling – of erotic warmth – in the habit of sensibility expressed in his verse'.

However, in spite of such differences, Wordsworth mattered immensely to Shelley; otherwise, says Leavis, he would not have been drawn to read him with 'that devoted intensity'. The one particular aspect of Wordsworth's achievement that was so relevant to Shelley and to Shelley's contemporaries is the way he, like Eliot later on, altered expression, which made it possible 'for *them* to achieve the means of expressing their own instinctive sensibilities'.

As to the identification between the Wanderer and Wordsworth, or between the 'I' of the poem and Wordsworth, Leavis argues how 'at this crucial moment of his creative career (indistinguishably, for him, of his life – his greatness as a poet is given in that identity), the thought of the poor woman's suffering is not a matter of "emotion recollected in tranquillity". The Wanderer, of whom we have been told, with the diagnostic verb italicized, "He could *afford* to suffer/With those whom he saw suffer", is the ideal Wordsworth he aspires, in an effort of imaginative realization, to be.' Leavis quotes another passage (starting from 'He spoke with somewhat of a solemn tone' and ending with 'He would resume his story') to illustrate how, with its dramatic immediacy, surprise and inevitableness, it evokes 'the compulsion, the whole complex state' of the actual Wordsworth who could not achieve the Wanderer's 'assured tranquillity' and who is 'tormented by a compulsion that makes him expose himself to the contemplating he can hardly endure'. This constitutes the main reason why the actual Wordsworth cannot contemplate, without profound emotional disturbance, 'the condition incident to human life in general, the condition made concretely present in the story of Margaret'. This, for Leavis, is the urgent personal problem Wordsworth is wrestling with in 'The Ruined Cottage' and his preoccupation with technique, poetic diction, versification, 'as he writes and ponders, identifies itself in his mind – and his fingers – with that'. The poem, thus, represents a 'vital equivocalness', a 'kind of tense equipoise' which no other poem by Wordsworth achieves, as no other poem embodies that 'painful pressure' which made the poet 'feed on disquiet'. But Wordsworth cannot hold 'this tense and difficult poise very long' and he settles down to the tranquillity of 'natural wisdom', 'natural effort' and 'the calm of nature' which he attributes to the Wanderer in 'The Ruined Cottage'. Commenting on the link between what Wordsworth settled down to and the lapse of creativity in him, Leavis conclusively points out how 'when, with his gift of piety, he had arrived at affording to suffer as easily and securely as the Wanderer did, there wasn't much to save his creativity from lapsing into habit, or the Wanderer's philosophic calm. It had lost its intransigence. It had lost, that is, its creativeness.'

To be articulate about the nature of Wordsworth's genius engaged Leavis, in his last years, in pondering and exploring how 'by the study of precisions created by poetic genius we advance our knowledge of ourselves' and how 'the fact of the "meeting" of individual sensibilities "out there" in the poem' entails 'shifting the emphasis in our thought from living individual being to life'. For all his 'personal' involvement in what he was writing, however, and in the author he was writing about, Leavis always aimed at achieving what he calls 'pure and real impersonality'. For not only the creative artist as such, but also the critic had to be 'a wholly pure individual (and an individual remains "I") in order to free himself from any egoistic taint and achieve pure and real impersonality'. That is why in examining a particular poem, a critic aims at 'making more adequate our knowing what it is and why it affects us – making more adequate by bettering our sense of it'. For Leavis the consciousness accompanying that greater adequacy in our knowing is not a matter of clear and distinctive ideas; 'Descartes was a mathematician', whereas 'art-speech inspiration is pledged to cultivate the concrete – aspires to precision in rendering the actual experience'.

It is precisely by virtue of his mastery over art-speech that Wordsworth succeeded in doing what Blake, for all his genius, could not – namely, 'liberate creative sensibility from the yoke of Augustanism'. Wordsworth succeeded, because of his debt to Shakespeare. In fact, Leavis argues, 'he couldn't have accomplished this liberation if he hadn't been so intensely interested in the language of poetry, or if English hadn't been the language of Shakespeare rather than the language of Dryden – or of Milton'. Eliot failed to appreciate this aspect of Wordsworth's poetry because, according to Leavis, he was not really interested in Wordsworth. In Eliot's introduction to Johnson's satires – according to Leavis his best essay on eighteenth-century poetry – 'there is nothing to make one guess that Wordsworth was the genius who liberated and thereby launched the great poets of the nineteenth century'. In fact, Eliot talks of Wordsworth's interest and achievement as having had the way prepared for them by Akenside, Cowper, and the eighteenth-century Miltonisers. But for Leavis the difference between Wordsworth and 'those versifiers' is 'in magnitude of gift' without which and without 'disciplined self-searching' Wordsworth could not have written 'The Ruined Cottage'; nor could he have realised those distinctive characteristics of his which 'make a creative genius push forward the frontiers of language, thought and perception'.

With Wordsworth's poetic achievement on the one hand and Eliot's on the other in mind, Leavis continued to sharpen his own response to poetry, developing his thought into value-judgement that can never have 'its rightness proved – or disproved'. The only thing to do, he would say, was 'to continue the battle while perception – while life – persists in one', something he himself did indefatigably till the very end. Being all too conscious of how the word 'creative' has been badly overworked, Leavis set out to define and demonstrate what creativity is for him as applied to poetry, in terms of words and thought. His comment, one of the last things he jotted down, on the first movement of Eliot's *Four Quartets*, is a characteristic example of the infallible union in his criticism between the personal and the impersonal, the individual and the universal, his concern for creative use of words and the nature of creative thought: 'the organic change has taken place; life has entered into the words – they are not words, but the livingness of the life of meaning; transmitted beyond my powers, but not beyond my perception, which is untiming and inexhaustible'.

In the Blake lecture Leavis revalues not only Blake, but also his own commitment to Blake's poetry. 'Blake is for me – has long been – a challenge and a reproach. He is a reproach because the challenge remains still untaken. To take it would mean a very ambitious self-commitment.' When taken, what that challenge and that commitment entail in terms of criticism is impressively exemplified in this lecture, where Blake is seen as embodying 'a major value, and one of peculiar importance for time'. But it is an order of importance that cannot be brought home by the Blake authorities and Blake literature. Nevertheless, Leavis finds Eliot's essay on Blake (*The Sacred Wood*) very helpful – 'a rare kind of help – not the less so for also presenting ... his distinctive limitations and weaknesses'. He discusses the implications of what Eliot says about Blake's 'peculiar honesty' and how it could never exist without 'great technical accomplishment'. However, in Eliot's recognition of 'the magnitude' of Blake's achievement Leavis finds something paradoxical and contradictory. For while registering his sense of Blake's genius – 'He was naked, and saw man naked, and from the centre of his crystal' – Eliot could, nevertheless, still write: 'His philosophy, like his visions, like his insight, like his technique, was his own. And accordingly, he was inclined to attach more importance to it than an artist should; that is what makes him eccentric and makes him inclined to formlessness.' Leavis rebuts Eliot's argument, by asking: 'What ... *could* Blake's philosophy have been but his own?' As to Blake's gifts, summarised in 'large quasi-cliché terms', Eliot observes: 'Had these been controlled by a respect for impersonal reason, for common sense, for the objectivity of science, it would have been better for him.' For Leavis, Eliot's remark, in its absurd gratuitousness, tells us more about Eliot himself than about Blake – Blake who had to wage a lifelong battle against the 'positive culture' of his time, with its respect for impersonal reason, for common sense, and for the objectivity of science, who intensely believed in human creativity, and who was 'dedicated to its vindication'. In this respect, Leavis contrasts Blake with Eliot who could not believe in creativity, because 'he hadn't the wholeness, with the courage it brings, which *is* belief, and at the best was equivocal'. *Four Quartets*, Eliot's 'most sustained and impressive work', embodies for Leavis, as we have seen, Eliot's 'essential paradox' where, 'offering to achieve the assurance he needs by creative means', he reveals 'his inveterate underlying will to discredit creativity'. And when Eliot remarks in the same essay on Blake, that 'what his genius required, and what it sadly lacked, was a framework of accepted and traditional ideas which would have prevented him from indulgence in a philosophy of his own, and concentrated his attention upon the problems of the poet', Leavis rebuts the remark by asking: 'What ... *are* the "problems of the poet"? The problems of a poet that are worth any intensity of study are the problems of a man – one open to being profoundly disturbed by experience, and capable of a troubled soul.'

In fact, the contrast Leavis finds between Blake and Eliot is, in a way, indicative of the contrast between Leavis himself and Eliot. For, even though he considers both Blake and Eliot important in what they communicate, 'highly important to us all who are troubled, as we have reason to be, about the way our civilization is going', he feels a closer kinship with the ethos of Blake's poetry and philosophy than with Eliot's, which explains, and is in turn explained by, the fact that Blake's attitude to life and civilization has 'a validity, a salutary and inspiring rightness' for him that Eliot's does not have.

Leavis also hints both at the parallel and the contrast between Blake and Wordsworth as repaying study, as well as at the 'unique Blakean relation' to Shakespeare, Blake being 'the only man who in the first age of bardolatory could read Shakespeare'. Another Shakespearean quality in Blake is the immense 'range and diversity of human life over which Blake's perception and intuition played'. As to Blake's simplicity and simplifying attitude, Leavis shows how what poems like 'Introduction' to *Songs of*

Innocence and 'The Echoing Green' communicate is presented 'as an actuality of human experience' and with a sureness of touch, because Blake has his 'vivid knowledge of what they exclude, and knows that he has it in him to write "The Tyger" '. While being in some sense the product of a labour of simplification, this poem exhibits 'marked complexity ... complexity of a kind that couldn't have been achieved in a poetry describable with Eliot's intention as "contemporary with Gray and Collins" '. The technical achievement of this poem, like that of other poems such as 'London', 'The Sick Rose', 'Ah! Sunflower', 'The Echoing Green', represents what was possible for Blake, not only because he escaped from the positive culture, but also because he succeeded in freeing his own genius from 'the language that had "undergone the discipline of prose" '.

As to Blake's philosophy, Leavis cautions us against its encouraging 'falsifying expectations and wrong-headed cults' such as the kind of Blake research Yeats inaugurated – a research of which Leavis considered Kathleen Raine to be the 'recognized high-priestess' in our time. 'Blind to Blake's genius', such a research 'generates blindness, and perpetuates a cult that, whatever it serves, doesn't serve Blake or humanity'. Even specialist scholars cannot provide the help we need, so that 'the fissions, coalescences, doublings, overlappings, and psychologico-symbolic subtleties of changing interrelation wear down our powers of attention'.

But criticism of Blake's philosophy and the way it works in his poetry is itself a kind of compliment to Blake – to his 'profound insight into human nature and *la condition humaine*' as well as to his being the master of an 'incomparably subtle psychological realism' such as is to be found only in the novels of Dickens, George Eliot, Tolstoy, Conrad and D.H. Lawrence. His reaction against Newton and Locke heralded the new knowledge as well as the new sense of the real; it heralded what Leavis calls 'the early momentous new development associated with the complex spiritual ideas, impulsions, and intransigently conscious human needs'.

In the essay 'Hardy the Poet', written in 1940 – that is, before Hardy's present reputation as a poet had begun to gain momentum – Leavis argues that, although Hardy was not a great poet, he wrote a certain amount of major poetry, and hence 'the need for strictly discriminating justice'. Only a very small proportion of Hardy's poetic output – 'Neutral Tones', 'A Broken Appointment', 'The Self-Unseeing', 'The Voice', 'After a Journey', 'During Wind and Rain' – are seen by Leavis as demonstrating that Hardy was a major poet.

What gives Hardy's poetry 'its solidest kind of emotional substance' is not only the lack of emotionality in it – the emotionality of 'Tears, Idle Tears' or 'Break, Break, Break' where the motion is 'an intoxication and the poignancy a luxury' – but 'the single-minded integrity of his preoccupation with a real world and a real past'.

In 'Gerard Manley Hopkins: Reflections After Fifty Years', Leavis strikes a personal note at the outset, telling us that he was 'contemporary with the beginnings and establishment of his [Hopkins'] reputation'. His coming to terms with Hopkins' work played an important part in his own development. Having written on him twice before – once in *New Bearings* which was intended to be 'a concentrated essential critique of Hopkins', and then on the occasion of the centenary of the poet's birth, his 'maturely considered estimate' in *Scrutiny* – Leavis starts in the present lecture by affirming that Hopkins is not Shakespeare and that 'the essential considerations are limited'. One such consideration is the regrettable way in which Hopkins has been made 'a minor academic industry'; another is the unhelpful nature of Hopkins' *Preface*, so that he would never send anyone to it as an introduction 'that would ease the way to an attempt at reading out Hopkins' poetry'. The third consideration is that, in spite of Hopkins' own reference to Greek in the *Preface*, study of Greek prosody, or 'the elaborated Welsh', does not help one appreciate his poetry or even his rhythmic experiments, and 'is academic in the bad sense'.

Leavis admires Hopkins above every other Victorian poet because he brought back into poetry 'the distinctive speech-strength of English', whereas an essential part of Tennyson's creative aim was to maintain 'a smooth canorousness, a quasi-musical play of vowels, in which English should be cured of its tendency to produce effects of consonantal "harshness" requiring marked effort to pronounce'. This, by its very nature, entailed 'a drastically exclusive specialization of poetic sensibility'. 'The extremeness of Hopkins' experimenting' was a reaction against as well as a response to Tennyson. Leavis quotes certain poems by way of illustrating 'the characteristic Hopkins effect' where Hopkins is closer to Keats than to any other Victorian poet – Keats with the 'unTennysonian sensuous concreteness in which the factual plays so essential a part' – and therefore belongs to 'the Shakespearean in the complex poetic tradition of the English language rather than to the Spenserian-Miltonic-Tennysonian'. This is manifested particularly in 'The Wreck of the Deutschland' which Bridges found 'repellingly difficult'. Hopkins' use of alliteration, too, is 'un-Swinburnian – or anti-Swinburnian'; for whereas Swinburne's alliterative habit is 'hypnoidal', Hopkins' alliterative and other formal and technical habits serve 'to intensify and enforce meaning; they organize, give edge and compel the realizing attention of the full waking mind'.

Leavis ends his lecture with a comparison, or rather a contrast between Hopkins and Eliot. The 'important power inherent in speech' – namely, the 'delicate command of shifting tone, tempo and movement' – that we find in Shakespeare and in Eliot alike, we do not find even in Hopkins' best work. As religious poets too, Hopkins and Eliot are different – a difference Leavis comments on with an eye on the ethos of Eliot's religious poetry and on Eliot's concern with technique which served his 'desperate need to foster in himself a positive nisus in a pertinacious exploration of what it may mean or imply, while holding scrupulously back from unequivocal affirmation'. But when in 'Little Gidding' Eliot moves into 'a sustained and final affirmation', Leavis' response, not so much to Eliot's poetry, as to what he affirms, takes the form of an adverse comment on how Eliot, in his 'heroic wrestling to discover what he is and what and how he believes', lapses into 'self-deception' to which he is exposed by his 'inner disunity'. Hopkins, on the other hand, presents 'an antithesis to this plight that gave Eliot's creative gift the "resistance" (Murry calls it in pointing to the lack of such in Hopkins's case) that evoked that paradoxical great poetry' which is Eliot's. Hopkins' poetry presents no such paradox. Who would suggest, Leavis asks in conclusion, 'that even in the "terrible sonnets" the anguish is in any way akin to that of "The Hollow Men" – insufferable emptiness and the impossibility of any kind of action?' If Leavis finds Hopkins, 'in a wholly unpejorative sense', simple, it is because 'there is nothing equivocal in his verse', whereas in his letters Hopkins' simplicity is that of a man 'of high intelligence, irresistible charm and complete integrity'.

In his critique on *Gwendolen Harleth* Leavis uses the opportunity offered him by a publisher to extricate the better part of *Daniel Deronda* for a drastically critical estimate of the novel as a whole. What makes the novel one of the major classics of English tradition is precisely that 'very substantial strong part' of the novel which he identifies as *Gwendolen Harleth*, even though he admits that it is impossible to purge *Gwendolen Harleth* completely of the 'voluminous clouds of Zionizing, altruism and Victorian nobility that Deronda trails and emits – and for the most part is'. In the character of Gwendolen Harleth, Leavis sees the hand of 'the great creative George Eliot'. But there is also the other George Eliot who gave for the title of the novel the name of Daniel Deronda, and to whom Leavis denies 'the insight, the disinterested intensity and the irresistible power of the major creative genius'. However, it is the purged part, so to speak, the very substantial part of *Daniel Deronda*, that Leavis considers greater even than *Middlemarch*. When George Eliot writes as a great genius, 'her truly noble and compassionate benignity is controlled by the intelligence and insight it informs', whereas in the case of the other George Eliot, 'her profound need to feel benignly and compassionately disinterested prevails as a kind of intoxication that licenses for self-indulgence the weak side of her femininity', and 'the egoism and falsity of day-dream manifest themselves as sentimentality'. Gwendolen is, thus, the creation of genuine compassion 'exemplified in penetrating intelligence'. The fact that she is as unlike George Eliot as she could well be, underlines all the more how 'the disinterestedness of sympathetic insight' could hardly go further than in *Gwendolen Harleth*. Moreover, whereas in the art of the great George Eliot, a certain stringency 'is seldom far away', in the treatment of Deronda and the Deronda world, so much of a kind of day-dream or fairy-tale as they are, there is no stringency at all. Leavis finds George Eliot guilty of 'a radical confusion', in so far as she presents Deronda to be taken 'as being real with a reality that qualifies him to exist in a world that contains Gwendolen, Grandcourt, Gascoigne, Herr Kles-

mer and Miss Arrowpoint'. Leavis' analysis of the characters of Gwendolen
and Grandcourt has the same creative urge and psychological insight
behind it as well as the same sense of the real in human affairs and human
relationships, that we find in his earlier critiques of the great novels and
novelists.

In 'Memories of Wittgenstein', what Leavis recaptures, in his characteristic mode of recollecting the lived past in its evocatively detailed and
circumstantial reality, tells us, in a certain way, as much about Leavis
himself as about Wittgenstein. For certain characteristics of Wittgenstein's character and personality – 'an intensity of concentration that
impressed itself on one as disinterestedness', his being 'a complete human
being, subtle, self-critical and un-self-exalting', his 'self-sufficiency, a robust single-mindedness', his embodying 'a centre of life, sentience and
human responsibility' – were, in different modes and degrees, what Leavis
himself shared.

His disagreements with Wittgenstein, too, throw light on Leavis no less
than on Wittgenstein. The only thing that is rather uncharacteristic of him
in his attitude to or dealings with Wittgenstein is his excessive regard, at
times almost bordering on reverence, for Wittgenstein. He even gives the
impression of defending Wittgenstein against his own criticism of what
Wittgenstein said, thought or did, so that it is Leavis rather than Wittgenstein who seems to be on the defensive. In fact, in his attitude to
Wittgenstein, there is a strange mixture of both what is characteristic and
what is patently uncharacteristic of Leavis. The feeling behind his admis-
sion 'Besides, I respected Wittgenstein too much' is rather too pervasive in
these 'Memories'.

At a certain point, though, Leavis himself pinpoints Wittgenstein's
failings: his 'disconcerting lack of consideration', his 'innocent egotism', his
'fundamental insecurity'. But he glosses over them, as if trying to explain
them away, by relating them to Wittgenstein's genius – something quite
different from his way of dealing with Eliot's failings and insecurity.

The nearest Leavis comes to an unqualified criticism of Wittgenstein is
when he refers to his negative influence – influence represented by 'the
immense vogue generated by Wittgenstein's genius', but that 'wasn't in
general the kind that has its proof in improved understanding of the
influencer and his theme, or in fortified intellectual powers'. At this point,
Leavis, himself a gifted teacher, both inspired and inspiring, avows that
he cannot believe Wittgenstein to have been a good teacher. 'I can't believe
that most (at any rate) of even the mature and academically officed
professionals who were present [at Wittgenstein's lectures] supposed that
they could sincerely claim to have followed, in the sense of having been
able to be even tacit collaborators (that is, serious questioners and critics),
the discussions carried on by Wittgenstein.' For Wittgenstein's 'discussions were discussions carried on *by* Wittgenstein' – something profoundly
at variance with what Leavis understood and practised as the collabora-

tive process in teaching as well as in criticism. Hence his belief that
university students of 'English' should be defended against the suggestion
that they stand to benefit, 'at any rate on balance, by having lectures and
seminars on Wittgenstein arranged for them'. Another conviction of his,
one central to his profession as a literary critic, is that 'the fullest use of
language is to be found in creative literature, and that a great creative
work is work of original exploratory thought'. Consequently, as he observed in his essay on Blake, 'philosophers are always weak on language'.
That is why he found Wittgenstein's genius hardly more relevant to his
own intellectual powers than 'a genius for chess'. Moreover, there was,
Leavis points out, 'this tacitly accepted difference between us – potentially
an intellectual incompatibility, and perhaps something like an antipathy
of temperament'. The difference, in essence, was between the critic and the
philosopher which, in the coming decades, would convince Leavis of the
fundamental antithesis between literary criticism and philosophy and
make him consider the critic as anti-philosopher. In any case – and in spite
of Leavis' genuine admiration for him – it is, frankly, not Wittgenstein but
the younger Leavis who comes out in these 'Memories' as a maturer,
completer and warmer human being and intellectual.

Leavis' essay on Montale's *Xenia* (a series of poems written after the
death of Montale's wife and dedicated to her) is, in my view, one of the most
illuminating and perceptive comments on the poem. He finds in *Xenia* a
'truly creative impersonality' as well as a 'profound movingness'. In his
Introduction to his translation of Valéry's *Ébauche d'un Serpent*, Eliot had
said: 'To English amateurs, rather inclined to dismiss poetry which appears reticent ... such an activity may seem no other than a *jeu de quilles*.
But Boileau was a fine poet, and he spoke in seriousness. To reduce one's
disorderly and mostly silly personality to the gravity of a *jeu de quilles*
would be to do an excellent thing.' Leavis refers to the suggestion of
'sophisticated naivety' behind this remark, the significance of which, he
tells us, 'lies in the personal insecurity it betrays – an insecurity that plays
a decisive part in his [Eliot's] creative drive'. For Leavis, however, there is
no such reticence or insecurity in Montale, which makes him as different
from Eliot as he is from Valéry. If *Xenia* brings out 'one's profoundest
response to experience', it is because the poet's intelligence 'determines
how the actual pondered sense of irrevocable loss can be defined and
communicated – two words that mean one thing to the poet'. Leavis refers
to the foreword to my translation of *Xenia* in which I had made a comparative reference to Hardy's *Poems 1912-1913* (written after the death of his
wife) and observes: 'There is point in the comparison: a direct simplicity of
personal feeling certainly relates the two poets, who in this essential
characteristic differ equally from Eliot. The point, however, is inseparable
from the constatation to which it leads – that of the striking unlikeness it
brings out.' He finds Montale 'immensely more subtle, more supple and
more diverse than Hardy', and analyses the nature of this diversity at the

verbal, stylistic and rhythmic level as well as in terms of the mood and manner in which both Hardy and Montale evoke the past and the kind of past they evoke. What particularly impresses Leavis in *Xenia* is 'exquisite and sure tact', 'sensitive precision', and the effect of 'spontaneous natural-ness, going with a great range of varying inflection, tone and distance' – qualities which set him apart from Hardy who had to fight 'an unending battle against Victorian "poetic diction" ' and who achieved 'major victo-ries' only in a handful of poems.

There is also another difference. Hardy's 'woman much missed' exists 'only as posited by the poet's nostalgic intensity', whereas Montale's wife 'Mosca' is 'the highly individual woman apart from whom daily life was inconceivable until the "catastrophe" of her loss, and is almost inconceiv-able now'. If Montale is more sophisticated – but 'in a wholly unpejorative sense' – than Hardy, his sophistication is to be found in 'the wit, irony and humour that intensify the effect of profound seriousness characterizing his poetry'. The 'evoked day-to-day ordinariness' in *Xenia* shows 'the art of a great novelist (which Hardy was not)'. Hence Leavis finds it easy to think of *Xenia* as an English poem, though, he admits, 'we have nothing like it in English'.

The two articles ' "Believing in" the University' and 'Mutually Neces-sary' were published in *The Human World* (Nos. 15-16, May-August 1974) and the *New Universities Quarterly* (Spring 1976) respectively. The first starts with a personal anecdote. Leavis was once attending a by-election meeting of the Liberal Party which he had hitherto backed. He heard its then leader Jeremy Thorpe say: 'The Liberal Party is in favour of compre-hensive schools.' 'The sentence was brief ', Leavis recalls, 'and he said no more about education. It's not for that alone that I resolved, there and then, not to expose myself to being counted in future as a loyal backer of the liberal party.' But it was during the subsequent speech by the candi-date to whose nomination paper Leavis had given his signature and to whose election fund he had made a modest contribution, that both Leavis and his wife walked out. This was Leavis' protest in the interest of education – a cause he had been committed to throughout his long teach-ing and writing career – and he would encounter the politicians' maxim: 'Politics is the art of the possible' with his own dictum '*We* create possibil-ity', thereby counteracting 'a cynically inert indifference in the face of contemporary politics'.

In the face of 'the prevailing Robbins' mentality and its consequences', Leavis reiterates the arguments he had been debating since *Education and the University* and even earlier, as to what the essential university function is and why it is important 'to keep alive the idea of what, for us, should be the essential university-function ... and the idea of what goes with it: the idea of an educated public'. Much of the article is Leavis' rebuttal, point by point, of what he was charged with: i.e. his 'believing in' the university, with the naivety of one wanting to build Jerusalem; i.e.

create an ideal university, 'the perfect and perfectly functioning' university.

'Mutually Necessary' is another exercise in rebuttal – in this case a rebuttal of the criticism of *The Living Principle* made by Michael Tanner in his article 'Literature and Philosophy', one of the contributions devoted to Leavis in the December 1975 issue of the *New Universities Quarterly*. One point of Tanner's criticism is that Leavis should have recommended Marjorie Grene's book *The Knower and the Known* for use to literary students as 'a classic of original philosophical thought' against the judgement of qualified philosophers. Denying any such presumption on his part, Leavis goes on to explain how, having eliminated Russell's *History of Western Philosophy* as wasteful of time and effort spent by the students on it, he came across Marjorie Grene's book in the Petty Cury bookshop, and having to rely on his own 'unprofessional' judgement, he found it useful and interesting, and offered it to the students as 'suggested' reading. A critically more weighty argument by Tanner is that in his 'famous' encounter with René Wellek, while giving 'an excellent account of how tastes are formed, become more or less firm, and so forth', Leavis had not offered 'a *justification* of the taste that has been formed' and had substituted 'biographical-psychological description for philosophical analyses'. Leavis rejects the assumption, as he had done in Wellek's case, that 'value-judgements in literary criticism are to be justified by philosophical analysis' – an assumption common to most philosophers. 'That is why', he tells us, 'I call myself an "anti-philosopher" '.

But while one cannot prove a value-judgement, one can generally get beyond 'the mere assertion of personal conviction'. The process of 'getting beyond', a 'tactical' one, is illustrated by Leavis in the practical criticism of short poems, as in 'Judgement and Analysis'. But what is illustrated is essentially a critical process: 'Putting a finger on this or that in the text, and moving tactically from point to point, you make at each a critical observation that hardly anyone in whom the power of critical perception exists, or is at least strongly potential wouldn't endorse ("This is so, isn't it?"). The ideal is (not usually for the critic, in important cases, a remote one) that when this tactical process has reached its final stage, there is no need for assertion; this "placing" judgement is left as established.'

Leavis also dismisses Tanner's use of the word 'taste' as 'merely the philosopher's ingrained habit taking over, and obscuring a reality which is basic for valid thought with a misconception'. For his own part he would rather use the word 'sensibility' or the phrase 'power of perception' in describing the way in which 'a poem that we meet in is established'. But together with perception which 'stresses the outward focus, which is on the printed words', there is the 'inward concern' – concern with what the words do in their 'complex organic interaction', and that concern is, for Leavis, a challenge to each critic to be more than ordinarily 'inward';

involving, as it does, 'a self-searching and self-testing – for a profoundly considered and wholly sincere response'.

Original critics, Leavis points out, echoing A.E. Housman, 'are rare; whether rarer than great creative writers (who are certainly rare) I won't discuss (it would be pointless in any case)'. It is they who testify and demonstrate how 'the surest insight into human nature, human potentiality and the human situation is that accessible in the great creative writers', and who establish 'what human centrality is'. These writers 'differ in timbre, but they all have genius, and their genius is capacity for experience and for profound and complete sincerity (which goes in them for self-knowledge)'. The rare real critic, too, has a 'more than average capacity for experience and a passion for sincerity and complete conviction'. He may not attain to 'the completeness that is finality', and some of his certitudes may be 'insufficiently grounded', but he is in possession of the 'basic major perceptions, intuitions and realizations communicated with consummate delicacy to the reader in the mastering of the creative work of a great writer'. Such certitude of possession is 'an ultimate; what could a proof, if proof were possible, add to it?' But the 'proof' Tanner asks for is philosophical, and his whole article is itself a proof of the difficulty that 'one habituated to philosophical discipline finds in realizing the nature of the discipline of thought I am contending for – a discipline developed out of literary criticism'.

As to Tanner's complaint about Leavis' not explaining, while dealing with *Four Quartets*, 'the relationship between poetry and what it is concerned to state', Leavis notes two flaws in this argument – he calls them 'portents': Tanner's assuming that poetry is concerned to state something, and that *Four Quartets* is concerned with stating a philosophy.

The first three *Quartets* exemplified as well as dealt with 'the felt basic difficulty of approach to the possibility of full Christian affirmation', which constitutes their nature, their originality and their strength, and the creative drive behind them was 'intensely and poignantly personal'. The poignancy is the result of what Leavis calls 'the dividedness that entailed in Eliot the refusal to know what he really knew about himself – that self-defensive inability to face the knowledge of what he was which didn't save him from self-contempt'. As to the fourth *Quartet*, 'Little Gidding', it shows Eliot in a relaxed mood: 'he is in heaven at last'. Leavis' comment on the *terza rima* passage in 'Little Gidding' based on Eliot's experience as an air-raid warden, is implicitly also a comment on the peculiarities in Eliot himself that 'limited and starved him in his firsthand living – precluded his having access to that comprehensive human experience without which he was incapacitated for the imagining and producing of a great creative work'. Towards the end of this passage Eliot 'comes to the verge of telling himself the nature of his guilt ("the shame of motives late revealed"); and then draws back, the rare moment's courage neatly disposed of in a demonstration of stern and comfortable Christian virtue'. If in his embarrassment he was too unemphatic in making this point in *The Living Principle*, it was, he tells Tanner, because his 'embarrassed modesty was complex' and because there was another factor. Apropos of this factor, he gives a detailed account of Eliot's coming to Cambridge and calling on him – an account that brings out, in a nutshell, the nature of the tension between him and Eliot and why they found each other 'so very uncongenial as to generate a great deal of awareness – on my side certainly diagnostic'. 'I was very surprised', Leavis writes,

> to receive a letter from Eliot intimating that he was coming to Cambridge and would like to call on me. The actual call must have taken place either late in 1940 or early in 1941 (it was unique). He stayed a very long while, and, when he finally went, left behind a small mound of cigarette-ash on the flat brick hearth in the room where we'd had tea. The pertinacious length of his stay was unmistakably explained by his wanting to feel sure that he had extracted something out of me that, actually, he couldn't get – signs interpretable as an assurance that I shouldn't in future take ill – from *him*, who would continue to think highly of me – his continuing to support the Desmond MacCarthys against me. I deduced later, when 'Little Gidding' was made accessible by being published, that he had been composing that Quartet at the time of his visit to my house. A number of things he said to me appear in that 'All Clear!' passage, and I was (with good reason) a major focus of the guilt-feelings expressed in *The Family Reunion*, the most revealingly personal of his works.
>
> I will add here that I know of several reasons, all different, given by Eliot for his not being among my friends. The first, a quarter of a century ago, was given to a Wykehamist of my acquaintance, who reported it to me. 'I went out of my way to call on him. No good! It must be that I didn't support him enough in the 1930s.' The last was passed on to me by a very intelligent friend of mine who cultivated Eliot, and put the question to him. Eliot answered (it was towards the end of his life): 'I think he hasn't forgiven me about Milton.'

The last remark was passed on to Leavis by me, first through my article 'Incontro con Eliot' (*Il Mondo*) which appeared not long after my meeting Eliot at his Faber and Faber office in August 1964; and then, later on, when I personally gave Leavis an account of that meeting.

Valuation in Criticism

In 1986 *Valuation in Criticism*, the second posthumously published volume of Leavis' essays, appeared with Cambridge University Press. There are four sections in the book. The first two sections contain Leavis' earliest writings from 1929 to 1933; the third Leavis' miscellaneous essays, prefaces or articles published or lectures delivered between 1955 and 1973; and the fourth some of Leavis' older essays going as far back as 1935 together with his more recent essays and 'Thought, Meaning and Sensibility: The Problem of Value Judgement', on which he was working in the last few months of his life.

Most of the essays in the fourth section, though published at different dates and on different occasions, have one unifying theme: 'Valuation in Criticism', which is the title of an essay (probably the text of a talk) as well as the title of the volume. Thus the fourth section is devoted very largely to defining and analysing what 'valuation' and value judgement mean, and how they are achieved – a problem that has always been at the core of Leavis' critical thought and practice, whether dealing with 'The Literary Discipline and Liberal Education', 'The Responsible Critic: or the function of criticism at any time', 'Literary Studies' or 'Standards of Criticism'.

Coming to the fourth and in many ways the most significant and even original section of this volume, we find Leavis discussing I.A. Richards' book *Coleridge on Imagination* in the first essay: 'Dr. Richards, Bentham and Coleridge'. While differing from Richards 'less essentially about the nature of Coleridge's greatness than about the ways of applying intelligence to poetry', Leavis demonstrates what valuation in criticism and the value judgement mean for him and what they amount to in terms of literary criticism as such. He compares Coleridge's position, as it was for his epoch, with Eliot's in our time, and pays Eliot more or less the same kind of tribute that Eliot himself, some years later, was to pay Pound (in his introduction to Pound's *Literary Essays*) and that Leavis himself would later on pay D.H. Lawrence. 'If anyone', Leavis tells us, 'may be said to have been for our time what Coleridge was for his, then it is Mr Eliot. Mr Eliot, like Coleridge, combined a creative gift with rare critical intelligence .... To have improved the situation for other poets is an achievement of decided importance, and, by his poetry and his criticism together, it is Mr Eliot's.'

In comparison, Leavis finds Richards an unsatisfactory guide both to Coleridge's criticism and to the 'different ways of thinking profitably about poetry'. For, especially in the book under review, Richards seems to be 'more interested in the "philosophical matter" than in the "critical theories" '. And for Leavis, it is one thing to observe, as Richards does, that 'to inquire about words is to inquire about everything' and that 'knowledge in all its varieties – scientific, moral, religious – has come to seem a vast mythology with its sub-orders divided according to their different pragmatic sections'; and 'much more another thing than Dr Richards seems to recognize to give such observations the rigour and precision of development and statement that are necessary if any problem is to be left where it wasn't before'. In Richards' thinking Leavis detects 'unacceptable compressions and ellipses in key places – failures to make, or to make clearly and hold to, essential distinctions – a debility sorting oddly with the show of analytic rigour, and, it seems, escaping the author's notice by reason of this semasiological zeal itself '. While exposing Richards' laxity of thought no less than of expression, he implicitly defines his own position as 'a person of literary interests who is nevertheless concerned for rigorous thinking', and who cannot but take cognisance of the fact that Richards is 'curiously prone to an uncritical satisfaction with words'. That is why he finds it impossible 'to pin Dr. Richards down locally to any precise meaning', a defect not unconnected with the latter's view of poetry which is 'unrealistic to a degree almost incredible'.

Even the theory of value as expounded by Richards in *Principles of Literary Criticism* is of little use to Leavis, contrasting, as it does, with Coleridge's interest in developing *his* theories. Coleridge's interest, Leavis tells us, 'was of a kind that did not tempt him to forget the nature of "experimental submission" (without which, whatever it is that is analysed, it is not poetry)'. Hence his theory could be developed 'only in an arduous and scrupulous exploration of the organic complexities of poetry by a developing analysis – by an analysis going deeper and deeper and taking wider and wider relations into account; that is, becoming less and less disguisable as laboratory technique'. Richards' procedure, on the contrary, 'heading away from the concrete, leaves him (it is an ironical fate for one who warns us so much against this sort of thing) the happy servant of a set of abstract terms'.

In his critique of *Coleridge on Imagination*, and incidentally also of *Principles of Criticism*, Leavis thus implicitly formulates his own concept, method and criteria of valuation in criticism. The profound divergence between him and Richards can be epitomised by the fact that Richards' literary interests 'derive from an interest in theory rather than his theory from his literary interests'.

In 'The Responsible Critic: or the function of criticism at any time', Leavis takes to task F.W. Bateson, editor of *Essays in Criticism*, which was supposed to be, 'in a positive way', a criticism of *Scrutiny* by combining scholarship and scholarly precision, that the Cambridge periodical was supposed to be lacking in, with a critical vigour 'not inferior to *Scrutiny's* might'. What *Essays in Criticism*, in fact, achieves, chiefly in the work of the editor himself, is a kind of scholarship which, under the guise of the 'discipline of contextual meaning', is 'inimical to criticism, that is to intelligence'. Discarding the way scholarship is generally set over against criticism, as, for instance, by Bateson himself, and the virtue of accuracy upheld, Leavis observes that in criticism the only accuracy that matters is synonymous with 'pointedness and precision of relevance' and with being intelligent about literature. 'Overemphasis on scholarly knowledge', in fact, tends to let in a great deal of what is 'critically irrelevant' and shut out 'the most essential kinds of knowledge', something amounting to critical irresponsibility.

As an example, Leavis examines what Bateson has to say by way of criticising Leavis' comments on the 'affinities' between the four lines of Marvell (from 'A Dialogue between the Soul and Body') and the four lines by Pope (from *Dunciad* IV). But whereas for Bateson Marvell's poem is 'the kind of allegory that was popularized in the early seventeenth century by the Emblem books', for Leavis it is one of Marvell's 'supreme things, profoundly original and a proof of genius', a 'profoundly critical and inquiring poem, devoted to some subtle exploratory thinking, and to the *questioning* of "conventional concepts" and current habits of mind'. Thus what ultimately comes out is the radically different way Leavis 'reads' or approaches a poem from the way Bateson does. Leavis backs his valuation of Marvell's poem and of what it means to him through a close critical analysis of the text aimed at invalidating Bateson's comments on it. For instance, apropos of Bateson's remark that 'slave', 'vassal' and 'dupe' in Pope's lines – 'First slave to Words, then vassal to a Name,/Then dupe to Party' are 'tautologies', Leavis observes: 'How can Mr Bateson so have anaesthetized himself as to be able to pronounce "slave", "vassal" and "dupe" "virtually interchangeable"? That the forces of these words should have something in common is essential to the intention: "child and man the same". But that the forces are different, and that each word has a felicity in its place, is surely apparent at once, without analysis.'

As to Bateson's 'apparatus of "contextual" aids' to the interpretation of a poem, with the aim of putting the poem 'back in its "total context" ', namely, this 'complex of religious, political and economic factors that may be called the social context', Leavis finds such an aim 'illusory' and the 'social' context an illusion. For him 'context' as 'something determinate' is 'nothing but his [Bateson's] postulate; the wider he goes in his ambition to construct it from his reading in the period, the more is it *his* construction (in so far as he produces anything more than a mass of heterogeneous information alleged to be relevant)'. But Bateson regards awareness of the 'appropriate social context' as 'the culminating desideratum', 'the final criterion of correctness', which for Leavis is tantamount to suggesting that 'one may reconstruct the "essential drama" of a poem correctly without responding to it correctly; that the taking possession of it is independent of valuing'. No wonder he finds what Bateson has to say concerning the nature of the process of judgement 'wholly unintelligible', and the whole passage (quoted by Leavis), in which Bateson says it, 'incompatible with any true account of value judgement'. For it is the nature of a value judgement, and how and on the basis of what one arrives at it, that is, for Leavis, the crux of the matter. 'One judges a poem by Marvell', he observes, 'not by persuading a hypothetical seventeenth-century "context", or any "social context", to take the responsibility, but, as one alone can, out of one's personal living (which inevitably is in the twentieth century)'.

In his dealings with contemporary writers, too, Bateson betrays what Leavis calls 'an inertia of judgement. His uncritical largeness of respect for the "splendid qualities" of what he styles the "new critical movement" might be taken for tact. But why should he "respect and admire" the criticism of Wyndham Lewis? That reputation was never grounded in anything but fashion, and fashion of the frothiest kind.' Leavis also reprimands Bateson for speaking of the 'thoroughness, the usefulness' and the 'general good sense' of Wellek and Warren's *Theory of Literature*. 'To have suggested', Leavis argues, 'that the student may go hopefully to it for help or enlightenment is an irresponsibility that ought to trouble Mr Bateson's conscience. There are too many of these conventional values which, once established, are perpetuated by inertia, and it is *not* the function of criticism to countenance them.'

Exercising that function, Leavis in 'Literary Studies: a reply' examines W.W. Robson's comments on what constitutes Literary Studies. He comes out sharply against Robson's notion of the 'separableness of criticism and literary history' based on the distinction between the 'descriptive' and the 'evaluative'. For Leavis such a separation is neither possible nor desirable, for 'only in so far as he is a critic can a historian – or an undergraduate – achieve the *intelligent* reading of a creative work. The intelligent reader, faced with describing a piece of creative literature, knows that, unless he had entered into it and attained to a kind of re-creative possession, he cannot give an intelligent description of it, and that the testing and verifying of the necessary possession is a work of critical intelligence.'

The various comments, convictions and approaches by other critics examined by Leavis gave him both the occasion and the incentive to expound his own view of what a critical reading of a creative work and its 're-creative possession' involves. A 'critical' reader, in the Leavisian sense of the term, could, for instance, see that 'the gravediggers' scene in *Hamlet* (which has to be saved from the comic actor – and the academic view that it is "comic relief" – rather than from the narcissistic mouther, whom it doesn't attract) is a truly profound and moving treatment of the theme of death, and great poetry (though it is in prose, and not prose of the "poetic" order)'.

In 'The Literary Discipline and Liberal Education', too, Leavis argues that 'to think, at all seriously and insistently, about the teaching of literature is to tackle the problem of liberal education' – a problem that is 'so desperately urgent and so desperately difficult'. But this problem is tied up with the problem of the teaching of literature, on the one hand, and with the Idea of a University, on the other. In dealing with these problems one has to be 'vigilant against the temptations of use and fatigue – inert acquiescences, concessions to social amenity, tacit agreements to take the form for the reality and the running of the machine for the movement of life'. Such vigilance Leavis himself relentlessly exercised throughout his career. Being 'avowedly concerned with the training of an élite', he expected everyone else concerned with liberal education at the university 'to be able to say the same'. For him the idea of liberal education and that of literary studies had one goal in common – the 'training of perception and critical judgement'.

But the concept of 'real and creative thinking' presupposes another concept, that of the 'standards of criticism' discussed in the essay of the same title. Suggesting why the term 'standards', in so far as it is applied to criticism, cannot be strictly or neatly defined, Leavis observes that they 'are not at all of the order of the standards in the Weights and Measures Office. They are not producible, they are not precise, and they are not fixed. But if they are not effectively "there" for the critic to appeal to, the function of criticism is badly disabled. In fact, it is always a part of the function of criticism to assert and maintain them; that is, to modify them, for to maintain is to vitalize, and to vitalize is almost inevitably to modify.'

Leavis' notion of what 'standards of criticism' are and how they function is rooted in his own practice as a critic – a critic whose evaluative judgements, or 'placings', are 'personal', but are, at the same time, also backed by a practical demonstration of their validity in terms of a close critical and analytical reading of the text, especially if the author or the work in question is a great one; say Tolstoy or D.H. Lawrence, T.S. Eliot or Henry James, Wordsworth or George Eliot. By judging such works, the very criteria by which one judges them are 'affected' and 'altered'. Thus, one can say that the criteria Leavis used in his earliest writings in order to judge Eliot or Lawrence were undoubtedly 'affected' and 'altered', when he discussed them subsequently, as a result of his contact with their other works, or with the works of other authors of comparable status. In fact, from *New Bearings* and *Revaluation* and *The Great Tradition* onwards, Leavis' critical criteria were inevitably affected by the achievement of those authors he had tackled in these three crucial books. Hence he could well say that, as compared with such masters as had been dealt with in these books, 'few even of the respectable admired writers of a given time are original in the important sense' and that writers 'found impressive in their effect of technical modernness and significant originality, writers such as Huxley and Auden, in their time, may be really *no more* original – no more so in any essential way. They may be significant only at the level of the journalistic intellectual who claims them, and thinks them original – profound interpreters of the modern human situation – because he can respond to them and feel advanced without having been called to make any effort of readjustment.' Hence for Leavis, whose own standards of criticism were 'affected' and moulded by the best and the most original in Lawrence and Eliot, writers like Huxley and Auden, for all their intelligence and talent, could not be the kind of writers 'because of whom literature matters'.

A critic who distinguishes, identifies and appreciates an original work is, for Leavis, engaged in performing the true function of criticism. For, since a work of art 'hasn't unrelated, standing by itself, its full significance', it is when the critic starts relating it, implicitly or explicitly, to other works, that the work attains its full significance. He performs his function 'not only when he wins recognition for contemporary works, but also when he helps to determine that works of the past shall be actively alive in the contemporary mind – when he alters accepted valuations', as Eliot and Leavis did. Such a critic, therefore, helps to form the contemporary sensibility which is ' "there" in a responsive educated public'. It is, if not 'precisely a collapse, or an abeyance, of standards in literary criticism ... something immediately and intimately related' that, for Leavis, accounts for 'the vulgar, brassy, fatuous and insulting demonstration of brightness that is kept up with mechanical pertinacity', as exemplified, for instance, by the phenomenon of the review headings of the *Times Literary Supplement*. But in the absence of critical standards for him to appeal to, if the critic challenges 'the accepted currency of valuations', or 'the social corruptions and betrayals of criticism', he is accused of 'anti-social ill-will, dogmatic assertion and bad manners'.

As examples of what the absence of standards of criticism entails, Leavis quotes 'recent appointments to prestige Lectureships and Chairs ... the election of Mr Kingsley Amis as Fellow of a distinguished and very selective college'; research projects on the time-patterns in Iris Murdoch's novels; or the philosophy of Angus Wilson – examples indicative of 'the presence of the enemy, at ease and at home, within the citadel; a state of affairs eloquent of that lapse of standards which, having made it possible, prevents its being recognized for what it is'. But even if standards were there for the critic to appeal to, they may not guarantee 'the immediate or swift recognition of the Wordsworth, the Hopkins, or the Lawrence, or exclude the possibility that the Thackeray, the Tennyson or the Meredith may be widely and for long overvalued. But they make it impossible for a Snow to be accepted even for six months as a profound mind, or for a Kingsley Amis to be defended by a Cambridge Custodian of the humanities as engaged in serious studies of amorality.'

Closely linked with and having a crucial bearing on 'Standards of Criticism' is Leavis' essay on 'Valuation in Criticism' – criticism conceived as 'a specific discipline' – where, among other things, he discusses how a judgement is both personal and, at the same time, something more than 'merely personal'. Essentially, a critical judgement for Leavis takes the form, 'This is so, isn't it?', so that of its nature the critical activity 'aims at, in fact, is an exchange, a collaborative exchange, a corrective and creative interplay of judgements'. Even the analysis of a given text in the course of 'practical criticism' is a 'creative or re-creative process' – that process of 'creation in response to the poet's words (a poem being in question) which any serious reading is'. Leavis distinguishes 'the re-created poem ... from the mere text on the page', so that it is neither merely private nor public in the sense that 'it can be pointed to'. It is 'neither: the alternatives are not exhaustive. There is a third realm and the poem belongs to that.'

As to language itself, language in its creative use – i.e. 'apart from the conventional signs and symbols for it' – it is 'really *there*, it really exists in full actuality, only in individual users'. It is a language that 'in the full concrete reality ... eludes any form of linguistic science' and is 'very largely the essential life of a culture'. Literature itself 'is a mode of manifestation of "language" '. Hence what Leavis says of value judgements concerning a work of creative literature may be applied to the value judgements concerning the language of that literature. 'Any reading of a poem', he tells us, 'that takes it *as* a poem involves an element of implicit valuation. The process, the kind of activity of inner response and discipline by which we take possession of the created work, is essentially the kind of activity that completes itself in full explicit value judgements. There is no such thing as neutral possession.' Valuation leads to 'a comprehensive "placing" '; i.e. placing of an author in terms of his relations to other contemporary authors as well as to the past. And where major value judgements are concerned, one of the criteria involved is indicated by the word 'moral' used by literary critics as diverse as Arnold and Lawrence. But when literary-critical judgement has a moral significance for a critic, it does not mean that he is 'subscribing to and applying some specific ethical theory or scheme – something other than his critical sensibility, other and apart from it, that takes over the function of critical judgement'. And yet the term 'moral' indicates one of the 'radical criteria' in criticism – a criterion in relation to which Lawrence, with 'his sureness and centrality in value judgement' and with his genius manifesting itself 'in a sure sense of what makes *for* life and what makes against it' has, for Leavis, an advantage over Eliot as a critic.

It is because of its moral dimension, therefore, that any significant work of art 'challenges us in the most disturbing and inescapable way to a radical pondering, a new profound realization, of the grounds of our most important determinations and choices', and why it is in creative literature that 'one finds the challenge to discover what one's real beliefs and values are'. But the critic himself, not less than the creative artist, is involved, while judging a particular work, in responding to the significance of that work at a moral level. In this respect, the literary critic, with his 'original creative conviction', is very different from the sociologist or the social psychologist. Through his conviction the critic manages to get 'the due recognition' for a neglected creative writer – a function that is, for Leavis, in itself creative. But this conviction is something the justice or injustice of which cannot be proved, just as the rightness of one's 'convinced' reading of a poem cannot be proved. 'One knows that', says Leavis, 'and yet doesn't acquiesce in the suggestion that one's poem is an arbitrary and merely personal thing'.

In the last few months of his life, Leavis continued to grapple with the concept of value judgement in literary criticism, as his essay, entitled 'Thought, Meaning and Sensibility: the problem of value judgement' and published for the first time in *Valuation in Criticism*, demonstrates. In this essay he starts by commenting on language as 'the product of human creativity', and points out that meaning itself is equally the product of human creativity. 'Unless someone means and someone else takes the meaning, there is no meaning ... in creating language human beings create the world they live in. When language is impoverished – and it is being impoverished today – *the world* is impoverished'. Such axiomatic simplicity and sureness of style in Leavis were dictated by a new intensity of conviction and a new clarity of vision and perception as to what he, in the course of his long and critically 'engaged' life, had succeeded in upholding, and how most of his value judgements had, in his own lifetime, come to be accepted. But at the same time he also realised how the modern civilisation (represented by the American World 'which we're all going to have to live in') was hostile to much of what he valued and stood for in life.

In such a mood, Leavis pondered again on what he considered to be plain truths regarding value judgements in literature and literary criticism, as distinguished from value judgements in other spheres such as 'the relation between great creative writers and the thought I credit them with – the most important kind of thought'; how value judgements, while being personal, 'aspire to a general validity', and how this validity is of a kind that philosophy 'of its very nature, its essential habit' cannot explain or establish. But in discussing and analysing thought, meaning and language, Leavis had great creative writers in mind, who are 'sharply concentrated in their individuality', and whose genius signifies 'intensity of aliveness'.

Another theme germane to 'thought, meaning and sensibility' is that of art-speech and how 'the precision sought in art-speech bears an ironical relation to the utterly different precision sought by science'. Precision in the field of science is associated with an ideal of impersonality, or with 'a superstitious belief in the attainableness of pure objectivity' – something quite different from the poet's 'achieved' precision. In discussing this Leavis was 'stimulated' by Lawrence's *Psychoanalysis and the Unconscious* – a book which, though neither a poem nor a 'creative master-piece', Leavis considered to be 'in its marvellous lucidity, which is irresistibly convincing, a work of genius'.

In his 'Notes on Wordsworth' – notes that were among the very last ones he jotted down – Leavis reflected on how creative genius 'forwards the frontiers of expression and in the perception which is thought achieves the new', as Wordsworth did – Wordsworth who, like Eliot, 'altered expression' and in whose case 'art-speech and purity of being are inseparable for us'. No wonder Leavis considered Wordsworth's best poems 'a good way of compelling oneself to think vitally, that is profitably, that is intelligently, about the *sui generis* nature of life' and 'to achieve articulate thought about meaning, value and art-speech'.

'Notes on Wordsworth' as well as 'Thought, Meaning and Sensibility' are indicative of the frame of mind of one engaged in the 'revaluation' of his own life's work as a critic, and struggling with the subtle complex distinctions and definitions arising out from that work.

13

The Leavises in Partnership

> The only way to escape misrepresentation is never to commit oneself
> to any critical judgement that makes an impact – that is, never to say
> anything.
>
> F.R. Leavis

What constituted, as *The Times* obituary described it, the 'formidable
critical partnership' between F.R. Leavis and his wife Q.D. Leavis was not
merely their interest in literature and literary criticism, but a sense of
shared values, convictions and principles, which bound them together and
which went far beyond their matrimonial tie and their profession of
letters. A commitment to critical standards was itself a corollary of the
values and principles the Leavises implicitly believed in and applied to the
business of living, so that what was upheld in the sphere of criticism – the
severest criteria professed disinterestedly – was inseparable from and
reflected in their actual life. 'The judgements the literary critic is concerned with', the Leavises firmly believed, 'are judgements about life' – a
belief that is at the core of their critical 'credo' and method and constitutes
the very essence of the spirit and drive behind whatever they wrote. To
Eliot's dictum – the only method in criticism is to be very intelligent – the
Leavises could well have added, *'and* very mature'.

Maturity, both moral and intellectual, and intelligence and sensibility
at their finest and most developed, are what the Leavises admired in
works of literature and what they aspired to achieve – and *did* achieve –
in their best criticism. Marxist or psychoanalytical, linguistic or sociological approaches to literature had little meaning for them, as had academic
scholarship for its own sake, unless directed by a critical awareness of, and
an intelligent interest in what not merely literature, but also what life
itself is really about. This is exemplified by Leavis' critiques of poets from
Shakespeare and Milton down to Yeats, Pound and Eliot, or of novelists
from Dickens to D.H. Lawrence; or in Q.D. Leavis' critiques of Jane
Austen, the Brontës, George Eliot, Hawthorne, Melville, Gissing and
Henry James. However, Q.D. Leavis' approach and the kind of research
and erudition that went into her writing were conspicuously different from
Leavis', as was her style. For Leavis, whether he was dealing with a work
of poetry or of fiction, an analysis of style and diction was an integral part

of his procedure, since he believed that a writer's language and technique are the surest tests not only of his sincerity but also of his originality. For Mrs Leavis, on the other hand, a writer's sociological and cultural background was at least as important as his style in determining the quality, moral as well as artistic, of his writing. Moreover, she was as much interested in inquiring into and analysing the factors that influenced the taste of the reading public as in determining the literary and artistic merit of a given author or work. Hence she wrote with as much interest about Mrs Oliphant or Trollope as about Dickens, about Charlotte Yonge as about George Eliot, about Edith Wharton as about Henry James; and history and biography on the one hand, and sociology and anthropology on the other, played a much more important part in her criticism than they did in her husband's. *Fiction and the Reading Public* (1932), a version of her doctoral thesis, is a pioneering work, as is much of what Mrs Leavis subsequently wrote, including her well-known prefaces to some English novels. Although she never held a permanent teaching post in her own university, she carried out all her life what she called 'ventriloquist work behind the scenes by directing research students, whose theses when published carry on my own lines in what I may call the sociology of literature'.

The collaboration between the Leavises started very early, as evidenced by the link between *Mass Civilization and Minority Culture* and *Culture and Environment* on the one hand, and *Fiction and the Reading Public* on the other. It was to become even closer with the founding of *Scrutiny*, in the running and editing of which Mrs Leavis played a crucial role. Not only did she, through her contributions, bring about a general change in the critical approach to the novel, and thus help establish the *Scrutiny* ethos so far as criticism of the novel is concerned, but she also bore the brunt of what Leavis calls the twenty-year battle for *Scrutiny's* survival – a battle against 'a new and triumphant academic institutionalism, the new kind of enemy this bred and empowered, and the whole massive movement of civilization'. If Leavis achieved a full university lectureship only in his forties, his chief collaborator and partner never obtained any university post. In the face of such odds the success of *Scrutiny* was a matter of particular pride to the Leavises, and all the more so when, a decade after its demise, Cambridge University Press reprinted the whole *Scrutiny* set in 20 volumes.

From the very outset of their married life the Leavises were conscious of the various modes in which their collaboration manifested itself. In his writings as well as in his correspondence Leavis often referred to his wife's critical powers and originality and to the fact of her never having been given a university post, even though she had taught and supervised generations of Cambridge post-graduates. In his Introduction to *English Literature in Our Time*, he described himself and his wife as the permanent devoted presences that kept *Scrutiny* going, and, in the one place and the only way in which it could be done, kept the contributing connection continually recruited and renewed (ensuring, in the course of doing it, that the pre-Faculty potentiality of creative life implicit in what I have called the 'charter' should be kept still living – to the resolutely prophylactic distrust of the new professional academics). One of the pair, my wife, has had no academic recognition of any kind since the publication of *Fiction and the Reading Public* (1932), and has recently, after a life devoted to scholarship and criticism, Cambridge English, and the service to that literary tradition which might today be this country's indisputable claim to honour, distinction and self-respect, received a final rebuff – a very pointed one.

In '*Scrutiny*: A Retrospect', too, he had commented on the nature of the impact *Fiction and the Reading Public* had made and the way it had influenced the ethos of and the intellectual climate around *Scrutiny*. Its appearance, says Leavis, 'was a contemporary event, worked in the intellectual climate as a pervasive and potent influence – the more potent because every one knew that the book had been written as a dissertation in the English School'. An early article of Leavis' – 'What's Wrong with Criticism?' – in which he sets out to examine 'the contemporary performance of the critical function at the level of the higher reviewing', was, in some respects, a parallel exercise based on *Fiction and the Reading Public*: for, if the latter incorporates 'documentation and analysis of the developments that had left our culture in the plight that disquieted and challenged us', Leavis' article dealt with that plight in so far as it affected contemporary criticism. In fact none of the *Scrutiny* collaborators shared with Leavis this sense of disquiet as the author of *Fiction and the Reading Public* did, and this common feeling, even more than the fact of their marriage, was the real basis of their intellectual partnership. No wonder Leavis could say that it was out of *Fiction and the Reading Public* that *Scrutiny* 'very largely took its start' and continued the work 'initiated and given so powerful an impulsion to' by Q.D. Leavis. It was a work that led to the new sociological approach to literature and to a new concept of the history and tradition of the English novel.

Leavis dedicated to her two of his most important and influential books – *New Bearings* (another co-dedicatee being Leavis' father Harry Leavis) and *The Common Pursuit*. And she herself dedicated *Fiction and the Reading Public* to her husband. Apart from being tokens of personal affection, their dedications were proofs of the moral as well as intellectual esteem in which the Leavises held each other and of their mutual indebtedness. And so far as *Fiction and the Reading Public* is concerned, although written as a dissertation under I.A. Richards' supervision, it owed much, by way of stimulus and encouragement, to Leavis' undergraduate supervision of her at Girton and to his own PhD thesis on 'The Relationship of Journalism to Literature: Studies in the Rise and Earlier Development of the Press in England'. Two chapters of this thesis (the fourth 'The Growing of a Reading Public', and the seventh 'The Age of Elizabeth: The Beginnings of Journalism') had obviously an important bearing both on *Fiction and the Reading Public* and on Leavis' own subsequent social and cultural criticism.

Thus, not only shared experience in daily living, teaching and discussion of literature, but also a spontaneous and deeply rooted affinity of temperaments, values and criteria, moral as well as literary, determined the nature of their collaboration – while allowing each of them the maximum freedom to develop his or her own individual bent and aptitude. Q.D. Leavis' predominant interest was in the novel – and in her husband's words, 'it's my wife (who's very different from me – hence our lifelong collaboration is historic) who's an authority on prose fiction though it did not preclude an interest in poetry. She's both critic and scholar. I think that on the novel, she has no rival in the world.'

Also the comments that the Leavises jotted down in their respective notebooks throw light on their collaboration and literary affinity. Q.D. Leavis, for instance, quotes Eliot's remark – 'Compared with James', other novelists' characters seem only accidentally in the same book' – and asks: 'But is this not true of *any* great novelist?' At times certain quotes were copied as possible exam questions or subjects for an essay or article, together with or without the Leavises' gloss on them. When Q.D. Leavis notes, for instance, what L.H. Myers had to say about the novel: 'Between a novel as a description of persons, and philosophy as a description of the universe, there is, I think, a natural connection', one might well surmise that, although she makes no comment, she would have concurred with that proposition and might have borne it in mind for future use. The same may be said of F.R. Leavis' jotting down a quote from V.S. Pritchett's article on Fielding (the *Listener*, 2 February 1950): 'It was Fielding who put the English novel on its feet and you can find his mark in Jane Austen, Thackeray, Dickens, George Eliot, Meredith, right down to Wells, W.W. Jacobs and P.G. Wodehouse, in all those novelists in whom the masculine is stronger than the feminine strain'; or from Gilbert Murray (*Euripides*, p. 203): 'In blank verse the language has to be tortured, or it will read like prose.' He also copies down a comment from William James: 'The most significant characteristic of modern civilization is the sacrifice of the future for the present and all the power of science has been prostituted to this purpose' – a remark that epitomises Leavis' own thinking on 'the plight of our civilization' which he discussed both in *Two Cultures?* and *Nor Shall My Sword*. Leavis' involvement in the cultural, social and educational issues of the day went further back than *Two Cultures?* It is outlined in a letter he wrote to Doctor Karl Mannheim in the early forties when, in spite of the uncertainties about his own future as well as that of *Scrutiny*, he was full of ideas concerning liberal education, literary criticism as a discipline of intelligence and sensibility, and how both could be linked with sociology as *Scrutiny* demonstrated number after number:

> I personally haven't used the term 'sociology' very much, but I recognize that it indicates a direction in which I have been led by my twin interests in literature and education … my conviction has become steadily stronger that a literary education won't do by itself; I've been preoccupied with the problem of working out a liberal education appropriate to the modern world, and you'll guess at once some of the ways in which that preoccupation has led me towards sociology.
>
> Actually, the development of our literary interests towards sociological study came early.

How early it came Leavis explains by tracing the association between his own work and that of his wife – especially her *Fiction and the Reading Public*. She had, he tells us, planned further studies to follow up *Fiction and the Reading Public* and had organised the material for at least one of them. But the work was brought to a stop by what he calls the 'academic history' in probing and analysing which he adduces relevant 'literary' facts:

> The club spirit (take this as a sociological observation) prevails in the 'Arts'; my kind of interest in literature and education was disapproved of, with practical consequences that meant that, though we contrived (God knows how) to run *Scrutiny*, we were, for the better part of a decade, too desperately occupied making a bare livelihood in a hostile environment to do anything else. We had, in the 1930s, been able, by discreet methods, to get sanctioned for 'English' research a number of sociologically-inclined subjects that we had formulated for young PhD students; but our influence soon became known, and that stopped.

And yet, at the time of writing this letter, in spite of the unfavourable, indeed positively hostile environment, Leavis was not without hope and confidence regarding his future. 'My position is now', he told Dr. Mannheim, 'in many ways a strong one. I have (what I hadn't) a college behind me; Downing backs whole-heartedly my work in connection with the English Tripos, and will do what it can to facilitate the attempts I shall make after the war at developing that work towards a more adequate notion of a university course of English studies than the English Tripos actually represents'. Not that there were not difficulties in his way – especially of a financial nature – which were aggravated by the fact of his

being, as he was the first to admit, 'out of step, and inevitably to some
extent at odds, with the regular institutional régime' and therefore often
'up against formidable difficulties'. And yet he nourished what he calls a
'daydream solution' – namely, that 'some plutocrat endows Downing as an
"Experimental College", so enabling it to support a couple of suitable
collaborators for me on the teaching staff, and to enlist from time to time
the necessary collaboration from outside the College'. Even though such a
prospect did not materialise – or materialised later on only partially –
Leavis was determined to go ahead and do what he could to 'contrive' such
contacts between literary studies and sociology – contrive them 'in the
interest of my "liberal education".' A couple of years later what Leavis
thought of the relation between sociology and literature found a more
explicitly analytical formulation in his review of Dr. Schücking's book *The
Sociology of Literary Taste*, first published in *Scrutiny* (XIII) and later
included in *The Common Pursuit*.

In the Leavises' intellectual life, thus, it is practically impossible to
determine as to who, on a given subject or in a given context, influenced
whom. But, so far as Q.D. Leavis is concerned, there is hardly any doubt
that in much of what she wrote, she had, at the back of her mind, her
husband as a model and as an example, both in terms of what he had
written and of what he believed in. This helped her define her own
position, beliefs and attitudes. For instance, when, in her essay 'The Novel
of the Religious Controversy in the Nineteenth Century', she indicates, at
the outset, her own position on such a controversial subject as one 'who is
not and never has been either a Protestant or an Anglican or a Roman
Catholic or a Nonconformist', she was well aware of her husband's Huguenot and Nonconformist background, even though it may not have had
much to do by way of influencing his thought or his criticism as such. Or
when (in 'The Development of Character in George Eliot's Novels'), she
brings out how George Eliot was 'an intellectual *and* a very intelligent
person (not by any means the same thing)', she is echoing the distinction
Leavis often made between intelligence and character, or between intelligence in the English and in the French sense of the term.

Leavis, for his part, was profoundly conscious of the role the novel as
social history played in Q.D. Leavis' criticism, and how her approach to the
novel influenced, up to a point, his own approach. For instance, in his
lecture on *The Two Cultures? The Significance of C.P. Snow*, he criticised
Snow for, among other things, not taking into account how there was more
social history dealing with the consequences of the Industrial Revolution
to be learnt from an imaginative and creative writer like Dickens, than
from all the historians of Victorian England and the Industrial Revolution
put together. Q.D. Leavis could not have concurred more, since she herself
was keen to establish, as in her essay on Mrs Oliphant's *Miss Mar-
joribanks*, that the value not only of that particular novel, but of the novel

in general as social history, was of 'the kind that, in default of the novelist, no history could supply'.

Another thing for which Leavis had criticised Snow's novels, was their dialogues, which are so far removed from how people in those circumstances actually speak. Q.D. Leavis, too, in criticising the Anglo-Irish novelist Gerard Griffin's masterpiece *The Collegians*, points out how the novel suffers from 'stilted dames in castles and young gentlemen conversing in set speeches that no one could have actually spoken'. Moreover, in her Introduction to Mrs Oliphant's *Autobiography and Letters*, when she analyses the author's style, she does so in terms of qualities that, in varying degrees, characterised her own as well as her husband's style. 'Her style', she tells us apropos of Mrs Oliphant, 'is the natural expression of such a character (i.e. the character of a poor but talented family of professional artists). It is witty, but the apt epithet, the adroit sentence, the telling phrase, the lively conversational manner, are never sought after or strained'. But style for its own sake – especially in the Patorian sense – or the search for the *mot juste* or the purely aesthetic qualities of language in the Flaubertian sense, meant no more to Q.D. Leavis than they did to her husband.

There are, she points out in her essay 'Literary value and the Novel', 'no such things as "literary values"; the values of great literature, I believe, can only be those of life itself, and the term "aesthetics", whatever use it may be to the connoisseur of sculpture and painting, is only misleading, and can have no function for the literary critic' – an observation that sums up Leavis' own thinking in the matter.

In the same essay Q.D. Leavis echoes another well-known concept of Leavis' as she comments on Swift's 'maniacal conceit and contempt for mankind, and morbid disgust with life, a turning of life against itself '. In yet another essay, 'Leslie Stephen: Cambridge Critic', while attesting to what the humanistic side of Cambridge Studies meant to her and what constituted its 'standing in the eyes of the great world', she traces its origin to Leslie Stephen. And in doing so she implicitly corroborates what Leavis himself had to say by way of vindicating the Cambridge critical tradition both in '*Scrutiny: A Retrospect*' and in '*Two Cultures?*'.

Similarly, in her review-article on Charlotte Yonge, Q.D. Leavis states her own view regarding theological or philosophical training vis-à-vis literary criticism along the lines of Leavis' well-known argument with René Wellek on philosophy vis-à-vis literary criticism. There is, she tells us, 'no reason to suppose that those trained in theology, or philosophy for that matter, are likely to possess, what is essential to the practice of literary criticism, that "sensitiveness of intelligence" described by Matthew Arnold as equivalent to conscience in moral matters'. And as the poet in Leavis' case, so the novelist in her case works differently from the theologian, in so far as he works in terms of concrete particularity and not in terms of abstract concepts. This makes practically every creative writer's style uniquely individual in so far as it expresses 'something real and personal', as, for instance, Thomas Hardy, even though Q.D. Leavis found his style often 'bad in the sense of being gauche, pedantic and so on'. She defends Hardy against Lord David Cecil's strictures that he was 'impervious to education' and lacked the 'native heritage of one bred from childhood in the atmosphere of a high culture'. Her defence is in line with Leavis' defence of Lawrence against Eliot's more or less similar strictures. Hardy, Q.D. Leavis observes,

> had a good Victorian education, was further equipped in the official arts and crafts of music and architecture, was generally well read, as his notebooks show, had a remarkably acute grasp of literary theory and a most intelligent response to its practice; (if) his style was often bad in the sense of being gauche, pedantic and so on, it was at least his own style and succeeded in expressing something real and personal; and he had a heritage more valuable than that of one based from childhood in the atmosphere of 'high culture' (whatever that may be, for the implication that Hardy's cultural milieu was a low one is preposterous).

In *After Strange Gods* Eliot, too, had criticised Hardy – an attack that Q.D. Leavis dismissed as an 'outrageous account of Hardy's work – which could hardly be more wrong in tone, intention and expression'.

In her article 'Gissing the Novelist', Q.D. Leavis implicitly invokes the critical concerns and criteria behind her husband's concept of 'the great tradition' of the novel. Her own contribution to the making of *The Great Tradition* and the kind of collaboration it entailed is hinted at by some of her comments on the novel. 'It is time', she tells us, 'the history of the English novel was rewritten from the point of view of the twentieth century (it is always seen from the point of view of the mid-nineteenth century), just as has been done for the history of English poetry'. *The Great Tradition* went a long way towards achieving the goal that had been achieved by *New Bearings* in the field of poetry. For one of the aims Leavis had in mind in conceiving and writing *The Great Tradition* was certainly that of enabling a student or a reader, in Q.D. Leavis' words, 'to reorganise his approval and revise the list of novels he had to accept as worth attention', which would really be 'a matter chiefly of leaving out, but also of substitution' as well as of shifting the emphasis from 'the middling practitioner' of the novel (such as Trollope, Charles Reade and Wells) on to the major practitioners (Jane Austen, Dickens, George Eliot, Henry James, Conrad and D.H. Lawrence).

Thus, there was much common ground between F.R. and Q.D. Leavis as to what constitutes 'the great tradition' of the English novel, which accounts for the similarity between some of their critical valuations of various novels and novelists – as, for instance, when Q.D. Leavis characterises the novels of Trollope or Wells as being 'rather contributions to the literary history of their time and to be read as material for the sociologists'. It reminds one of Leavis' equally reductive view of Thackeray, Trollope and Priestley: Thackeray a greater Trollope, *Vanity Fair* a matter of going on and on, or life being too short for reading Priestley's novels. For Q.D. Leavis, too, was as much concerned as Leavis about challenging the conventional and academic view of the novels generally accepted 'as worth attention'. 'I don't know', she observes, 'who will dare touch off the first charge to blow up those academic values. Mr. Forster had made an attempt on Scott and the response in the academic world was most interesting; the subsequent Scott centenary was a rally of the good men and true to batten down the hatches on Mr. Forster's wholesome efforts to have that reputation reconsidered.' A more radical effort that had a more lasting effect on the criticism of the novel was made by Leavis in *The Great Tradition* and *D.H. Lawrence: Novelist* – books which did not so much directly engage in demolishing novels and novelists 'which (like Scott's and Robert Louis Stevenson's and George Moore's) perpetrate or perpetuate bogus traditions', as critically demonstrate how it was George Eliot, Henry James, Conrad and D.H. Lawrence who '*did* belong to and enrich "the real tradition of the English novel" '. In other words, these books did in the field of the novel what *New Bearings* and *Revaluation* had done in that of poetry – namely, undertake a convincing revaluation of the novels.

A fight against academic and conventional values, therefore, entailed both for Q.D. Leavis and for F.R. Leavis a fight against the literary establishment and the social and cultural milieu as represented by Bloomsbury. While reviewing Edwin Muir's autobiography, Q.D. Leavis called Bloomsbury 'a little world in which social life made the exercise of critical judgement bad taste; every member accruing to the group became entitled to eminence as it were'. And, with reference to Edwin Muir, she observed: 'to be born outside any such group and to have to make his way by hard work and native endowment has its own reward for a man of letters.'

Q.D. Leavis' critical esteem for Muir and the qualities that characterised his work and personality – 'decent impartiality and personal judgement (not the glib currency of a social group) ... and an integrity that comes from not being committed to compromises' – was all the greater because she saw those qualities embodied in her own husband, and because she herself shared them. It was her conviction no less than her husband's that 'to be a man of letters of any worth you must be a man of character too, in the sense that Hardy and Lawrence were'. The same emphasis on character and integrity is there in her comparison between Orwell and Spender. Orwell's varied writings, she tells us, 'bear an unvarying stamp: they are responsible, adult and decent – compare *The Road to Wigan Pier* with Spender's *Forward from Liberalism*, which is a comparison between the testament of an honest man and a helping of flap

doodle' -- a judgement on Spender in line with F.R. Leavis', in his review
of Spender's *World Within World*.

But no piece of Q.D. Leavis' writing is so indicative of the parallel
between the career and the character of the subject she is writing about
and F.R. Leavis, as her review of A.H. Quiggin's *Life of A.C. Hadden*, the
Cambridge anthropologist. Hence when, with regard to Hadden, she tells
us that 'though the universities were originated by great teachers and are
only kept alive by them (not only spiritually but in a very material sense
since it is they who attract students to the schools), yet to arouse enthusiasm as a teacher is not the way to become *persona grata* in the academic
world', Leavis' own example springs to mind. And while commenting on
the odds that were to frustrate Hadden's initial efforts to establish the
study of Anthropology at Cambridge – not unlike the opposition to *Scrutiny* and to Leavis' efforts to establish the 'English school' and propagate
the idea of literary criticism as a serious intellectual discipline – Q.D.
Leavis observes that 'there was indeed a considerable period of his life
when the motto of his University must have seemed to him a bitter joke'.
Nevertheless Hadden, like Leavis, had 'his *work*, his teaching and his
enthusiastic students and, as time went on, his grateful old pupils all over
the world'. Among the hardships Hadden was up against, Q.D. Leavis
includes a 'campaign of personal calumny and social ostracism' – something to which the Leavises themselves were no strangers. And yet
Hadden 'held on' in Cambridge, as Leavis was to do, believing that by so
doing 'he might get Anthropology permanently endowed there'. But, Q.D.
Leavis points out, with an eye on her own case and experience, 'the real
burden fell on his wife, who had to raise a family under the most difficult
conditions and financial and psychological strain'.

But there is this difference between Hadden's career and Leavis' –
Hadden's subject belonged to the world of science rather than to that of the
humanities, which means that he had the 'disinterested world of science
behind him'. But, as Q.D. Leavis pointedly remarks, 'the real tragedies lie
elsewhere'. They lie in the humanities where

> careers founded on log-rolling and social contacts are not unknown,
> and keeping the right company is in many fields the best, if not the
> indispensable means of advancement. There is a pretty general
> recognition that the further the subject is from being a science the
> less have real qualifications to do with appointments or influential
> position in the academic world of the humanities.

There is, therefore, no doubt that while writing about Hadden, Q.D.
Leavis had her own as well as her husband's case at Cambridge very much
in mind. Her tribute to Hadden – 'in spite of everything, or rather everybody, he had achieved much of what he had wanted and more than could
possibly have been expected in the circumstances' – might just as well

have applied to F.R. Leavis. Being herself one of those Cambridge free-lances who supported themselves without fellowships or faculty posts, Q.D. Leavis knew all too well what those circumstances were, and how difficult it was to force one's way into 'the stronghold of vested interests that faculties inevitably become'.

The intellectual and critical partnership between the Leavises revealed itself also in the use of individual terms and the particular significance they attached to them. Take, for instance, the word 'intelligence' and the different interpretations they attributed to it. Commenting on Peter Quennell's remark on Aldous Huxley that 'his intelligence is properly considered to be so great that it inhibits his other powers as novelist, particularly his ability to "feel" ' – Q.D. Leavis states: 'But supreme intelligence in other literary artists – Shakespeare, Blake, for instance – is not a handicap or disability: on the contrary, it is the condition of their outstanding achievement. It is obvious that "intelligence" here needs examining. There must be different kinds of intelligence and Mr Huxley's is an inferior and inherently defective kind.'

Another critical concept that plays a crucial role both in Q.D. Leavis' criticism and Leavis' is that of the sensitive response to literature. So what Q.D. Leavis says about Dorothy Sayers' knowingness about literature 'without any sensitiveness to it or any feeling for quality – that is, she has an academic literary taste over and above having no general taste at all' – is akin to Leavis' remark on René Wellek: 'He may be said to know something about literature but doesn't know what literature is.' Similarly Q.D. Leavis' assessment of Dorothy Sayers' qualification as a fiction writer has an unmistakable affinity with Leavis' assessment of C.P. Snow. Sayers, Q.D. Leavis points out,

proudly admits to having 'the novelist's habit of thinking of every-thing in terms of literary allusion'. What a give-away! This is a habit that gets people like Harriet Vane firsts in English examinations no doubt, but no novelist with such a parasitic, stale, adulterated way of feeling and living could ever amount to anything. And Miss Sayers' fiction, when it isn't mere detective-story of an unimpressive kind, is exactly that: stale, second-hand, hollow. Her wit consists in literary references. Her deliberate indecency is not shocking or amusing, it is odious merely, as so much Restoration Comedy is, because the breath of life was never in it and it is only that emanation of a 'social' mind wanting to raise a snigger; you sense behind it a sort of female smoking-room (see the girlish dedication to *Busman's Honeymoon*) convinced that this is to be emancipated. (How right, you feel, Jane Austen was not to attempt male conversation unless ladies are present.)

In this commentary we find criticism both of the literary merit of a particular novel and of the kind of ethos and sensibility it represents. It is the kind of criticism that Leavis applied to Snow. In fact, Dorothy Sayers' *Gaudy Night* – 'a peepshow of the senior university world, especially of the women's college' – may be regarded as being in some respects a precursor of C.P. Snow's novels. Miss Sayers, Q.D. Leavis points out,

> produces for our admiration an academic world which is the antithesis of the great world of bustle and Big Business that her readers know.... In their world ... everything is 'unsound, unscholarly, insincere' – the implication being that the academic world is sound and sincere because it is scholarly .... If such a world ever existed, and I should be surprised to hear as much, it does no longer, and to give substance to a lie or to perpetuate a dead myth is to do no one any service really. It is time that a realistic account of the older universities was put into circulation.

Such an account did get into circulation with Leavis' lecture *Two Cultures?* as well as with his elaborate explanation in *'Scrutiny*: A Retrospect' as to why this periodical was considered to be 'an outlaw's enterprise', and what the circumstances were that made it possible. Thus, the Leavises shared a common ethos which is behind their critical principles and convictions – the ethos that, for example, dictates Q.D. Leavis' comments on the kind of writers Dorothy Sayers admires: 'Edward Lear and Ernest Bramah's *Kai Lung* (delicious humour), Charles Morgan and C.E. Montague (stylists), Rupert Brooke (or Humbert Wolfe or some equivalent)' alongside whom she herself can take her place 'without raising any blushes'. And she asks: 'What is the value of this scholarly life Miss Sayers hymns if it doesn't refine the perceptions of those leading it? If your work was of any value to you would you want, would you be able to relax on Edgar Wallace (much less on Dorothy Sayers)?'

The ethos that the Leavises embodied in their life and work did not, of course, make for an easy life for them, and they were dogged by misrepresentation all their life. 'I am used to being misrepresented, but not resigned to it', said Leavis, and Q.D. Leavis could have echoed him. Such representations continued even after their deaths. An *Observer* reviewer of Q.D. Leavis' posthumously published first volume of essays, *The Englishness of the English Novel*, had, for instance, this to say about her appreciation of what is typically English about English literature and about the English novel: 'It seems to me reasonable to wonder, whether this intense concern with Englishness may not have been connected with a desire on Mrs Leavis' part to distance herself from her Jewish background' – a misrepresentation that deserves no comment.

Another misrepresentation through innuendo, and without naming Leavis, was C.S. Lewis' comment on certain critics 'for whom the great classics of English literature were like a lamp-post to a dog'. Sometimes the misrepresentation was disguised as pondered objective judgement; as, for instance, when Kingsley Amis adjudicated that Leavis and *Scrutiny* 'have, on balance, done more harm than good to literature and its study'. For Lord Annan, too, Leavis' critical, analytical and perceptive powers were just so many manifestations of 'rancour, hatred of people, spitefulness, and destruction'. The causes of such misrepresentations were manifold, including resentment of Leavis' growing fame and impact. Some senior colleagues in the English Faculty of his university even encouraged him to apply for Chairs of English elsewhere. Had there been a university in the Falkland Islands, Leavis used to say, they would have created a Chair for him there. But he and his wife were not to move from Cambridge where, in the interest of English literature and English criticism, there was so much at stake for them. Leavis' influence on Cambridge teaching and Cambridge undergraduates soon came to be recognised to the point of being resented.

As regards Q.D. Leavis, it was often suggested that she suffered from persecution mania. The only way, Leavis said, 'not to suffer from a persecution mania is not to be persecuted'. Thus, throughout his life, Leavis had been aware, not only of the invaluable collaboration between him and his wife, but also of the grounds for resentment and bitterness in her because of the way the academic world had treated her. But neither in his case nor in hers, did the sense of bitterness and resentment interfere with their devotion to literature or affect their value-judgements in any way. And whatever literary differences there might have been between them their fundamental judgements about life and literature were basically identical.

In her public lecture given, just a few months before her death, at the Cheltenham Festival on 'The Englishness of the English Novel', Q.D. Leavis analysed the decline of standards in terms of the decline of the novel. Her sense of the moral values implicit in such an analysis was the same as F.R. Leavis'. In the past, Q.D. Leavis argued, the novel, traditionally 'the product of an essentially Protestant culture', was concerned, especially in the hands of such masters as Jane Austen, Dickens and George Eliot, with 'radical and responsible inquiry into the human condition'. It was the art 'most influenced by national life in all its particulars as well as the art that has been most influential upon English national life'. But now with the emergence of radio, television and the cinema – 'institutions which seem to have some connection with, though by no means all the responsibility for, what is commonly recognized to be the decay and approaching death of the English novel as a major art (though not of course of English fiction as commercial entertainment)' – what one is witnessing is 'the withdrawal of moral responsibility of novelists. We see a parody of it in the novels of Graham Greene or *Brideshead Revisited* – and a consequent lapse of the novel into triviality or, in the cases of novelists like Greene and Waugh, spiritual pedantry.' 'The England that produced the classical English novel' had gone for ever for Q.D. Leavis. For in a country of 'high-rise flat-dwellers, office workers and factory robots and unassimilated multi-racial minorities, with a suburbanized country-side, factory farming, sexual emancipation without responsibility, rising crime and violence, and the Trade Union mentality', literature comparable with 'the novel tradition of a so different past' was no longer possible. 'How diminished', Q.D. Leavis concluded, 'the tradition of the novel has become in the hands of the most well-known practitioners of this age, who have uncritically been accepted as classics – as well as how commercialized.' Her mode of analysing both the novel and the spirit of the times was often quite different from Leavis', but the ethos behind what she wrote was unmistakably Leavisian.

In what was probably her very last public lecture, given at Queen's University, Belfast in 1980, on 'Jane Austen: Novelist of a Changing Society', Q.D. Leavis was introduced to the audience by the then Vice-Chancellor Professor (now Sir) Peter Froggatt in a manner which sums up the nature and the essence of the partnership and collaboration between the Leavises. With an apt metaphorical felicity, he called them 'twin stars of the first magnitude who for years orbited together as one of literature's most formidable binary stars, each casting its own light undwarfed by the other, yet each drawing from its partner power and inspiration to fuel its own brightness and like all sources of brightness producing some heat as well as light, or more accurately, attracting heat from many of the lesser stars in the constellations around them'.

14

Leavis and his Publishers

Not only does the individual *need* relations with others, but the vital relations are creative – and creative of a reality that transcends language.

F.R. Leavis

'I should hate to fall short in any way towards Chatto, with whom we are so much more than satisfied', Leavis, speaking also on behalf of his wife, wrote to Ian Parsons in an early letter of his (7 September 1933). And what he wrote then seems to have remained true throughout his and his wife's life. In fact, few authors have enjoyed a happier or a smoother relationship with their publishers or the latter with their authors than the Leavises did with Chatto and especially with its director Ian Parsons. It was, indeed, after the relationship with his wife and children, the longest and most constructive relationship for Leavis – a relationship that spanned the whole of his working life. Parsons started as an admirer of Leavis and soon found himself negotiating with him the terms of the publication of his first book *New Bearings in English Poetry*. He admired Leavis' critical views, his approach to life and literature and above all what he stood for. Both as publisher and admirer, he offered Leavis suggestions, advice, information and even criticism which the recipient found useful and which was, more often than not, accepted. This paved the way for a long uninterrupted collaboration between the author and the publisher.

The correspondence Leavis had with Chatto, and almost exclusively with Ian Parsons, forms an important and substantial part of the letters he wrote in his lifetime. After *Mass Civilization* and *D.H. Lawrence* – two minority pamphlets published by Gordon Fraser in 1932 – Chatto brought out all Leavis' books, including the first of his two posthumously published works, *The Critic as Anti-Philosopher* (1982) (the other, *Valuation in Criticism*, was published by Cambridge University Press in 1986). Most of the correspondence relates to the various stages of the publication of these books from the manuscript stage, to the negotiation of the contract. But a great many letters by Leavis also contain critical comments regarding the books themselves as well as matters of general or autobiographical interest, so that they may be regarded as an important chapter in Leavis' literary biography, enabling one to trace the genesis of his books.

Leavis' attitude to the suggestions and comments made by Parsons was dictated by a friendly but critically forthright co-operation: if he accepted them it was not at all as an expedient for paving the way to the timely publication of a particular book, but because he found them constructive and, from the point of view of enhancing both the sales and the impact of the book in question, practical.

What appears to be the first letter Leavis wrote to Chatto, telling them that he was on the point of finishing *New Bearings in Modern Poetry* (as he had originally intended it to be called) is dated 12 August 1931. He describes the nature of the book and inquires if they would be interested in publishing it.

> It's short, but, I hope, weighty (anyway, it represents the fruit of some years' specialization). I'm wondering whether it's any use submitting it to your firm. I know, of course, that there can be no commitment beforehand, but if there is no chance of your considering it favourably I would rather not waste the time of either party.
>
> The book is not a general survey of the verse turned out in our time: nothing on the same lines has yet appeared, I think. This is a brief sketch of it.

After giving details of the various chapters of the book, Leavis adds: 'I have argued that the tradition has been revised and that we have witnessed a new start. Well, what follows? – And I make a few notes on some younger people, and risk some general prognostications'. In the same letter Leavis also congratulated Parsons on having brought out Empson's book *Seven Types of Ambiguity* (1930).

> It's magnificent and is, I am quite sure, going to be a classic. I'm pushing it as hotly as is discreet in lectures and supervision, and have sent it to various parts of the world.
>
> It's a book that I confess (I'm afraid this is not modest) I should like to be in company with.

Together with the typescript of *New Bearings* or soon after having dispatched it, Leavis must have sent Parsons a copy of *Mass Civilization and Minority Culture*, for on 25 August, he wrote to say:

> I'm glad you liked my pamphlet. I was lucky to get in before Bennett died. I had contemplated a whole pamphlet upon him as Enoch Arnold Babbitt, but decided that the subtler way was better.

p.s. We're looking forward with excitement to *Unclay* – if only Eliot would give it to me for review!

On receiving *Unclay* from Chatto, Leavis started reading it at once, and wrote to Parsons to say that judging by the opening chapters he would be able to propagand *Unclay* as a worthy successor to *Mr Weston*:

> (I can think of no higher praise): the writing is magnificently sure. It will also be pleasant to be able to write early to Powys and tell him so. He told me last time I saw him that I was right in my guess at the kind of development 'Unclay' would show. I'm sorry I can't review it for the 'Cambridge Review': I've done with the 'C.R.' since last winter it invited me to spend much time over reviews which it put in the waste-paper basket – including one (of which I'd told Powys before-hand) of 'The White Paternoster'.
>
> If Eliot can be moved by a hint, so much the better. I often suspect (and seeing the average quality of it, hope) that he hasn't much to do with the running of the 'Criterion'. He has, by the way, had an essay of mine on Powys these two months.

Leavis acknowledged Parsons' letter offering the terms for *New Bearings in English Poetry* which he found 'quite agreeable' and commented: 'Yes, the book is on the short side: I aimed at the highest possible degree of concentration.' Apropos of Parsons' having extracted a promise from T.S. Eliot (to let Leavis review *Unclay*), he remarked: 'There's a chance he may remember it. He is full of the Christian virtues, but no one I know who has had anything to do with him commends his business efficiency.' Leavis also alluded to Powys' work: 'Having now read *Unclay* through I can say that it would be pleasure to me to review it. *Mr Weston* remains Powys's great book; he's not so sure of what he is doing in *Unclay*; but it contains some of his best work, and exhibits very interesting developments in his art.'

In another letter, while commenting on Parsons' suggestion that he give further Empson references in his chapter 'Epilogue' (in *New Bearings*), Leavis observed: 'I had thought of giving further Empson references but wondered whether they would help much; and in any case, only a small proportion of the other poems seems to me worth attention. I had qualms about increasing the suggestion of coterie, tackling, as I am, two Cambridge men [Empson and Bottrall]. But I will think it over.' Leavis eventually decided not to give further Empson references – the poems by Empson referred to and quoted from being 'Arachne', 'Legal Fiction' and 'To an Old Lady'. Four days later, while thanking Parsons for his notes and suggestions, Leavis insisted on keeping the word 'minify' rather than substitute it with 'minimize', saying 'I want "minify" which doesn't mean the same as "minimize". The word is current enough to be in the *Oxford*

Concise Dictionary. When quarrelling with Eliot I feel inclined to be meticulous in expression.'

On 11 December, Leavis wrote to Parsons to ask him not to put his degree after his name on the title-page.

> I never bothered to take an M.A., Ph.D. being senior to it; but 'Ph.D' certainly won't do; it would raise the worst suspicions, and, anyway, looks comic.
>
> And, for strong reasons which I could give, but prefer not to commit to paper, I would rather my college were left out too.
>
> I hope you don't feel that I'm making myself awkward. But my formal academic status (such as it is) wouldn't help the sale of the book anyway and my connection with Cambridge can, if you think fit, be indicated by a note on the dust-cover.

New Bearings came out at the beginning of 1932. On 9 February Leavis wrote to Parsons to suggest some names to whom review copies could be sent. As to complimentary copies to be sent on Leavis' own behalf, he was quite explicit:

> I know of no eminent person to whom it seems worth sending a copy of *New Bearings*. I had thought of asking you to send one to Eliot with a private note from me, but have decided against it: he will, I think, appreciate the abstinence more than he would the compliment.

As to the book itself, Leavis was pleased with the way it was produced and wrote to thank Parsons:

> This is just a hurried scrawl to you for the splendid job you've made of 'New Bearings'. Everything is admirable: it couldn't be better. The dust-jacket is perfect in its quiet originality. I should like to express my gratitude to the designer.

The book came at a time when Leavis was busy launching *Scrutiny* of which the first number was to come out in May. He confided to Parsons why he was 'formally' keeping out of it.

> As for *Scrutiny*, of course the more support the better. Formally, for politic reasons (you know enough about Cambridge to understand) I'm keeping out of it. Actually (*in confidence*, again) most of the planning goes on at my house; of course, I'm in a position to supply the special connections that will constitute the differentia of *Scrutiny*.

In the meantime Leavis was sounding out Chatto about *Culture and*

Environment, which he and his collaborator (Denys Thompson) had initially offered to a publisher 'with an educational connection, and which the publisher had accepted to publish'. In his letter of 1 October 1932, Leavis wrote to Parsons to say:

> It now strikes us that it was mistaken tactics to go to an 'educational' house at all. We might have been certain that its 'experience' would make it quite unable to understand an educational aim like ours. And we cannot now trust this particular house (or any other educational one) to do well by the book either as 'educational' or 'general'. If the book had been merely 'general' in intention we should, of course, have gone straight to Chatto's, and we feel now that we would very much rather Chatto's did it than anyone else. As for the 'educational connection', what is not supplied by Chatto's high 'intellectual' reputation will be supplied by *Scrutiny* (which goes marvellously: No. 2 nearly sold out weeks before Term).

Chatto agreed to publish the book, which came out in 1933. In the meantime, the March 1934 issue of *Scrutiny* announced the publication of Basil Willey's *The Seventeenth Century Background* by Chatto & Windus. Leavis was sent a copy which, he wrote to Parsons (22 February 1934) to say: 'I look forward to reading. The lecture-course was one of the *very* few worth sending men to (though I was depressed by the chapter that appeared in the *Criterion* – outside his real scope, no doubt). The book will in any case be sure of a steady sale. Yes, certainly we're going to review it. You may recall that I approached Grierson, and that he has agreed to have it sent to him.' (Grierson's review, under the title 'What is Truth?' appeared in the December 1934 issue of *Scrutiny*.)

Leavis' own book that he had been working on since the publication of *New Bearings*, and that had been actually planned as a background to it, was to be ready around the middle of 1936. But while writing this book, as with other books of his, uncertainty about his job and position at Cambridge was a constant worry to Leavis. Referring to the atmosphere as well as to the state of mind in which his present book was written, Leavis wrote to Parsons:

> I hope my bundle of stuff reveals no silly blunders when it's undone. I checked and re-checked, but I'm so tired that I may have done something as silly as leave out a chapter. What with constant overwork and worry, I'm about dead-beat, and this is a peculiarly worrying moment: the gentlemen of Cambridge are about to bring off, I'm afraid, the final blackballing, and it's practically impossible to make a living.

In another letter Leavis again mentioned the Cambridge situation:

I'm afraid there's nothing to be done, thank you very much all the
same. The Faculty have never yielded an inch, and they've only to
stand firm on the 10th when the Appointments Committee meets, to
be able to face public opinion henceforward with a *non possumus*.
Quiller-Couch's friendly, but apparently helpless .... It's all very
squalid, and, for me, worse. But we shall soon know.

On 14 July (his forty-first birthday) Leavis wrote to Parsons again:

Nothing official from Cambridge, but the report reaches me today
that Friday's meeting ended in deadlock and adjournment. That's
better than I feared, it means the old man stuck to his guns, and at
least some educational work will have been done .... Anyway they're
giving me my money's worth of interest in life. I could do with a
modicum of security instead.

However, Leavis did get appointed Assistant Lecturer in the University
and a Fellow of Downing. Soon after this *Revaluation* came out.
    It was typical of Leavis to use his contact with Chatto and his by now
personal acquaintance with its director to help other authors he regarded
as promising and to recommend their works for publication. For instance,
on 20 February 1937, he wrote to Parsons about W.H. Mellers – a *Scrutiny*
collaborator:

I don't know whether you noticed the things on music by W.H. Mellers in recent numbers of *Scrutiny*. They're parts (adapted) of a book
he has now finished, and which I've suggested he should try on
Chatto's. It seems to me extraordinarily good. I, of course, am not
qualified in music, but that makes me a good witness to the non-tech-
nical interest of the book. Of his technical qualifications there can be
no doubt: he is a fine pianist, he composes, and he has been a leading
figure in Cambridge undergraduate music in the last three years ....
The book offers a general survey of the present situation in music
(and the immediate antecedents); and I never saw writing on music
that so obviously came from a man of fine general cultivation and fine
general intelligence. I should think that the book would be liked by
(say) both Constant Lambert (whose *Music Ho* Mellers likes) and
W.J. Turner.

The frank exchange of opinions – whether by way of agreement or
disagreement – between Leavis and Parsons was a hall-mark of their
correspondence. Sometimes Parsons would recommend books for reviewing in *Scrutiny*, but for one reason or another, they could not be reviewed.
For instance, in April 1937 Leavis wrote to Parsons to say that he could

not in conscience accept his kind offer of Low's *Gibbon* since it was difficult to find a suitable *Scrutiny* reviewer for it.

With *New Bearings*, *Culture and Environment* and *Revaluation* behind him, Leavis, while engaged in teaching and in running *Scrutiny*, was also busy writing what he intended to be another book, as he wrote to Parsons (25 August 1938) in reply to a query:

> I am actually (you made a by-the-way inquiry a little while ago) getting down to a new book – my practical criticism one (whatever I may call it). Since I have all the stuff (and more) already worked out, it shouldn't take long.

But in the course of writing this book, Leavis was faced with a problem that would be a recurrent source of worry to him throughout his career – namely, that of obtaining permission to quote from contemporary writings on which he was going to make a critically adverse comment. He asked Parsons if there were going to be 'insuperable or grave difficulties':

> Shortish passages of prose – parts of poems I suppose could be used pretty freely? Or within what expectations ought I to work? It would be pleasant and desirable – to be able to use (random examples these) say Auden, Spender, *The Shropshire Lad* and some Georgian bits. Ideally, of course, I should be able now and then to deal with a whole poem, but – ?
>
> Don't, however, suppose that I intend to specialize in destructive analysis! I shall like to use some modern work for other purposes. My idea is to deal with general questions – imagery, sincerity, sentimentality, impersonality, etc. etc. – almost wholly in terms of particular analysis.

But a book on practical criticism as such was never to materialise. However, Leavis continued working on and had already negotiated the publication of *Education and the University* with Chatto. Its forthcoming publication was announced in the *TLS*. On seeing the advertisement where his name was tagged with 'PhD', Leavis wrote (21 September 1943) to Chatto to dissuade them from using this tag, as he had done in the case of *New Bearings*, explaining why:

> To tag my name with 'Ph.D.' isn't good policy (which is a way of saying that I'm sure my personal abhorrence isn't merely personal abhorrence). At Cambridge and Oxford 'Ph.D.', unless after a German name, has something of a comic effect, and for the educational world at large it isn't really a useful hall-mark: I'm known well enough there already, and the tag makes the name slightly odd and unfamiliar. So I do hope you'll keep it out where you're not irretriev-

ably committed to it. It would be especially lamentable to have it anywhere on the book or jacket. 'Fellow of Downing' does everything necessary there.

I hope I don't seem to you absurdly fussy, but I'm sure I'm right. I'm sometimes tempted to put in for the Litt.D. (for which I have no desire) to protect myself, since the 'Doctor' now seems inescapable.

Leavis was asked to suggest names to whom review copies of *Education and the University* might be sent. He suggested the *Dublin Review*, *Blackfriars*, *Anglican Theology*, *Journal of Education*, the *Kenyon Review*, and the *New Republic*, explaining the choice of some of the periodicals by saying that 'for some reason or other the Catholic intellectuals tend to be well-disposed to me'.

Leavis' next book, *The Great Tradition*, was to come out five years later, but some of the essays that were going to form part of it had been published beforehand in *Scrutiny*. In 1947 he wrote to Parsons (14 May) saying that he had received a visit from Professor Gordon Haight who had called on him to express approval of his George Eliot critique in *Scrutiny*. 'He's bringing out a new edition of the Journals and Letters: he earnestly hoped, he said, my book would be soon out. It is the right time, he said, since there's going to be a George Eliot boom in America.'

Leavis was by no means indifferent to his own growing reputation in America, which he thought helped his reputation in England. In a letter to Parsons (14 May 1947), he said he was 'a bit exasperated to think of the sales *New Bearings* would have had in America'. However, he did not see any point now in bringing out *New Bearings* in America. 'Naturally I think the book a classic!' he wrote to Parsons (16 May 1947),

> but it was addressed to a situation that is past. It can't just be brought up to date. Later it might, perhaps, be reissued with a retrospective essay, commenting on the situation to which the book was addressed and what has happened since. But that wouldn't be a bringing-up-to-date chapter.

However, Leavis was quite enthusiastic about the American edition of *Education and the University*, though not so much from the business point of view: 'My plans (at Downing and University education generally) make it highly desirable that the formidable American support and collaboration I'm now getting should be consolidated. That means that *Education and the University* must be current in the American universities – as it now will be.'

Leavis' sense of editorial practicality and opportunism was quite sound. He could assess the context and the circumstances in which what he wrote would have the most telling effect. In this respect, he at times even went beyond the publisher, however shrewd and commercially minded; and this largely because he knew the value of his writings not only in themselves, but also, and above all, in terms of their appeal and relevance in a given literary or cultural milieu.

Apart from teaching and *Scrutiny*, as well as his Chairmanship of Tripos Part II, Leavis had what he called 'a heavy burden of correspondence which avalanches eternally on me'. Moreover, he had his writing projects in mind including the 'Prefixed – Epilogue', as he called it, to the new edition of *New Bearings* as well as his long projected book *Judgement and Analysis*. But he could not complete any one of them before the year was out, even though he was pressurised about the first by Parsons. He declined, as he had already done before, to bring *New Bearings* 'up to date' – 'I don't think the criticism has been superseded (Heaven knows other writers go on finding it useful)', he wrote to Parsons (3 April 1949), 'but the book stands as a historical document. It was written, that is, at a given point in history, and was addressed to given circumstances. As such it has its place – and that will go on record.' However, Leavis promised to say 'what of this can be said, and say briefly, giving my general reasons, why I don't think there *is* much subsequent history of English poetry to be written: saying, that is, how the situation looks now compared with 1930'.

While he was still trying to write this 'Epilogue', Leavis had already started getting Chatto interested in another book: *The Common Pursuit*. He broached the subject of this book in a letter to Parsons (24 April 1949):

I'm always being asked why I don't make this, that and the other available. The new factor is that I published last December in America a 10,000-word reply to Eliot on Milton. I'm told it's as good a thing as I've done. We never re-print in *Scrutiny* – and anyway it's too long; but I want it to be current on this side. The solution, it occurs to me, would be to lead up a new volume with it. I've matter not wanted for other books amounting to substantially more than Knights' volume contained, I believe.

Leavis went on to enumerate the various essays that were to go into this volume, including the one on Swift which appeared in *Determinations* and of which he said: 'It's (if I may say so) a classic and it should go with the Milton and the Johnson'.

In the meantime, *Mill on Bentham and Coleridge*, with Leavis' Introduction, came out the following year. Leavis continued to struggle in order to find time for 'that "Epilogue" for *New Bearings*', to settle the question of the selection of essays for his proposed new volume and to finish *Judgement and Analysis*. But none of these projects was completed, as both Leavis and Parsons had hoped they would be, by the end of the year, since Leavis had, even during the summer vacation, as he wrote to Parsons (1 August 1949), 'an awful lot of other things on hand'. One thing, however, that he did achieve, as he wrote in the same letter, was getting

H.A. Mason appointed as his collaborator at Downing and for *Scrutiny*. 'It has taken years to bring it off, and the problems, practical and diplomatic, have especially drained my energy this past year. But it's done; and I'm hopeful that my energizings in future will be more fruitful.'

At the beginning of January 1950 Leavis sent away the 'Epilogue' or the 'Retrospective Preface' for *New Bearings*. Once the 'Epilogue' was out of the way, he concentrated on getting his new book of essays ready. In a letter to Parsons (17 January 1950), he reported that he had drawn up a list of the things he wanted to include and added: 'It builds up very impressively in its coherence and variety, and will be recognized as something apart from the usual run of collected essays'. In another letter to Parsons, after he had sent him the material for the new book *The Common Pursuit*, Leavis further explained that 'there is reason in the arrangement: there is a build-up and development, and the total effect is to define a position and a conception of literary criticism and its place in the scheme of things .... (My severest critic, Q.D.L. has been through the collection – has helped to select it – and is unaffectedly and unwontedly impressed.)'

At about this time Parsons had written to Leavis, suggesting a reprint of *Fiction and the Reading Public*. After consulting Q.D. Leavis, Leavis replied (6 March 1950):

A new *Fiction and the Reading Public* would, of course, be highly desirable. But the job as done for 1930 *was* done, and is acknowledged to be *classical*, and remains the basis for all later work in the field. For method, and history and essential conclusions it remains current – and should be made properly and freely so.

Some three weeks later (30 March 1950) Q.D. Leavis herself wrote to Parsons to suggest that the nine to a dozen articles on the sociology of the novel she had written since the publication of *Fiction and the Reading Public* might be added to the book to make it 'more useful'. But eventually, after further discussions, this idea was dropped and the book was reprinted in 1950, with a new preface by Q.D. Leavis.

Together with *Fiction and the Reading Public*, however, Leavis was also trying to persuade Chatto to reprint John Speirs' book *The Scots Literary Tradition*. In the postscript of a letter to Parsons, he wrote: 'Eliot, to whom I had recommended it, took Speirs' *Chaucer* for Fabers. Mark my prophecy – it will be a classic. It occurs to me to ask (unknown to Speirs) whether you're still interested in *The Scots Literary Tradition*. I believe in Speirs and see some point in its going with the Faber if you weren't keen on keeping it in print'.

Another author Leavis wanted to help was Marius Bewley – an American ex-student of his who had contributed to *Scrutiny* and who had brought out a book of essays on the American novel – *The Complex Fate*.

Parsons approached Leavis asking him if he would do a brief introduction to the book. 'I don't do these things, however slight they may appear, easily', replied Leavis (8 November 1950), 'and heaven knows I'm always putting off getting on with what I ought to be getting on with. But, as I said, I believe in Bewley, and would do an introduction if you thought that would help.'

In the same letter Leavis expressed his reluctance to being photographed, as he had been asked for a photograph by Mr. Brown of Chatto's:

> The fact is that there isn't one to hand at present. For twenty years I've resisted the pressure to be photographed. Because of that, *The Bookman* fifteen years ago sent down Robert Austin who did a drawing which is the only portrait of me – I mean the recognizable me – extant. I had some pulls of the block that was made, but they have gone. So there it is. I suppose I must think about the matter; but at the moment I'm desperately busy – and there are always good reasons for putting off so distasteful a business.

The photograph was required in connection with the forthcoming publication of *The Common Pursuit*. There was also a difficulty, as has already been indicated, in securing the permission from the Society of Jesus to reprint Leavis' essay (originally published in the *Kenyon Review*) on Hopkins, which annoyed Leavis.

Eventually the permission was granted and the essay included in *The Common Pursuit*. The publication was welcomed by Leavis, coming, as he said, 'at an apt moment'; for it gave his wife, who had been ill, 'a needed stimulus'. Leavis also hoped '(without much confidence) that the incipient improvement in "Press" continues – or enough. It's really extraordinary (if I – ego – may say it) how I've "come" to be recognized to be there, quite a feature on the map, without ever having been given corresponding "recognition" '. One thing Leavis was particularly hopeful about was that the *Times Literary Supplement* would take the opportunity to show that it had no anti-*Scrutiny* bias.

Even before *The Common Pursuit* came out, Leavis had already started working on his book on D.H. Lawrence. 'I've just got back', he wrote to Parsons (18 March 1951), 'from giving the D.H. Lawrence lecture at Nottingham. The D.H. Lawrence book is shaping. If only I can get at last an undisturbed summer: there are two books all-but done, and the D.H. Lawrence coming'.

The more distracted and rushed Leavis was, the more intensely he concentrated on what he was working on. Explaining why he was so vague on the telephone when Parsons rang, he observed (29 May 1951): 'You caught me deep in the agony of trying to finish off my *Women in Love* essay: it's always difficult for me to pull out of one of these fierce concentrations it costs me to write (I don't mean note-take, or think generally about, but write)'.

One of the things Parsons had sounded Leavis about was the book he had been trying to get ready over the previous few years – *Judgement and Analysis*. Leavis still could not provide any definite answer and for the same reason: 'deep in Lawrence. I have too many things going; placed as I am, am bound to have too many things going. You've heard my hopeful protestations before, but I'm at last in sight of the month or so of non-distraction and I need to finish that job.' But there was also the difficulty 'about permission for pieces to be mauled: I had naturally worked out the book in terms of pieces used in "teaching" and lecturing'. Still another difficulty was the actual process of writing. 'What always takes my time is the final *writing*. It's absurd, in a sense, when I think of the thinking and organizing that's actually *done*, and how other people produce what pass for books.'

No wonder that with all these pressures and difficulties, Leavis did nothing by way of supplying Chatto with a photograph. However he did ask his wife to send the various photos of him in her possession. 'I shall be glad', she wrote to Parsons, 'to have them back when you have done with them. I must say I think it a very good idea to put one or both of these into circulation, specially on the dust-jacket of *The Common Pursuit*, as there seems a general impression in the academic world that he has a tail and horns!'

The Common Pursuit came out in January 1952 and was widely reviewed. Soon after its publication Leavis asked Parsons if he would consider the reprint of *Towards Standards of Criticism* – a selection of criticism from the old *Calendar of Modern Letters*, with a long introductory essay by him, that had come out some twenty years earlier, adding: 'I personally very much want to have the book in print, both for its intrinsic use as criticism and for its value as a document as history, and as contemporary "sociological" illumination. I should propose to add a recent article from *Scrutiny* that complements the Introduction with a survey of scene taken 20 years after. Also a brief preface.' Such a project, however, was to be shelved until 1976 when it was eventually published not by Chatto but by Lawrence and Wishart.

In the meantime Leavis was busy working on his book on D.H. Lawrence. 'It would be bad policy', he wrote to Parsons (27 March 1952), 'to delay the book long ("the time is ripe", as Mr Eliot has said). I shall stick at it as steadily as possible.' At the same time he kept repeating the old promise about finishing off *Judgement and Analysis* – a promise, however, he was never to fulfil. However, he sent Parsons his preface to Marius Bewley's *The Complex Fate* and his two interpolations. The book came out before the end of the year.

At the beginning of April Professor V. de Sola Pinto of Nottingham University had written to Leavis for permission to quote from *Revaluation* in his book on Rochester. Leavis wrote to Parsons (8 April 1952) to say that the 'Muses Library' (name of the series edited by de Sola Pinto) Rochester

> will be *the* current Rochester, and, as you know, the series has a high scholarly standing. Naturally, I'm all in favour of being recognized by the scholar.
>
> There's no doubt about the spirit of Pinto's request. He has implicitly based his School of Nottingham on *Education and the University* – which (may I tell the publisher?) will, for all the conspiracy to smother it, go down as one of their historic publications – small as it is (but containing how much of my life!).
>
> Forgive this brag – made with conviction.

American literature and what constituted its distinctive creative individuality were, at this time, very much part of Leavis' critical concern. Hence when Parsons suggested that he might consider doing an Introduction to Mark Twain's *Pudd'nhead Wilson* for use in schools, Leavis wrote back (18 June 1952), saying that while it would 'certainly *not* do as school reading – at least that would inevitably be the official view (though it wouldn't hurt anyone! – I mean the book)', it was 'wholly adult' and offered to do the Introduction he thought the book 'badly needs'. In another letter he suggested the possibility of adding *Life on the Mississippi* – one of the three major recognised classics 'I much admire (so did my old headmaster, W.H.D. Rouse, who discussed it with us in Greek, observing tonic accent as well as quantity and stress)'. But in the following letter (8 July 1952), he changed his mind, thinking that *Pudd'nhead Wilson* would be 'best by itself – I mean from the literary point of view' and promised to send the Introduction to Parsons by the end of August at the latest. But soon after, Leavis started having doubts as to the kind of Introduction he was going to write or was supposed to write, and wrote to Parsons about what he called 'the *Pudd'nhead Wilson* problem':

> I never thought of it as a quite simple one. I never supposed one could just say 'Here is a great neglected masterpiece!'. On the other hand I was right in supposing that the book was extremely interesting and illuminating in respect of Mark Twain's genius (and the nature of American literature), and ought to be current. For an English critic, of limited knowledge too, there were questions of delicacy, tactics, and so on and so on (and the need to keep the Introduction within decent proportionate limits). Last night I felt what a presumptuous fool I was – and wondered how I could do anything like the kind of introduction you would judge necessary. Since then, (having done a morning's teaching!) I think I see the kind of thing that can be suitably done – and Queenie has turned up some useful matter

confirming some of my divinations .... You see, I'm not the sort of writer who dashes off an 'Introduction' – and *Pudd'nhead Wilson* is a case for just the right thing which, for an Englishman above all, *is* difficult.

Leavis' doubts persisted and the deeper he went into the actual act of writing the Introduction the more uncertain he became. However, he finished and sent it to Parsons on 30 March 1953 with a note: 'I've tried hard to introduce *Pudd'nhead Wilson* effectively, and hope the result isn't too disappointing.'

Some months later, Chatto were approached by Yale University Press asking if they would be interested in handling the British rights of a six-volume edition of the George Eliot letters that Gordon Haight was editing for them, and Parsons turned for advice to Leavis, who replied to say that

Gordon Haight has long been known as on that job. About 'scholarship' I'm not enthusiastic, but I think there's every reason for supposing that he represents the well-known high standards of scholarship.

As to the letters themselves, Leavis commented:

The fact is, the already published letters are dull, what liveliness there might have been having been immolated to virtue and decorum. And we [Leavis and his wife] suspect that the good (or 'wicked') and interesting letters have disappeared for ever. Haight [when he had called on the Leavises some ten years earlier] encouraged that suspicion.

But we imagine he has done the job thoroughly – final, standard, and so on.

Surely, though, there'll be only the most exiguous sale in this country. We haven't scores and scores of university and college libraries that will buy the set. As for George Eliot specialists to that tune – how many are there? I should like to know that there was a set in the University Library here.

But, as adviser to the house, I shouldn't dare recommend the plunge.

Leavis' advice had its effect: Chatto did not take on the letters which were then published by Oxford University Press.

For his own part, Leavis was still working on his book on D.H. Lawrence. He wrote to Parsons (5 July 1954):

I've been working hard and steadily at D.H. Lawrence.... My problem is leaving – without leaving out anything essential. And there are some very difficult problems of formulation – which isn't to say that I don't know my mind about Lawrence. I've worked very hard (I never do things easily) and I've little in a sense to show; but yet I *have* done something and see the end in sight.

A month or so later he was still wrestling with the problem of 'a long (and, I think, major, in relation to D.H. Lawrence and my work) opening chapter', which he was 'determined' to ensure was going to be 'incisive and concentrated'.

The Lawrence book came out at the end of September 1955. 'There'll be', Leavis warned Parsons (17 September 1955) 'some very unfriendly reviews, but they'll do no harm. Even the *New Statesman* these days doesn't suppress me.'

But even before the book came out – and perhaps in anticipation of it – there was an attack by Raymond Mortimer on Leavis and Downing in the *Sunday Times*. 'I saw it', Leavis wrote to Parsons (17 September 1955),

because Leonard Russell sent me a wire beforehand, and offered me 20 guineas for 700 words reply. Reply prepaid: 'Not at any price. It's too late for Raymond Mortimer's kind of malice to harm anyone but his own party. And I see that even the TLS (this current one) feels that F.L. Lucas hasn't the world with him. – All the same the Faculty keeps me out of examining.

'Sorry to decline the invitation, for which many thanks.'

The Lawrence book was also to appear in America to be published by Knopf, and the American publishers had suggested using a new title – a suggestion Leavis refused to consider, and he wrote to Parsons (16 October 1955) accordingly:

If D.H. Lawrence's name coupled with mine doesn't provide the right kind of selling title for America, I'm truly at a loss to know what could. I can't believe that a 'Flaming Phoenix' (or 'Immortal Phoenix') kind would help, and anyway I can't and won't fake up one of that kind. The title must bring in Lawrence's name, and must surely indicate that it is the novels I deal with. *Our* title does it.

An even more curious request for Leavis to consider came from the American publisher's 'stylist', that a particular sentence in his book was obscure and should be clarified. 'The sentence', said Leavis – giving, by the way, a glimpse into his own mode of writing, besides explaining its drift –

has a context and in the context it's perfectly clear to anyone who is capable of reading the book. In my characteristic (I hope) condensed way I do a good deal of comparing of Lawrence with George Eliot. Focussed on Ursula, I say that Lawrence has obviously been impressed by *Mill on the Floss*. But the insight he has shown in presenting Maggie comes not from literature, but from life. And now I pick up a point I developed in *The Great Tradition* ('the comparison reminds us'): George Eliot's Maggie is given too much from Maggie's (the adolescent girl's) point of view – i.e. it's too much as if Maggie, and not an adult mind (the mind of a clairvoyant genius), had herself written the book. With Ursula, I point out, it's different ...

I'm *not* going to attempt that kind of paraphrase for the American, or any reader. It's like being asked to have a different kind of mind and to have written a different kind of book. There, I stand, and as Luther said, 'I can no other'. I tried the sentence on Q.D. Leavis (my severest critic), and she says it would give no trouble to anyone who can read the book.

The sentence can't be 'clarified' by *re-writing* it, as the 'stylist' suggests.
P.S. It wasn't a stylist that was wanted – least of all one from Bronx via Columbia – but someone who could follow the argument, and was intent on that.

The American edition of *D.H. Lawrence: Novelist* was published by Knopf in Spring 1956. When Leavis received a copy he was again annoyed to see that without consulting him they had cut out the dedication and one of the epigraphs and had ignored some of the emendations he had made in the original text. He wrote to Parsons (14 April 1956) to say that he was 'sad about the dedication (having many American friends), mad about the epigraph (which very much makes a point), and embarrassed about Katherine Mansfield, the more so since I want to stand in unreproachable rectitude *vis-à-vis* the *unqualifiable* Mr. Mansfield.'

Another link in Leavis' American connection was the publication in the following year of *The Importance of 'Scrutiny'*, a book of selections from *Scrutiny* edited by Eric Bentley. In his reply (6 April 1957) to Parsons' query concerning this book, Leavis commented:

We had various objections to that at that time: it wasn't the selection *we* should have made, for one thing, – it wasn't representative in the way we should have liked ....

On the other hand *The Importance of 'Scrutiny'* has the advantage of having been done in America, and disinterestedly, by someone who is neither me nor allegeably a 'Leavisite'. Similarly the problem of tact and delicacy in including and excluding hardly arose.

However, Leavis found Bentley's book 'thick with bad and often insidious misprints' and was irritated by the fact that the author had, without consulting him, dedicated it to John Crowe Ransom.

Regarding a book of his own he had been currently working on, Leavis told Parsons that he had

> kept it warm (delivered part of it, successfully, as a lecture three weeks ago). The book is not *Judgement and Analysis*, but the one represented by the three essays on critics (Johnson, Coleridge and Arnold) that Bentley reprints. These will be revised; and there's much other matter, including a long, general introductory section (written) that makes the book – and makes it one of my books. I haven't yet hit on the title, but the book is conceived as the companion to *Judgement and Analysis*: it's to give the full complex idea of criticism as I see it – to define the intelligent man's concern with History and Theory for the Tripos (which doesn't of course mean that the book is academic).

In the same letter he also told Parsons that he had been 'waiting for some American foundation to finance a complete reprint of *Scrutiny* (that's the solution – there is the demand all right)', something that was to happen half a dozen years later under the aegis not of an American foundation, but of Cambridge University Press.

One note Leavis frequently struck in his correspondence with Chatto was his backing of the more promising among his pupils by recommending their works for publication. Thus on 18 August 1957, he wrote to Parsons from his holiday address in Aldeburgh, Suffolk, to say that he had just been called on by an old pupil of his 'who was at Christ's 25 years ago' – Reuben Brower, now Professor at Harvard, who had finished a book on Pope which he – Leavis – would very much like to see in Chatto's list:

> I haven't seen the book, but I know Brower and his work very well: it will be, I'm confident, thorough, sound, and intelligent on the critical side. Ben Brower isn't one of the creative minds in criticism; but how many of them *are* then? He's uncommonly intelligent in his unpretentious way.

Reporting on his own 'creative labours', Leavis said that they were 'much impeded' and this largely because of Q.D. Leavis' illness during the last two years which had been 'agonizing – directly for her, and "psychologically" for me. I have her here for a month in a charming bungalow a mile out of Aldeburgh (having hooked Lord Fairbank's cook – who's pretty poor: my God! English cooking!).'

The year 1961 started well for Leavis. Not only was *The Common Pursuit* reprinted, but Cambridge University Press offered to undertake a total reprint of *Scrutiny* with Leavis' Introduction. For the new edition of

The Common Pursuit Leavis wanted a third epigraph – a sentence from Knut Hamsun's obituary – to be added to the existing epigraphs from Henry James and Robert Graves, and so he wrote to Parsons (28 March 1961): 'The challenge is so important that to get in one more name (2 major writers in sum it would be) is worth a little trouble. *All* great writers feel like that – but we live in the world of T.S. Eliot.' Three months later, Leavis also suggested the idea of reprinting Leslie Stephen's *English Literature and Society* (28 June 1961).

> It is a distinguished classic with a distinction and value not recognized. It's immensely relevant to the conception of University 'English' for which I'm the great campaigner – and so is Leslie Stephen, the Cambridge Critic and *real* literary reader. I should happily write an essay on that Leslie Stephen as an introduction to *English Literature and Society*. Leslie Stephen badly needs reclaiming and vindicating after the too effective relegating work of his daughter and her Bloomsbury pals. I shall in any case, in one way or another, take opportunities of putting the multiplying English students of our universities on to Leslie Stephen and this book – which may still be obtainable (or may not), but hasn't my Introduction.

Leavis' interest in Leslie Stephen is one of several instances of what one might call literary cross-fertilisation between him and his wife who had herself written an important essay on Leslie Stephen in *Scrutiny*. It was not, Leavis explained to Parsons,

> that I'm short of work. I'm getting down to the next book, and the Introduction I'm to write to the Cambridge University Press total reprint of *Scrutiny* (irony!) won't at all get in the way of that: it should in fact help – crystallization, economy, etc.
>
> If only we could find the right small house to move into I could sail ahead. Tripos-tired and cursed with pilgrims and correspondence.

For one reason or another Leavis didn't find time to get down to the Introduction to Leslie Stephen's *English Literature and Society*: nor was the book published by Chatto. All he actually wrote on Leslie Stephen are a few paragraphs incorporated in his later writings.

Leavis had two more years to go before retiring and the most widely publicised thing he did during this period was the Richmond Lecture on *Two Cultures? The Significance of C.P. Snow*, which originally appeared in the *Spectator* and subsequently as a book together with Michael Yudkin's essay, published by Chatto in 1962. But before Chatto published it, Leavis was pressing upon Parsons to expedite the publication and also to explore the possibility of 'the pamphlet – opusculum' appearing in America, 'the sooner the lecture is available the better.'

The publication of the lecture in the *Spectator* caused a heated controversy in the pages of the weekly. One of the letters published in the Correspondence columns was by Parsons, and Leavis wrote to thank him (29 March 1962):

Your letter was really telling – the more so that what it said wasn't news to anyone: there are things that everyone knows but at the same time has agreed to unknow. For the everyone of that world, I both exist (to the extent of obsession) and don't exist. In the same way everyone knows I can't write and have no humour.

The note of irony at his own expense – 'everyone knows I can't write and have no humour', which he regarded as 'a very odd comparative judgement' – was followed up by Leavis with such questions as: '*Who* can write? and is writing? Gerhardi? Or any of the Snowmen?' The correspondence in the *Spectator* columns – which Leavis called 'abuse' and which, he thought, did not hurt him, but the Editor of the *Spectator* – made it desirable for the lecture to be published as a book. Chatto brought it out in 1962. A year later the American edition of the book came out, published by Random House, and two years later the lecture was published by Feltrinelli of Milan in my Italian translation in the periodical *Il Verri*.

With the publication of *Two Cultures?* now out of the way, Leavis went on to deal with other 'exhausting battles on the academic fronts ("crucial for my causes")' as well as with 'the imminence of date-lines'. He declined the opportunity offered him by Parsons for a trip to Florence to give a lecture at the British Institute. He was busy finishing the Introduction to the *Scrutiny* reprint; and the 'Florence jaunt' would have created other problems. 'I've been less than my normal vestige of digestion', he explained to Parsons, 'and should have to be virtually a total abstainer (from eating) while at Florence. Moreover my spontaneities don't work at their best in British Institute Society. My well-known "vivid talk" is apt to go rogue .... So, with gratitude, I *have* to decline.'

Leavis was also trying to put together material for his next book '*Anna Karenina' and Other Essays*. He sent Parsons the preliminary list of contents which included 'Joyce and "The Revolution of the Word" '. But this was eventually taken out to make room for 'The Orthodoxy of Enlightenment', first published in the *Spectator* (February 1961) under the title 'The New Orthodoxy'.

Leavis also received an invitation from John Sparrow, Warden of All Souls, Oxford, to give the Chichele lectures on Dickens in the Michaelmas Term. This meant that he could give only two lectures, whereas he would have liked to give half a dozen. But, he told Parsons, 'I shouldn't really have wanted to give my summer to them: there's so much else fuming and waiting.'

The Common Pursuit and *The Great Tradition* were reprinted in Peregrine Books. Leavis supplied a footnote to *The Great Tradition* indicating his changed view of Dickens. 'In the last twenty years', Leavis wrote to Mrs Smallwood of Chatto, 'I've been changing my view of Dickens, and am now (have been for years) his vindicator. I contend that *he* created the modern novel. He did.'

There were also suggestions from some people, including Parsons, that Leavis might add something new to, or bring out an enlarged edition of *Education and the University*. But he categorically refused to do so: 'I stand by it and it will stand in history. But in form it was a product of those war-time circumstances, and wouldn't there be something comic about adding still another make-weight?' Instead of writing something new, he suggested including his essay 'The "Great Books" and a Liberal Education' if there were going to be 'a re-issued and baited *Education and the University*. It is immediately relevant *and* it adds something (and would be properly preserved there) .... It's, if I may say so, one of my good things and seems to be a good deal in request.' (One such request came from me, as I wanted to include the essay in *Sotto che re, briccone?* – a request to which Leavis promptly acceded.) In view of the fact that 'there has been much history since', Leavis offered to write a brief explanatory note to accompany 'The "Great Books" and a Liberal Education'. However, neither the idea of a reprint of the book nor of Leavis' writing a note for it materialised. The essay was eventually included in *The Critic as Anti-Philosopher* (1982).

The following year (1967) *'Anna Karenina' and Other Essays* was published by Chatto in England and by Random House in America. Just a year before the publication of this book, Leavis had given a lecture on Yeats – 'Yeats: The Problem and The Challenge' – at Queen's University, Belfast. He chose not to include it in *'Anna Karenina' and Other Essays*, since he had made an agreement with Queen's that it would appear in a book along with other Yeats centenary lectures given at Queen's, to be edited by the then Professor of English at Queen's, the late W.J. Harvey. But after Harvey's unexpected death and there being no indication given as to the possible date of publication of the Yeats book, Leavis started worrying about the fate of his lecture. 'I gave that lecture', he told Parsons (22 September 1967), 'over which I took great pains, fifteen or sixteen months ago. It was wholly original and was heard by a great many people', and suggested the possibility of its being published together with the Eliot lecture – 'Eliot's Classical Standing' – which he had given in America. (Both these lectures were, therefore, included in *Lectures in America* which came out a couple of years later and which contained another lecture given in America: 'Luddites? Or, There is Only One Culture?'.)

In 1967 Leavis also gave six Clark lectures, with Lord Butler, the then Master of Christ's, in the Chair. For the publication of these lectures with

Chatto, under the title *English Literature in Our Time and the University*, Leavis added three appendices: 'The Function of the University'; 'Rilke on Vacuity'; and 'Research in English'. During the latter part of the year there was another project that kept Leavis busy, the two-volume selection from *Scrutiny*. He reassured Parsons that his use of his part in *Scrutiny* was not restricted in any way by the reprint, and that nothing of what was in any of his books figured in the *Selections*. When *'Anna Karenina' and Other Essays* came out, Leavis wrote to Parsons that Q.D. Leavis enthusiastically approved of it. Also his views on University education had 'a galaxy of avowed supporters among the mature and distinguished in education, including three ex-Ministers-of-Education: Eccles, Boyle and Butler'.

In the following year Leavis gave Chatto permission to say 'yes' to the project of a German translation of *The Great Tradition*, though refusing Oxford Ohio permission to reprint the book in America. 'One *has* to make exceptions sometimes, but the more one makes, the weaker do one's defences become, and these book-making requests come in eternally. Would you please invoke the rule I've been forced to lay down? The habit spreads in this country as our universities multiply and become more and more democratic – or Americanized.'

An even more important decision both on Leavis' and Q.D. Leavis' part concerned their Dickens book which they wanted to 'go forward energetically', so that it might come out in 1969-70, as they were hoping it to be '*the* book for the [Dickens] Centenary'. At the same time, Leavis was also 'brooding on a book on *Four Quartets* (talked at York) and a possible essay (book) on Blake (do). Possibly one on *Hamlet* too.'

Another question that engaged his mind at this time was the publication of his and his wife's American lectures. Both Cornell and Harvard University Presses wanted to publish them in America, but Leavis wanted the book to appear with Chatto: 'Queenie and I were concerned (intensely) to escape from our embarrassment without offending either University, and (even more intensely) to escape having *any* of our work entombed (and compromised) in a Cornell Collective Volume.'

Eventually, it was decided, both to the Leavises' satisfaction and to that of the American presses, that *Lectures in America* would appear in England with Chatto & Windus. The solution of this problem enabled the Leavises to plunge into their Dickens book. Leavis suggested to Chatto that the chapter on *Hard Times* be transferred from *The Great Tradition* to the book on Dickens: 'I see that essay referred to (in that curious way I've been so much treated to) as "famous", and in fact it set off the present "revival" of Dickens. There it is, classical! It would be ridiculous to leave it out of a book by us on Dickens.'

Before the publication of the Dickens book, the only distraction the Leavises allowed themselves was a visit to Italy where, at the invitation of the British Council, they gave lectures on Yeats, Eliot and Jane Austen at Milan, Rome, Padua and Bologna. 'Take the air for Italy on Wednesday', Leavis wrote to Parsons (5 April 1969), 'and preparation involves more than providing ourselves with special lecture scripts.' This was his way of intimating not only his confidence in himself, but also in his wife who represented 'a unique combination of devoted scholarship with critical intelligence' as well as being 'an incomparable authority on the novel'.

Leavis started discussing with Parsons the idea of a new book – not a collection of essays so much as 'a closely-worked book (appealing for its wider context to *Education and the University* and the Clark Lectures)'. It was to include his public lectures 'Two Cultures?', 'Luddites?', ' "English", Unrest and Continuity', ' "Literarism" versus "Scientism" ', 'Pluralism, Compassion and Social Hope', 'Élites, Oligarchies and an Educated Public', delivered at various universities (York, Bristol, Wales, Oxford, Cambridge, Durham, Hull), and to be called *Nor Shall My Sword*.

But even before *Nor Shall My Sword* came out, Leavis had already started working on *Four Quartets* – a work which was to be entitled: *Eliot and the Human World*. However, this was not the only work to engage his mind. He was also working on his Blake lecture ('extremely arduous, but, to me, repaying') delivered at Bristol University in November 1971. He found his work on Blake very relevant to his work on Eliot. 'These things bring out and strengthen the unity of my whole *oeuvre*. I expect a Blake book will follow, but not at once'. (Leavis never finished such a book and his lecture on 'Justifying One's Sense of Blake' was included in *Critic as Anti-Philosopher*.)

Another book he wanted to write, but which, too, never got written was on George Eliot, which Q.D. Leavis thought she and her husband could do in collaboration as they did their Dickens book. Before mentioning it to F.R. Leavis, however, she discussed the idea with Parsons:

> I wonder what you think of an idea I've been chewing over for a similar book [similar to *Dickens the Novelist*], but not so long, on *George Eliot* by us jointly. There are several original essays I want an excuse for writing on her work as a whole and on individual aspects of it, the influences on her work (not investigated to my knowledge so far) and so on: and I daresay, I could get F.R.L. to revise, rewrite, extend and add to, his previous numerous writings on George Eliot, as I did for the Dickens book.

When Parsons reacted enthusiastically to the idea, Q.D. Leavis wrote to him again: 'I'll start trying to sell my husband the idea at Christmas, when he'll have time to pay attention to it – in term he is at York half of the week, and writing lectures and answering letters the other half.' But she did not want the idea to get leaked for fear that someone somewhere could ultimately say to him ' "I hear you're writing a book on George Eliot", to which he'd reply: "No, I'm not", and set his back up against it. I *could* do the book on my own, but I'm sure you'd agree it would do better under the collaborative signatures.' Q.D. Leavis' plan for a collaborative book did not materialise, but much of what she wrote on George Eliot was later included in the first volume of her posthumously published essays: *The Englishness of the English Novel*, whereas F.R. Leavis' essays on George Eliot appeared in *The Critic as Anti-Philosopher* and *Valuation in Criticism*.

Throughout his literary career, Leavis was, from time to time, involved, together with his publishers, in editorial and decision-making problems. One such problem arose in 1973 when John Tasker approached first Leavis and then Chatto about the possibility of bringing out a selection of his published letters. At first Leavis was dubious as to the utility of such a project and vetoed it. But subsequently he agreed. However, he did not want Tasker's introduction to be too long: 'I can't see a reason for a long one', he wrote to Parsons (28 April 1973); 'as I shall find myself telling him: the essential things can be said briefly, I think.' But when the Introduction was sent to Parsons he had serious doubts about it which he explained to Leavis, observing, among other things, that 'you don't *need* to be introduced' and that Tasker's 'over-emphasis would merely add fuel to your opponents' fires, while acutely embarrassing your supporters'. Consequently the Introduction was modified and *Letters in Criticism* appeared in 1974.

In the same year appeared – without Leavis' consent or approval – *F.R. Leavis: A Checklist* by McKenzie and Allum, published, again without Leavis' prior knowledge, by Chatto, bearing the formula in front about the profits of the book going to the Leavis Trust Fund. The publication of this checklist – in view of the Leavis Trust Fund involvement in its publication – caused Leavis intense annoyance and frustration or, as he put it, in a long letter to Parsons, 'an insufferably tense complex of felt responsibilities in an exhausted man – isolated too'.

In spite of such frustration and the controversial reviews of *Letters in Criticism*, Leavis continued working on what he had assured his publishers was going to be a new book – one dedicated to *Four Quartets*. By now, however, his idea as to the kind of book it was going to be had changed. What he had in mind now was a more comprehensive project of which his elucidation of *Four Quartets*, something drastically different from Helen Gardner's, was going to form the last of the three parts, with a short Appendix dismissing Wittgenstein. At first the title was to be *Judgement, Analysis and the Living Principle*, of which Part II was going to be 'the actual familiar (mostly) "Judgement and Analysis" exercises (*Scrutiny*)' and Part I 'Thought, Objectivity and Language'. Although not a philosopher, he had become aware of his growing prestige among the professional philosophers. And yet he was determined '*not* to be classed as a Wittgensteinian'. However, the new book was not yet ready: 'Nothing went wrong; merely being (in spite of 55 or 6 years of no digestion) fit, my thought naturally goes on developing. I'm always up and down about work in progress; but most of the book is written. How long the finishing will take I can't be sure.'

It took Leavis another ten months to finish the book, which became *The Living Principle*. The typescript was dispatched to Chatto on 15 February 1974, and in the covering letter Leavis explained how and why things had gone on taking longer than he had calculated: 'the working out and the actual composition had been complex and arduous. You see, then, that while the book has all my work behind it, it's a new development. I hope the originality will be recognized (though recognition won't be on a large scale). I aim at enlarging my beach-head in the philosophical domain, but this entails tackling the problem of making *some* philosophers see that language isn't what their linguistics implies. At the same time I had to convey what "educated public" means – and what "meaning"!'

As to the longest chapter in the book – his critique of *Four Quartets* – Leavis considered it to be 'unrivalled and final', a kind of commentary that 'establishes a classic'. Nevertheless, he was apprehensive about Chatto not getting permission from Mrs. T.S. Eliot for the lengthy Eliot quotes so indispensable to his book. 'I've been as tactful as possible with the "buts" ', he assured Parsons, hoping that, though Mrs. Eliot might resent them, she would be able to see that 'they serve to enforce my insistence that he is a major classic and a living power (at any rate, my book will ensure his being that)'.

About this time a book of essays on Blake, containing Leavis' 'Justifying One's Sense of Blake', edited by Sir Geoffrey Keynes, was reviewed in the *Times Literary Supplement*, in which 'a superlative tribute' was paid to Leavis. This was particularly pleasing to him, given that he had had 'several ups and downs in morale – worse than usual', and was trying 'even in my very bad nights to hold the Devil at bay – most of the time'.

Even before *The Living Principle* was out Leavis announced his intention of writing another book that was to deal with some tales and *nouvelles* of D.H. Lawrence, 'the great master', whose criticism 'bears the same relation as my own does to the theme of *thought* and *the creative use of language*. He is the greatest – incomparably – of all critics.' But, in addition to the new Lawrence book, there were other projects – so tirelessly active his mind was in the last years – that he wanted to discuss with Chatto. For instance, the reprint of *Towards Standards of Criticism*, a selection of *Calendar of Modern Letters* he had made in 1933, and that included, among other things, 'a characteristically intelligent but to-be-argued-with review of the novel'. Recommending the *Calendar* Leavis suggested that 'apart from the educational campaign, the *Calendar* is a crucial fact in history', and wanted the contents of his 'Selection' (from the

Calendar) to be made 'accessible, and in wide circulation, for its sheer critical quality which is incomparable'. However, in spite of Leavis' faith in its importance and his campaign to make it available as a classic, *Towards Standards of Criticism* was reprinted, as we have seen, not by Chatto, but by Lawrence and Wishart in 1976 – the year which also saw the publication with Chatto of *Thought, Words and Creativity: Art and Thought in Lawrence.*

15

Remembering F.R. Leavis

Leavis' poetic gospel has spread into every cranny of the English studies across the globe.

G. Wilson Knight

I have known personally two men who were great in their respective fields and extraordinary as men: one was Ezra Pound; the other, F.R. Leavis. For all the reservations about *The Cantos* and about Pound himself, Leavis had much in common with him. Courage, integrity and disinterestedness characterised everything Pound said, did or wrote; and the same may be said of Leavis. The Pound who came to England in 1908, says Leavis, 'showed a wonderful energy of disinterested intelligence and public spirit. Never, in the literary world, has there been a more courageous single-mindedness.' 'Until someone is honest we get nothing clear.' 'It is only when a few men who know get together and *disagree* that any sort of criticism is born.' 'Isn't it worthwhile having *one* critic who won't say a thing is good until he is ready to stake his whole position on the decision?' Leavis' choice of such quotes from Pound's letters is significant in that it tells us as much about Leavis himself as about Pound. They epitomise both the spirit and the drive behind *Scrutiny*. Both Pound and Leavis stuck out their necks for what they believed in; and both paid, although in different ways, the price for doing so. Nevertheless Pound as poet and critic, and Leavis as critic, educationist and university teacher, exercised a greater influence in their respective fields than did any other poet, critic or educationist in this century.

Leavis' commitment to literature and literary criticism was as much an expression of his character and personality as a matter of career or vocation. And he shared this commitment with his wife. Although Leavis' writings played an important part in my studies, I first met him a few months after he had delivered the Richmond lecture on C.P. Snow. Our meeting lasted for nearly an hour. We talked about numerous things, two of which stand out in my memory. One was the way he pointed out, with a certain degree of pride and satisfaction, the room in which he had given the lecture, which, as he was to tell me years later, had cost him more time, thought and energy than any other single piece of writing. The other was the spontaneous way he recited Leopardi's poem 'L'infinito' in Italian

when I told him of my interest in that poet. (He knew, he told me, hundreds
of lines from Dante and Leopardi by heart, and the effort to memorise
them had served as an antidote to insomnia.) He recited Leopardi's poem
with great accuracy, observing the pauses, caesuras and cadence. However, I was still not in a position to recognise – as I was to do in later years
– Leavis' incomparable ability to read out poetry, whether Shakespeare's,
Pope's, Hopkins', Hardy's, Pound's or Eliot's. Another thing I particularly
like to remember is his making me feel at ease in his company; and yet
there was no contrived air of informality about him. It was the unconscious
air of natural authority which did not have to be consciously exercised.

In subsequent years, my contacts with Leavis – both through correspondence and through my visits to Cambridge – became more frequent. I
called on him and his wife five or six times a year during the last thirteen
years of his life. The contact originated, in the first place, with my project
to edit a selection of his critical essays which was published (by Bo
Cavefors) in Sweden in 1966. A couple of years later I translated into
Italian another selection of some of his essays and reviews (published by
De Donato, Bari) under the title *Sotto che re, briccone?* (*Under Which King,
Bezonian?*) A third selection in my Italian translation, *Da Swift a Pound:
Saggi letterari di F.R. Leavis* (*From Swift to Pound: Literary Essays of F.R.
Leavis*), appeared with Einaudi of Turin in 1973, with Leavis' preface. In
translating Leavis' work I could not have wished for greater co-operation
from him, and the way he helped me render into Italian certain idiomatic
particularities of his English made me appreciate his thought processes
and the form of expression, with its subtlety, suppleness and tautness, all
the more.

The ruthless severity of his critical judgements may at times have given
the impression of harshness; but when you came to know him personally
nothing could have been farther from the truth. Even behind his most
severe critical judgements or dismissals, there was no personal animus.
He believed too seriously in what he regarded to be the proper function of
literary criticism to entertain any personal animus against what or whom
he criticised. One example of his moral wisdom and humaneness combined
with critical acumen and a sense of responsibility can be seen when he
takes issue with Sarah Gainham who, while reviewing a German author
in the *Spectator*, had this to say: 'She was used to well-being, yet it is
materialism for the mass of people to get used to well-being. This is a
familiar resentment and envy, often seen in Britain, that working people
should be going to Florence and Majorca, and buying Beethoven long-play-
ing records. This ought not to be dressed up as moral indignation.' With a
firm and clear grasp on the moral as well as social issues involved,
together with some rare bits of autobiography thrown in, Leavis retorts:

> Of course it oughtn't, as far as it exists. And possibly the writer could
> back her 'familiar' by adducing instances known to her. But to

suggest that such resentment and envy are representative, so that
she can reasonably dismiss in this way all questioning uneasiness
about the human consequences of the technological revolution and
the affluent society – is that to promote clear vision and intelligent
thought? The unrealism, the disturbing emotional intention, or per-
versity, betrays itself clearly enough in those 'Beethoven long-play-
ing records'. I myself, after an unaffluent and very much 'engaged'
academic life, am not familiar with Majorca or Florence, but in those
once very quiet places very much nearer Cambridge to which my wife
and I used to take our children the working-class people now everywhere to be met with in profusion carry transistors round with them
almost invariably. The music that comes from these, like that one
hears in greater volume in the neighbourhood of the Bingo establishments (of which the smallest coast-hamlet has at least one –
Bingo being the most pathetic of vacuum-fillers) doesn't at all suggest
aspirations towards Beethoven. If working-class people did, characteristically, or in significant numbers, show a bent that way, who
would be found deploring it? – except, of course, Kingsley Amis and
his admirers (and there you have a significant cultural phenomenon
that Miss Gainham would do well to ponder). But as for the actual
working-class people who *can* be regarded as characteristic, it's not
anything in the nature of moral indignation one feels towards *them*,
but shame, concern and apprehension at the way our civilization has
let them down – left them to enjoy a 'high standard of living' in a
vacuum of disinheritance. The concern, I imagine, is what all decent
people capable of sympathetic perception must feel: the apprehension is for the future of humanity.

The moral force behind Leavis' 'high standard of living' and 'a vacuum of
disinheritance' argument is of the same kind as the one behind
Wordsworth's contrast between 'low living' and 'high thinking'. It emphasises the basically humane character of Leavis' concern in the face of
challenges and dilemmas presented by the technologico-Benthamite civilisation.

And yet his efforts to project his ethical and intellectual preoccupations
with the problems of our civilization into the sphere of social and literary
criticism were often misunderstood. For instance, a *Times Literary Supplement* reviewer once suggested that the Leavises, instead of castigating
the opposition to *Scrutiny*, should have ignored it. For, he argued, had they
set up on their own desks 'the comforting sentence: "Fret not thyself
because of evil-doers"', and, instead of attempting to serve the full function
of criticism, confined themselves to the display of their gifts in appreciating what they admired, they wouldn't have been misunderstood or
incurred any resentment. But to believe this, Leavis argues, 'is to underrate the percipient prudence of established mediocrity – the instinctive

and cultivated habit that makes it quick and decided in its reaction to the signs of disturbing intelligence, unacceptable genuineness and unaccommodating disinterestedness'.

Such qualities accompanied Leavis' commitment not only to literary criticism, but also to criticism of society, culture and civilisation. It is in this sense that Leavis as a critic may be regarded as a moralist, as Eliot regarded him. The fusion in his work between the values of life and the values of literature, between what is moral and what is artistic, was the natural outcome of a conviction that was no less Leavis' than Arnold's – namely, that literature is at bottom a criticism of life, and that poetry divorced from morality is poetry divorced from life. Few critics since Arnold have held this conviction so firmly as Leavis; and in the case of few critics has it been so central to their work, their life and their personality as in his case. That is why he did not evaluate literature solely in terms of its technical, aesthetic or stylistic qualities, but also, and above all, in terms of its relevance to life. In so doing he brought to bear upon it his own experience and personality as well as his own individuality and character.

In fact, apart from Pound, there are few critics in the twentieth century of whom it can be said, as it can be of Leavis, that every principle, concept or criterion which he adopted in his criticism and which determined its tone and ethos emerged from his character and temperament as well as from his personal beliefs and convictions. One can well understand Leavis' refusal to write his autobiography, for a factually and circumstantially detailed account of his life, personality and career could not give a better glimpse into his character and into what really mattered to him than do his critical writings.

I shall remember Leavis for the way in which his critical and intellectual powers were matched by his moral powers – courage, integrity, selflessness; I shall remember him for a rare kind of honesty and consistency, so that whatever he said, wrote or did was never out of character; I shall remember him as an inspiring teacher and a critic endowed with an extraordinary faculty of thought, perception and analysis and with a corresponding mastery over style and expression; but above all I shall remember him as a man – a man larger than the business of letters and criticism he professed, capable of true friendship and utterly incapable of duplicity, disloyalty or ingratitude which, if so common in the world at large, are not altogether unknown in the literary and academic world.

Bibliography of the Works of F.R. Leavis

Leavis' articles, introductions, reviews, etc. are not included here, as the more important ones have all been included in his books.

Mass Civilization and Minority Culture, Minority Pamphlet No. 1, Gordon Fraser, The Minority Press: Cambridge, 1930.

New Bearings in English Poetry: A Study of the Contemporary Situation, Chatto & Windus: London, 1932.

How to Teach Reading: A Primer for Ezra Pound, Gordon Fraser, The Minority Press: Cambridge, 1932.

D.H. Lawrence, Gordon Fraser, The Minority Press: Cambridge, 1932.

For Continuity, Gordon Fraser, The Minority Press: Cambridge, 1933.

Towards Standards of Criticism, selections from *The Calendar of Modern Letters*, with an Introduction by F.R. Leavis, Lawrence & Wishart: London, 1933.

Culture and Environment: The Training of Critical Awareness (with Denys Thompson), Chatto & Windus: London; Oxford University Press: Toronto, 1933.

Determinations: Critical Essays, edited with an Introduction by F.R. Leavis, Chatto & Windus: London, 1934.

Revaluation: Tradition and Development in English Poetry, Chatto & Windus: London; Macmillan: Toronto, 1936.

Education and the University: A Sketch for an 'English School', Chatto & Windus: London; Macmillan: Toronto, 1943.

The Great Tradition: George Eliot, Henry James, Joseph Conrad, Chatto & Windus: London; Clarke Irwin: Toronto, 1948.

Mill on Bentham and Coleridge, with an Introduction by F.R. Leavis (pp. 1-38), Chatto & Windus: London, 1950.

The Common Pursuit, Chatto & Windus: London; Clarke, Irwin: Toronto, 1952.

D.H. Lawrence: Novelist, Chatto & Windus: London; Clarke, Irwin: Toronto, 1955.

Two Cultures? The Significance of C.P. Snow, Being the Richmond Lecture, 1962, with an Essay on Sir Charles Snow's Rede Lecture by Michael Yudkin, Chatto & Windus: London; Clarke, Irwin: Toronto, 1962.

Scrutiny: A Reprint, 20 volumes, Cambridge University Press: Cambridge, 1963.

'Anna Karenina' and Other Essays, Chatto & Windus: London, 1967.

A Selection from 'Scrutiny', 2 volumes, Cambridge University Press: Cambridge, 1968.

English Literature in Our Time and the University, Chatto & Windus: London, 1969.

Lectures in America (with Q.D. Leavis), Chatto & Windus: London, 1969.

Dickens the Novelist (with Q.D. Leavis), Chatto & Windus: London, 1970.

Nor Shall My Sword: Discourses on Pluralism, Compassion and Social Hope, Chatto & Windus: London, 1972.

Letters in Criticism, edited with an Introduction by John Tasker, Chatto & Windus: London, 1974.

The Living Principle: 'English' as a Discipline of Thought, Chatto & Windus: London, 1975.

Towards Standards of Criticism: Selections from *The Calendar of Modern Letters*, chosen and with Introductions by F.R. Leavis, Lawrence & Wishart: London, 1976.

Thought, Words and Creativity: Art and Thought in Lawrence, Chatto & Windus: London, 1976.

The Critic as Anti-Philosopher, edited by G. Singh, Chatto & Windus: London, 1982.

Valuation in Criticism and Other Essays, edited by G. Singh, Cambridge University Press: Cambridge, 1986.

Index